Discovering
Ideas
An Anthology
for Writers

Jean Wyrick
Colorado State University

Holt, Rinehart and Winston
New York   Chicago   San Francisco   Philadelphia
Montreal   Toronto   London   Sydney   Tokyo
Mexico City   Rio de Janeiro   Madrid

Credits

Introduction: "Our Youth Should Serve," by Steven Muller. Copyright 1978, by Newsweek, Inc. All rights reserved. **1-1** "A Halfway House," from *Close to Home*, by Ellen Goodman. Copyright © 1979 by The Washington Post Company. Reprinted by permission of Simon & Schuster, a Division of Gulf and Western Corporation. **1-2** "Graduation," from *I Know Why the Caged Bird Sings*, by Maya Angelou. Copyright © 1969 by Maya Angelou. Reprinted by permission of Random House, Inc. "Lift Ev'ry Voice and Sing"—words by James Weldon Johnson and music by J. Rosamond Johnson. © Copyright: Edward B. Marks Music Corporation. Used by permission. **1-3** "What's Wrong with 'Me, Me, Me'?" by Margaret Halsey. Copyright 1978, by Newsweek, Inc. All rights reserved. Reprinted by permission. **1-4** "A Few Words About Breasts," copyright © 1972 by Nora Ephron. Reprinted from *Crazy Salad: Some Things About Women*, by Nora Ephron, by permission of Alfred A. Knopf, Inc. **1-5** "The Miseducation of a Former Fat Boy," by Louie Crew. Copyright © 1973 by *Saturday Review*. All rights reserved. Reprinted with permission. **1-6** "A & P," copyright © 1962 by John Updike. Reprinted from *Pigeon Feathers and Other Stories*, by John Updike, by permission of Alfred A. Knopf, Inc. Originally appeared in *The New Yorker*. **2-1** "Masculine/Feminine," from *Thundering Sneakers*, by Prudence Mackintosh. Copyright © 1977, 1981 by Prudence Mackintosh. Reprinted by permission of Doubleday & Company, Inc. Excerpt from *Undoing Sex Stereotypes*, by Marcia Guttentag and Helen Bray. Copyright © 1976 McGraw-Hill, Inc. Used with the permission of McGraw-Hill Book Company. **2-2** "Confessions of a Female Chauvinist Sow," by Anne Roiphe. Published in *New York Magazine*. Copyright © 1972 by Anne Roiphe. Reprinted by permission of Brandt & Brandt Literary Agents, Inc. **2-3** "Let 'em Eat Leftovers," by Mike McGrady. Copyright © 1976 by Mike McGrady. Reprinted by permission of The Sterling Lord Agency, Inc. **2-4** "Omnigamy: The New Kinship System," by Lionel Tiger. Copyright © 1978 by Lionel Tiger. Reprinted by permission of Lionel Tiger % International Creative Manage-

(continued on p. iv)

Library of Congress Cataloging in Publication Data
Main entry under title:

Discovering ideas.

Includes index.
1. College reader. 2. English language—Rhetoric.
I. Wyrick, Jean.
PE1417.D57   808'.0427   81-13459
ISBN 0-03-056158-2   AACR2

CBS COLLEGE PUBLISHING
Holt, Rinehart and Winston
The Dryden Press
Saunders College Publishing

*This book is for
David and Sarah*

(continued on p. 364)

To the Teacher

Discovering Ideas was compiled and written in response to teachers who have been listening to their students complain, "I have nothing to write about." Many of these teachers have turned to essay anthologies not only to illustrate good prose styles but also to help their students find interesting essay topics. Unfortunately, they have been disappointed too often in the past by textbook authors who have chosen essays that illustrate particular rhetorical strategies—but at the expense of engaging subject matter that would encourage class discussion and lead naturally to writing assignments. "Ever tried to get a stirring class discussion going on the Declaration of Independence? Impossible!" laments one new teacher of composition who uses a popular rhetorical reader.

This text is called *Discovering Ideas* for two reasons. First, like most anthologies, it is designed to help students find new approaches, new techniques and strategies they can analyze and incorporate into their writing. But the book is also so titled because it is a collection of essays, stories, and poems carefully selected *to help young writers discover new ideas and formulate new opinions that they will want to talk and write about.* Each selection was deliberately chosen because it has proven that it can generate discussion, evoke varied responses, and encourage fresh, imaginative thinking on issues students can react to. And, in turn, each one can help motivate students to discover thoughtful essay topics that avoid the mechanical, pointless, or just plain boring compositions writing teachers are so tired of. In other words, these selections try to inspire rather than intimidate, to stimulate rather than subdue.

The fifty-nine selections are divided into nine categories that interest students: Growing up; Men and Women; People at Leisure; Education: Teaching and Learning; Life Confronts Death; Perceiving Our Environment; Social Issues; Scenes of the Past; and Language: Reading, Writing, Talking. (A slightly unusual section, Scenes of the Past, grew from the realization that today's students know surprisingly little about their country's history but would like to know more.) The sections themselves are arranged in a sequence that moves from immediate to more abstract or symbolic experience—a sequence that parallels the movement in most composition courses from writing about personal experience to writing with a broader perspective. Each of the nine sections contains five essays and ends with one or two pieces of literature that complement the prose selections. Each section contains selections by both old favorites, such as George Orwell, James Thurber, and Mark Twain, and contemporary writers, such as Prudence Mackintosh, Mike McGrady, and Michael Mewshaw. The selections present a variety of styles, tones, and organizational patterns, offering students opportunities to read and study not only traditional essays but also speeches, editorials, newspaper articles, satire, journal entries, autobiographical narratives, short stories, and poems. Most of the selections are brief, and the reading level of each is appropriate for college freshmen (unusual words and unfamiliar references are footnoted).

An annotated thematic table of contents makes the choice of essays, poems, or stories easy for teachers who wish to assign individual selections rather than entire sections. A second table of contents is also included in this text to aid those instructors who wish to emphasize rhetorical modes and strategies as well as thematic concerns. Essays are listed in the rhetorical table of contents under their primary strategy of development, with the major secondary strategies noted in parentheses for quick reference.

Next in importance to the selections themselves in any college anthology is the apparatus that enables both the teachers and students to use the text more efficiently. This book offers a number of helpful additions not always available in other texts. "Modes and Strategies: An Introduction to Essays" provides a brief overview of the kinds of writing the students will most likely study in their freshman composition class. "Why Read Essays?" explains to the students the purposes of studying other people's writing, and "How to Read an Essay" then shows them how to become critical readers. The step-by-step process for marking and analyzing the essays in this text should prepare the students for class discussions and help train them to recognize and remember important techniques and ideas. A sample essay, marked according to the steps in the how-to-read process, is included as a model.

Each selection in this text is accompanied by a brief biographical note on its author, publication information, a vocabulary list, questions on content, style, and structure, and suggestions for writing. The questions are *not* divided into separate sections on "content" and "form" because to do so not only leads to repetition but also implies to the student that *what* one says can be easily distinguished from *how* one says it. Instead, the questions generally follow the order of the selection itself so that as a student rereads he or she can quickly answer the questions. Many of the suggestions for writing ask the students to write short essays based on personal experiences; others ask for longer essays drawn from local interviews or library research. Topics call for developing papers by a variety of strategies so that the students may practice organizing their writing in a number of ways.

Finally, an instructor's manual containing the answers to each set of questions and brief teaching tips on each selection is available upon request from Holt, Rinehart, and Winston, 383 Madison Avenue, New York, New York 10017.

Discovering Ideas is a text that can be used in any college composition course and especially by those teachers who wish to take a thematic, rhetorical, or literary approach. By simultaneously providing models of good writing and provocative, challenging ideas, this book should help teachers guide their students from analytical reading to thoughtful discussions, and, ultimately, to the writing of their own insightful essays.

Acknowledgments

I would like to thank Kenney Withers and Susan Katz with whom I began this project. Sincere gratitude goes to Anne Boynton-Trigg, associate English editor, who patiently guided the book to completion. I also appreciate the helpful advice of Professor Richard Beal and the excellent work of Harriet Sigerman, project editor, and Renee Cafiero, copy editor. For their assistance and suggestions I am grateful to Professors Stephen Reid, Colorado State University; Chris Antonides, Lansing Community College; Larry Champion, North Carolina State University; Robert Cosgrove, Texas Tech University; Barnett Guttenberg, University of Miami; William Hamlin, University of Missouri, St. Louis; Francis Hubbard, University of Wisconsin, Milwaukee; Robert C. Johnson, Miami University; Joseph LaBriola, Sinclair Community College; Richard Larson, Lehman College, CUNY; David Skwire, Cuyahoga Community College; Frederick C. Stern, University of Illinois at Chicago Circle; Joseph Trimmer, Ball State University; and John R. Wallace, Coastal Carolina Community College.

And, finally, I wish to thank my husband, David Hall, for giving me the time and encouragement I needed.

Contents

I   Growing Up

II   Men and Women

III   People at Leisure

(*) Denotes short story.
(+) Denotes poetry.

IV   Education: Teaching and Learning

V   Life Confronts Death

VII   Social Issues

VIII   Scenes of the Past

IX   Language: Reading, Writing, Talking

Rhetorical Contents

The essays in this text are listed here according to their primary mode or strategy of development. Other important modes and strategies found in each essay are noted in parentheses below the selection's title.

I Description

II Narration

III Examples

IV Comparison and Contrast

V Definition

IX   Persuasion and Argument

Why Read Essays?

Studying the essays in this text should help you become a better writer in several ways. First, a close reading of the opinions and arguments expressed by these authors may spark new thoughts and reactions that will lead you to devise interesting essay topics of your own; secondly, discovering the various ways others have organized, developed, and explained their material should give you some new ideas about selecting your own strategies and supporting details. Familiarizing yourself with the effective stylistic devices and diction of other writers may also stimulate you to use language in ways you've never tried before. And, finally, evaluating the prose of others should make you more aware of the writing process itself. Each writer represented in this book faced a series of problems similar to those you face when you write; each had to make decisions regarding organization, development, coherence, sentence style, tone, and so forth, just as you do. By asking questions ("Why did the writer begin the essay this way?" "Why is this term defined here?" "Why compare this study to that one?" and so forth), you will begin to see how the writer put the essay together—and that knowledge in turn can help you put *your* essay together.

Questioning the choices of other writers should also help you become a better editor as you rewrite and polish your prose because you will acquire the habit of asking yourself questions such as the following: does this point need more supporting evidence? is my reasoning clear and logical here? does my conclusion fall flat? In other words, the skills you practice as a critical reader are some of the very ones you'll need to become a skillful writer.

How to Read an Essay

How do you become a critical reader? One way you can better understand not only the content but also the composition of the essays in this text is by practicing a process of analysis involving the steps explained below. This analytical process demands at least two readings, some marking of the text, and some brief note-taking. While this procedure may seem time-consuming at first, the benefits to you as both reader and writer are well worth the extra minutes.

First, read the essay through without marking anything. Then jot down a sentence or two summarizing your general impression. Consider what you think the author was trying to do and how well he or she succeeded (a typical response might be "argued for tuition hike—unconvincing, boring—too many confusing statistics"). Then return to the beginning of the essay and, as you reread, follow these steps and answer these questions:

1. Note any *publication information* and biographical data on the *author.* Knowing the source of the material you're reading may make a difference in your evaluation. Is the author qualified to discuss this subject? Is he or she obviously biased in any way? To whom was the essay written? Is the essay out of date?

2. Look at the *title* and *introduction.* Do they draw you into the essay? Do they help set up the essay's tone?

3. Frequently writers will present their main point (*thesis*) early in the essay; the thesis may be stated plainly in one or more sentences or it may be implied. Once you've located the main point, underline the sentence or note the area in which it is implied with a capital "T" in the margin, so that you can refer to it easily.

4. As you reread the essay, you will discover important statements that support the thesis. These statements are usually found in *topic sentences,* which often occur near the beginning or at the end of body paragraphs. So that you can quickly find each of these supporting points later, number each one and place two or three key words in the margin by each number. (Hint: writers often use subheadings to announce a new point; watch for these and also for any italicized or underlined words.) Writing down these key words will also help you remember the *content* of the essay.

5. Each time you discover one of the essay's key statements, ask yourself how the author *develops* that idea. For instance, does he or she try to support or prove the point by providing examples, statistics, or testimony; by comparing or contrasting it to something else; or by describing, classifying, or defining the subject? A writer can use one method of development or any combination, but each major point in an essay should be explained clearly and logically. Underdeveloped ideas or ones supported only by generalizations, biased sources, or emotional outpourings are not ultimately convincing.

6. As you move through the essay, circle any words you don't know that you feel are essential to the author's meaning. Look these up in a dictionary if their context does not provide a definition. Next, underline or put a star by important or especially effective statements; put a question mark by those passages you think are weak, exaggerated, or untrue. Use the top and bottom margins to jot brief responses, raise questions, or make note of new ideas (or possible essay topics?). Most of these markings and notes will help you assess the essay's effectiveness in your final evaluation.

7. To help you structure your own essay, you may find it useful to note how the writer moved from one point to the next. Bracketing the *transition devices* that link the paragraphs can make you aware of the ways a good writer subtly creates a smooth flow from idea to idea. (You probably won't have time to do this throughout the essay, but you might try marking a few paragraphs.)

8. Look closely at the essay's *conclusion*. Does it sum up the author's thesis without being boring or repetitive?

9. Consider the essay's *tone*. Is it ironic, sarcastic, serious, informal, humorous, or what? An inappropriate tone can undercut an author's intended effect on the reader. For instance, a flippant, overly informal tone may offend the reader who takes seriously the subject in question; a sarcastic tone may signal a writer who's too angry to be logical. On the other hand, a coolly rational tone can be convincing, and sometimes humor can be persuasive in a way that nothing else can. Creating the right tone is important.

10. The author's *style* is important, too. Does he or she use figurative language (for example, similes, metaphors, personification) in an arresting way? Literary allusions? Specialized diction? Does he or she use any sentence patterns that are especially effective? Writers use a variety of stylistic devices to make their prose vivid and memorable; you may want to study some of the devices you find so that you can try using them in your own essays.

Once you have completed the ten steps above, you're ready to make your final evaluation of the essay. Review your notes and markings; they should help you quickly locate the important parts of the essay and your impressions of those parts. Is the essay's thesis supported by enough logically developed, persuasive points? Is each point as clear, convincing, and well stated as it should be? Is the essay organized effectively? What strengths and weaknesses did you find after this critical reading? Has your original *evaluation* changed? If so, write a new assessment of the essay. Add any other comments you want to remember about this piece of writing.

Finally, after this critical reading of the essay, have you discovered any new ideas, strategies, or techniques you wish to incorporate into *your* writing?

Here is an essay marked and annotated according to the criteria listed on pages 1–3.

Our Youth Should Serve

STEVEN MULLER is the president of Johns Hopkins University. This essay appeared in *Newsweek* in 1978.

title forecasts thesis

educator writing about young people

general audience, educated

1   Too many young men and women now leave school without a well-developed sense of purpose. If they go right to work after high school, many are not properly prepared for careers. But if they enter college instead, many do not really know what to study or what to do afterward. Our society does not seem to be doing much to encourage and use the best instincts and talents of our young.

introduction sets up the problem

2   [On the one hand,] I see the growing problems of each year's new generation of high-school graduates. After twelve years of schooling—and television— many of them want to participate actively in society; but they face either a job with a limited future or more years in educational institutions. Many are wonderfully idealistic: they have talent and energy to offer, and they seek the meaning in their lives that comes from giving of oneself to the common good. But they feel almost rejected by a society that has too few jobs to offer them and that asks nothing of them except to avoid trouble. They want to be part of a new solution; instead society perceives them as a problem. They seek a cause; but their elders preach only self-advancement. They need experience on which to base choice; yet society seems to put a premium on the earliest possible choice, based inescapably on the least experience.

the problem for young people

Style: note parallelism stressing the difficult situation

Necessary Tasks

3 [On the other hand,] I see an American society
sadly in need of <u>social services</u> that we can afford
less and less at prevailing costs of labor. Some tasks
are necessary but constitute no career; they should
be carried out, but not as anyone's lifetime occupation. Our democracy profoundly needs public
spirit, but the economy of our labor system primarily encourages self-interest. The Federal government
spends billions on opportunity grants for post-secondary education, but some of us wonder about
money given on the basis only of need. <u>We ask the
young to volunteer for national defense,</u> but not for
the improvement of our society. As public spirit and
public services decline, so does the quality of life.
So I ask myself why cannot we put it all together
and ask our young people to volunteer in peacetime
to serve America?

4   I recognize that at first mention, universal national youth service may sound too much like compulsory military service or the Hitler Youth or the
Komsomol. I do not believe it has to be like that at
all. It need not require uniforms or camps, nor a vast
new Federal bureaucracy, nor vast new public expenditures. And it should certainly not be compulsory.

5   A voluntary program of universal national youth
service does of course require <u>compelling</u> incentives.
Two could be provided. <u>Guaranteed job training</u>
would be one. <u>Substantial Federal assistance toward
post-secondary education</u> would be the other. This
would mean that today's complex measures of Federal aid to students would be ended, and that there
would also be no need for tuition tax credits for post-
secondary education. Instead, prospective students
would *earn* their assistance for post-secondary education by volunteering for national service, and
only those who earned assistance would receive it.
Present Federal expenditures for the assistance of
students in post-secondary education would be con-
verted into a simple grant program, modeled on the
post-World War II GI Bill of Rights.

Volunteers

6 But what, you say, would huge numbers of high-
school graduates do as volunteers in national ser-

the problem for society
? such as ?

⟩ ?

} Thesis

clarifies his proposal—tells what it isn't (contrast, definition)

youth section of the Soviet Communist Party

1. incentives
a. job training
b. Federal assistance for education

(contrast)

(comparison)

2. Duties

vice? They could be interns in public agencies, local, state and national. They could staff day-care programs, neighborhood health centers, centers to counsel and work with children; help to maintain public facilities, including highways, railbeds, waterways and airports; engage in neighborhood-renewal projects, both physical and social. Some would elect <u>military service,</u> others the Peace Corps. Except for the latter two alternatives and others like them, they could live anywhere they pleased. They would not wear uniforms. They would be employed and supervised by people already employed locally in public-agency careers.

(examples)

?How would this differ from the present volunteer army?

7   Volunteers would be paid only a subsistence wage, because they would receive the benefits of job training (not necessarily confined to one task) as well as assistance toward post-secondary education if they were so motivated and qualified. If cheap mass <u>housing</u> for some groups of volunteers were needed, supervised participants in the program could rebuild decayed dwellings in metropolitan areas.

3. Low pay (cites reasons)

But how could the volunteers afford essentials like food?

8   [All that] might work. But perhaps an even more attractive version of universal national youth service might include private industrial and commercial enterprise as well. A private employer would volunteer to select a stated number of volunteers. He would have their labor at the universally applied subsistence wage; in return he would offer guaranteed job training as well as the exact equivalent of what the Federal government would have to pay for assistance toward post-secondary education. The inclusion of volunteer private employers would greatly amplify job-training opportunities for the youth volunteers, and would greatly lessen the costs of the program in public funds.

4. Role of private employers

(description of benefits to both employers & employees)

Direct Benefits

5.

9   The direct benefits of [such a universal national-youth-service program] would be significant. Every young man and woman would face a meaningful role in society after high school. Everyone would receive job training, and the right to earn assistance toward post-secondary education. Those going on to post-secondary education would have their education interrupted by a constructive work experience. <u>There is evidence that</u> they would thereby become <u>more highly motivated and successful students, par-</u>

> projects results

from where?

ticularly if their work experience related closely to subsequent vocational interests. Many participants might locate careers by means of their national-service assignments.

10   No union jobs need be lost, because skilled workers would be needed to give job training. Many public services would be performed by cheap labor, but there would be no youth army. And the intangible, indirect benefits would be the greatest of all. Young people could regard themselves as more useful and needed. They could serve this country for a two-year period as volunteers, and *earn* job training and/or assistance toward post-secondary education. There is more self-esteem and motivation in earned than in unearned benefits. Universal national youth service may be no panacea. But in my opinion the idea merits serious and imaginative consideration.

counters a possible problem

6. Indirect Benefits

✱ a remedy for all ills

Conclusion: stresses benefits & calls for consideration of proposal

First Impression: Muller wants a volunteer youth corps to provide certain public services – many benefits – clearly organized arguments –

Final evaluation: Muller is persuasive, although the low pay would be a problem for many. I especially like the idea of getting work experience before college – working might have helped me decide on the major and career I wanted. (Possible essay topic: Some people [or just me?] should work a year before starting college –)

Other Notes:
Organization and development: Muller's essay is an argument – good use of examples, reasons, comparison, contrast, description, cause-effect relationships. Many specific details. Essay flows smoothly – uses transition words and repeats key terms.
Style and tone: Muller is serious, straight-forward, forceful, sincere. No jargon or pompous language. Note parallelism for emphasis (#2). Might have given essay more of a personal tone by adding some testimony from students or by citing some real experiences.

Modes and Strategies:
An Introduction to Essays

Communication may be divided into four types (or "modes" as they are often called): exposition, argumentation, description, and narration. The four modes may be defined briefly as follows:

exposition: the writer intends to explain or inform
narration: the writer intends to tell a story or recount an event
description: the writer intends to create in words a picture of a person, place, object, or feeling
argumentation: the writer intends to convince or persuade

While we commonly refer to exposition, argumentation, description, and narration as the basic types of prose, in reality it is difficult to find any one mode in a pure form. In fact, almost all essays are combinations of two or more modes; it would be virtually impossible, for instance, to write a story—narration—without including description or to argue without also giving some information. Nevertheless, by determining a writer's *main* purpose, we can usually identify an essay or prose piece as primarily exposition, argumentation, description, or narration. In other words, an article may include a brief description of a new mousetrap, but if the writer's main intention is to explain how the trap works, then we may designate the essay as exposition. In almost all cases, the primary mode of any essay will be readily apparent to the reader.

Here, then, is a brief introduction to the modes and the most frequently used patterns of organization. Learning to recognize and analyze prose patterns as they appear in the essays in this text will ultimately help you select the most effective plan for organizing and developing your own writing.

I. Exposition

There are a variety of ways to organize an expository essay, depending upon the writer's purpose. The most common *strategies,* or patterns, of organization include development by example, comparison and contrast, definition, classi-fication, process analysis, and causal analysis. An essay may be identified as having a primary strategy of development (for instance, an essay telling how to change a tire is a piece of process analysis), or an essay may use a variety of strategies to explain its points.

STRATEGY ONE: *Development by Example*

Using examples to illustrate, clarify, or support an idea is probably the most common method of development. If a writer wants to make a point about the dangers of nuclear wastes, he or she must cite specific examples—actual harm done to people or experts' opinions of possible hazards—to support his or her claims rather than relying on vague generalizations. In addition to making gen-eral statements specific and thus more convincing, good examples can explain and clarify unfamiliar, abstract, or difficult concepts for the reader. Examples also make prose more vivid and interesting by giving readers something con-crete to think about as they note each point in the essay. A general statement decrying child abuse, for instance, is probably not as effective as a paragraph citing several instances of brutal treatment.

Sometimes writers use a number of brief examples to support or explain their ideas; at other times one long, detailed example (called an extended example) or a combination of the two types is more useful. Regardless of the number, the writer should always select examples that are clear, persuasive, and relevant to the subject under discussion.

STRATEGY TWO: *Development by Comparison and Contrast*

Comparison (pointing out similarities) and contrast (pointing out differences) is another common expository method. Writers frequently use comparison and contrast to make a point ("the many similarities in style clearly suggest that Ernest Hemingway was influenced by Stephen Crane"), assert superiority or advantages ("Mom's is a better place to eat than McHenry's"), or clarify the unfamiliar ("the new aid-to-education plan will be set up like the GI Bill").

Essays of comparison and contrast are often organized one of two ways. The writer may present all the information on subject A and then turn to all the information on subject B, being careful to make the basis for comparison/con-trast clear through use of connecting phrases, such as "unlike those responsible for the friendly service at restaurant A, the employees of restaurant B are cold, distant, and uncooperative." Or the writer may choose to compare/contrast the two subjects on one point, then another, and then another and so forth. Which-ever plan the writer adopts, he or she probably will use numerous examples to clarify his or her points; the writer will also employ transition devices wisely to avoid a choppy, "seesaw" effect.

STRATEGY THREE: *Development by Definition*

When readers do not understand a particular term central to a writer's point, the entire meaning of the essay may be lost or clouded. For instance, a writer arguing for the repeal of a law he or she considers too liberal must first make clear his or her use of "liberal" before the readers know whether they agree. Other essays may define new or unusual words found in slang, dialects, or jargon, or they may provide interpretations of vague, abstract, or controversial terms (such as "pornography," "success," or "mercy killing"). Depending upon the subject, a writer might define a word or expression by giving synonyms, stating some examples, comparing or contrasting to similar terms, explaining a process, presenting the history, describing the parts, or using any combination of these and other methods.

STRATEGY FOUR: *Development by Classification*

We classify knowledge to make it easier to comprehend. For example, if the classified ads in the newspaper were not listed under categories such as "houses to rent" and "help wanted," we would have to search through countless ads to find the service or item we wanted. Classification essays approach a subject by separating it into groups, types, or categories for a particular purpose. Such essays may be serious (kinds of plants native to Colorado) or humorous (blind dates to avoid).

STRATEGY FIVE: *Development by Process Analysis*

Process analysis identifies and explains what steps must be taken to complete an operation or procedure. A *directional* process tells the reader how to do or make something; a directional process essay might explain how to buy a used car or how to knit a sweater. An *informative* process tells how something is or was made or done that could not be duplicated by the reader. For example, an informative process essay might describe how the French Revolution started or how scientists created DNA in the laboratory or how a particular machine operates. Both kinds of essays should state the steps of the process clearly and accurately in logical, chronological order.

STRATEGY SIX: *Development by Causal Analysis*

Casual analysis explains the cause-and-effect relationship between two elements. Essays that discuss the conditions producing X analyze *causes* (political events leading to Pearl Harbor); essays that discuss the results produced by X analyze *effects* (jogging's benefits to potential heart-attack victims). Some essays, of course, discuss both causes and effects of an event or condition. In any case, the writer must make the analysis clear enough so that the reader is convinced the cause-effect relationship does, in fact, exist.

II. Narration

Not all narratives are fictional, nor are they all synonymous with short stories or novels. Essay writers often use stories to illustrate, explain, or support some larger point; for instance, an essay narrating a childhood event might stress the importance of an understanding teacher. Shorter narratives may also illustrate ideas within expository and argumentative essays. A successful narrative, regardless of length, frequently depends upon the writer's ability to create believable characters, settings, and dialogue through the use of vivid details. The narrative should also maintain a consistent point of view, an appropriate time sequence, and a smooth pace.

III. Description

The writer of description creates a word picture of persons, places, objects, abstract qualities, and emotions, using a careful selection of details to make an impression on the reader. An essay can be almost entirely description, but more often than not description is used in expository, narrative, and argumentative essays to make them more vivid, understandable, and convincing. Sometimes the writer of description tries to be *objective* (the factual detailing of a business transaction or cancer operation), but frequently the writer wants to convey a particular attitude toward the subject; this approach is called *subjective* or *impressionistic* (the joyful description of a baby at play). In both kinds of description the writer selects only those details that will communicate the appropriate mood to the readers, and those details should be arranged in an order that will most effectively present the picture. Good description uses specific, sensory details to help the reader understand and imagine the subject the writer wants to reproduce. Frequently, a writer will use figurative language, such as metaphors or similes, to clarify the unfamiliar or abstract subject or simply to make the description more distinct and memorable.

IV. Argumentation

An argumentative essay presents the writer's stand on some subject and then offers reasons to support that position. The writer may want the reader to agree, to support a cause, to change behavior, or to take action—but whatever the goal, the essay must be convincing and persuasive. Consequently, the writer must provide more than mere opinion; he or she must offer enough logical evidence to back up the essay's position. Writers may use any of a number of expository methods to develop their arguments, such as definition, comparison, cause and effect, and illustration. They may argue *inductively* (move from specific evidence to a generalization) or *deductively* (move from an accepted generality to a specific claim), and they may also employ testimony from authorities, statistics, factual information, or personal experience. Many writers of argument find it useful to state and refute the opposition's major points, a practice that not only helps convince the readers but also shows them that the writer has thoroughly investigated and thought out his or her position. No matter what sort of evidence or organization of that evidence a writer selects, he or she should maintain a sincere, rational tone and should avoid making any logical fallacies, such as hasty generalizations (conclusions based on insufficient or unrepresentative evidence), *non sequiturs* (conclusions that do not follow from the facts), or arguments *ad hominem* (attacks on the opponent's character rather than on the argument).

Section 1
Growing Up

A Halfway House
Ellen Goodman

Ellen Goodman worked as a reporter for *Newsweek* and the *Detroit Free Press* before becoming a columnist for *The Boston Globe*. Her columns, syndicated by the Washington Post Writers Group since 1976, won her a Pulitzer Prize in 1980 for distinguished commentary. She is the author of *Turning Points* (1979) and *Close to Home* (1979), a collection of her columns from which this selection was taken. It originally appeared in November of 1976.

1   For many years I was certain that Thanksgiving was a plot devised by the Turkey Population Growth lobby. But, more recently, I have decided that it is truly brought to us by the American Family Psychoanalytic Association, in order to study midlife-crisis parents and their identity-crisis children.

2   For those of you unfamiliar with the middle-class American Life Cycle patterns, every September, at enormous expense, a large segment of the population send their children off to Institutions of Higher Adolescence, known as universities. These institutions are charged with the responsibility of managing the transition of America's youth into adulthood.

3   Ideally, they are to produce totally delightful twenty-two-year-old graduates who are independent but caring, articulate but agreeable, and fully appreciative of their parents' wonderfulness. In short, "the children we would have regretted not having when we were older." These institutions, like all modern rehabilitative centers, allow the wards out on furloughs at carefully managed intervals known as holidays.

4   During each of these furloughs—of which Thanksgiving is the first— the issue is to discover how the new lessons fit into the old setting. Not to mention vice versa.

5   The kiddies come home with a mixed agenda. They want to be taken care of on the one hand, and prove their independence on the other. They drop their laundry in the utility room and their opinions in the dining room.

6   They are hurt if their parents have forgotten to stock up on their special brand of low-calorie soda, and horrified if these same parents expect them to eat their favorite roast, since they "don't touch meat anymore." They want to be treated like visitors who get clean sheets, while conveniently forgetting that visitors ask before they use the car.

7   Their parents meanwhile have their own adjustments to make. You see, those who were prepared for an attack of the empty-nest syndrome

in September are aghast at the symptoms of a full-nest syndrome in November.

8   In the past six weeks they have discovered what it's like to have sex when you don't have to outwait your teenage children—"Not now, *they* are still awake"—and what it's like to have dinner-time conversation instead of arbitration. After years of "running a household," they are learning to live together. Now, vaguely distressed at having a household of children, they have reams of guilt—"Does this mean I don't miss my children? Does this mean I don't love them?"—which leads them into overdosing their young with nurturing and role-playing.

9   The separate issues of parents and children meet across the groaning board known as Thanksgiving Dinner. Next to this encounter of generations, the University of Texas football field is as calm as a chessboard.

10   There is, for example, one daughter who has come home with a definitive analysis of her parents' relationship—"sexist"—and now wants to institute a plan for changing it: "Mother, you carve the turkey." Then, there is the son who is taking an American history course on the sixties and informs his father that "Jack Kennedy was a fascist" (an opinion his father calculates costs $465, not including books).

11   To add to the family fun, there is a son who has decided that it is time for him to be honest and direct with grandma, so that "she will know where I'm coming from," which is generally an X-rated dictionary. And, finally, there is daughter's Mystery Guest, whom she introduces to eighty-three-year-old Aunt Jane as "my lover," in case anyone had not noticed.

12   Mother, in turn, tells her daughter (in front of the lover) to brush her hair. Father reminds his son to "Kiss your Aunt Polly hello," and in glorious unison they tell their twenty-year-old to "Finish your peas or no dessert."

13   Dinner thus ends in a draw, and the turkey ends in a curry. Or a fricassee. Or a salad. Everyone is momentarily aghast at the speed with which they fell into their old roles, but the beat goes on.

14   The holiday home is a halfway house between childhood and adulthood, between parenthood and friendship, and it's difficult to work out these transitions in a 108-hour furlough. But this is just a beginning. If Thanksgiving can be handled without a major bloodletting, give thanks for that. Remember, there are only thirty recovery days until Christmas.

A Halfway House

Questions on Content, Style, and Structure

1. How does Goodman characterize universities in her second and third paragraphs? Why does she begin this way?

2. Why is the first Thanksgiving at home so important for both college students and their parents?

3. Goodman compares and contrasts what subjects in this essay?

4. How does Goodman make her comparison and contrast vivid to the reader? Support your answer with examples.

5. How does the sentence construction in paragraphs 5 and 6 emphasize the contrasts Goodman presents?

6. What conflict is discussed in paragraph 9? How does the contrast presented in paragraphs 10 through 12 differ from those in paragraphs 5 through 8?

7. What does the use of dialogue add to this essay?

8. Identify the transition devices Goodman uses to link paragraphs 10–13.

9. Because this essay was written for a newspaper, its paragraphs are very short. If you were writing this for your composition class, which paragraphs would you combine?

10. How does Goodman end her essay? Is it an effective conclusion?

11. Describe the tone of this essay; how is it produced?

12. What is a halfway house? Is it an appropriate title for this essay?

Vocabulary

articulate (3)   syndrome (7)
furloughs (4)   arbitration (8)
aghast (7)

Suggestions for Writing

1. Describe your first visit home after leaving for college. Explain why it was a better (or worse) visit than you expected.

2. Write an essay in which you compare and contrast your relationship with your parents when you were in high school to the relationship you now have with them.

3. Write an essay analyzing the one or two major changes you've undergone since you began attending college. Your essay might focus on the causes of these changes or the effects, or both. (If your assignment is a short essay of three to five pages, you should probably not try to describe both the causes and effects of more than one change.)

Graduation
Maya Angelou

Maya Angelou is an American author, actress, journalist, and
civil rights activist. Raised in Stamps, Arkansas, Angelou has
traveled and performed in Europe and Africa as well as in the
United States. She has written two volumes of poetry and three
popular autobiographies. This essay is a chapter from her first
autobiography, *I Know Why the Caged Bird Sings* (1969).

1   The children in Stamps[1] trembled visibly with anticipation. Some adults
were excited too, but to be certain the whole young population had come
down with graduation epidemic. Large classes were graduating from both
the grammar school and the high school. Even those who were years
removed from their own day of glorious release were anxious to help
with preparations as a kind of dry run. The junior students who were
moving into the vacating classes' chairs were tradition-bound to show
their talents for leadership and management. They strutted through the
school and around the campus exerting pressure on the lower grades.
Their authority was so new that occasionally if they pressed a little too
hard it had to be overlooked. After all, next term was coming, and it
never hurt a sixth grader to have a play sister in the eighth grade, or a
tenth-year student to be able to call a twelfth grader Bubba. So all was
endured in a spirit of shared understanding. But the graduating classes
themselves were the nobility. Like travelers with exotic destinations on
their minds, the graduates were remarkably forgetful. They came to
school without their books, or tablets or even pencils. Volunteers fell
over themselves to secure replacements for the missing equipment.
When accepted, the willing workers might or might not be thanked, and
it was of no importance to the pregraduation rites. Even teachers were
respectful of the now quiet and aging seniors, and tended to speak to
them, if not as equals, as beings only slightly lower than themselves.
After tests were returned and grades given, the student body, which acted
like an extended family, knew who did well, who excelled, and what
piteous ones had failed.

2   Unlike the white high school, Lafayette County Training School distinguished itself by having neither lawn, nor hedges, nor tennis court,
nor climbing ivy. Its two buildings (main classrooms, the grade school
and home economics) were set on a dirt hill with no fence to limit either
its boundaries or those of bordering farms. There was a large expanse to
the left of the school which was used alternately as a baseball diamond

[1]A small town in Arkansas

or a basketball court. Rusty hoops on the swaying poles represented the permanent recreational equipment, although bats and balls could be borrowed from the P.E. teacher if the borrower was qualified and if the diamond wasn't occupied.

3 Over this rocky area relieved by a few shady tall persimmon trees the graduating class walked. The girls often held hands and no longer bothered to speak to the lower students. There was a sadness about them, as if this old world was not their home and they were bound for higher ground. The boys, on the other hand, had become more friendly, more outgoing. A decided change from the closed attitude they projected while studying for finals. Now they seemed not ready to give up the old school, the familiar paths and classrooms. Only a small percentage would be continuing on to college—one of the South's A & M (agricultural and mechanical) schools, which trained Negro youths to be carpenters, farmers, handymen, masons, maids, cooks and baby nurses. Their future rode heavily on their shoulders, and blinded them to the collective joy that had pervaded the lives of the boys and girls in the grammar school graduating class.

4 Parents who could afford it had ordered new shoes and ready-made clothes for themselves from Sears and Roebuck or Montgomery Ward. They also engaged the best seamstresses to make the floating graduating dresses and to cut down secondhand pants which would be pressed to a military slickness for the important event.

5 Oh, it was important, all right. Whitefolks would attend the ceremony, and two or three would speak of God and home, and the Southern way of life, and Mrs. Parsons, the principal's wife, would play the graduation march while the lower-grade graduates paraded down the aisles and took their seats below the platform. The high school seniors would wait in empty classrooms to make their dramatic entrance.

6 In the Store I was the person of the moment. The birthday girl. The center. Bailey had graduated the year before, although to do so he had had to forfeit all pleasures to make up for his time lost in Baton Rouge.

7 My class was wearing butter-yellow piqué dresses, and Momma launched out on mine. She smocked the yoke into tiny crisscrossing puckers, then shirred the rest of the bodice. Her dark fingers ducked in and out of the lemony cloth as she embroidered raised daisies around the hem. Before she considered herself finished she had added a crocheted cuff on the puff sleeves, and a pointy crocheted collar.

8 I was going to be lovely. A walking model of all the various styles of fine hand sewing and it didn't worry me that I was only twelve years old and merely graduating from the eighth grade. Besides, many teachers in Arkansas Negro schools had only that diploma and were licensed to impart wisdom.

9 The days had become longer and more noticeable. The faded beige of former times had been replaced with strong and sure colors. I began to

see my classmates' clothes, their skin tones, and the dust that waved off pussy willows. Clouds that lazed across the sky were objects of great concern to me. Their shiftier shapes might have held a message that in my new happiness and with a little bit of time I'd soon decipher. During that period I looked at the arch of heaven so religiously my neck kept a steady ache. I had taken to smiling more often, and my jaws hurt from the unaccustomed activity. Between the two physical sore spots, I suppose I could have been uncomfortable, but that was not the case. As a member of the winning team (the graduating class of 1940) I had outdistanced unpleasant sensations by miles. I was headed for the freedom of open fields.

10   Youth and social approval allied themselves with me and we trammeled memories of slights and insults. The wind of our swift passage remodeled my features. Lost tears were pounded to mud and then to dust. Years of withdrawal were brushed aside and left behind, as hanging ropes of parasitic moss.

11   My work alone had awarded me a top place and I was going to be one of the first called in the graduating ceremonies. On the classroom blackboard, as well as on the bulletin board in the auditorium, there were blue stars and white stars and red stars. No absences, no tardinesses, and my academic work was among the best of the year. I could say the preamble to the Constitution even faster than Bailey. We timed ourselves often: WethepeopleoftheUnitedStatesinordertoformamoreperfectunion . . ."   I had memorized the Presidents of the United States from Washington to Roosevelt in chronological as well as alphabetical order.

12   My hair pleased me too. Gradually the black mass had lengthened and thickened, so that it kept at last to its braided pattern, and I didn't have to yank my scalp off when I tried to comb it.

13   Louise and I had rehearsed the exercises until we tired out ourselves. Henry Reed was class valedictorian. He was a small, very black boy with hooded eyes, a long, broad nose and an oddly shaped head. I had admired him for years because each term he and I vied for the best grades in our class. Most often he bested me, but instead of being disappointed I was pleased that we shared top places between us. Like many Southern Black children, he lived with his grandmother, who was as strict as Momma and as kind as she knew how to be. He was courteous, respectful and soft-spoken to elders, but on the playground he chose to play the roughest games. I admired him. Anyone, I reckoned, sufficiently afraid or sufficiently dull could be polite. But to be able to operate at a top level with both adults and children was admirable.

14   His valedictory speech was entitled "To Be or Not to Be." The rigid tenth-grade teacher had helped him to write it. He'd been working on the dramatic stresses for months.

15   The weeks until graduation were filled with heady activities. A group of small children were to be presented in a play about buttercups and daisies and bunny rabbits. They could be heard throughout the building practicing their hops and their little songs that sounded like silver bells.

The older girls (non-graduates, of course) were assigned the task of making refreshments for the night's festivities. A tangy scent of ginger, cinnamon, nutmeg and chocolate wafted around the home economics building as the budding cooks made samples for themselves and their teachers.

16   In every corner of the workshop, axes and saws split fresh timber as the woodshop boys made sets and stage scenery. Only the graduates were left out of the general bustle. We were free to sit in the library at the back of the building or look in quite detachedly, naturally, on the measures being taken for our event.

17   Even the minister preached on graduation the Sunday before. His subject was "Let your light so shine that men will see your good works and praise your Father, Who is in Heaven." Although the sermon was purported to be addressed to us, he used the occasion to speak to backsliders, gamblers and general ne'er-do-wells. But since he had called our names at the beginning of the service we were mollified.

18   Among Negroes the tradition was to give presents to children going only from one grade to another. How much more important this was when the person was graduating at the top of the class. Uncle Willie and Momma had sent away for a Mickey Mouse watch like Bailey's. Louise gave me four embroidered handkerchiefs. (I gave her three crocheted doilies.) Mrs. Sneed, the minister's wife, made me an underskirt to wear for graduation, and nearly every customer gave me a nickel or maybe even a dime with the instruction "Keep on moving to higher ground," or some such encouragement.

19   Amazingly the great day finally dawned and I was out of bed before I knew it. I threw open the back door to see it more clearly, but Momma said, "Sister, come away from that door and put your robe on."

20   I hoped the memory of that morning would never leave me. Sunlight was itself still young, and the day had none of the insistence maturity would bring it in a few hours. In my robe and barefoot in the backyard, under cover of going to see about my new beans, I gave myself up to the gentle warmth and thanked God that no matter what evil I had done in my life He had allowed me to live to see this day. Somewhere in my fatalism I had expected to die, accidentally, and never have the chance to walk up the stairs in the auditorium and gracefully receive my hard-earned diploma. Out of God's merciful bosom I had won reprieve.

21   Bailey came out in his robe and gave me a box wrapped in Christmas paper. He said he had saved his money for months to pay for it. It felt like a box of chocolates, but I knew Bailey wouldn't save money to buy candy when we had all we could want under our noses.

22   He was as proud of the gift as I. It was a soft-leather-bound copy of a collection of poems by Edgar Allan Poe, or, as Bailey and I called him, "Eap." I turned to "Annabel Lee" and we walked up and down the garden rows, the cool dirt between our toes, reciting the beautifully sad lines.

23   Momma made a Sunday breakfast although it was only Friday. After we finished the blessing, I opened my eyes to find the watch on my plate. It was a dream of a day. Everything went smoothly and to my credit. I

didn't have to be reminded or scolded for anything. Near evening I was too jittery to attend to chores, so Bailey volunteered to do all before his bath.

24 Days before, we had made a sign for the Store and as we turned out the lights Momma hung the cardboard over the doorknob. It read clearly: CLOSED. GRADUATION.

25 My dress fitted perfectly and everyone said that I looked like a sunbeam in it. On the hill, going toward the school, Bailey walked behind with Uncle Willie, who muttered, "Go on, Ju." He wanted him to walk ahead with us because it embarrassed him to have to walk so slowly. Bailey said he'd let the ladies walk together, and the men would bring up the rear. We all laughed, nicely.

26 Little children dashed by out of the dark like fireflies. Their crepe-paper dresses and butterfly wings were not made for running and we heard more than one rip, dryly, and the regretful "uh uh" that followed.

27 The school blazed without gaiety. The windows seemed cold and un-friendly from the lower hill. A sense of ill-fated timing crept over me, and if Momma hadn't reached for my hand I would have drifted back to Bailey and Uncle Willie, and possibly beyond. She made a few slow jokes about my feet getting cold, and tugged me along to the now-strange build-ing.

28 Around the front steps, assurance came back. There were my fellow "greats," the graduating class. Hair brushed back, legs oiled, new dresses and pressed pleats, fresh pocket handkerchiefs and little handbags, all homesewn. Oh, we were up to snuff, all right. I joined my comrades and didn't even see my family go in to find seats in the crowded auditorium.

29 The school band struck up a march and all classes filed in as had been rehearsed. We stood in front of our seats, as assigned, and on a signal from the choir director, we sat. No sooner had this been accomplished than the band started to play the national anthem. We rose again and sang the song, after which we recited the pledge of allegiance. We re-mained standing for a brief minute before the choir director and the principal signaled to us, rather desperately I thought, to take our seats. The command was so unusual that our carefully rehearsed and smooth-running machine was thrown off. For a full minute we fumbled for our chairs and bumped into each other awkwardly. Habits change or solidify under pressure, so in our state of nervous tension we had been ready to follow our usual assembly pattern: the American National Anthem, then the pledge of allegiance, then the song every Black person I knew called the Negro National Anthem. All done in the same key, with the same passion and most often standing on the same foot.

30 Finding my seat at last, I was overcome with a presentiment of worse things to come. Something unrehearsed, unplanned, was going to happen, and we were going to be made to look bad. I distinctly remember being explicit in the choice of pronoun. It was "we," the graduating class, the unit, that concerned me then.

31   The principal welcomed "parents and friends" and asked the Baptist minister to lead us in prayer. His invocation was brief and punchy, and for a second I thought we were getting back on the high road to right action. When the principal came back to the dais, however, his voice had changed. Sounds always affected me profoundly and the principal's voice was one of my favorites. During assembly it melted and lowed weakly into the audience. It had not been in my plan to listen to him, but my curiosity was piqued and I straightened up to give him my attention.

32   He was talking about Booker T. Washington, our "late great leader," who said we can be as close as the fingers on the hand, etc. . . . Then he said a few vague things about friendship and the friendship of kindly people to those less fortunate than themselves. With that his voice nearly faded, thin, away. Like a river diminishing to a stream and then to a trickle. But he cleared his throat and said, "Our speaker tonight, who is also our friend, came from Texarkana to deliver the commencement address, but due to the irregularity of the train schedule, he's going to, as they say, 'speak and run.' " He said that we understood and wanted the man to know that we were most grateful for the time he was able to give us and then something about how we were willing always to adjust to another's program, and without more ado—"I give you Mr. Edward Donleavy."

33   Not one but two white men came through the door offstage. The shorter one walked to the speaker's platform, and the tall one moved over to the center seat and sat down. But that was our principal's seat, and already occupied. The dislodged gentleman bounced around for a long breath or two before the Baptist minister gave him his chair, then with more dignity than the situation deserved, the minister walked off the stage.

34   Donleavy looked at the audience once (on reflection, I'm sure that he wanted only to reassure himself that we were really there), adjusted his glasses and began to read from a sheaf of papers.

35   He was glad "to be here and to see the work going on just as it was in the other schools."

36   At the first "Amen" from the audience I willed the offender to immediate death by choking on the word. But Amens and Yes, sir's began to fall around the room like rain through a ragged umbrella.

37   He told us of the wonderful changes we children in Stamps had in store. The Central School (naturally, the white school was Central) had already been granted improvements that would be in use in the fall. A well-known artist was coming from Little Rock to teach art to them. They were going to have the newest microscopes and chemistry equipment for their laboratory. Mr. Donleavy didn't leave us long in the dark over who made these improvements available to Central High. Nor were we to be ignored in the general betterment scheme he had in mind.

38   He said that he had pointed out to people at a very high level that one of the first-line football tacklers at Arkansas Agricultural and Mechanical

College had graduated from good old Lafayette County Training School. Here fewer Amen's were heard. Those few that did break through lay dully in the air with the heaviness of habit.

39   He went on to praise us. He went on to say how he had bragged that "one of the best basketball players at Fisk sank his first ball right here at Lafayette County Training School."

40   The white kids were going to have a chance to become Galileos and Madame Curies and Edisons and Gauguins, and our boys (the girls weren't even in on it) would try to be Jesse Owenses and Joe Louises.

41   Owens and the Brown Bomber were great heroes in our world, but what school official in the white-goddom of Little Rock had the right to decide that those two men must be our only heroes? Who decided that for Henry Reed to become a scientist he had to work like George Washington Carver, as a bootblack, to buy a lousy microscope? Bailey was obviously always going to be too small to be an athlete, so which concrete angel glued to what country seat had decided that if my brother wanted to become a lawyer he had to first pay penance for his skin by picking cotton and hoeing corn and studying correspondence books at night for twenty years?

42   The man's dead words fell like bricks around the auditorium and too many settled in my belly. Constrained by hard-learned manners I couldn't look behind me, but to my left and right the proud graduating class of 1940 had dropped their heads. Every girl in my row had found something new to do with her handkerchief. Some folded the tiny squares into love knots, some into triangles, but most were wadding them, then pressing them flat on their yellow laps.

43   On the dais, the ancient tragedy was being replayed. Professor Parsons sat, a sculptor's reject, rigid. His large, heavy body seemed devoid of will or willingness, and his eyes said he was no longer with us. The other teachers examined the flag (which was draped stage right) or their notes, or the window which opened on our now-famous playing diamond.

44   Graduation, the hush-hush magic time of frills and gifts and congratulations and diplomas, was finished for me before my name was called. The accomplishment was nothing. The meticulous maps, drawn in three colors of ink, learning and spelling decasyllabic words, memorizing the whole of *The Rape of Lucrece*—it was nothing. Donleavy had exposed us.

45   We were maids and farmers, handymen and washerwomen, and anything higher that we aspired to was farcical and presumptuous. Then I wished that Gabriel Prosser and Nat Turner had killed all whitefolks in their beds and that Abraham Lincoln had been assassinated before the signing of the Emancipation Proclamation, and that Harriet Tubman had been killed by that blow on her head and Christopher Columbus had drowned in the *Santa Maria*.

46   It was awful to be Negro and have no control over my life. It was brutal to be young and already trained to sit quietly and listen to charges

brought against my color with no chance of defense. We should all be dead. I thought I should like to see us all dead, one on top of the other. A pyramid of flesh with the whitefolks on the bottom, as the broad base, then the Indians with their silly tomahawks and teepees and wigwams and treaties, the Negroes with their mops and recipes and cotton sacks and spirituals sticking out of their mouths. The Dutch children should all stumble in their wooden shoes and break their necks. The French should choke to death on the Louisiana Purchase (1803) while silkworms ate all the Chinese with their stupid pigtails. As a species, we were an abomination. All of us.

47   Donleavy was running for election, and assured our parents that if he won we could count on having the only colored paved playing field in that part of Arkansas. Also—he never looked up to acknowledge the grunts of acceptance—also, we were bound to get some new equipment for the home economics building and the workshop.

48   He finished, and since there was no need to give any more than the most perfunctory thank-you's, he nodded to the men on the stage, and the tall white man who was never introduced joined him at the door. They left with the attitude that now they were off to something really important. (The graduation ceremonies at Lafayette County Training School had been a mere preliminary.)

49   The ugliness they left was palpable. An uninvited guest who wouldn't leave. The choir was summoned and sang a modern arrangement of "Onward, Christian Soldiers," with new words pertaining to graduates seeking their place in the world. But it didn't work. Elouise, the daughter of the Baptist minister, recited "Invictus," and I could have cried at the impertinence of "I am the master of my fate: I am the captain of my soul."

50   My name had lost its ring of familiarity and I had to be nudged to go and receive my diploma. All my preparations had fled. I neither marched up to the stage like a conquering Amazon, nor did I look in the audience for Bailey's nod of approval. Marguerite Johnson, I heard the name again, my honors were read, there were noises in the audience of appreciation, and I took my place on the stage as rehearsed.

51   I thought about colors I hated: ecru, puce, lavender, beige and black.

52   There was shuffling and rustling around me, then Henry Reed was giving his valedictory address, "To Be or Not to Be." Hadn't he heard the whitefolks? We couldn't *be,* so the question was a waste of time. Henry's voice came out clear and strong. I feared to look at him. Hadn't he got the message? There was no "nobler in the mind" for Negroes because the world didn't think we had minds, and they let us know it. "Outrageous fortune"? Now, that was a joke. When the ceremony was over I had to tell Henry Reed some things. That is, if I still cared. Not "rub," Henry, "erase." "Ah, there's the erase." Us.

53   Henry had been a good student in elocution. His voice rose on tides of promise and fell on waves of warnings. The English teacher had helped

him to create a sermon winging through Hamlet's soliloquy. To be a man, a doer, a builder, a leader, or to be a tool, an unfunny joke, a crusher of funky toadstools. I marveled that Henry could go through with the speech as if we had a choice.

54   I had been listening and silently rebutting each sentence with my eyes closed; then there was a hush, which in an audience warns that something unplanned is happening. I looked up and saw Henry Reed, the conservative, the proper, the A student, turn his back to the audience and turn to us (the proud graduating class of 1940) and sing, nearly speaking,

> Lift ev'ry voice and sing
> Till earth and heaven ring
> Ring with the harmonies of Liberty . . .[2]

It was the poem written by James Weldon Johnson. It was the music composed by J. Rosamond Johnson. It was the Negro National Anthem. Out of habit we were singing it.

55   Our mothers and fathers stood in the dark hall and joined the hymn of encouragement. A kindergarten teacher led the small children onto the stage and the buttercups and daisies and bunny rabbits marked time and tried to follow:

> Stony the road we trod
> Bitter the chastening rod
> Felt in the days when hope, unborn, had died.
> Yet with a steady beat
> Have not our weary feet
> Come to the place for which our fathers sighed?

56   Every child I knew had learned that song with his ABC's and along with "Jesus Loves Me This I Know." But I personally had never heard it before. Never heard the words, despite the thousands of times I had sung them. Never thought they had anything to do with me.

57   On the other hand, the words of Patrick Henry had made such an impression on me that I had been able to stretch myself tall and trembling and say, "I know not what course others may take, but as for me, give me liberty or give me death."

58   And now I heard, really for the first time:

> We have come over a way that with tears has been watered,
> We have come, treading our path through the blood of the slaughtered.

59   While echoes of the song shivered in the air, Henry Reed bowed his head, said "Thank you," and returned to his place in the line. The tears that slipped down many faces were not wiped away in shame.

---

[2]"Lift Ev'ry Voice and Sing"—words by James Weldon Johnson and music by J. Rosamond Johnson.© Copyrighted: Edward B. Marks Music Corporation. Used by permission.

60   We were on top again. As always, again. We survived. The depths had been icy and dark, but now a bright sun spoke to our souls. I was no longer simply a member of the proud graduating class of 1940; I was a proud member of the wonderful, beautiful Negro race.

61   Oh, Black known and unknown poets, how often have your auctioned pains sustained us? Who will compute the lonely nights made less lonely by your songs, or the empty pots made less tragic by your tales?

62   If we were a people much given to revealing secrets, we might raise monuments and sacrifice to the memories of our poets, but slavery cured us of that weakness. It may be enough, however, to have it said that we survive in exact relationship to the dedication of our poets (include preachers, musicians and blues singers).

Graduation

Questions on Content, Style, and Structure

1. In paragraph 1, how does Angelou characterize the members of the graduating classes?

2. Study paragraphs 9 and 10; what level of diction is used there? Why?

3. Why are the students confused when they are signaled to sit down after reciting the pledge of allegiance? Why is Angelou upset?

4. What is Angelou's reaction to Donleavy's speech?

5. Why does she make the wishes she does in paragraphs 45 and 46? How has her mood changed from the earlier part of the day?

6. Why is the reading of the poem "Invictus" particularly ironic to her?

7. Why does Angelou "hear" the words of the Negro National Anthem for the first time? What effect do they have on her?

8. Why does Angelou end this selection by addressing "Black known and unknown poets"? How does the tone in the last two paragraphs differ from the rest of the essay?

9. In this story why does Angelou spend so much time describing the graduation preparations of both her family and the other students?

10. Does Angelou use enough detail in her story to make it vivid and believable? Support your answer with some examples.

11. What was Angelou's purpose in telling about this incident?

Vocabulary

trammeled (10)   presumptuous (45)
explicit (30)   perfunctory (48)
penance (41)   palpable (49)
meticulous (44)   impertinence (49)
farcical (45)   rebutting (54)

Suggestions for Writing

1. Write an essay explaining what Angelou learned from this experience and how, through her use of characterization and description, she communicates this lesson to her reader.

2. Write an essay describing an incident that you feel taught you something important about your view of yourself.

3. Consider your own high school graduation. In what ways, if any, did you share Angelou's feelings? Write an essay analyzing what your graduation meant to you.

What's Wrong with "Me, Me, Me"?
Margaret Halsey

> Margaret Halsey is the author of six books, including *With Malice toward Some* (1938), *Color Blind* (1946), *The Folks at Home* (1952), and *No Laughing Matter: The Autobiography of a WASP* (1977). She has contributed many articles to magazines such as *The New Republic*, *The New Yorker*, and *Newsweek*, where this essay appeared in 1978.

1   Tom Wolfe* has christened today's young adults the "me" generation, and the 1970s—obsessed with things like consciousness expansion and self-awareness—have been described as the decade of the new narcissism. The cult of "I," in fact, has taken hold with the strength and impetus of a new religion. But the joker in the pack is that it is all based on a false idea.

2   The false idea is that inside every human being, however unprepossessing, there is a glorious, talented and overwhelmingly attractive personality. This personality—so runs the erroneous belief—will be revealed in all its splendor if the individual just forgets about courtesy, cooperativeness and consideration for others and proceeds to do exactly what he or she feels like doing.

3   Nonsense.

4   Inside each of us is a mess of unruly primitive impulses, and these can sometimes, under the strenuous self-discipline and dedication of art, result in notable creativity. But there is no such thing as a pure, crystalline

---

*Wolfe is a popular American journalist-author whose books include *The Kandy-Kolored Tangerine-Flake Streamlined Baby* (1965), *The Electric Kool-Aid Acid Test* (1968), *The Right Stuff* (1979), and *From Bauhaus to Our House* (1981).

and well-organized "native" personality, though a host of trendy human-potential groups trade on the mistaken assumption that there is. And backing up the human-potential industry is the advertising profession, which also encourages the idea of an Inner Wonderfulness that will be unveiled to a suddenly respectful world upon the purchase of this or that commodity.

5   However, an individual does not exist in a vacuum. A human being is not an isolated, independent thing-in-itself, but inevitably reflects the existence of others. The young adults of the "me" generation would never have lived to grow up if a great many parents, doctors, nurses, farmers, factory workers, teachers, policemen, firemen and legions of others had not ignored their human potential and made themselves do jobs they did not perhaps feel like doing in order to support the health and growth of children.

6   And yet, despite the indulgence of uninhibited expression, the "self" in self-awareness seems to cause many new narcissists and members of the "me" generation a lot of trouble. This trouble emerges in talk about "identity." We hear about the search for identity and a kind of distress called an identity crisis.

7   "I don't know who I am." How many bartenders and psychiatrists have stifled yawns on hearing that popular threnody for the thousandth time!

8   But this sentence has no meaning unless spoken by an amnesia victim, because many of the people who say they do not know who they are actually *do* know. What such people really mean is that they are not satisfied with who they are. They feel themselves to be timid and colorless or to be in some way or other fault-ridden, but they have soaked up enough advertising and enough catch-penny ideas of self-improvement to believe in universal Inner Wonderfulness. So they turn their backs on their honest knowledge of themselves—which with patience and courage could start them on the road to genuine development—and embark on a quest for a will-o'-the-wisp called "identity."

9   But a *search* for identity is predestined to fail. Identity is not found, the way Pharaoh's daughter found Moses in the bulrushes. Identity is built. It is built every day and every minute throughout the day. The myriad choices, small and large, that human beings make all the time determine identity. The fatal weakness of the currently fashionable approach to personality is that the "self" of the self-awareness addicts, the self of Inner Wonderfulness, is static. Being perfect, it does not need to change. But genuine identity changes as one matures. If it does not, if the 40-year-old has an identity that was set in concrete at the age of 18, he or she is in trouble.

10   The idea of a universal Inner Wonderfulness that will be apparent to all beholders after a six-week course in self-expression is fantasy.

11   But how did this fantasy gain wide popular acceptance as a realizable fact?

12   Every society tries to produce a prevalent psychological type that will best serve its ends, and that type is always prone to certain emotional malfunctions. In early capitalism, which was a producing society, the ideal type was acquisitive, fanatically devoted to hard work and fiercely repressive of sex. The emotional malfunctions to which this type was liable were hysteria and obsession. Later capitalism, today's capitalism, is a consuming society, and the psychological type it strives to create, in order to build up the largest possible markets, is shallow, easily swayed and characterized much more by self-infatuation than self-respect. The emotional malfunction of this type is narcissism.

13   It will be argued that the cult of "I" has done some individuals a lot of good. But at whose expense? What about the people to whom these "healthy" egoists are rude or even abusive? What about the people over whom they ride roughshod? What about the people they manipulate and exploit? And—the most important question of all—how good a preparation for inevitable old age and death is a deliberately cultivated self-love? The psychologists say that the full-blown classic narcissists lose all dignity and go mad with fright as they approach their final dissolution. Ten or fifteen years from now—when the young adults of the "me" generation hit middle age—will be the time to ask whether "self-awareness" really does people any good.

14   A long time ago, in a book called *Civilization and Its Discontents*, Freud pointed out that there is an unresolvable conflict between the human being's selfish, primitive, infantile impulses and the restraint he or she must impose on those impulses if a stable society is to be maintained. The "self" is not a handsome god or goddess waiting coyly to be revealed. On the contrary, its complexity, confusion and mystery have proved so difficult that throughout the ages men and women have talked gratefully about *losing* themselves. They *lose* the self in contemplating a great work of art, or in nature, or in scientific research, or in writing poetry, or in fashioning things with their hands or in projects that will benefit others rather than themselves.

15   The current glorification of self-love will turn out in the end to be a no-win proposition, because in questions of personality or "identity," what counts is not who you are, but what you do. "By their fruits, ye shall know them." And by their fruits, they shall know themselves.

What's Wrong with "Me, Me, Me"?

Questions on Content, Style, and Structure

1. What, according to Halsey, is the idea underlying the new search for self-awareness? What is her attitude toward this idea?

2. How do such phrases as "trendy human-potential groups," "catch-penny ideas of self-improvement," and "self-awareness addicts" affect the tone of this essay?

3. Who are two of the major contributors to the belief in "Inner Wonderfulness"?

4. What is Halsey's argument against always following one's own desires?

5. Why is a *search* for identity doomed to fail?

6. What is the purpose of paragraph 12?

7. How does Halsey refute her opposition in paragraph 13? Is her response convincing?

8. Why does Halsey refer to Freud?

9. How does Halsey conclude her essay? Is it an appropriate ending?

10. Overall, how effective is Halsey's argument? Would it persuade someone about to enroll in a self-awareness course? Why/why not?

Vocabulary

narcissism (1)	predestined (9)
unprepossessing (2)	myriad (9)
erroneous (2)	static (9)
unruly (4)	prevalent (12)
threnody (7)	

Suggestions for Writing

1. Write an essay in which you argue against Halsey's views. What benefits are there to "self-awareness" books and courses?

2. Halsey notes that certain advertisements encourage the belief that Inner Wonderfulness "will be unveiled to a suddenly respectful world upon the purchase of this or that commodity." Find a number of these advertisements, and write an essay analyzing their various appeals.

3. Write an essay describing someone you know who has undertaken a "search for identity." Was the search successful? What were the main causes and/or effects of the search?

A Few Words about Breasts
Nora Ephron

Nora Ephron has written articles and essays for many magazines and newspapers, such as *Esquire, McCall's, Cosmopolitan,* and the *New York Post.* Her books include *Wallflower at the Orgy* (1970), *Crazy Salad* (1975), and *Scribble Scribble* (1978); this essay, reprinted in *Crazy Salad* with twenty-four other essays on women, originally appeared in *Esquire* in 1972.

1   I have to begin with a few words about androgyny. In grammar school, in the fifth and sixth grades, we were all tyrannized by a rigid set of rules that supposedly determined whether we were boys or girls. The episode in *Huckleberry Finn* where Huck is disguised as a girl and gives himself away by the way he threads a needle and catches a ball—that kind of thing. We learned that the way you sat, crossed your legs, held a cigarette, and looked at your nails—the way you did these things instinctively was absolute proof of your sex. Now obviously most children did not take this literally, but I did. I thought that just one slip, just one incorrect cross of my legs or flick of an imaginary cigarette ash would turn me from whatever I was into the other thing; that would be all it took, really. Even though I was outwardly a girl and had many of the trappings generally associated with girldom—a girl's name, for example, and dresses, my own telephone, an autograph book—I spent the early years of my adolescence absolutely certain that I might at any point gum it up. I did not feel at all like a girl. I was boyish. I was athletic, ambitious, outspoken, competitive, noisy, rambunctious. I had scabs on my knees and my socks slid into my loafers and I could throw a football. I wanted desperately not to be a mixture of both things, but instead just one, a girl, a definite indisputable girl. As soft and as pink as a nursery. And nothing would do that for me, I felt, but breasts.

2   I was about six months younger than everyone else in my class, and so for about six months after it began, for six months after my friends had begun to develop (that was the word we used, develop), I was not particularly worried. I would sit in the bathtub and look down at my breasts and know that any day now, any second now, they would start growing like everyone else's. They didn't. "I want to buy a bra," I said to my mother one night. "What for?" she said. My mother was really hateful about bras, and by the time my third sister had gotten to the point where she was ready to want one, my mother had worked the whole business into a comedy routine. "Why not use a Band-Aid in-

stead?" she would say. It was a source of great pride to my mother that she had never even had to wear a brassiere until she had her fourth child, and then only because her gynecologist made her. It was incomprehensible to me that anyone could ever be proud of something like that. It was the 1950s, for God's sake. Jane Russell. Cashmere sweaters. Couldn't my mother see that? *"I am too old to wear an undershirt."* Screaming. Weeping. Shouting. "Then don't wear an undershirt," said my mother. "But I want to buy a bra." "What for?"

3   I suppose that for most girls, breasts, brassieres, that entire thing, has more trauma, more to do with the coming of adolescence, with becoming a woman, than anything else. Certainly more than getting your period, although that, too, was traumatic, symbolic. But you could see breasts; they were there; they were visible. Whereas a girl could claim to have her period for months before she actually got it and nobody would ever know the difference. Which is exactly what I did. All you had to do was make a great fuss over having enough nickels for the Kotex machine and walk around clutching your stomach and moaning for three to five days a month about The Curse and you could convince anybody. There is a school of thought somewhere in the women's lib/women's mag/gynecology establishment that claims that menstrual cramps are purely psychological, and I lean toward it. Not that I didn't have them finally. Agonizing cramps, heating-pad cramps, go-down-to-the-school-nurse-and-lie-on-the-cot cramps. But, unlike any pain I had ever suffered, I adored the pain of cramps, welcomed it, wallowed in it, bragged about it. "I can't go. I have cramps." "I can't do that. I have cramps." And most of all, gigglingly, blushingly: "I can't swim. I have cramps." Nobody ever used the hard-core word. Menstruation. God, what an awful word. Never that. "I have cramps."

4   The morning I first got my period, I went into my mother's bedroom to tell her. And my mother, my utterly-hateful-about-bras mother, burst into tears. It was really a lovely moment, and I remember it so clearly not just because it was one of the two times I ever saw my mother cry on my account (the other was when I was caught being a six-year-old kleptomaniac), but also because the incident did not mean to me what it meant to her. Her little girl, her firstborn, had finally become a woman. That was what she was crying about. My reaction to the event, however, was that I might well be a woman in some scientific, textbook sense (and could at least stop faking every month and stop wasting all those nickels). But in another sense—in a visible sense—I was as androgynous and as liable to tip over into boyhood as ever.

5   I started with a 28AA bra. I don't think they made them any smaller in those days, although I gather that now you can buy bras for five-year-olds that don't have any cups whatsoever in them; trainer bras they are called. My first brassiere came from Robinson's Department Store in

Beverly Hills. I went there alone, shaking, positive they would look me over and smile and tell me to come back next year. An actual fitter took me into the dressing room and stood over me while I took off my blouse and tried the first one on. The little puffs stood out on my chest. "Lean over," said the fitter. (To this day, I am not sure what fitters in bra departments do except to tell you to lean over.) I leaned over, with the fleeting hope that my breasts would miraculously fall out of my body and into the puffs. Nothing.

6   "Don't worry about it," said my friend Libby some months later, when things had not improved. "You'll get them after you're married."

7   "What are you talking about?" I said.

8   "When you get married," Libby explained, "your husband will touch your breasts and rub them and kiss them and they'll grow."

9   That was the killer. Necking I could deal with. Intercourse I could deal with. But it had never crossed my mind that a man was going to touch my breasts, that breasts had something to do with all that, petting, my God, they never mentioned petting in my little sex manual about the fertilization of the ovum. I became dizzy. For I knew instantly—as naïve as I had been only a moment before—that only part of what she was saying was true: the touching, rubbing, kissing part, not the growing part. And I knew that no one would ever want to marry me. I had no breasts. I would never have breasts.

10   My best friend in school was Diana Raskob. She lived a block from me in a house full of wonders. English muffins, for instance. The Raskobs were the first people in Beverly Hills to have English muffins for breakfast. They also had an apricot tree in the back, and a badminton court, and a subscription to *Seventeen* magazine, and hundreds of games, like Sorry and Parcheesi and Treasure Hunt and Anagrams. Diana and I spent three or four afternoons a week in their den reading and playing and eating. Diana's mother's kitchen was full of the most colossal assortment of junk food I have ever been exposed to. My house was full of apples and peaches and milk and homemade chocolate-chip cookies—which were nice, and good for you, but-not-right-before-dinner-or-you'll-spoil-your-appetite. Diana's house had nothing in it that was good for you, and what's more, you could stuff it in right up until dinner and nobody cared. Bar-B-Q potato chips (they were the first in them, too), giant bottles of ginger ale, fresh popcorn with melted butter, hot fudge sauce on Baskin-Robbins jamoca ice cream, powdered-sugar doughnuts from Van de Kamp's. Diana and I had been best friends since we were seven; we were about equally popular in school (which is to say, not particularly), we had about the same success with boys (extremely intermittent), and we looked much the same. Dark. Tall. Gangly.

11   It is September, just before school begins. I am eleven years old, about to enter the seventh grade, and Diana and I have not seen each other all summer. I have been to camp and she has been somewhere like Banff

with her parents. We are meeting, as we often do, on the street midway between our two houses, and we will walk back to Diana's and eat junk and talk about what has happened to each of us that summer. I am walking down Walden Drive in my jeans and my father's shirt hanging out and my old red loafers with the socks falling into them and coming toward me is . . . I take a deep breath . . . a young woman. Diana. Her hair is curled and she has a waist and hips and a bust and she is wearing a straight skirt, an article of clothing I have been repeatedly told I will be unable to wear until I have the hips to hold it up. My jaw drops, and suddenly I am crying, crying hysterically, can't catch my breath sobbing. My best friend has betrayed me. She has gone ahead without me and done it. She has shaped up.

12   Here are some things I did to help:

13   Bought a Mark Eden Bust Developer.

14   Slept on my back for four years.

15   Splashed cold water on them every night because some French actress said in *Life* magazine that that was what *she* did for her perfect bustline.

16   Ultimately, I resigned myself to a bad toss and began to wear padded bras. I think about them now, think about all those years in high school I went around in them, my three padded bras, every single one of them with different-sized breasts. Each time I changed bras I changed sizes: one week nice perky but not too obtrusive breasts, the next medium-sized slightly pointy ones, the next week knockers, true knockers; all the time, whatever size I was, carrying around this rubberized appendage on my chest that occasionally crashed into a wall and was poked inward and had to be poked outward—I think about all that and wonder how anyone kept a straight face through it. My parents, who normally had no restraints about needling me—why did they say nothing as they watched my chest go up and down? My friends, who would periodically inspect my breasts for signs of growth and reassure me—why didn't they at least counsel consistency?

17   And the bathing suits. I die when I think about the bathing suits. That was the era when you could lay an uninhabited bathing suit on the beach and someone would make a pass at it. I would put one on, an absurd swimsuit with its enormous bust built into it, the bones from the suit stabbing me in the rib cage and leaving little red welts on my body, and there I would be, my chest plunging straight downward absolutely vertically from my collarbone to the top of my suit and then suddenly, wham, out came all that padding and material and wiring absolutely horizontally.

18   Buster Klepper was the first boy who ever touched them. He was my boyfriend my senior year of high school. There is a picture of him in my high-school yearbook that makes him look quite attractive in a Jewish, horn-rimmed-glasses sort of way, but the picture does not show the pim-

ples, which were air-brushed out, or the dumbness. Well, that isn't really fair. He wasn't dumb. He just wasn't terribly bright. His mother refused to accept it, refused to accept the relentlessly average report cards, refused to deal with her son's inevitable destiny in some junior college or other. "He was tested," she would say to me, apropos of nothing, "and it came out a hundred and forty-five. That's near-genius." Had the word "underachiever" been coined, she probably would have lobbed that one at me, too. Anyway, Buster was really very sweet—which is, I know, damning with faint praise, but there it is. I was the editor of the front page of the high-school newspaper and he was editor of the back page; we had to work together, side by side, in the print shop, and that was how it started. On our first date, we went to see *April Love*, starring Pat Boone. Then we started going together. Buster had a green coupe, a 1950 Ford with an engine he had hand-chromed until it shone, dazzled, reflected the image of anyone who looked into it, anyone usually being Buster polishing it or the gas-station attendants he constantly asked to check the oil in order for them to be overwhelmed by the sparkle on the valves. The car also had a boot stretched over the back seat for reasons I never understood; hanging from the rearview mirror, as was the custom, was a pair of angora dice. A previous girl friend named Solange, who was famous throughout Beverly Hills High School for having no pigment in her right eyebrow, had knitted them for him. Buster and I would ride around town, the two of us seated to the left of the steering wheel. I would shift gears. It was nice.

19   There was necking. Terrific necking. First in the car, overlooking Los Angeles from what is now the Trousdale Estates. Then on the bed of his parents' cabana at Ocean House. Incredibly wonderful, frustrating necking, I loved it, really, but no further than necking, please don't, please, because there I was absolutely terrified of the general implications of going-a-step-further with a near-dummy and also terrified of his finding out there was next to nothing there (which he knew, of course; he wasn't that dumb).

20   I broke up with him at one point. I think we were apart for about two weeks. At the end of that time, I drove down to see a friend at a boarding school in Palos Verdes Estates and a disc jockey played "April Love" on the radio four times during the trip. I took it as a sign. I drove straight back to Griffith Park to a golf tournament Buster was playing in (he was the sixth-seeded teen-age golf player in southern California) and presented myself back to him on the green of the 18th hole. It was all very dramatic. That night we went to a drive-in and I let him get his hand under my protuberances and onto my breasts. He really didn't seem to mind at all.

21   "Do you want to marry my son?" the woman asked me.

22   "Yes," I said.

23   I was nineteen years old, a virgin, going with this woman's son, this big strange woman who was married to a Lutheran minister in New Hampshire

and pretended she was gentile and had this son, by her first husband, this total fool of a son who ran the hero-sandwich concession at Harvard Business School and whom for one moment one December in New Hampshire I said—as much out of politeness as anything else—that I wanted to marry.

24   "Fine," she said. "Now, here's what you do. Always make sure you're on top of him so you won't seem so small. My bust is very large, you see, so I always lie on my back to make it look smaller, but you'll have to be on top most of the time."

25   I nodded. "Thank you," I said.

26   "I have a book for you to read," she went on. "Take it with you when you leave. Keep it." She went to the bookshelf, found it, and gave it to me. It was a book on frigidity.

27   "Thank you," I said.

28   That is a true story. Everything in this article is a true story, but I feel I have to point out that that story in particular is true. It happened on December 30, 1960. I think about it often. When it first happened, I naturally assumed that the woman's son, my boyfriend, was responsible. I invented a scenario where he had had a little heart-to-heart with his mother and had confessed that his only objection to me was that my breasts were small; his mother then took it upon herself to help out. Now I think I was wrong about the incident. The mother was acting on her own, I think: that was her way of being cruel and competitive under the guise of being helpful and maternal. You have small breasts, she was saying; therefore you will never make him as happy as I have. Or you have small breasts; therefore you will doubtless have sexual problems. Or you have small breasts; therefore you are less woman than I am. She was, as it happens, only the first of what seems to me to be a never-ending string of women who have made competitive remarks to me about breast size. "I would love to wear a dress like that," my friend Emily says to me, "but my bust is too big." Like that. Why do women say these things to me? Do I attract these remarks the way other women attract married men or alcoholics or homosexuals? This summer, for example. I am at a party in East Hampton and I am introduced to a woman from Washington. She is a minor celebrity, very pretty and Southern and blond and outspoken, and I am flattered because she has read something I have written. We are talking animatedly, we have been talking no more than five minutes, when a man comes up to join us. "Look at the two of us," the woman says to the man, indicating me and her. "The two of us together couldn't fill an A cup." Why does she say that? It isn't even true, dammit, so why? Is she even more addled than I am on this subject? Does she honestly believe there is something wrong with her size breasts, which, it seems to me, now that I look hard at them, are just right? Do I unconsciously bring out competitiveness in women? In that form? What did I do to deserve it?

29   As for men.

30   There were men who minded and let me know that they minded. There were men who did not mind. In any case, *I* always minded.

31   And even now, now that I have been countlessly reassured that my figure is a good one, now that I am grown-up enough to understand that most of my feelings have very little to do with the reality of my shape, I am nonetheless obsessed by breasts. I cannot help it. I grew up in the terrible fifties—with rigid stereotypical sex roles, the insistence that men be men and dress like men and women be women and dress like women, the intolerance of androgyny—and I cannot shake it, cannot shake my feelings of inadequacy. Well, that time is gone, right? All those exaggerated examples of breast worship are gone, right? Those women were freaks, right? I know all that. And yet here I am, stuck with the psychological remains of it all, stuck with my own peculiar version of breast worship. You probably think I am crazy to go on like this: here I have set out to write a confession that is meant to hit you with the shock of recognition, and instead you are sitting there thinking I am thoroughly warped. Well, what can I tell you? If I had had them, I would have been a completely different person. I honestly believe that.

32   After I went into therapy, a process that made it possible for me to tell total strangers at cocktail parties that breasts were the hang-up of my life, I was often told that I was insane to have been bothered by my condition. I was also frequently told, by close friends, that I was extremely boring on the subject. And my girl friends, the ones with nice big breasts, would go on endlessly about how their lives had been far more miserable than mine. Their bra straps were snapped in class. They couldn't sleep on their stomachs. They were stared at whenever the word "mountain" cropped up in geography. And *Evangeline*, good God what they went through every time someone had to stand up and recite the Prologue to Longfellow's *Evangeline*: "... stand like druids of eld ... / With beards that rest on their bosoms." It was much worse for them, they tell me. They had a terrible time of it, they assure me. I don't know how lucky I was, they say.

33   I have thought about their remarks, tried to put myself in their place, considered their point of view. I think they are full of shit.

A Few Words about Breasts

Questions on Content, Style, and Structure

1. How does Ephron introduce her subject?
2. Why does Ephron refer in paragraph 2 to the 1950s and Jane Russell as part of her explanation for wanting a bra?
3. Why is the story of Diana Raskob included in this essay?
4. How is this essay unified? What sort of chronology is followed?
5. Study paragraphs 12–17. How does Ephron make her writing vivid?
6. How does Ephron show the reader the ways she was traumatized as a young woman by her flat chest and how she is obsessed by it even now?

7. Why does Ephron use dialogue in her story about her boyfriend's mother? Is it effective?

8. Analyze the effectiveness of Ephron's conclusion. Is the last sentence necessary?

9. Characterize the tone of this essay. What role does humor play?

10. Do you sympathize with Ephron or find her "thoroughly warped" as she fears? Defend your answer.

Vocabulary

androgyny (1)   intermittent (10)   protuberances (20)
rambunctious (1)   gangly (10)   gentile (23)
indisputable (1)   apropos (18)   guise (28)

Suggestions for Writing

1. Almost everyone has experiences or hang-ups like Ephron's that, in retrospect, seem to symbolize the hardships of growing up. Write an essay in which you discuss an "obsession" you had in adolescence and how it has affected you.

2. Ephron blames part of her obsession with breasts on growing up in the 1950s, "an era when you could lay an uninhabited bathing suit on the beach and someone would make a pass at it." Are today's standards for women different? Would Ephron have a different attitude toward her body were she a young woman today? Defend your response in an essay.

3. Do young men have pressures similar to the one Ephron describes for young women? Write an essay explaining and illustrating your answer.

The Physical Miseducation of a Former Fat Boy
Louie Crew

Louie Crew is an associate professor of English at the University of Wisconsin, Stevens Point. He has written *Sunspots* (1976) and *The Gay Academic* (1978). This essay appeared in *Saturday Review* in 1973.

1   When I was six, a next-door neighbor gave me my first candy bar, and I fattened immediately in a home where food was love. It is hardly surprising that when I first entered physical education courses in the eighth grade my coaches were markedly unimpressed or that thereafter I compensated by working harder at books, where I was more successful. Although I did learn to take jokes about my size and experienced the

"bigness" of being able to laugh at myself (the standard fat man's reward), at thirty-five I am furious to recall how readily and completely my instructors defaulted in their responsibilities to me. Some remedies I have learned in my thirties persuade me that it is not inevitable that the system will continue to fail other fat boys.

2   My personal remedies for physical ineptitude have a firm base in ideas. Four years ago I weighed 265 pounds. Only my analyst needs to know how much I consequently hated myself. In six months I took off 105 pounds and initiated a regular jogging and exercising schedule that has gradually, very gradually, led to increased self-confidence. Yet my physical education teachers in secondary school and college never showed the least interest in my physical problems, never sat down and initiated the simplest diagnosis of my physical needs, never tempted me into the personal discoveries that I had to wait more than a decade to make for myself.

3   Instead, my physical educators offered two alternatives. Either I could enter the fierce competitive sports that predominate in our culture and therein make and accept the highest mark I could achieve; or I could opt for the less-competitive intramurals, modeled after the big boys' games, and accept my role as a physically incompetent human being, sitting on the sidelines to cheer for a chosen team of professionals. These limited alternatives were repeatedly justified as teaching me how it is out in the "real world," in "the game of life," allegedly divided between the participators and the watchers.

4   Now, as I jog in midwinter dawn, all muffled with socks over my hands, making tracks with the rabbits in Carolina dew, I am not competing with anyone, unless I whimsically imagine Father Time having to add another leaf to my book. I am celebrating me, *this* morning, *this* pair of worn-out tennis shoes, the tingle in my cheeks, the space being cleared in my stomach for my simple breakfast when I get back. . . . I was very articulate at fourteen—fat but articulate—and I believe that a sympathetic, interested coach could have shared this type of insight, this type of reality, with me, and perhaps thereby he could have teased me into the discoveries I had to make many years later. But the coach would have had to love kids like me more than he loved winning if he had hoped to participate in my physical education. I had no such coach.

5   Perhaps an athletic friend could have shared insights into my physical needs and suggested alternative fulfillments. I certainly had many athletic friends, because I sought avidly to compensate for my physical failures by liking and being liked by athletes. Unfortunately, these friends were all schooled in the competitive rules of keeping trade secrets and of enjoying and hoarding compliments. Human sharing had not been a part of their education.

6   I recall how at thirty-two I tentatively jogged around a block for the first time, how the fierce hurt in my gut was less bothersome than the fear that I would not make it. I had to learn to love myself for making it, and for making it again the next day, rather than to participate in my

hecklers' mockery of the sweating fat man. I remember jogging no faster at sixteen and being laughed at by the coach, who kept me that much longer a prisoner in my role as the jovial class clown.

7   I became a water boy and trainer, winning the school's award for "most unselfish service." Is not the role familiar? I even served two summers as a camp counselor. I could not walk to first base without puffing, but I could call a kid "out" with a tongue of forked lightning. I had been taught well.

8   My physical educators were signally unimaginative. We played only the few sports that had always been played in our area. Further, they maintained a rigid separation between "sports" and "play." Football, baseball, basketball, and track were "sports." Fishing, hiking, boating, and jogging were "play." Golf was "play" until you had a team that won five trophies; then you developed the cool rhetoric of "sport."

9   I remember going on a boy-scout trip in the Talledega National Forest in Alabama for a week. My anticipation was immense. I liked the woods. I liked walking. I liked the sky, trees, rocks, ferns. . . . We were to walk only about five or ten miles a day through a wilderness, camping out around an authentic chuck wagon that would move in advance during the day. The trip itself, however, was a nightmare for me. The coach/scoutmaster led at a frantic pace, because he wanted to get each lap done with and, as he said, he wanted "to make men" out of us. The major activity was to race ahead so as to enjoy "breathers" while waiting to heckle us slower folk when we caught up. When we came to a clearing overlooking the vast chasms of blue-green shimmer, the biggest breach of the unwritten code would have been to stop to look for ten minutes. The trip was to get somewhere (nobody quite knew why or where), not to be somewhere.

10   For a long time I treasured illusions that my experiences with physical miseducation resulted merely from my provincial isolation, that real professionals elsewhere had surely identified and rectified these ills. But as I have moved from south to west to east, even to England, I have found very few real physical educators. Almost no one is interested in educating individuals to discover their own physical resources and to integrate them with all other personal experiences. Almost everyone is interested in developing ever-better professionals to provide vicarious entertainment for a physically inept society.

11   Most of the professional literature describes the training of professional sportsmen and evaluates the machinery developed to serve this training. My favorite example of this perverse pedantry is my friend's M.A. thesis studying the effects of various calisthenics on sweat samples. One is scared to imagine what secretions he will measure for his doctoral dissertation. Yet it is fashionable to mock medieval scholars for disputing how many angels could stand on the head of a pin!

12   Once while working out in a gymnasium at the University of Alabama, I jestingly asked some professionals how many pounds I would have to be able to lift to be a man. To my surprise, I received specific answers:

one said 280 pounds (he could lift 285); another said, "one's own weight"; another. . . . But I was born a man! It is surely perverse for a man to trap himself by confusing *being* with *becoming*.

The Physical Miseducation of a Former Fat Boy

Questions on Content, Style, and Structure

1. What is Crew's attitude toward physical education teachers? Why?
2. What choices did the P.E. teachers offer Crew? How were these choices justified?
3. What roles did Crew assume in high school?
4. What is the unstated point of the comparison of "sport" to "play" in paragraph 8?
5. How does Crew illustrate his coach's lack of understanding?
6. What is the effect of the three parallel sentences in paragraph 9?
7. According to Crew, the interest in physical training unfortunately is focused on which people?
8. Why does Crew refer to his friend's M.A. thesis?
9. Why does Crew end with the story of the gym conversation? How does the last sentence relate to Crew's subject?
10. Characterize the tone of this essay. Is it appropriate?
11. Overall, is Crew's essay convincing?

Vocabulary

compensated (1)	provincial (10)
defaulted (1)	rectified (10)
inevitable (1)	vicarious (10)
ineptitude (2)	perverse (11)
predominate (3)	pedantry (11)
articulate (4)	

Suggestions for Writing

1. Write an essay in which you illustrate your own experience with physical education classes. Do you share some of Crew's hostility?
2. Write an essay explaining why you feel negatively about some other subject, such as math or English.
3. Being overweight or underweight or having some other physical problems can cause great unhappiness for teenagers. Write an essay showing the effects of such problems or, if you know of a case, write an essay that tells how someone (you?) overcame such a problem, as Crew did.

A & P
John Updike

John Updike began his writing career as a staff member of *The New Yorker* from 1955 to 1957. Since that time he has written numerous short stories and over a dozen novels, including *Rabbit Run* (1964), *Couples* (1968), *The Coup* (1978), and *The Centaur,* which won the 1964 National Book Award for Fiction. "A & P" was originally published in *The New Yorker* and then appeared in *Pigeon Feathers and Other Stories* (1962).

1   In walks these three girls in nothing but bathing suits. I'm in the third checkout slot, with my back to the door, so I don't see them until they're over by the bread. The one that caught my eye first was the one in the plaid green two-piece. She was a chunky kid, with a good tan and a sweet broad soft-looking can with those two crescents of white just under it, where the sun never seems to hit, at the top of the backs of her legs. I stood there with my hand on a box of HiHo crackers trying to remember if I rang it up or not. I ring it up again and the customer starts giving me hell. She's one of these cash-register-watchers, a witch about fifty with rouge on her cheekbones and no eyebrows, and I know it made her day to trip me up. She'd been watching cash registers for fifty years and probably never seen a mistake before.

2   By the time I got her feathers smoothed and her goodies into a bag— she gives me a little snort in passing, if she'd been born at the right time they would have burned her over in Salem—by the time I get her on her way the girls had circled around the bread and were coming back, without a pushcart, back my way along the counters, in the aisle between the checkouts and the Special bins. They didn't even have shoes on. There was this chunky one, with the two-piece—it was bright green and the seams on the bra were still sharp and her belly was still pretty pale so I guessed she just got it (the suit)—there was this one, with one of those chubby berry-faces, the lips all bunched together under her nose, this one, and a tall one, with black hair that hadn't quite frizzed right, and one of these sunburns right across under the eyes, and a chin that was too long—you know, the kind of girl other girls think is very "striking" and "attractive" but never quite makes it, as they very well know, which is why they like her so much—and then the third one, that wasn't quite so tall. She was the queen. She kind of led them, the other two peeking around and making their shoulders round. She didn't look around, not this queen, she just walked straight on slowly, on these long white prima-donna legs. She came down a little hard on her heels, as if she didn't walk in bare feet that much, putting down her heels and then letting the weight move along to her toes as if she was testing the floor with every

step, putting a little deliberate extra action into it. You never know for
sure how girls' minds work (do you really think it's a mind in there or
just a little buzz like a bee in a glass jar?) but you got the idea she had
talked the other two into coming in here with her, and now she was
showing them how to do it, walk slow and hold yourself straight.

3   She had on a kind of dirty-pink—beige maybe, I don't know—bathing
suit with a little nubble all over it and, what got me, the straps were
down. They were off her shoulders looped loose around the cool tops of
her arms, and I guess as a result the suit had slipped a little on her, so
all around the top of the cloth there was this shining rim. If it hadn't
been there you wouldn't have known there could have been anything
whiter than those shoulders. With the straps pushed off, there was nothing between the top of the suit and the top of her head except just *her*,
this clean bare plane of the top of her chest down from the shoulder
bones like a dented sheet of metal tilted in the light. I mean, it was more
than pretty.

4   She had a sort of oaky hair that the sun and salt had bleached, done
up in a bun that was unravelling, and a kind of prim face. Walking into
the A & P with your straps down, I suppose it's the only kind of face
you *can* have. She held her head so high her neck, coming up out of
those white shoulders, looked kind of stretched, but I didn't mind. The
longer her neck was, the more of her there was.

5   She must have felt in the corner of her eye me and over my shoulder
Stokesie in the second slot watching, but she didn't tip. Not this queen.
She kept her eyes moving across the racks, and stopped, and turned so
slow it made my stomach rub the inside of my apron, and buzzed to the
other two, who kind of huddled against her for relief, and then they all
three of them went up the cat-and-dog-food–breakfast-cereal–macaroni–
rice–raisins–seasonings–spreads–spaghetti–soft-drinks–crackers-and-
cookies aisle. From the third slot I look straight up this aisle to the meat
counter, and I watched them all the way. The fat one with the tan sort
of fumbled with the cookies, but on second thought she put the package
back. The sheep pushing their carts down the aisle—the girls were walking against the usual traffic (not that we have one-way signs or anything)—were pretty hilarious. You could see them, when Queenie's white
shoulders dawned on them, kind of jerk, or hop, or hiccup, but their eyes
snapped back to their own baskets and on they pushed. I bet you could
set off dynamite in an A & P and the people would by and large keep
reaching and checking oatmeal off their lists and muttering "Let me see,
there was a third thing, began with A, asparagus, no, ah, yes, applesauce!"
or whatever it is they do mutter. But there was no doubt, this jiggled
them. A few houseslaves in pin curlers even looked around after pushing
their carts past to make sure what they had seen was correct.

6   You know, it's one thing to have a girl in a bathing suit down on the
beach, where what with the glare nobody can look at each other much
anyway, and another thing in the cool of the A & P, under the fluorescent

lights, against all those stacked packages, with her feet padding along naked over our checkerboard green-and-cream rubber-tile floor.

7   "Oh Daddy," Stokesie said beside me. "I feel so faint."

8   "Darling," I said. "Hold me tight." Stokesie's married, with two babies chalked up on his fuselage already, but as far as I can tell that's the only difference. He's twenty-two, and I was nineteen this April.

9   "Is it done?" he asks, the responsible married man finding his voice. I forgot to say he thinks he's going to be manager some sunny day, maybe in 1990 when it's called the Great Alexandrov and Petrooshki Tea Company or something.

10   What he meant was, our town is five miles from a beach, with a big summer colony out on the Point, but we're right in the middle of town, and the women generally put on a shirt or shorts or something before they get out of the car into the street. And anyway these are usually women with six children and varicose veins mapping their legs and nobody, including them, could care less. As I say, we're right in the middle of town, and if you stand at our front doors you can see two banks and the Congregational church and the newspaper store and three real-estate offices and about twenty-seven old freeloaders tearing up Central Street because the sewer broke again. It's not as if we're on the Cape; we're north of Boston and there's people in this town haven't seen the ocean for twenty years.

11   The girls had reached the meat counter and were asking McMahon something. He pointed, they pointed, and they shuffled out of sight behind a pyramid of Diet Delight peaches. All that was left for us to see was old McMahon patting his mouth and looking after them sizing up their joints. Poor kids, I began to feel sorry for them, they couldn't help it.

12   Now here comes the sad part of the story, at least my family says it's sad, but I don't think it's so sad myself. The store's pretty empty, it being Thursday afternoon, so there was nothing much to do except lean on the register and wait for the girls to show up again. The whole store was like a pinball machine and I didn't know which tunnel they'd come out of. After a while they come around out of the far aisle, around the light bulbs, records at discount of the Caribbean Six or Tony Martin Sings or some such gunk you wonder they waste the wax on, six-packs of candy bars, and plastic toys done up in cellophane that fall apart when a kid looks at them anyway. Around they come, Queenie still leading the way, and holding a little gray jar in her hand. Slots Three through Seven are unmanned and I could see her wondering between Stokes and me, but Stokesie with his usual luck draws an old party in baggy gray pants who stumbles up with four giant cans of pineapple juice (what do these bums *do* with all that pineapple juice? I've often asked myself) so the girls come to me. Queenie puts down the jar and I take it into my fingers icy cold. Kingfish Fancy Herring Snacks in Pure Sour Cream: 49¢. Now her

hands are empty, not a ring or a bracelet, bare as God made them, and I wonder where the money's coming from. Still with that prim look she lifts a folded dollar bill out of the hollow at the center of her nubbled pink top. The jar went heavy in my hand. Really, I thought that was so cute.

13   Then everybody's luck begins to run out. Lengel comes in from haggling with a truck full of cabbages on the lot and is about to scuttle into that door marked MANAGER behind which he hides all day when the girls touch his eye. Lengel's pretty dreary, teaches Sunday school and the rest, but he doesn't miss that much. He comes over and says, "Girls, this isn't the beach."

14   Queenie blushes, though maybe it's just a brush of sunburn I was noticing for the first time, now that she was so close. "My mother asked me to pick up a jar of herring snacks." Her voice kind of startled me, the way voices do when you see the people first, coming out so flat and dumb yet kind of tony, too, the way it ticked over "pick up" and "snacks." All of a sudden I slid right down her voice into her living room. Her father and the other men were standing around in ice-cream coats and bow ties and the women were in sandals picking up herring snacks on toothpicks off a big glass plate and they were all holding drinks the color of water with olives and sprigs of mint in them. When my parents have somebody over they get lemonade and if it's a real racy affair Schlitz in tall glasses with "They'll Do It Every Time" cartoons stencilled on.

15   "That's all right," Lengel said. "But this isn't the beach." His repeating this struck me as funny, as if it had just occurred to him, and he had been thinking all these years the A & P was a great big dune and he was the head lifeguard. He didn't like my smiling—as I say he doesn't miss much—but he concentrates on giving the girls that sad Sunday-school-superintendent stare.

16   Queenie's blush is no sunburn now, and the plump one in plaid, that I liked better from the back—a really sweet can—pipes up, "We weren't doing any shopping. We just came in for the one thing."

17   "That makes no difference," Lengel tells her, and I could see from the way his eyes went that he hadn't noticed she was wearing a two-piece before. "We want you decently dressed when you come in here."

18   "We *are* decent," Queenie says suddenly, her lower lip pushing, getting sore now that she remembers her place, a place from which the crowd that runs the A & P must look pretty crummy. Fancy Herring Snacks flashed in her very blue eyes.

19   "Girls, I don't want to argue with you. After this come in here with your shoulders covered. It's our policy." He turns his back. That's policy for you. Policy is what the kingpins want. What the others want is juvenile delinquency.

20   All this while, the customers had been showing up with their carts but, you know, sheep, seeing a scene, they had all bunched up on Stokesie, who shook open a paper bag as gently as peeling a peach, not

wanting to miss a word. I could feel in the silence everybody getting nervous, most of all Lengel, who asks me, "Sammy, have you rung up their purchase?"

21   I thought and said "No" but it wasn't about that I was thinking. I go through the punches, 4, 9, GROC, TOT—it's more complicated than you think, and after you do it often enough, it begins to make a little song, that you hear words to, in my case "Hello (*bing*) there, you (*gung*) happy *pee*-pul (*splat*)!"—the *splat* being the drawer flying out. I uncrease the bill, tenderly as you may imagine, it just having come from between the two smoothest scoops of vanilla I had ever known there were, and pass a half and a penny into her narrow pink palm, and nestle the herrings in a bag and twist its neck and hand it over, all the time thinking.

22   The girls, and who'd blame them, are in a hurry to get out, so I say "I quit" to Lengel quick enough for them to hear, hoping they'll stop and watch me, their unsuspected hero. They keep right on going, into the electric eye; the door flies open and they flicker across the lot to their car, Queenie and Plaid and Big Tall Goony-Goony (not that as raw material she was so bad), leaving me with Lengel and a kink in his eyebrow.

23   "Did you say something, Sammy?"

24   "I said I quit."

25   "I thought you did."

26   "You didn't have to embarrass them."

27   "It was they who were embarrassing us."

28   I started to say something that came out "Fiddle-de-do." It's a saying of my grandmother's, and I know she would have been pleased.

29   "I don't think you know what you're saying," Lengel said.

30   "I know you don't," I said. "But I do." I pull the bow at the back of my apron and start shrugging it off my shoulders. A couple of customers that had been heading for my slot begin to knock against each other, like scared pigs in a chute.

31   Lengel sighs and begins to look very patient and old and gray. He's been a friend of my parents' for years. "Sammy, you don't want to do this to your Mom and Dad," he tells me. It's true, I don't. But it seems to me that once you begin a gesture it's fatal not to go through with it. I fold the apron, "Sammy" stitched in red on the pocket, and put it on the counter, and drop the bow tie on top of it. The bow tie is theirs, if you've ever wondered. "You'll feel this for the rest of your life," Lengel says, and I know that's true, too, but remembering how he made that pretty girl blush makes me so scrunchy inside I punch the No Sale tab and the machine whirs "pee-pul" and the drawer splats out. One advantage to this scene taking place in summer, I can follow this up with a clean exit, there's no fumbling around getting your coat and galoshes, I just saunter into the electric eye in my white shirt that my mother ironed the night before, and the door heaves itself open, and outside the sunshine is skating around on the asphalt.

32   I look around for my girls, but they're gone, of course. There wasn't

anybody but some young married screaming with her children about some candy they didn't get by the door of a powder-blue Falcon station wagon. Looking back in the big windows, over the bags of peat moss and aluminum lawn furniture stacked on the pavement, I could see Lengel in my place in the slot, checking the sheep through. His face was dark gray and his back stiff, as if he's just had an injection of iron, and my stomach kind of fell as I felt how hard the world was going to be to me hereafter.

A & P

Questions on Content, Style, and Structure

1. Who narrates this story? Why did Updike pick this narrator instead of another character?
2. Characterize Sammy's view of women by pointing out some of his opinions and descriptions of them.
3. Who are "sheep"? What is Sammy's attitude toward them? toward his boss?
4. How does he see Queenie and her friends?
5. What do Sammy's opinions about other people reveal about *him*?
6. Why does Sammy quit his job? Are his motives entirely what he says they are?
7. Is his action admirable or misguided? Why?
8. What does Sammy mean in the last line of the story when he says he knows "how hard the world was going to be to me hereafter"? To what, if any, extent is Sammy exaggerating?
9. Is this a humorous or serious story? Defend your answer.
10. An "initiation story" is a tale in which a young person learns something important—and often disillusioning—about becoming an adult. Such stories often deal with a loss of innocence or youthful naïveté. Would you call "A & P" an initiation story? Why/why not?

Vocabulary

crescents (1)   nubble (3)
prima donna (2)   fuselage (8)
deliberate (2)

Suggestions for Writing

1. Write an essay describing an experience from your adolescence that convinced you that the world was going to be harder on you than you had imagined.

2. Write an essay comparing Sammy's attitude toward his job to your attitude toward any job you have held.

3. Study Sammy's description of his customers. In a short essay, describe the customers of a different kind of store, imitating Sammy's diction and attitude.

Section 2

Men and Women

Masculine/Feminine
Prudence Mackintosh

Prudence Mackintosh is the author of many magazine articles and the humorous book *Thundering Sneakers* (1981). For several years she wrote a column on family life for *Texas Monthly*; this essay was first published in that magazine in 1977.

1   I had every intention to raise liberated, nonviolent sons whose aggressive tendencies would be mollified by a sensitivity and compassion that psychologists claim were denied their father's generation.

2   I did not buy guns or war toys (although Grandmother did). My boys even had a secondhand baby doll until the garage sale last summer. I did buy Marlo Thomas' *Free to Be You and Me* record, a collection of non-sexist songs, stories, and poems, and I told them time and time again that it was okay to cry and be scared sometimes. I overruled their father and insisted that first grade was much too early for organized competitive soccer leagues. They know that moms *and dads* do dishes and diapers. And although they use it primarily for the convenient bathroom between the alley and the sandpile, my boys know that the storeroom is now mother's office. In such an environment, surely they would grow up free of sex-role stereotypes. At the very least wouldn't they pick up their own socks?

3   My friends with daughters were even more zealous. They named their daughters strong, cool unisex names like Blakeney, Brett, Brook, Lindsay, and Blair, names that lent themselves to corporate letterheads, not Tupperware party invitations. These moms looked on Barbie with disdain and bought trucks and science kits. They shunned frilly dresses for overalls. They subscribed to Feminist Press and read stories called "My Mother the Mail Carrier" instead of "Sleeping Beauty." At the swimming pool one afternoon, I watched a particularly fervent young mother, ironically clad in a string bikini, encourage her daughter. "You're so strong, Blake! Kick hard, so you'll be the strongest kid in this pool." When my boys splashed water in Blakeney's eyes and she ran whimpering to her mother, this mom exhorted, "You go back in that pool and shake your fist like this and say, 'You do that again and I'll bust your lights out.'" A new generation of little girls, assertive and ambitious, taking a backseat to no one?

4   It's a little early to assess the results of our efforts, but when my seven-year-old son, Jack, comes home singing—to the tune of *"Frère Jacques"*—"Farrah Fawcett, Farrah Fawcett, I love you" and five minutes later asks Drew, his five-year-old brother, if he'd like his nose to be a blood foun-

tain, either we're backsliding or there's more to this sex-role learning than the home environment can handle.

5   I'm hearing similar laments from mothers of daughters. "She used to tell everyone that she was going to grow up to be a lawyer just like Daddy," said one, "but she's hedging on that ambition ever since she learned that no one wears a blue fairy tutu in the courtroom." Another mother with two sons, a daughter, and a very successful career notes that, with no special encouragement, only her daughter keeps her room neat and loves to set the table and ceremoniously seat her parents. At a Little League game during the summer, fearful that this same young daughter might be absorbing the stereotype "boys play while girls watch," her parents readily assured her that she too could participate when she was eight years old. "Oh," she exclaimed with obvious delight, "I didn't know they had cheerleaders."

6   How does it happen? I have my own theories, but decided to do a little reading to see if any of the "experts" agreed with me. I was also curious to find out what remedies they recommended. The books I read propose that sex roles are culturally induced. In simplistic terms, rid the schools, their friends, and the television of sexism, and your daughters will dump their dolls and head straight for the boardroom while your sons contemplate nursing careers. *Undoing Sex Stereotypes* by Marcia Guttentag and Helen Bray is an interesting study of efforts to overcome sexism in the classroom. After reading it, I visited my son's very traditional school and found it guilty of unabashedly perpetuating the myths that feminists abhor. Remember separate water fountains? And how, even if the line was shorter, no boy would be caught dead drinking from the girls' fountain and vice versa? That still happens. "You wouldn't want me to get cooties, would you, Mom?" my son says, defending the practice. What did I expect in a school where the principal still addresses his faculty, who range in age from 23 to 75, as "girls"?

7   Nevertheless, having been a schoolteacher myself, I am skeptical of neatly programmed nonsexist curriculum packets like Guttentag and Bray's. But if you can wade through the jargon ("people of the opposite sex hereafter referred to as POTOS"), some of the observations and exercises are certainly thought-provoking and revealing. In one exercise fifth-grade students were asked to list adjectives appropriate to describe women. The struggle some of the children had in shifting their attitudes about traditional male roles is illustrated in this paragraph written by a fifth-grade girl who was asked to write a story about a man using the adjectives she had listed to describe women:

> Once there was a boy who all his life was very *gentle*. He never hit anyone or started a fight and when some of his friends were not feeling well, he was *loving* and *kind* to them. When he got older he never changed. People started not liking him because he was *weak, petite,* and he wasn't like any of the other men—not strong or tough. Most of his life he sat alone thinking about why no one liked him. Then one day he went out and tried to act like the other men. He joined a baseball team, but he was no good, he always got out.

Then he decided to join the hockey team. He couldn't play good. He kept on breaking all the rules. So he quit the team and joined the soccer team. These men were *understanding* to him. He was really good at soccer, and was the best on the team. That year they won the championship and the rest of his life he was happy.*

8   After reading this paragraph it occurred to me that this little girl's self-esteem and subsequent role in life would be enhanced by a teacher who spent less time on "nonsexist intervention projects" and more time on writing skills. But that, of course, is not what the study was meant to reveal.

9   The junior high curriculum suggested by *Undoing Sex Stereotypes* has some laudable consciousness-raising goals. For example, in teaching units called "Women's Roles in American History" and "The Socialization of Women and the Image of Women in the Media" teenagers are encouraged to critically examine television commercials, soap operas, and comic books. But am I a traitor to the cause if I object when the authors in another unit use *Romeo and Juliet* as a study of the status of women? Something is rotten in Verona when we have to consider Juliet's career possibilities and her problems with self-actualization. The conclusions of this project were lost on me; I quit reading when the author began to talk about ninth-graders who were "cognitively at a formal-operational level." I don't even know what my "external sociopsychological situation" is. However, I think I did understand some of the conclusions reached by the kids:

> "Girls are smart."
> "If a woman ran a forklift where my father works, there would be a walk-out."
> "Men cannot be pom-pom girls."

10   Eminently more readable, considering that both authors are educators of educators, is *How to Raise Independent and Professionally Successful Daughters*, by Drs. Rita and Kenneth Dunn. The underlying and, I think, questionable assumption in this book is that little boys have been reared correctly all along. Without direct parental intervention, according to the Dunns, daughters tend to absorb and reflect society's values. The Dunns paint a dark picture indeed for the parents who fail to channel their daughters toward professional success. The woman who remains at home with children while her husband is involved in the "real world" with an "absorbing and demanding day-to-day commitment that brings him into contact with new ideas, jobs, and people (attractive self-actualized females)" is sure to experience lowered IQ, according to the Dunns. They go on to predict the husband's inevitable affair and the subsequent divorce, which leaves the wife emotionally depressed and probably financially dependent on her parents.

---

* From *Undoing Sex Stereotypes* by Marcia Guttentag and Helen Bray © 1976 McGraw-Hill, Inc. Used with permission of McGraw-Hill Book Co.

11   Now I'm all for women developing competency and self-reliance, but the Dunns' glorification of the professional is excessive. Anyone who has worked longer than a year knows that eventually any job loses most of its glamour. And the world is no less "real" at home. For that matter, mothers at home may be more "real" than bankers or lawyers. How is a corporate tax problem more real than my counseling with the maid whose boyfriend shot her in the leg? How can reading a balance sheet compare with comforting a five-year-old who holds his limp cat and wants to know why we have to lose the things we love? And on the contrary, it is my husband, the professional, who complains of lowered IQ. Though we wooed to Faulkner, my former ace English major turned trial lawyer now has time for only an occasional *Falconer* or Peter Benley thriller. Certainly there is value in raising daughters to be financially self-supporting, but there is not much wisdom in teaching a daughter that she must achieve professional success or her marriage probably won't last.

12   In a chapter called "What to Do from Birth to Two," the authors instruct parents to introduce dolls only if they represent adult figures or groups of figures. "Try not to give her her own 'baby.' A baby doll is acceptable only for dramatizing the familiar episodes she has actually experienced, like a visit to the doctor." If some unthinking person should give your daughter a baby doll, and she likes it, the Dunns recommend that you permit her to keep it without exhibiting any negative feelings, "but do not lapse into cuddling it or encouraging her to do so. Treat it as any other object and direct attention to other more beneficial toys." I wonder if the Dunns read an article by Anne Roiphe called "Can You Have Everything and Still Want Babies?" which appeared in *Vogue* a couple of years ago. Ms. Roiphe was deploring the extremes to which our liberation has brought us. "It is nice to have beautiful feet, it may be desirable to have small feet, but it is painful and abusive to bind feet. It is also a good thing for women to have independence, freedom and choice, movement, and opportunity; but I'm not so sure that the current push against mothering will not be another kind of binding of the soul. . . . As women we have thought so little of ourselves that when the troops came to liberate us we rushed into the streets leaving our most valuable attributes behind as if they belonged to the enemy."

13   The Dunns' book is thorough, taking parents step-by-step through the elementary years and on to high school. Had I been raising daughters, however, I think I would have flunked out in the chapter "What to Do from Age Two to Five." In discussing development of vocabulary, the Doctors Dunn prohibit the use of nonsensical words for bodily functions. I'm sorry, Doctors, but I've experimented with this precise terminology and discovered that the child who yells "I have to defecate, Mom" across four grocery aisles is likely to be left in the store. A family without a few poo-poo jokes is no family at all.

14   These educators don't help me much in my efforts to liberate my sons. And although I think little girls are getting a better deal with better

athletic training and broader options, I believe we're kidding ourselves if we think we can raise our sons and daughters alike. Certain inborn traits seem to be immune to parental and cultural tampering. How can I explain why a little girl baby sits on a quilt in the park thoughtfully examining a blade of grass, while my baby William uproots grass by handfuls and eats it? Why does a mother of very bright and active daughters confide that until she went camping with another family of boys, she feared that my sons had a hyperactivity problem? I'm sure there are plenty of rowdy, noisy little girls, but I'm not just talking about rowdiness and noise. I'm talking about some sort of primal physicalness that causes the walls of my house to pulsate on rainy days. I'm talking about something inexplicable that makes my sons fall into a mad, scrambling, pull-your-ears-off-kick-your-teeth-in heap just before bedtime, when they're not even mad at each other. I mean something that causes them to climb the doorjamb with honey and peanut butter on their hands while giving me a synopsis of *Star Wars* that contains only five intelligible words: "And then this guy, he 'pssshhhhhhh.' And then this thing went 'vrongggggg.' But this little guy said, 'Nong-neeee-nonh-neee.' " When Jack and Drew are not kicking a soccer ball or each other, they are kicking the chair legs, the cat, the baby's silver rattle, and, inadvertently, Baby William himself, whom they have affectionately dubbed "Tough Eddy." Staying put in a chair for the duration of a one-course meal is torturous for these boys. They compensate by never quite putting both feet under the table. They sit with one leg doubled under them while the other leg extends to one side. The upper half of the body appears committed to the task at hand—eating—but the lower extremities are poised to lunge should a more compelling distraction present itself. From this position, I have observed, one brother can trip a haughty dessert-eating sibling who is flaunting the fact he ate all his "sweaty little peas." Although we have civilized them to the point that they dutifully mumble, "May I be excused, please?" their abrupt departure from the table invariably overturns at least one chair or whatever milk remains. This sort of constant motion just doesn't lend itself to lessons in thoughtfulness and gentleness.

15   Despite my encouragement, my sons refuse to invite little girls to play anymore. Occasionally friends leave their small daughters with us while they run errands. I am always curious to see what these females will find of interest in my sons' roomful of Tonka trucks and soccer balls. One morning the boys suggested that the girls join them in playing Emergency with the big red fire trucks and ambulance. The girls were delighted and immediately designated the ambulance as theirs. The point of Emergency, as I have seen it played countless times with a gang of little boys, is to make as much noise with the siren as possible and to crash the trucks into each other or into the leg of a living-room chair before you reach your destination.

16   The girls had other ideas. I realized why they had selected the ambulance. It contained three dolls: a driver, a nurse, and sick man on the stretcher. My boys have used that ambulance many times, but the dolls

were always secondary to the death-defying race with the fire trucks; they were usually just thrown in the back of the van as an afterthought. The girls took the dolls out, stripped and re-dressed them tenderly, and made sure that they were seated in their appropriate places for the first rescue. Once the fire truck had been lifted off the man's leg, the girls required a box of Band-Aids and spent the next half hour making a bed for the patient and reassuring him that he was going to be all right. These little girls and my sons had seen the same NBC *Emergency* series, but the girls had apparently picked up on the show's nurturing aspects, while Jack and Drew were interested only in the equipment, the fast driving, and the sirens. . . .

17   Of course, I want my sons to grow up knowing that what's inside a woman's head is more important than her appearance, but I'm sure they're getting mixed signals when I delay our departure for the swimming pool to put on lipstick. I also wonder what they make of their father, whose favorite aphorism is "beautiful women rule the world." I suppose what we want for these sons and the women they may marry someday is a sensitivity that enables them to be both flexible and at ease with their respective roles, so that marriage contracts are unnecessary. When my sons bring me the heads of two purple irises from the neighbor's yard and ask, "Are you really the most beautiful mama in the whole world like Daddy says, and did everyone want to marry you?" do you blame me if I keep on waffling?

Masculine/Feminine

Questions on Content, Style, and Structure

1. What was Mackintosh's intention in raising her three sons? Did she succeed?

2. What did Mackintosh do to raise "liberated" sons?

3. According to the experts, why isn't the home environment enough to break sexual stereotyping?

4. How does Mackintosh show cultural stereotyping in her son's schools?

5. What complaint does Mackintosh have about the advice in *How to Raise Independent and Professionally Successful Daughters*?

6. Why does Mackintosh quote Anne Roiphe in paragraph 12?

7. Ultimately, does Mackintosh think it's possible to raise children free of sex-role differences? How does she support her opinion? Are the characteristics she describes in paragraphs 14–16 all "inborn traits"?

8. Throughout the essay, what is the main source of support Mackintosh offers for her thesis? In what ways does she try to broaden her support?

9. Characterize the tone of this essay. Is it appropriate? What role does humor play?

10. Point out ways Mackintosh tries to appear fair and evenhanded when she criticizes the "experts."

Vocabulary

mollified (1)	laments (5)	synopsis (14)
disdain (3)	unabashedly (6)	inadvertently (14)
fervent (3)	laudable (9)	aphorism (17)
exhorted (3)	eminently (10)	

Suggestions for Writing

1. Mackintosh believes that there are natural sex differences, certain inborn traits that are immune to change. Do you agree? Write an essay defending your position.

2. Write an essay in which you agree or disagree with the author's opinion that mothers at home may be more involved in the "real" world than women with careers.

3. Think back to your childhood; describe an incident or time when you feel you were trained to follow a stereotype. How has this training affected you as you are now?

Confessions of a Female Chauvinist Sow
Anne Roiphe

Anne Roiphe has published three books: *Digging Out* (1968), *Up the Sandbox* (1971), and *Long Division* (1973). Her articles appear in a variety of magazines, such as *Vogue* and *The New York Times Magazine*; this essay is reprinted from a 1972 issue of *New York Magazine*.

1   I once married a man I thought was totally unlike my father and I imagined a whole new world of freedom emerging. Five years later it was clear even to me—floating face down in a wash of despair—that I had simply chosen a replica of my handsome daddy-true. The updated version spoke English like an angel but—good God!—underneath he was my father exactly: wonderful, but not the right man for me.

2   Most people I know have at one time or another been fouled up by
their childhood experiences. Patterns tend to sink into the unconscious
only to reappear, disguised, unseen, like marionette strings, pulling us
this way or that. Whatever ails people—keeps them up at night, tossing
and turning—also ails movements no matter how historically huge or
politically important. The women's movement cannot remake consciousness, or reshape the future, without acknowledging and shedding
all the unnecessary and ugly baggage of the past. It's easy enough now
to see where men have kept us out of clubs, baseball games, graduate
schools; it's easy enough to recognize the hidden directions that limit
Sis to cake-baking and Junior to bridge-building; it's now possible for
even Miss America herself to identify what *they* have done to us, and,
of course, *they* have and *they* did and *they* are. . . . But along the way
we also developed our own hidden prejudices, class assumptions and an
anti-male humor and collection of expectations that gave us, like all
oppressed groups, a secret sense of superiority (co-existing with a poor
self-image—it's not news that people can believe two contradictory
things at once).

3   Listen to any group that suffers materially and socially. They have a
lexicon with which they tease the enemy: ofay, goy, honky gringo. "Poor
pale devils," said Malcolm X loud enough for us to hear, although blacks
had joked about that to each other for years. Behind some of the women's
liberation thinking lurk the rumors, the prejudices, the defense systems
of generations of oppressed women whispering in the kitchen together,
presenting one face to their menfolk and another to their card clubs, their
mothers and sisters. All this is natural enough but potentially dangerous
in a revolutionary situation in which you hope to create a future that
does not mirror the past. The hidden anti-male feelings, a result of the
old system, will foul us up if they are allowed to persist.

4   During my teen years I never left the house on my Saturday night
dates without my mother slipping me a few extra dollars—mad money,
it was called. I'll explain what it was for the benefit of the new generation
in which people just sleep with each other: the fellow was supposed to
bring me home, lead me safely through the asphalt jungle, protect me
from slithering snakes, rapists and the like. But my mother and I knew
young men were apt to drink too much, to slosh down so many rye-and-
gingers that some hero might well lead me in front of an oncoming bus,
smash his daddy's car into Tiffany's window or, less gallantly, throw up
on my new dress. Mad money was for getting home on your own, no
matter what form of insanity your date happened to evidence. Mad
money was also a wallflower's rope ladder; if the guy you came with
suddenly fancied someone else, well, you didn't have to stay there and
suffer, you could go home. Boys were fickle and likely to be unkind; my
mother and I knew that, as surely as we knew they tried to make you do
things in the dark they wouldn't respect you for afterwards, and in fact

would spread the word and spoil your rep. Boys like to be flattered; if you made them feel important they would eat out of your hand. So talk to them about their interests, don't alarm them with displays of intelligence—we all knew that, we groups of girls talking into the wee hours of the night in a kind of easy companionship we thought impossible with boys. Boys were prone to have a good time, get you pregnant, and then pretend they didn't know your name when you came knocking on their door for finances or comfort. In short, we believed boys were less moral than we were. They appeared to be hypocritical, self-seeking, exploitative, untrustworthy and very likely to be showing off their precious masculinity. I never had a girl friend I thought would be unkind or embarrass me in public. I never expected a girl to lie to me about her marks or sports skill or how good she was in bed. Altogether—without anyone's directly coming out and saying so—I gathered that men were sexy, powerful, very interesting, but not very nice, not very moral, humane and tender, like us. Girls played fairly while men, unfortunately, reserved their honor for the battlefield.

5   Why are there laws insisting on alimony and child support? Well, everyone knows that men don't have an instinct to protect their young and, given half a chance, with the moon in the right phase, they will run off and disappear. Everyone assumes a mother will not let her child starve, yet it is necessary to legislate that a father must not do so. We are taught to accept the idea that men are less than decent; their charms may be manifold but their characters are riddled with faults. To this day I never blink if I hear that a man has gone to find his fortune in South America, having left his pregnant wife, his blind mother and taken the family car. I still gasp in horror when I hear of a woman leaving her asthmatic infant for a rock group in Taos because I can't seem to avoid the assumption that men are naturally heels and women the ordained carriers of what little is moral in our dubious civilization.

6   My mother never gave me mad money thinking I would ditch a fellow for some other guy or that I would pass out drunk on the floor. She knew I would be considerate of my companion because, after all, I was more mature than the boys that gathered about. Why was I more mature? Women just are people-oriented; they learn to be empathetic at an early age. Most English students (students interested in humanity, not artifacts) are women. Men and boys—so the myth goes—conceal their feelings and lose interest in anybody else's. Everyone knows that even little boys can tell the difference between one kind of a car and another—proof that their souls are mechanical, their attention directed to the non-human.

7   I remember shivering in the cold vestibule of a famous men's athletic club. Women and girls are not permitted inside the club's door. What are they doing in there, I asked? They're naked, said my mother, they're sweating, jumping up and down a lot, telling each other dirty jokes and

bragging about their stock market exploits. Why can't we go in? I asked. Well, my mother told me, they're afraid we'd laugh at them.

8   The prejudices of childhood are hard to outgrow. I confess that every time my business takes me past that club, I shudder. Images of large bellies resting on massage tables and flaccid penises rising and falling with the Dow Jones average flash through my head. There it is, chauvinism waving its cancerous tentacles from the depths of my psyche.

9   Minorities automatically feel superior to the oppressor because, after all, they are not hurting anybody. In fact, they feel morally better. The old canard that women need love, men need sex—believed for too long by both sexes—attributes moral and spiritual superiority to women and makes of men beasts whose urges send them prowling into the night. This false division of good and bad, placing deforming pressures on everyone, doesn't have to contaminate the future. We know that the assumptions we make about each other become a part of the cultural air we breathe and, in fact, become social truths. Women who want equality must be prepared to give it and to believe in it, and in order to do that it is not enough to state that you are as good as any man, but also it must be stated that he is as good as you and both will be humans together. If we want men to share in the care of the family in a new way, we must assume them as capable of consistent loving tenderness as we.

10   I rummage about and find in my thinking all kinds of anti-male prejudices. Some are just jokes and others I will have a hard time abandoning. First, I share an emotional conviction with many sisters that women given power would not create wars. Intellectually I know that's ridiculous; great queens have waged war before; the likes of Lurleen Wallace, Pat Nixon and Mrs. General Lavelle can be depended upon in the future to guiltlessly condemn to death other people's children in the name of some ideal of their own. Little girls, of course, don't take toy guns out of their hip pockets and say "Pow, pow" to all their neighbors and friends like the average well-adjusted little boy. However, if we gave little girls the six-shooters, we would soon have double the pretend body count.

11   Aggression is not, as I secretly think, a male-sex-linked characteristic: brutality is masculine only by virtue of opportunity. True, there are 1,000 Jack the Rippers for every Lizzie Borden, but that surely is the result of social forms. Women as a group are indeed more masochistic than men. The practical result of this division is that women seem nicer and kinder, but when the world changes, women will have a fuller opportunity to be just as rotten as men and there will be fewer claims of female moral superiority.

12   Now that I am entering early middle age, I hear many women complaining of husbands and ex-husbands who are attracted to younger females. This strikes the older woman as unfair, of course. But I remember a time when I thought all boys around my age and grade were creeps and bores. I wanted to go out with an older man: a senior or, miraculously,

a college man. I had a certain contempt for my coevals, not realizing that the freshman in college I thought so desirable was some older girl's creep. Some women never lose that contempt for men of their own age. That isn't fair either and may be one reason why some sensible men of middle years find solace in young women.

13   I remember coming home from school one day to find my mother's card game dissolved in hysterical laughter. The cards were floating in black rivers of running mascara. What was so funny? A woman named Helen was lying on a couch pretending to be her husband with a cold. She was issuing demands for orange juice, aspirin, suggesting a call to a specialist, complaining of neglect, of fate's cruel finger, of heat, of cold, or sharp pains on the bridge of the nose that might indicate brain involvement. What was so funny? The ladies explained to me that all men behave just like that with colds, they are reduced to temper tantrums by simple nasal congestion, men cannot stand any little physical discomfort—on and on the laughter went.

14   The point of this vignette is the nature of the laughter—us laughing at them, us feeling superior to them, us ridiculing them behind their backs. If they were doing it to us we'd call it male chauvinist pigness; if we do it to them, it is inescapably female chauvinist sowness and, whatever its roots, it leads to the same isolation. Boys are messy, boys are mean, boys are rough, boys are stupid and have sloppy handwriting. A cacophony of childhood memories rushes through my head, balanced, of course, by all the well-documented feelings of inferiority and envy. But the important thing, the hard thing, is to wipe the slate clean, to start again without the meanness of the past. That's why it's so important that the women's movement not become anti-male and allow its most prejudiced spokesmen total leadership. The much-chewed-over abortion issue illustrates this. The women's-liberation position, insisting on a woman's right to determine her own body's destiny, leads in fanatical extreme to a kind of emotional immaculate conception in which the father is not judged even half-responsible—he has no rights, and no consideration is to be given to his concern for either the woman or the fetus.

15   Woman, who once was abandoned and disgraced by an unwanted pregnancy, has recently arrived at a new pride of ownership or disposal. She has traveled in a straight line that still excludes her sexual partner from an equal share in the wanted or unwanted pregnancy. A better style of life may develop from an assumption that men are as human as we. Why not ask the child's father if he would like to bring up the child? Why not share decisions, when possible, with the male? If we cut them out, assuming an old-style indifference on their part, we perpetuate the ugly divisiveness that has characterized relations between the sexes so far.

16   Hard as it is for many of us to believe, women are not really superior to men in intelligence or humanity—they are only equal.

Confessions of a Female Chauvinist Sow

Questions on Content, Style, and Structure

1. Roiphe wants a future of equality that "does not mirror the past."
What feelings must be shed before a better future can be created for
everyone?

2. What audience is Roiphe primarily addressing?

3. Characterize the male stereotype Roiphe was taught. Contrast this
stereotype to the female myth she also learned. What are the dangers of
these myths?

4. What is the effect in paragraphs 4, 5, and 6 of so many sentences that
state "everyone knows," "we knew," "mother and I knew," etc.?

5. What is the purpose of paragraph 9?

6. What is Roiphe's point in telling the story about the woman pretending to be her husband with a cold?

7. According to Roiphe, how might abortion be reconsidered?

8. How effective is the concluding paragraph?

9. Is Roiphe's title appropriate? effective?

10. Characterize the tone of this essay. Is the tone appropriate? Why/
why not? What does the use of such words and phrases as "spoil your
rep" (4), "ditch a fellow" (6), "to slosh down so many rye-and-gingers"
(4), and "creeps" (12) add to the tone?

11. Find examples of Roiphe's imagery and humor. What do these add
to her essay?

Vocabulary

marionette (2)	canard (9)
lexicon (3)	coevals (12)
exploitative (4)	solace (12)
empathetic (6)	vignette (14)
flaccid (8)	cacophony (14)

Suggestions for Writing

1. Roiphe admits that the "prejudices of childhood are hard to outgrow."
Write an essay discussing a prejudice you once held against a group or a
person and how you overcame your belief.

2. The author notes that most people she knows have "at one time or
another been fouled up by their childhood experiences." Explain a way
you feel a childhood experience has adversely affected you.

3. Are there any "myths" about males or females Roiphe discusses that you still think are true? Defend your position in an essay developed by example.

Let 'em Eat Leftovers
Mike McGrady

Mike McGrady is the author of *The Kitchen Sink Papers—My Life as a Househusband* (1975) and *The Husband's Cookbook* (1979). This essay was published in *Newsweek* in 1976.

1   Last year my wife and I traded roles. Every morning she went off to an office and earned the money that paid the bills. I cooked and cleaned, picked up after three kids, went head-to-head with bargain-hunting shoppers, pleaded for a raise in allowance and lived the generally hellish life that half the human race accepts as its lot.

2   The year is over now but the memories won't go away. What is guaranteed to stir them up is any of those Total Woman or Fascinating Womanhood people singing the praises of the happy housewife—that mythical woman who manages a spotless house, runs herd over half a dozen kids, whips up short-order culinary masterpieces, smells good and still finds time to read Great Books and study Japanese line engraving.

3   I never qualified. Never even came close. In fact, I never quite mastered that most basic task, the cleaning of the house. Any job that requires six hours to do and can be undone in six minutes by one small child carrying a plate of crackers and a Monopoly set—this is not a job that will long capture my interest. After a year of such futility, I have arrived at a rule of thumb—if the debris accumulates to a point where small animals can be seen to be living there, it should be cleaned up, preferably by someone hired for the occasion.

4   Housekeeping was just one facet of the nightmare. I think back to a long night spent matching up four dozen bachelor socks, all of them wool, most of them gray. Running an all-hours taxi service for subteens. Growing older in orthodontists' waiting rooms. Pasting trading stamps into little booklets. Oh, the nightmare had as many aspects as there were hours in the day.

Empress of Domestic Arts

5   At the heart of my difficulty was this simple fact: for the past two decades I had been paid for my work. I had come to feel my time was valuable. Suddenly my sole payment was a weekly allowance given to me with considerable fanfare by my bread-winning wife. I began to see that as a trap, a many-strings-attached offering that barely survived a single session in the supermarket and never got me through a neighborhood poker game.

6   The pay was bad and the hours were long but what bothered me most was my own ineptitude, my inability to apply myself to the business of managing a home. No longer do I feel guilty about my failure as a home-maker. I would no more applaud the marvelously efficient and content housewife than I would applaud the marvelously efficient and content elevator operator. The image strikes me as useful on several levels but the point is this: it is always someone else who goes up, someone else who gets off.

7   Some people seem to feel that the housewife's lot would be bettered if she were given a new title, one that takes into account the full range and complexity of her role, something along the lines of "household engineer" or, perhaps, "domestic scientist." Wonderful. You come and take care of my house and my kids and you can be the Empress of the Domestic Arts, the Maharanee of the Vacuum Cleaner.

Try a Little Neglect

8   A more intriguing suggestion is that husbands pay their wives salaries for housework. I suggested this to my wife and she said I don't make enough money to pay her to do that job again. Neither, according to her, does J. Paul Getty. I am coming to the feeling that this is a job that should not be done by any one person for love or for money.

9   This is not to put down the whole experience. By the end of the year, I had succeeded in organizing my time so that there were a few hours for the occasional book, the random round of golf. Then, too, it was a pleasure to be more than a weekend visitor in my kids' lives. While my wife and I are now willing to de-emphasize housekeeping, neither of us would cut back on what some people call parenting and what I look at as the one solid reward in this belated and male motherhood of mine.

10   Of course, I had it easy—relatively easy anyway. This was my little experiment, not my destiny. There is a considerable difference between a year in prison and a life sentence.

11   It will be argued: well, *someone* has to do these things. Not necessarily. In the first place, some two can do most of these things. Secondly, I can think of no area in modern life that could more easily sustain a policy of benign neglect than the home. I'm arguing here in favor of letting the dust gather where it may; in favor of making greater use of

slow cookers and nearby fish-and-chips stands; of abolishing, as far as possible, the position of unpaid servant in the family.

12   Many men surely will find this line of thought threatening. That's just as it should be. Few plantation owners were enthusiastic about the Emancipation Proclamation. What is more surprising is that these thoughts will prove equally threatening to many women. OK. Those females who demand the right to remain in service should not necessarily be discouraged—we all know how hard it is to find decent household help these days.

13   I suspect the real reason for many women's reluctance to break bonds is fear of the world that exists outside the home. They sense the enormous complexity of their husbands' lives, the tremendous skills required to head up a team of salesmen or to write cigarette commercials or to manufacture lawn fertilizer. The mind that feels these fears may be beyond the reach of change. It is another sort of mind, the mind that finds itself in constant rebellion against the limitations of housewifery, that concerns me more here.

The Life You Save

14   To this mind, this person, we should say: go ahead. There is a world out here, a whole planet of possibilities. The real danger is that you won't do it. If Gutenberg had been a housewife, I might be writing these words with a quill pen. And if Edison had been a housewife, you might be reading them by candlelight.

15   No escape is simple and a certain amount of toughness will be required. How do you do it? You might start by learning how to sweep things under the rug. You might have to stop pampering the rest of the family—let 'em eat leftovers. And be prepared for the opposition that will surely develop. Even the most loving family hates to lose that trusted servant, that faithful family retainer, that little old homemaker, you. No one enjoys it when the most marvelous appliance of them all breaks down. But if it will be any comfort to you, the life you save will surely be your own.

Let 'em Eat Leftovers

Questions on Content, Style, and Structure

1. After a year as a homemaker, McGrady has some advice for the woman who finds herself in rebellion against housewifery. What does he suggest she do?

2. Characterize McGrady's attitude toward housekeeping by selecting

key words and phrases. Who is "the most marvelous appliance of them all"?

3. McGrady begins his essay by describing his personal experiences. Why?

4. Many of the personal experiences are described humorously. Identify several examples of McGrady's humor and tell what you think such humor adds to the essay.

5. How does McGrady feel about new titles for housewives?

6. What, according to McGrady, were the worst aspects of being a home-maker? the best?

7. In many argumentative essays, the writer will try to anticipate objections and problems and then answer them. Where and how does McGrady do this?

8. McGrady makes frequent use of colorful comparisons, such as house-wives to elevator operators and husbands to plantation owners. What, if anything, do such images add to his argument?

9. Evaluate the effectiveness of the essay's conclusion. Why does McGrady direct his comments to "you"? What famous quotations are parodied in the last paragraph and the title? Why does he conclude on a line borrowed from a safe-driving campaign of earlier times?

Vocabulary

culinary (2)	belated (9)
facet (4)	benign (11)
ineptitude (6)	retainer (15)

Suggestions for Writing

1. Do you agree with McGrady that "no area in modern life . . . could more easily sustain a policy of benign neglect than the home"? Are all homemakers "unpaid servants"? Write an essay defending your position.

2. Using your imagination or experiences, write a humorous account of a day in the life of typical househusband.

3. Pretend you are a housewife who has decided to take a job or go back to school. Write an essay in which you not only explain the reasons for your decision but also counter the objections of your imaginary family.

Omnigamy: The New Kinship System
Lionel Tiger

Lionel Tiger is currently director of the graduate programs in anthropology at Rutgers University. He has written several books, including *Men in Groups* (1969), *Women in the Kibbutz* (1975), and *Optimism: The Biology of Hope* (1980). This essay was published in *Psychology Today* in 1978.

1   A hapless British cabinet minister responsible for the hapless UK telephone system once complained that the more phones installed in his country, the more there were to call, and so the demand for phones increased: supply creates demand. Somewhat the same thing is happening with marriage in America. The more divorces there are, the more experienced marriers exist, ready to remarry—and many do. The divorce rate has jumped 250 percent in the past 21 years; about 80 percent of the formerly married remarry. With each new marriage, the parents and children involved acquire a whole new set of relatives, friends, and associations—in effect, they stretch their kinship system. Many people are married to people who have been married to other people who are now married to still others to whom the first parties may not have been married, but to whom somebody has likely been married. Our society, once based on the principle of solid monogamy until death do us part, has shifted toward a pattern of serial polygamy, in which people experience more than one spouse, if only one at a time. Thus we appear to be moving to a new and imprecise system we might call omnigamy, in which each will be married to all.

2   People keep marrying, even though happy marriages are regarded as surprising and much-envied occurrences. The not-so-stately pageant of marriage goes on, heedless of the cautionary cries of pain and the clenched question: Why? Various responsible estimators expect that from a third to a half of the marriages formed in this decade will end in divorce sometime. That is astonishing. It is also astonishing that, under the circumstances, marriage is still legally allowed. If nearly half of anything else ended so disastrously, the government would surely ban it immediately. If half the tacos served in restaurants caused dysentery, if half the people learning karate broke their palms, if only 6 percent of people who went on roller-coasters damaged their middle ears, the public would be clamoring for action. Yet the most intimate of disasters—with consequences that may last a lifetime for both adults and children—happens over and over again. Marriage has not yet gone underground.

3   To an anthropologist, the emergence of a new kinship system should

be as exciting as the discovery of a new comet to an astronomer. But in the case of omnigamy, the developing pattern is still unclear, the forces shaping it unanalyzed, the final structure difficult to predict. We know the numbers of marriages and remarriages, but what about the apparent acceleration of the process? The new system permits—perhaps even demands—that its members repair themselves quickly after crises of vast personal proportion. In the slapdash, overpraised, and sentimental film *An Unmarried Woman*, Jill Clayburgh explains to her (quite nauseating) therapist how agonizing and lonely it was when her husband of umpteen years left her, and how she has been without sexual congress for such a long, long time. When the therapist hears this dreadful fact, she earnestly recommends that this casualty of a massive private accident return immediately to the sexual fray. It has, after all, been *seven weeks*.

4   The heroine subsequently decides to reject an offer to join an attractive and apparently quite suitable artist. Instead she chooses to lead an independent life as a part-time secretary in a SoHo art gallery, which makes her somewhat radical with respect to the omnigamous system. For her obligation seems clear: she must form some sturdy response, one way or the other, to the ambient fact of marriage and remarriage. To remain haunted by grief and inhibited by a sense of failure is taken as a mere expression of cowardice or restlessness. When anthropology first started out, the difficult trick in studying any culture was to discover just what the kinship system was—who was married to whom, and why, and what connections counted for inheritance, status, and authority. We found that marriage was the instrument for creating the extended family, which provided for most human needs in the tribal societies. If an anthropologist from the Trobriand Islands came here now, he or she could well conclude that by stimulating further marriages, divorce has come to be an important organizing principle in our society, since kinship alliances among divorced people are so extensive and complex.

5   When parents divorce and remarry, the new family connections extend the reach of family life to dimensions a Baganda or Trobriander or Hopi could well understand. Take an example: after the divorce of A and B, siblings A1 and B1 live with A and her new husband, C, but visit B and his new wife, D, on weekends. C's children, C1, C2, and C3, like to go to basketball games with A1 and B1. D's children by her first marriage also enjoy the company of A1 and B1, and take them along on visits to their father, E, a former star athlete who becomes an important hero and role model to the children of A, who has never met him and probably never will.

6   Nor is it only marriage that binds. In a world where all Mom and Dad's companions are potential mates, Dad's live-in girl friend may turn up for parents' night at school when he's out of town. She also may have a brother—a kind of stepuncle to the kids—with a 40-foot sloop. (The spreading network can put children in touch with a dislocating variety of styles.)

7   What this means for children, and how it affects their sense of what is stable, what is optional, what is fast, slow, brisk, or stately, is, of course, difficult to say. The generation of children spawned by the Age of Omnigamy has not yet made its mark on the social system in any clear way; we cannot know whether they are immune, immunized, or carriers of the bug across generational lines. In the old days, people were titillated by the polygamous habits of Hollywood celebrities, but few were tempted to emulate them. Parents, grandparents, aunts, and uncles seem to be more important role models for children. When they keep changing partners, it will likely increase the child's sense of the tentativeness in all relations that the new system reflects.

8   While I am not implying that omnigamous parents set a bad example, they surely set some example. The consequences for their own children and for those others with whom they come in contact must be considerable. Divorce as a recurrent aspect of life may make it relatively easier for children to accept when they are young, but harder to avoid when they become adults. And who has calculated the effect of omnigamy on grandparents, whose connections with their grandchildren suddenly come to be mediated by strangers—stepparents who might even move them to some distant city?

9   I do not mean to be alarmist and implacably negative about all this. The existence of relatively civilized divorce options is as much a sign of human freedom as it is of sanctioned personal confusion and pain. Who, after all, would wish to confirm in their desperate plight the countless real-world descendants of Madame Bovary?

10   Surely, too, there is a value in the extension of personal experience to wider circles of people than strict and permanent monogamy permits. And there is presumably an enhancement of personal vividness, which the new, relatively unstructured world permits—if not coerces.

11   Omnigamy may have interesting economic implications as well. Adrienne Harris of York University in Toronto has pointed out that each marital separation stimulates the repurchase of those items left in one household and needed in the next. Like amoebas splitting, one dishwasher becomes two, one vacuum cleaner becomes two, one television becomes two; domestic purchases even become impetuous ("Why shouldn't I have my Cuisinart to do my fish mousse when he/she has *our* Cuisinart for hers/his?") One can't help speculating that the rapid increase in retail outlets selling cooking equipment reflects the doubled demands of the new kinship system.

12   And where would the real estate market be without house sales to accommodate people who can no longer accommodate each other? And has anyone wondered why the garage sale has recently become so common? The economic shifts that depend on the breakup and re-forming of marital units are a form of internal colonialism: at the same time that the United States can no longer control foreign markets, it is expanding its internal ones. The family system, which both Engels and Marx saw

as the stimulus for the development of capitalism, may even, in the new form, turn out to be one of its props. As with all colonialisms, however, many people come to be exploited. Taking up the options omnigamy offers strains the financial and emotional resources both.

13   Can it be said that these comments apply mostly to a small group of self-involved persons inhabiting the Upper East and West Sides of Manhattan, where the production of novels and articles about marriage and anguished personal failure is a major cottage industry? No. If the divorce rates persist and cities continue to export their social patterns, as in the past, other communities still complacently conventional and relatively monogamous will make a gradual but perceptual shift to omnigamy. The pattern will broaden unless there is soon—and there could be—a renewed commitment to monogamous fidelity, and possibly even to the importance of virginity as a factor in marital choice (this possibility seems rather remote). What does seem clear is that many changes will derive from these many changes, perhaps even a return to notions of marriage based on economic convenience and an agreement to mount a common assault on loneliness. Marriage could be on its way to becoming a generalized corporate, if small-scale, experience capable of providing some sense of community and some prospect of continuity. But it may also become a relatively planless arrangement and rearrangement of fickle magnets inexplicably and episodically drawn into each other's orbits for varying purposes and periods.

Omnigamy: The New Kinship System

Questions on Content, Style, and Structure

1. According to Tiger, what new kinship system has evolved?
2. What has become a new, "important organizing principle in our society"? Why?
3. Why does Tiger find it "astonishing" that marriage is still legally allowed? Is he serious? What is the purpose of the comparisons in paragraph 2? How effective are they?
4. Characterize the tone of this essay. What is the effect of such sentences as "Many people are married to people who have been married to other people who are now married to still others to whom the first parties may not have been married, but to whom somebody has likely been married"?
5. Why does Tiger begin his essay with the story about the British telephone system?
6. How does Tiger use the film *An Unmarried Woman* to make his point in paragraphs 3–4? What is the purpose of the example in paragraph 5?

7. What negative effects does Tiger suggest omnigamy will have on the children of this generation?

8. What positive effects does he suggest? Economic results? Are such results really benefits?

9. According to Tiger, how may marriage be regarded if the current pattern is not halted?

10. How did Tiger form the word "omnigamy"? From what root words is it made?

Vocabulary

hapless (1)	ambient (4)	cottage industry (13)
monogamy (1)	emulate (7)	complacently (13)
polygamy (1)	implacably (9)	inexplicably (13)
heedless (2)	enhancement (10)	episodically (13)
congress (3)		

Suggestions for Writing

1. Have you ever been affected by a divorce? Write an essay in which you analyze the effects of this divorce on your life.

2. Many people have noted that it takes only three minutes to marry but usually several months to divorce; some critics feel the reverse should be true. Write an essay in which you agree or disagree.

3. Write a research paper explaining the major causes of divorce in the United States.

Is Love an Art?
Erich Fromm

Erich Fromm was awarded a Ph.D. in psychology from the University of Heidelberg and has taught at many universities, including Columbia and Yale. Some of his well-known books are *Escape from Freedom* (1941), *Sigmund Freud's Mission* (1958), *Life without Illusions* (1962), and *Anatomy of Human Destructiveness* (1973). This essay is excerpted from *The Art of Loving* (1956).

1   Is love an art? Then it requires knowledge and effort. Or is love a pleasant sensation, which to experience is a matter of chance, something one "falls into" if one is lucky? This little book is based on the former premise, while undoubtedly the majority of people today believe in the latter.

2   Not that people think that love is not important. They are starved for it; they watch endless numbers of films about happy and unhappy love stories, they listen to hundreds of trashy songs about love—yet hardly anyone thinks that there is anything that needs to be learned about love.

3   This peculiar attitude is based on several premises which either singly or combined tend to uphold it. Most people see the problem of love primarily as that of *being loved*, rather than that of *loving*, of one's capacity to love. Hence the problem to them is how to be loved, how to be lovable. In pursuit of this aim they follow several paths. One, which is especially used by men, is to be successful, to be as powerful and rich as the social margin of one's position permits. Another, used especially by women, is to make oneself attractive, by cultivating one's body, dress, etc. Other ways of making oneself attractive, used both by men and women, are to develop pleasant manners, interesting conversation, to be helpful, modest, inoffensive. Many of the ways to make oneself lovable are the same as those used to make oneself successful, "to win friends and influence people." As a matter of fact, what most people in our culture mean by being lovable is essentially a mixture between being popular and having sex appeal.

4   A second premise behind the attitude that there is nothing to be learned about love is the assumption that the problem of love is the problem of an *object*, not the problem of a *faculty*. People think that to *love* is simple, but that to find the right object to love—or to be loved— is difficult. This attitude has several reasons rooted in the development of modern society. One reason is the great change which occurred in the twentieth century with respect to the choice of a "love object." In the Victorian age, as in many traditional cultures, love was mostly not a spontaneous personal experience which then might lead to marriage. On the contrary, marriage was contracted by convention—either by the respective families, or by a marriage broker, or without the help of such intermediaries; it was concluded on the basis of social considerations, and love was supposed to develop once the marriage had been concluded. In the last few generations the concept of romantic love has become almost universal in the Western world. In the United States, while considerations of a conventional nature are not entirely absent, to a vast extent people are in search of "romantic love," of the personal experience of love which then should lead to marriage. This new concept of freedom in love must have greatly enhanced the importance of the *object* as against the importance of the *function*.

5   Closely related to this factor is another feature characteristic of contemporary culture. Our whole culture is based on the appetite for buying, on the idea of a mutually favorable exchange. Modern man's happiness consists in the thrill of looking at the shop windows, and in buying all that he can afford to buy, either for cash or on installments. He (or she) looks at people in a similar way. For the man an attractive girl—and for

the woman an attractive man—are the prizes they are after. "Attractive"
usually means a nice package of qualities which are popular and sought
after on the personality market. What specifically makes a person attractive depends on the fashion of the time, physically as well as mentally. During the twenties, a drinking and smoking girl, tough and sexy,
was attractive; today the fashion demands more domesticity and coyness.
At the end of the nineteenth and the beginning of this century, a man
had to be aggressive and ambitious—today he has to be social and tolerant—in order to be an attractive "package." At any rate, the sense of
falling in love develops usually only with regard to such human commodities as are within reach of one's own possibilities for exchange. I am
out for a bargain; the object should be desirable from the standpoint of
its social value, and at the same time should want me, considering my
overt and hidden assets and potentialities. Two persons thus fall in love
when they feel they have found the best object available on the market,
considering the limitations of their own exchange values. Often, as in
buying real estate, the hidden potentialities which can be developed play
a considerable role in this bargain. In a culture in which the marketing
orientation prevails, and in which material success is the outstanding
value, there is little reason to be surprised that human love relations
follow the same pattern of exchange which governs the commodity and
the labor market.

6   The third error leading to the assumption that there is nothing to be
learned about love lies in the confusion between the initial experience
of *"falling"* in love, and the permanent state of *being* in love, or as we
might better say, of "standing" in love. If two people who have been
strangers, as all of us are, suddenly let the wall between them break
down, and feel close, feel one, this moment of oneness is one of the most
exhilarating, most exciting experiences in life. It is all the more wonderful and miraculous for persons who have been shut off, isolated, without love. This miracle of sudden intimacy is often facilitated if it is
combined with, or initiated by, sexual attraction and consummation.
However, this type of love is by its very nature not lasting. The two
persons become well acquainted, their intimacy loses more and more its
miraculous character, until their antagonism, their disappointments,
their mutual boredom kill whatever is left of the initial excitement. Yet,
in the beginning they do know all of this: in fact, they take the intensity
of the infatuation, this being "crazy" about each other, for proof of the
intensity of their love, while it may only prove the degree of their preceding loneliness.

7   This attitude—that nothing is easier than to love—has continued to
be the prevalent idea about love in spite of the overwhelming evidence
to the contrary. There is hardly any activity, any enterprise, which is
started with such tremendous hopes and expectations, and yet, which
fails so regularly, as love. If this were the case with any other activity,

people would be eager to know the reasons for the failure, and to learn how one could do better—or they would give up the activity. Since the latter is impossible in the case of love, there seems to be only one adequate way to overcome the failure of love—to examine the reasons for this failure, and to proceed to study the meaning of love.

8   The first step to take is to become aware that *love is an art*, just as living is an art; if we want to learn how to love we must proceed in the same way we have to proceed if we want to learn any other art, say music, painting, carpentry, or the art of medicine or engineering.

9   What are the necessary steps in learning any art?

10   The process of learning an art can be divided conveniently into two parts: one, the mastery of the theory; the other, the mastery of the practice. If I want to learn the art of medicine, I must first know the facts about the human body, and about various diseases. When I have all this theoretical knowledge, I am by no means competent in the art of medicine. I shall become a master in this art only after a great deal of practice, until eventually the results of my theoretical knowledge and the results of my practice are blended into one—my intuition, the essence of the mastery of any art. But, aside from learning the theory and practice, there is a third factor necessary to becoming a master in any art—the mastery of the art must be a matter of ultimate concern; there must be nothing else in the world more important than the art. This holds true for music, for medicine, for carpentry—and for love. And, maybe, here lies the answer to the question of why people in our culture try so rarely to learn this art, in spite of their obvious failures: in spite of the deep-seated craving for love, almost everything else is considered to be more important than love: success, prestige, money, power—almost all our energy is used for the learning of how to achieve these aims, and almost none to learn the art of loving.

11   Could it be that only those things are considered worthy of being learned with which one can earn money or prestige, and that love, which "only" profits the soul, but is profitless in the modern sense, is a luxury we have no right to spend much energy on?

Is Love an Art?

Questions on Content, Style, and Structure

1. According to Fromm, what do most people mean by being "lovable"?
2. What are the misconceptions behind the attitude that there is nothing to be learned about love?
3. What is the difference between the function of love and the object of love?

4. Explain the metaphor in paragraph 5. What does it add to Fromm's point?

5. How does Fromm illustrate his point in paragraph 6?

6. What, says Fromm, is the only one way to overcome the failure of love?

7. What steps must be taken in the study of love?

8. Why, according to Fromm, do people fail to study the art of loving?

9. Identify the transition devices which connect one paragraph to another in this essay.

10. How does Fromm use analysis and classification to add coherence and clarity to his essay?

Vocabulary

premise (1)
faculty (4)
intermediaries (4)
domesticity (5)
commodities (5)

overt (5)
potentialities (5)
facilitated (6)
antagonism (6)
prevalent (7)

Suggestions for Writing

1. Fromm says people mistakenly focus on making themselves lovable instead of on learning how to love. Study a series of advertisements in magazines like *Playboy, Cosmopolitan,* or *Glamour.* Write an essay arguing that these ads do/do not illustrate the "paths" described in paragraph 3.

2. Write an essay defining "sex appeal."

3. Analyze a close personal relationship you have had with someone recently. Did you experience a failure of expectations for any of the reasons Fromm notes? Write an essay explaining the causes and/or effects of your disappointment.

Living in Sin
Adrienne Rich

Adrienne Rich is an American poet who has been active in the women's movement for many years. She has published over half a dozen books of poetry, including *Snapshots of a Daughter-in-Law* (1963) and *Diving into the Wreck* (1973), and the prose work *Of Woman Born* (1977). This poem appeared in *Poems, Selected and New, 1950–1974.*

```
     She had thought the studio would keep itself;
     no dust upon the furniture of love.
     Half heresy, to wish the taps less vocal,
     the panes relieved of grime. A plate of pears,
  5  a piano with a Persian shawl, a cat
     stalking the picturesque amusing mouse
     had risen at his urging.
     Not that at five each separate stair would writhe
     under the milkman's tramp; that morning light
 10  so coldly would delineate the scraps
     of last night's cheese and three sepulchral bottles;
     that on the kitchen shelf among the saucers
     a pair of beetle-eyes would fix her own—
     Envoy from some village in the moldings . . .
 15  Meanwhile, he, with a yawn,
     sounded a dozen notes upon the keyboard,
     declared it out of tune, shrugged at the mirror,
     rubbed at his beard, went out for cigarettes;
     while she, jeered by the minor demons,
 20  pulled back the sheets and made the bed and found
     a towel to dust the table-top,
     and let the coffee-pot boil over on the stove.
     By evening she was back in love again,
     though not so wholly but throughout the night
 25  she woke sometimes to feel the daylight coming
     like a relentless milkman up the stairs.
```

Living in Sin

Questions on Content, Style, and Structure

1. Who is the "she" of the poem? What was her fantasy about her relationship? How would you characterize her expectations?
2. Describe the studio as it actually is.

3. Who is the man in the poem? What do the short phrases in lines 15–18 communicate about his interest in the relationship?

4. What does she do while he is gone? How do these activities compare with her fantasy about the studio?

5. Explain the uses of evening and daylight as metaphors in this poem. Why is daylight like "a relentless milkman up the stairs"? Why does she wake throughout the night?

6. Summarize in one or two sentences what this poem is about.

7. Find examples of alliteration and personification. What do they add to the poem?

8. Is the title ironic in any way?

Vocabulary

delineate (10)
sepulchral (11)
envoy (14)
relentless (26)

Suggestions for Writing

1. Should young couples live together before marriage? Defend your answer in a well-written essay.

2. Have you ever been disillusioned about love? Write an essay contrasting your expectations to reality.

3. Write an essay describing your expectations of the perfect mate. Are your expectations realistic?

The Story of an Hour
Kate Chopin

Kate Chopin was a nineteenth-century writer whose stories appeared in such magazines as *The Atlantic Monthly, Century,* and *Saturday Evening Post.* She published two collections of short stories and two novels; one of her novels, *The Awakening* (1899), was considered so shocking in its story of a married woman who desired a career of her own that it was removed from some library shelves. "The Story of an Hour" was first published in *Vogue* in 1894.

1   Knowing that Mrs. Mallard was afflicted with a heart trouble, great care was taken to break to her as gently as possible the news of her husband's death.

2   It was her sister Josephine who told her, in broken sentences, veiled hints that revealed in half concealing. Her husband's friend Richards was

there, too, near her. It was he who had been in the newspaper office when intelligence of the railroad disaster was received, with Brently Mallard's name leading the list of "killed." He had only taken the time to assure himself of its truth by a second telegram, and had hastened to forestall any less careful, less tender friend in bearing the sad message.

3   She did not hear the story as many women have heard the same, with a paralyzed inability to accept its significance. She wept at once, with sudden, wild abandonment, in her sister's arms. When the storm of grief had spent itself she went away to her room alone. She would have no one follow her.

4   There stood, facing the open window, a comfortable, roomy armchair. Into this she sank, pressed down by a physical exhaustion that haunted her body and seemed to reach into her soul.

5   She could see in the open square before her house the tops of trees that were all aquiver with the new spring life. The delicious breath of rain was in the air. In the street below a peddler was crying his wares. The notes of a distant song which some one was singing reached her faintly, and countless sparrows were twittering in the eaves.

6   There were patches of blue sky showing here and there through the clouds that had met and piled each above the other in the west facing her window.

7   She sat with her head thrown back upon the cushion of the chair quite motionless, except when a sob came up into her throat and shook her, as a child who has cried itself to sleep continues to sob in its dreams.

8   She was young, with a fair, calm face, whose lines bespoke repression and even a certain strength. But now there was a dull stare in her eyes, whose gaze was fixed away off yonder on one of those patches of blue sky. It was not a glance of reflection, but rather indicated a suspension of intelligent thought.

9   There was something coming to her and she was waiting for it, fearfully. What was it? She did not know; it was too subtle and elusive to name. But she felt it, creeping out of the sky, reaching toward her through the sounds, the scents, the color that filled the air.

10   Now her bosom rose and fell tumultuously. She was beginning to recognize this thing that was approaching to possess her, and she was striving to beat it back with her will—as powerless as her two white slender hands would have been.

11   When she abandoned herself a little whispered word escaped her slightly parted lips. She said it over and over under her breath: "Free, free, free!" The vacant stare and the look of terror that had followed it went from her eyes. They stayed keen and bright. Her pulses beat fast, and the coursing blood warmed and relaxed every inch of her body.

12   She did not stop to ask if it were not a monstrous joy that held her. A clear and exalted perception enabled her to dismiss the suggestion as trivial.

13   She knew that she would weep again when she saw the kind, tender hands folded in death; the face that had never looked save with love upon

her, fixed and gray and dead. But she saw beyond that bitter moment a long procession of years to come that would belong to her absolutely. And she opened and spread her arms out to them in welcome.

14   There would be no one to live for during those coming years; she would live for herself. There would be no powerful will bending her in that blind persistence with which men and women believe they have a right to impose a private will upon a fellow creature. A kind intention or a cruel intention made the act seem no less a crime as she looked upon it in that brief moment of illumination.

15   And yet she had loved him—sometimes. Often she had not. What did it matter! What could love, the unsolved mystery, count for in face of this possession of self-assertion which she suddenly recognized as the strongest impulse of her being.

16   "Free! Body and soul free!" she kept whispering.

17   Josephine was kneeling before the closed door with her lips to the keyhole, imploring for admission. "Louise, open the door! I beg; open the door—you will make yourself ill. What are you doing, Louise? For heaven's sake open the door."

18   "Go away. I am not making myself ill." No; she was drinking in a very elixir of life through that open window.

19   Her fancy was running riot along those days ahead of her. Spring days, and summer days, and all sorts of days that would be her own. She breathed a quick prayer that life might be long. It was only yesterday she had thought with a shudder that life might be long.

20   She arose at length and opened the door to her sister's importunities. There was a feverish triumph in her eyes, and she carried herself unwittingly like a goddess of Victory. She clasped her sister's waist, and together they descended the stairs. Richards stood waiting for them at the bottom.

21   Some one was opening the front door with a latchkey. It was Brently Mallard who entered, a little travel-stained, composedly carrying his gripsack and umbrella. He had been far from the scene of accident, and did not even know there had been one. He stood amazed at Josephine's piercing cry; at Richards' quick motion to screen him from the view of his wife.

22   But Richards was too late.

23   When the doctors came they said she had died of heart disease—of joy that kills.

The Story of an Hour

Questions on Content, Style, and Structure

1. According to her doctors, what kills Mrs. Mallard? Do you agree with their diagnosis?

2. Why is the ending of the story ironic?

3. What is Mrs. Mallard's immediate reaction to the news of her husband's death?

4. During what season is the story set? Why?

5. What is the feeling Mrs. Mallard senses "creeping out of the sky"?

6. What does Mrs. Mallard recognize as the "strongest impulse of her being"?

7. Chopin uses what kind of imagery to describe Mrs. Mallard after her revelation?

8. Is Mr. Mallard a villain in this story?

9. Is this story critical of men only? Support your views with reference to the story.

10. If you did not know that this story was published in 1894, what year or era would you have guessed? Why?

Vocabulary

forestall (2) imploring (17)
aquiver (5) elixir (18)
elusive (9) importunities (20)
tumultuously (10)

Suggestions for Writing

1. Write an essay analyzing the use of setting in this story.

2. Write an essay analyzing Chopin's use of physical imagery to show Mrs. Mallard's transformation.

3. Write an essay of personal experience that illustrates "that blind persistence with which men and women believe they have a right to impose a private will upon a fellow creature."

Section **3**

People at Leisure

Fear of Dearth
Carll Tucker

Carll Tucker was a theater critic and columnist for *The Village Voice* during 1974–77; he has been the editor of *Saturday Review* since 1977. This essay appeared in that magazine in 1979.

1   I hate jogging. Every dawn, as I thud around New York City's Central Park reservoir, I am reminded of how much I hate it. It's so tedious. Some claim jogging is thought conducive; others insist the scenery relieves the monotony. For me, the pace is wrong for contemplation of either ideas or vistas. While jogging, all I can think about is jogging—or nothing. One advantage of jogging around a reservoir is that there's no dry shortcut home.

2   From the listless looks of some fellow trotters, I gather I am not alone in my unenthusiasm: Bill-paying, it seems, would be about as diverting. Nonetheless, we continue to jog; more, we continue to *choose* to jog. From a practically infinite array of opportunities, we select one that we don't enjoy and can't wait to have done with. Why?

3   For any trend, there are as many reasons as there are participants. This person runs to lower his blood pressure. That person runs to escape the telephone or a cranky spouse or a filthy household. Another person runs to avoid doing anything else, to dodge a decision about how to lead his life or a realization that his life is leading nowhere. Each of us has his carrot and stick. In my case, the stick is my slackening physical condition, which keeps me from beating opponents at tennis whom I overwhelmed two years ago. My carrot is to win.

4   Beyond these disparate reasons, however, lies a deeper cause. It is no accident that now, in the last third of the 20th century, personal fitness and health have suddenly become a popular obsession. True, modern man likes to feel good, but that hardly distinguishes him from his predecessors.

5   With zany myopia, economists like to claim that the deeper cause of everything is economic. Delightfully, there seems no marketplace explanation for jogging. True, jogging is cheap, but then not jogging is cheaper. And the scant and skimpy equipment which jogging demands must make it a marketer's least favored form of recreation.

6   Some scout-masterish philosophers argue that the appeal of jogging and other body-maintenance programs is the discipline they afford. We live in a world in which individuals have fewer and fewer obligations. The work week has shrunk. Weekend worship is less compulsory. Technology gives us more free time. Satisfactorily filling free time requires

imagination and effort. Freedom is a wide and risky river; it can drown the person who does not know how to swim across it. The more obligations one takes on, the more time one occupies, the less threat freedom poses. Jogging can become an instant obligation. For a portion of his day, the jogger is not his own man; he is obedient to a regimen he has accepted.

7   Theologists may take the argument one step further. It is our modern irreligion, our lack of confidence in any hereafter, that makes us anxious to stretch our mortal stay as long as possible. We run, as the saying goes, for our lives, hounded by the suspicion that these are the only lives we are likely to enjoy.

8   All of these theorists seem to me more or less right. As the growth of cults and charismatic religions and the resurgence of enthusiasm for the military draft suggest, we do crave commitment. And who can doubt, watching so many middle-aged and older persons torturing themselves in the name of fitness, that we are unreconciled to death, more so perhaps than any generation in modern memory?

9   But I have a hunch there's a further explanation of our obsession with exercise. I suspect that what motivates us even more than a fear of death is a fear of dearth. Our era is the first to anticipate the eventual depletion of all natural resources. We see wilderness shrinking; rivers losing their capacity to sustain life; the air, even the stratosphere, being loaded with potentially deadly junk. We see the irreplaceable being squandered, and in the depths of our consciousness we are fearful that we are creating an uninhabitable world. We feel more or less helpless and yet, at the same time, desirous to protect what resources we can. We recycle soda bottles and restore old buildings and protect our nearest natural resource—our physical health—in the almost superstitious hope that such small gestures will help save an earth that we are blighting. Jogging becomes a sort of penance for our sins of gluttony, greed, and waste. Like a hairshirt or a bed of nails, the more one hates it, the more virtuous it makes one feel.

10   That is why *we* jog. Why *I* jog is to win at tennis.

Fear of Dearth

Questions on Content, Style, and Structure

1. How does Tucker attract the reader's attention in paragraph 1? Is the introduction effective?

2. What does the author mean when he says that each jogger has "his carrot and stick"?

3. Tucker suggests several theories to account for the jogging craze. What are they?

4. Does Tucker agree with all the theorists?

5. Explain the river metaphor in paragraph 6.

6. What, according to Tucker, is the most important motive for jogging? Do you agree? Why/why not?

7. Identify the transition devices that hold the essay together. How does Tucker move from paragraph to paragraph?

8. Why did the author write part of this essay using the singular first-person "I" and other parts using the plural first-person "we"?

9. In paragraph 9, why does Tucker begin so many of his sentences in the same way?

10. What is the "hairshirt" Tucker refers to in paragraph 9?

11. Describe the tone of this essay. Is it formal or informal?

Vocabulary

conducive (1)   regimen (6)   dearth (9)
listless (2)   theologists (7)   blighting (9)
myopia (5)   charismatic (8)   penance (9)

Suggestions for Writing

1. If you jog or are involved in any sort of exercise program, write an essay, like Tucker's, in which you try to account for either your motivation or the exercise's popularity in general.

2. Write an essay using one of the following as your thesis:

"Freedom is a wide and risky river; it can drown the person who does not know how to swim across it."

"We are unreconciled to death, more so perhaps than any generation in modern memory."

"_____ becomes a sort of penance for our sins of gluttony, greed, and waste. . . the more one hates it, the more virtuous it makes one feel."

3. Write a process essay in which you tell someone how to begin a program of jogging or some other exercise.

The Disco Style: Love Thyself
Albert Goldman

Albert Goldman has written *Carnival in Rio* (1976), *Disco* (1979), and *Grass Roots: Marijuana in America Today* (1979) in addition to many articles on music for a variety of magazines; he was also the music critic for *Esquire,* in which this article appeared in 1978.

1   Studio 54—the hottest ticket in town—is a private club. That gives it a license to discriminate. Discrimination is the name of its game. Not the subtle Waspy discrimination of the old Stork Club or El Morocco but the blatant *you*-can-come-in-but-*you*-gotta-stay-out style of an eight-year-old's tree house. All night long, Marc, the blond, elegant, willowy front-door man of this feverishly popular establishment in midtown Manhattan, has been standing bareheaded out in the cold, flanked by his flunkies and backed by his man-mountain muscle, picking and choosing and barring and losing. His job is the most important in the whole joint. It even has a special name. It's called "painting the picture."

2   Painting the picture is the secret of a successful disco operation. You don't get to be the number one hot spot in New York just by installing a quarter-million dollars' worth of lighting equipment or seventy thousand dollars' worth of burgundy-red British broadloom or even by getting some postgrad sound engineer with steel-rimmed spectacles to design you a special custom-built hi-fi system with enough decibels to smash your middle ear to oyster jelly but so soft and stimulating in actual effect that it makes you feel like you've stepped into a supersonic vapor bath. No, what makes a joint like Studio 54 the vortex of New York's whirling night life is not so much the accommodations as the crowd, and not so much the crowd per se as the way this ever changing melee of fashionably casual, strikingly good-looking, celebrity-studded young men and women is selected, composed, and matched up every night so that when these hundreds of randomly arriving strangers bump into one another on the vast dance floor or on the black-strapped silver gas-tank cushions of the downstairs lounge or up in the dusky crimson bordello-like parlor of the smoking lounge, they will virtually fall into one another's arms with the head-on excitement of love at first sight.

3   First, they dance, dance, dance, till their legs go into cramps, and their teeth are numb and their heads are about to fly off. Then, some get so hot to slot that they run up into the great dark, steep balcony that lowers over the dance floor like a massive thunderhead; and there, with Halston gowns wrenching and tearing and St. Laurent velvet tuxedos popping

their buttons, the flower of New York's party people *get it on*, while around them sprawl a few luded-out voyeurs who dig these scenes like strokers in a Forty-second Street grind house.

4   Night after night, this is the action as disco becomes America's foremost form of live entertainment and participatory culture. In just one short year, disco has exploded from an underground scene down on the New York waterfront or out in the heavily ethnic nabes of Brooklyn and the Bronx into a vast international entertainment industry. Today, disco is right up there with spectator sports and tennis and skiing as one of the ideally contemporary forms of recreation. Specially composed and recorded disco music plays night and day on disco-oriented radio stations in every city of the country. Lavishly equipped disco entertainment centers are springing up all over the world like supermarkets. Disco stars like Barry White, Donna Summer, and Grace Jones are competing ever more successfully with the fading stars of rock. Now the first of the new disco movies, *Saturday Night Fever*, is carrying the disco ambience into cinema. Other films will follow soon, beginning with *Thank God It's Friday*. A $4-billion-a-year industry, with its own franchises, publications, top-forty charts, three-day sales conventions, catalogs of special equipment, and keenly competitive marketing agents—who are aiming to make every finished basement and rumpus room in America into a mini-disco—the new beat for the feet is sending up all the familiar signals that betoken a new wave of mass culture.

5   The reasons for this unexpected triumph are not hard to discover once you start looking for them. The current decade, so slow to declare itself, has finally crystallized as a fascinating amalgam of hip and square, conservative and radical, primitive and futuristic. On the one hand, it's now hip to be square: to be self-disciplined, self-denying, hardworking, hard-driving, keen on getting ahead in either the race against your fellow careerists or against the clock you set clicking as your private challenge.

6   On the other hand, when his day gig is over, when the coiled spring of careerism has been screwed up to the bursting point, your sharp young competitor craves the release of getting out on the town and exploring its nocturnal mysteries to the bottom. Because he has cleaned up his act for the day shift, he is more intent than ever before on getting wrecked at night.

7   To the ghetto-inspired pleasure grabbing of the Sixties, the multiple drug abuse, and the off-the-wall screwing have been added all those refinements that come with maturity and money. Now every night the big cars with their uniformed chauffeurs stand by the curb for hours while expensively catered suppers are served in lavishly decorated pads in SoHo or the East Seventies. Now to the pharmacopoeia of pills, mushrooms, and native grasses that got people high in the days of the hippie have

been added the vastly more expensive and difficult to obtain white powders that fly up the nostrils so fast that a man can easily spend a thousand dollars a week on nosegays.

8   The disco beat that throbs under the surface of modern life is as ingeniously designed, as finely tooled and professionally manufactured, as the engine of a BMW. Its phallicly probing bass line is from soul; its fast, flying tempo is from jazz; its thumping, mechanically insistent beat is from rock; and its characteristic tachycardic *ta-ta-tum*, *ta-ta-tum* hallmark is the gallop, yes, the gallop: the same effervescent, high-stepping rhythm that was employed by Strauss to evoke Gay Vienna and by Offenbach to put the froth on his *Gaieté Parisienne*.

9   Disco music is not meant to be confronted head on as something you sit down and listen to. Disco is meant to be experienced subliminally, not so much in the mind as in the body, which it exhorts ceaselessly to dance, dance, dance. The disco mix says nothing but suggests a great deal.

10   The only game in town so far as disco is concerned is the mating game. The songs, which are written to formulas, like the old Tin Pan Alley product, are directed ostensibly at a lover, typically someone the singer has just spotted on the dance floor. But the real thrust of disco culture is not toward love of another person but toward love of the self, the principal object of desire in this age of closed-circuit, masturbatory, vibrator sex. Outside the entrance to every discotheque should be erected a statue to the presiding deity: Narcissus.

11   Looking out on the floor of the modern dance hall, you don't see any of the interpersonal intimacy so glowingly described in the fashion magazines or on the screen during *Saturday Night Fever* (which like all Hollywood efforts to deal with the trendy is hopelessly out-of-date). The idea that disco has been built on a revival of "touch dancing" (what a hideously clammy word!) or that it is focused on a step called the Latin Hustle—all this kind of talk—is either wishful thinking by instructors at the Arthur Murray schools or just bad women's-page journalism. The truth is that today's hip disco dancer is into the kind of one-man show that John Travolta puts on in the most exciting sequence of *Saturday Night Fever*: a film that speaks the truth despite itself by demonstrating unwittingly how totally fulfilling it is to dance by yourself as opposed to how frustrating and infuriating it is to have to work out something as intimate as the way you dance with some cranky bitch.

12   That everybody sees himself as a star today is both a cliché and a profound truth. Thousands of young men and women have the looks, the clothes, the hairstyling, the drugs, the personal magnetism, the self-confidence, and the history of conquest that proclaims the star. The one thing they lack—talent—is precisely what is most lacking in those other, nearly identical, young people whom the world has acclaimed as stars. Never in the history of show biz has the gap between the amateur and

the professional been so small. Nor ever in the history of the world has there been such a rage for exhibitionism. The question is, therefore, what are we going to do with all these showoffs? Disco provides the best answer to date. Every night, the stage is set, the lights are lit, the audience is assembled, and the floor will clear magically for anyone who really is intent on getting out there and doing his solo version of *Soul Train*. That's what makes the modern discotheque so different from the traditional ballroom: the fact that the people out on the floor are really serious about their dancing and determined to do their thing—whether it be Fred Astaire, James Brown, or the Whirling Dervish—just as hard and as far as their well-conditioned bodies will carry them.

13   Getting yourself up to do your thing, however, is not such a simple matter—as any professional will confirm. Self-expression is less a matter of mood, energy, practice, and pep pills than it is of feeling that the people around you are *with* you. The highly burnished people who are the disco droids have founded countless psychedelic country clubs smack in the heart of the big city, where they can revel in the supportiveness of their own crowd. After the anarchic hugger-mugger of the Sixties, Americans are really into segregation: a trend that was launched, incidentally, by blacks, not whites. As there are so many races, classes, and cliques demanding to be segregated in any big American city, the number and variety of these exclusive dancing clubs has to be enormous. Recently, *Discothekin' Magazine* estimated that in New York City alone there are over a thousand of them.

14   A discotheque can be a little supper club with a patch of dance floor, or a big tastelessly Art Deco tourist trap, like Régine's on Park Avenue, where all the rich Europeans who don't know their way around town pay six dollars a drink to stare at the other rich Europeans.

15   The one thing that binds all these otherwise dissimilar establishments together is the music and the common atmosphere of overstimulation. If disco is emblematic of where it's all at today, then the stunning profusion of lights, sounds, rhythms, motions, drugs, spectacles, and illusions that comprise the disco ambience must be interpreted as the contemporary formula for pleasure and high times. Examining the formula, one soon sees that its essence is the concentration of extremes. Everything is taken as far as it can be taken; then it is combined with every other extreme to produce the final rape of the human sensorium. Why?

16   One answer is that modern man has so dulled and dimmed his senses by living in an overstimulating industrial environment that nothing but sensory overkill can turn him on. Another, more sympathetic, interpretation is that the search for pleasure in the modern world is not a case of decadent and insatiable hedonism but precisely its opposite: a displaced quest for certain spiritual values that can only be attained by breaching the barriers of the senses through overstimulation. What modern man craves most cannot be obtained through moderation. "The path

of excess leads to the palace of wisdom," proclaimed William Blake. The kind of wisdom that Blake was thinking about was not the "once burnt, twice cautious" prudence of the self-preservative middle class. What Blake meant was the genuine wisdom of the man who transcends the normal limits of human experience and attains, thereby, not only a detached and philosophic view of this world but even a glimpse of the mysteries beyond.

17   The truth is that all through the history of Western civilization there has always been a buried life, an underground tradition of primitive tribal religious rites and ecstasies that has burst out again and again in epidemic manias that have puzzled the learned.

18   What differentiates discomania from most of its predecessors is its overt tendency to spill over into orgy, as it has done already in the gay world. All disco is implicitly orgy: the question is whether this impulse should be resisted or encouraged. Orgiastic encounters can be animalistic and degrading, decadent and debauching. But they can also be genuine love feasts or even drastic devices for stilling the distracting clamor of the senses and training the mind, especially its most religious organ, the imagination, on the ultimate vistas of the spiritual world. By offering the instant and total gratification of all sexual desires in an atmosphere of intense imaginative excitement, the disco-inspired orgy promotes the dawning of an exalted state of consciousness, of literal *exstasis*, or standing outside the body, that allows us to experience with their full force the higher energies of the universe, which may else teem down upon us with as little effect as the fabled influences of the stars.

The Disco Style: Love Thyself

Questions on Content, Style, and Structure

1. Why does Goldman begin his essay with a description of Studio 54?
2. How is disco a "fascinating amalgam of hip and square"?
3. Describe the disco beat as Goldman presents it. How does he try to make the reader understand its sound?
4. The major point in Goldman's analysis of disco appears in paragraph 10. What is the "real thrust of disco culture"? Who is Narcissus and why should he be the presiding deity of disco? Do you agree?
5. What, according to Goldman, is the reason for so many discos in cities? What are the common denominators of discotheques?
6. What reasons does Goldman suggest for the popularity of disco? Do you agree with any of them?
7. How is discomania different from other "manias"? What might its effects be? Do you agree with Goldman's conclusion? Why/why not?

8. List the various ways Goldman tries to explain and define the phenomenon of disco. If you were from another culture and had never heard of disco, would you understand it from reading this essay?

9. Part of the effectiveness of describing any trend is the author's use of detail to make the reader see, hear, and sense the fad. How successful is Goldman's description throughout the essay? Cite some examples to support your answer.

10. Point out some examples of slang, colloquialisms, and "street language." Why does Goldman use these? Is his choice effective?

Vocabulary

bordello (2)	subliminally (9)	decadent (16)
amalgam (5)	exhorts (9)	hedonism (16)
noctural (6)	exhibitionism (12)	implicitly (18)
phallicly (8)	burnished (13)	debauching (18)
effervescent (8)	anarchic (13)	

Suggestions for Writing

1. Write an essay in which you agree or disagree with Goldman's thesis. Is disco essentially narcissistic? Is it decadent? Defend your view.

2. Select another fad or kind of music and write an essay explaining it.

3. Compare/contrast disco music to some other kind of music. Consider rhythm, lyrics, and singers, if you wish. Which kind of music do you prefer?

The Plug-In Drug: TV and the American Family
Marie Winn

Marie Winn is the author of ten books for children and many articles for such publications as *The New York Times Magazine* and *The Village Voice*. This essay is an excerpt from her book *The Plug-In Drug: Television, Children and Family*, published in 1977.

1 A quarter of a century after the introduction of television into American society, a period that has seen the medium become so deeply ingrained in American life that in at least one state the television set has attained the rank of a legal necessity, safe from repossession in case of debt along with clothes, cooking utensils, and the like, television viewing has be-

come an inevitable and ordinary part of daily life. Only in the early years
of television did writers and commentators have sufficient perspective
to separate the activity of watching television from the actual content
it offers the viewer. In those early days writers frequently discussed the
effects of television on family life. However, a curious myopia afflicted
those early observers: almost without exception they regarded television
as a favorable, beneficial, indeed, wondrous influence upon the family.

2   "Television is going to be a real asset in every home where there are
children," predicts a writer in 1949.

3   "Television will take over your way of living and change your children's habits, but this change can be a wonderful improvement," claims
another commentator.

4   "No survey's needed, of course, to establish that television has brought
the family together in one room," writes *The New York Times* television
critic in 1949.

5   Each of the early articles about television is invariably accompanied
by a photograph or illustration showing a family cozily sitting together
before the television set, Sis on Mom's lap, Buddy perched on the arm of
Dad's chair, Dad with his arm around Mom's shoulder. Who could have
guessed that twenty or so years later Mom would be watching a drama
in the kitchen, the kids would be looking at cartoons in their rooms,
while Dad would be taking in the ball game in the living room?

6   Of course television sets were enormously expensive in those early
days. The idea that by 1975 more than 60 percent of American families
would own two or more sets was preposterous. The splintering of the
multiple-set family was something the early writers could not foresee.
Nor did anyone imagine the number of hours children would eventually
devote to television, the common use of television by parents as a child
pacifier, the changes television would effect upon child-rearing methods,
the increasing domination of family schedules by children's viewing requirements—in short, the *power* of the new medium to dominate family
life.

7   After the first years, as children's consumption of the new medium
increased, together with parental concern about the possible effects of so
much television viewing, a steady refrain helped to soothe and reassure
anxious parents. "Television always enters a pattern of influences that
already exist: the home, the peer group, the school, the church and culture generally," write the authors of an early and influential study of
television's effects on children. In other words, if the child's home life
is all right, parents need not worry about the effects of all that television
watching.

8   But television does not merely influence the child; it deeply influences
that "pattern of influences" that is meant to ameliorate its effects. Home
and family life has changed in important ways since the advent of television. The peer group has become television-oriented, and much of the
time children spend together is occupied by television viewing. Culture

generally has been transformed by television. Therefore it is improper to assign to television the subsidiary role its many apologists (too often members of the television industry) insist it plays. Television is not merely one of a number of important influences upon today's child. Through the changes it has made in family life, television emerges as *the* important influence in children's lives today.

9   Television's contribution to family life has been an equivocal one. For while it has, indeed, kept the members of the family from dispersing, it has not served to bring them *together*. By its domination of the time families spend together, it destroys the special quality that distinguishes one family from another, a quality that depends to a great extent on what a family *does*, what special rituals, games, recurrent jokes, familiar songs, and shared activities it accumulates.

10   "Like the sorcerer of old," writes Urie Bronfenbrenner[1], "the television set casts its magic spell, freezing speech and action, turning the living into silent statues so long as the enchantment lasts. The primary danger of the television screen lies not so much in the behavior it produces— although there is danger there—as in the behavior it prevents: the talks, the games, the family festivities and arguments through which much of the child's learning takes place and through which his character is formed. Turning on the television set can turn off the process that transforms children into people."

11   Yet parents have accepted a television-dominated family life so completely that they cannot see how the medium is involved in whatever problems they might be having. A first-grade teacher reports:

12   "I have one child in the group who's an only child. I wanted to find out more about her family life because this little girl was quite isolated from the group, didn't make friends, so I talked to her mother. Well, they don't have time to do anything in the evening, the mother said. The parents come home after picking up the child at the baby-sitter's. Then the mother fixes dinner while the child watches TV. Then they have dinner and the child goes to bed. I said to this mother, 'Well, couldn't she help you fix dinner? That would be a nice time for the two of you to talk,' and the mother said, 'Oh, but I'd hate to have her miss "Zoom." It's such a good program!' "

13   Even when families make efforts to control television, too often its very presence counterbalances the positive features of family life. A writer and mother of two boys aged 3 and 7 described her family's television schedule in an article in *The New York Times*:

We were in the midst of a full-scale War. Every day was a new battle and every program was a major skirmish. We agreed it was a bad scene all around and were ready to enter diplomatic negotiations. . . . In principle we have

[1]Urie Bronfenbrenner is a professor in the Department of Human Development at Cornell University.

agreed on 2½ hours of TV a day, "Sesame Street," "Electric Company" (with dinner gobbled up in between) and two half-hour shows between 7 and 8:30 which enables the grown-ups to eat in peace and prevents the two boys from destroying one another. Their pre-bedtime choice is dreadful, because, as Josh recently admitted, "There's nothing much on I really like." So . . . it's "What's My Line" or "To Tell the Truth." . . . Clearly there is a need for first-rate children's shows at this time. . . .

14   Consider the "family life" described here: Presumably the father comes home from work during the "Sesame Street"—"Electric Company" stint. The children are either watching television, gobbling their dinner, or both. While the parents eat their dinner in peaceful privacy, the children watch another hour of television. Then there is only a half-hour left before bedtime, just enough time for baths, getting pajamas on, brushing teeth, and so on. The children's evening is regimented with an almost military precision. They watch their favorite programs, and when there is "nothing much on I really like," they watch whatever else is on—because *watching* is the important thing. Their mother does not see anything amiss with watching programs just for the sake of watching; she only wishes there were some first-rate children's shows on at those times.

15   Without conjuring up memories of the Victorian era with family games and long, leisurely meals, and large families, the question arises: isn't there a better family life available than this dismal, mechanized arrangement of children watching television for however long is allowed them, evening after evening?

16   Of course, families today still do *special* things together at times: go camping in the summer, go to the zoo on a nice Sunday, take various trips and expeditions. But their *ordinary* daily life together is diminished—that sitting around at the dinner table, that spontaneous taking up of an activity, those little games invented by children on the spur of the moment when there is nothing else to do, the scribbling, the chatting, and even the quarreling, all the things that form the fabric of a family, that define a childhood. Instead, the children have their regular schedule of television programs and bedtime, and the parents have their peaceful dinner together.

17   The author of the article in *The Times* notes that "keeping a family sane means mediating between the needs of both children and adults." But surely the needs of adults are being better met than the needs of the children, who are effectively shunted away and rendered untroublesome, while their parents enjoy a life as undemanding as that of any childless couple. In reality, it is those very demands that young children make upon a family that lead to growth, and it is the way parents accede to those demands that builds the relationships upon which the future of the family depends. If the family does not accumulate its backlog of shared experiences, shared *everyday* experiences that occur and recur and change and develop, then it is not likely to survive as anything other than a caretaking institution.

Family Rituals

18 Ritual is defined by sociologists as "that part of family life that the family likes about itself, is proud of and wants formally to continue." Another text notes that "the development of a ritual by a family is an index of the common interest of its members in the family as a group."

19 What has happened to family rituals, those regular, dependable, re-current happenings that gave members of a family a feeling of *belonging* to a home rather than living in it merely for the sake of convenience, those experiences that act as the adhesive of family unity far more than any material advantages?

20 Mealtime rituals, going-to-bed rituals, illness rituals, holiday rituals, how many of these have survived the inroads of the television set?

21 A young woman who grew up near Chicago reminisces about her childhood and gives an idea of the effects of television upon family rituals:

22 "As a child I had millions of relatives around—my parents both come from relatively large families. My father had nine brothers and sisters. And so every holiday there was this great swoop-down of aunts, uncles, and millions of cousins. I just remember how wonderful it used to be. These thousands of cousins would come and everyone would play and ultimately, after dinner, all the women would be in the front of the house, drinking coffee and talking, all the men would be in the back of the house, drinking and smoking, and all the kids would be all over the place, playing hide and seek. Christmas time was particularly nice be-cause everyone always brought all their toys and games. Our house had a couple of rooms with go-through closets, so there were always kids running in a great circle route. I remember it was just wonderful.

23 "And then all of a sudden one year I remember becoming suddenly aware of how different everything had become. The kids were no longer playing Monopoly or Clue or the other games we used to play together. It was because we had a television set which had been turned on for a football game. All of that socializing that had gone on previously had ended. Now everyone was sitting in front of the television set, on a holiday, at a family party! I remember being stunned by how awful that was. Somehow the television had become more attractive."

24 As families have come to spend more and more of their time together engaged in the single activity of television watching, those rituals and pastimes that once gave family life its special quality have become more and more uncommon. Not since prehistoric times when cave families hunted, gathered, ate, and slept, with little time remaining to accumulate a culture of any significance, have families been reduced to such a same-ness.

Real People

25 It is not only the activities that a family might engage in together that are diminished by the powerful presence of television in the home. The

relationships of the family members to each other are also affected, in both obvious and subtle ways. The hours that the young child spends in a one-way relationship with television people, an involvement that allows for no communication or interaction, surely affect his relationships with real-life people.

26   Studies show the importance of eye-to-eye contact, for instance, in real-life relationships, and indicate that the nature of a person's eye-contact patterns, whether he looks another squarely in the eye or looks to the side or shifts his gaze from side to side, may play a significant role in his success or failure in human relationships. But no eye contact is possible in the child-television relationship, although in certain children's programs people purport to speak directly to the child and the camera fosters this illusion by focusing directly upon the person being filmed. (Mr. Rogers is an example, telling the child "I like you, you're special," etc.) How might such a distortion of real-life relationships affect a child's development of trust, of openness, of an ability to relate well to other *real* people?

27   Bruno Bettelheim[2] writes:

> Children who have been taught, or conditioned, to listen passively most of the day to the warm verbal communications coming from the TV screen, to the deep emotional appeal of the so-called TV personality, are often unable to respond to real persons because they arouse so much less feeling than the skilled actor. Worse, they lose the ability to learn from reality because life experiences are much more complicated than the ones they see on the screen. . . .

28   A teacher makes a similar observation about her personal viewing experiences:

29   "I have trouble mobilizing myself and dealing with real people after watching a few hours of television. It's just hard to make that transition from watching television to a real relationship. I suppose it's because there was no effort necessary while I was watching, and dealing with real people always requires a bit of effort. Imagine, then, how much harder it might be to do the same thing for a small child, particularly one who watches a lot of television every day."

30   But more obviously damaging to family relationships is the elimination of opportunities to talk, and perhaps more important, to argue, to air grievances, between parents and children and brothers and sisters. Families frequently use television to avoid confronting their problems, problems that will not go away if they are ignored but will only fester and become less easily resolvable as time goes on.

31   A mother reports:

32   "I find myself, with three children, wanting to turn on the TV set when they're fighting. I really have to struggle not to do it because I feel

---

[2]Bruno Bettelheim is a well-known psychologist and author who frequently writes about children.

that's telling them this is the solution to the quarrel—but it's so tempting that I often do it."

33   A family therapist discusses the use of television as an avoidance mechanism:

34   "In a family I know the father comes home from work and turns on the television set. The children come and watch with him and the wife serves them their meal in front the set. He then goes and takes a shower, or works on the car or something. She then goes and has her own dinner in front of the television set. It's a symptom of a deeper-rooted problem, sure. But it would help them all to get rid of the set. It would be far easier to work on what the symptom really means without the television. The television simply encourages a double avoidance of each other. They'd find out more quickly what was going on if they weren't able to hide behind the TV. Things wouldn't necessarily be better, of course, but they wouldn't be anesthetized."

35   The decreased opportunities for simple conversation between parents and children in the television-centered home may help explain an observation made by an emergency room nurse at a Boston hospital. She reports that parents just seem to sit there these days when they come in with a sick or seriously injured child, although talking to the child would distract and comfort him. "They don't seem to know *how* to talk to their own children at any length," the nurse observes. Similarly, a television critic writes in *The New York Times*: "I had just a day ago taken my son to the emergency ward of a hospital for stitches above his left eye, and the occasion seemed no more real to me than Maalot or 54th Street, south-central Los Angeles. There was distance and numbness and an inability to turn off the total institution. I didn't behave at all; I just watched. . . ."

36   A number of research studies substantiate the assumption that television interferes with family activities and the formation of family relationships. One survey shows that 78 percent of the respondents indicated no conversation taking place during viewing except at specified times such as commercials. The study notes: "The television atmosphere in most households is one of quiet absorption on the part of family members who are present. The nature of the family social life during a program could be described as 'parallel' rather than interactive, and the set does seem to dominate family life when it is on." Thirty-six percent of the respondents in another study indicated that television viewing was the only family activity participated in during the week.

37   In a summary of research findings on television's effect on family interactions James Gabardino states: "The early findings suggest that television had a disruptive effect upon interaction and thus presumably human development. . . . It is not unreasonable to ask: 'Is the fact that the average American family during the 1950's came to include two parents, two children and a television set somehow related to the psychosocial characteristics of the young adults of the 1970's?' "

Undermining the Family

38   In its effect on family relationships, in its facilitation of parental with-drawal from an active role in the socialization of their children, and in its replacement of family rituals and special events, television has played an important role in the disintegration of the American family. But of course it has not been the only contributing factor, perhaps not even the most important one. The steadily rising divorce rate, the increase in the number of working mothers, the decline of the extended family, the breakdown of neighborhoods and communities, the growing isolation of the nuclear family—all have seriously affected the family.

39   As Urie Bronfenbrenner suggests, the sources of family breakdown do not come from the family itself, but from the circumstances in which the family finds itself and the way of life imposed upon it by those circumstances. "When those circumstances and the way of life they gen-erate undermine relationships of trust and emotional security between family members, when they make it difficult for parents to care for, educate and enjoy their children, when there is no support or recognition from the outside world for one's role as a parent and when time spent with one's family means frustration of career, personal fulfillment and peace of mind, then the development of the child is adversely affected," he writes.

40   But while the roots of alienation go deep into the fabric of American social history, television's presence in the home fertilizes them, encour-ages their wild and unchecked growth. Perhaps it is true that America's commitment to the television experience masks a spiritual vacuum, an empty and barren way of life, a desert of materialism. But it is television's dominant role in the family that anesthetizes the family into accepting its unhappy state and prevents it from struggling to better its condition, to improve its relationships, and to regain some of the richness it once possessed.

41   Others have noted the role of mass media in perpetuating an unsat-isfactory *status quo*. Leisure-time activity, writes Irving Howe[3], "must provide relief from work monotony without making the return to work too unbearable; it must provide amusement without insight and pleasure without disturbance—as distinct from art which gives pleasure through disturbance. Mass culture is thus oriented toward a central aspect of industrial society: the depersonalization of the individual." Similarly, Jacques Ellul[4] rejects the idea that television is a legitimate means of educating the citizen: "Education . . . takes place only incidentally. The clouding of his consciousness is paramount. . . ."

42   And so the American family muddles on, dimly aware that something is amiss but distracted from an understanding of its plight by an endless

[3]Irving Howe is an author, historian, critic, and professor of English at Hunter College in New York.
[4]Jacques Ellul is the author of eight books on religion and on our technological society.

stream of television images. As family ties grow weaker and vaguer, as children's lives become more separate from their parents', as parents' educational role in their children's lives is taken over by television and schools, family life becomes increasingly more unsatisfying for both parents and children. All that seems to be left is Love, an abstraction that family members *know* is necessary but find great difficulty giving each other because the traditional opportunities for expressing love within the family have been reduced or destroyed.

43   For contemporary parents, love toward each other has increasingly come to mean successful sexual relations, as witnessed by the proliferation of sex manuals and sex therapists. The opportunities for manifesting other forms of love through mutual support, understanding, nurturing, even, to use an unpopular word, *serving* each other, are less and less available as mothers and fathers seek their independent destinies outside the family.

44   As for love of children, this love is increasingly expressed through supplying material comforts, amusements, and educational opportunities. Parents show their love for their children by sending them to good schools and camps, by providing them with good food and good doctors, by buying them toys, books, games, and a television set of their very own. Parents will even go further and express their love by attending PTA meetings to improve their children's schools, or by joining groups that are acting to improve the quality of their children's television programs.

45   But this is love at a remove, and is rarely understood by children. The more direct forms of parental love require time and patience, steady, dependable, ungrudgingly given time actually spent *with* a child, reading to him, comforting him, playing, joking, and working with him. But even if a parent were eager and willing to demonstrate that sort of direct love to his children today, the opportunities are diminished. What with school and Little League and piano lessons and, of course, the inevitable television programs, a day seems to offer just enough time for a good-night kiss.

The Plug-In Drug: TV and the American Family

Questions on Content, Style, and Structure

1. How does Winn use the comments from early television critics to introduce her subject?
2. According to Winn, television does more than influence the child viewer. What larger effect does it have on the family?
3. How does Winn try to show that too often parents have accepted a "television-dominated family life"? Does she succeed?

4. What kinds of family rituals have been undermined by television?

5. How might television affect a child's relationships with people in general?

6. What other factors have contributed to the disintegration of the American family?

7. According to Winn, television anesthetizes the family into accepting what?

8. In Winn's opinion, how do some parents mistakenly demonstrate their love for their children? What should they do instead?

9. Evaluate Winn's use of evidence throughout the essay. What methods are most effective?

10. Winn argues the detrimental effects of watching too much television in general, in contrast to many critics who are opposed only to certain kinds of programs. Does this distinction hurt her argument?

Vocabulary

inevitable (1)	advent (8)	facilitation (38)
myopia (1)	equivocal (9)	perpetuating (41)
ameliorate (8)	shunted (17)	ungrudgingly (45)

Suggestions for Writing

1. Write an essay in which you discuss the effects of television on your family. Do you agree with Winn's thesis?

2. Write an essay in defense of television. What are some of its most positive effects?

3. Write an essay describing a family ritual and its effect on you.

Obsessed with Sport: On the Interpretation of a Fan's Dreams
Joseph Epstein

Joseph Epstein is a member of Northwestern University's English department and the editor of *The American Scholar*. His books include *Divorced in America* (1975) and *Ambition: The Secret Passion* (1981). This essay appeared in *Harper's* in 1976.

1 I cannot remember when I was not surrounded by sports, when talk of sports was not in the air, when I did not care passionately about sports. As a boy in Chicago in the late Forties, I lived in the same building as

the sister and brother-in-law of Barney Ross, the welterweight champion. Half a block away, down near the lake, the Sullivan High School football team worked out in the spring and autumn. Summers the same field was given over to baseball and men's softball on Sundays. A few blocks to the north was the Touhy Avenue Fieldhouse, where basketball was played, and lifeguards trained, and behind which, in a softball field frozen over in winter, crack-the-whip, hockey, and speed skating took over. To the west, a block or so up Morse Avenue, was the Morse Avenue "L" Recreations, a combined pool hall and bowling alley. Life, in short, was games.

2   My father had no interest in sports. He had grown up, one of the ten children of Russian Jewish immigrant parents, on tough Notre Dame Street in Montreal, where the major sports were craps, poker, and petty larceny. He left Montreal at seventeen to come to Chicago, where he worked hard and successfully so that his sons might play. Two of his boyhood friends from Notre Dame Street, who had the comic-book names of Sammy and Danny Spunt, had also come to Chicago, where they bought the Ringside Gym on Dearborn Street in the Loop. All the big names worked out at Ringside for their Chicago fights: Willie Pep, Tony Zale, Joe Louis. At eight or nine I would take the El downtown to the Ringside, be introduced around by Danny Spunt ("Tony Zale, I'd like you to meet the son of an old friend of mine. Kid, I'd like you to meet the middleweight champion of the world"), and return home with an envelope filled with autographed 8-by-10 glossies of Gus Lesnevich, Tammy Mauriello, Kid Gavilan, and the wondrous Sugar Ray. *

3   I lived on, off, and in sports. *Sport* magazine had recently begun publication, and I gobbled up its issues cover to cover, soon becoming knowledgeable not only about the major sports—baseball, football, and basketball—but about golf, hockey, tennis, and horse racing, so that I scored reputably on the Sport Quiz, a regular department at the front of the magazine. Another regular department was the Sport Classic, which featured longish profiles of the legendary figures in the history of sports: Ty Cobb, Jim Thorpe, Bobby Jones, Big Bill Tilden, Red Grange, Man o' War. I next moved on to the sports novels of John R. Tunis—*All-American, The Iron Duke, The Kid from Tomkinsville, The Kid Comes Back, World Series,* the lot—which I read with as much excitement as any books I have read since.

4   The time was, as is now apparent, a splendid era in sports. Ted Williams, Joe DiMaggio, and Stan Musial were afield; first Jack Kramer, then Pancho Gonzales, dominated tennis; George Mikan led the Minneapolis Lakers, and the Harlem Globetrotters could still be taken seriously; Doc Blanchard and Glen Davis, Mr. Inside and Mr. Outside, were playing for Army, Johnny Lujack was at Notre Dame; in the pros, Sammy Baugh, Bob Waterfield, and Sid Luckman were the major T-formation quarterbacks; Joe Louis and Sugar Ray Robinson fought frequently; the two

* Sugar Ray Robinson, former middleweight champion (1951)

Willies, Mosconi and Hoppe, put in regular appearances at Bensinger's in the Loop; Eddie Arcaro seemed to ride three, four winners a day. Giants, it truly seemed, walked the earth.

5   All learning of craft—which sport, like writing, most assuredly is— involves imitation, especially in the early stages; and I was an excellent mimic. By the time I was ten years old I had mastery over all the big-time moves: the spit in the mitt, the fluid infield chatter, the knocking of dirt from the spikes; the rhythmic barking out of signals, hands high under the center's crotch to take the ball; the three bounces and deep breath before shooting the free throw (on this last, I regretted not being a Catholic, so that I might be able to make the sign of the cross before shooting, as was then the fashion among Catholic high-school and college players). I went in for athletic haberdashery in a big way, often going beyond mimicry to the point of flat-out phoniness—wearing, for example, a knee pad while playing basketball, though my knees were always, exasperatingly, intact.

6   I always looked good, which was important, because form is intrinsic to sports; but in my case it was doubly important, because the truth is that I wasn't really very good. Or at any rate not good enough. Two factors accounted for this. The first was that, without being shy about body contact, I lacked a certain indispensable aggressiveness; the second, connected closely to the first, was that, when it came right down to it, I did not care enough about winning. I would rather lose a point attempting a slashing cross-court backhand than play for an easier winner down the side; the long jump shot always had more allure for me than the safer drive to the basket. Given a choice between the two vanities of winning and looking good, I almost always preferred looking good.

7   I shall never forget the afternoon, sometime along about my thirteenth year, when, shooting baskets alone, I came upon the technique for shooting the hook. Although today it has nowhere near the consequence of the jump shot—an innovation that has been to basketball what the jet has been to air travel—the hook is still the single most beautiful shot in the game. The rhythm and grace of it, the sway of the body off the pivot, the release of the ball behind the head and off the fingertips, the touch and instinct involved in its execution, make the hook altogether a balletic thing, and to achieve it is to feel one of the most delectable sensations in sports. That afternoon, on a deserted side street, shooting on a rickety wooden backboard and a black rim without a net, I felt it and grew nearly drunk on the feeling. Rain came down, dirt washed in the gutters, flecks of it spattering my clothes and arms and face, but, soaked and cold though I was, I do not think I would have left that basket on that afternoon for anything. I threw up hook after hook, from every angle, from farther and farther out, off the board, without the board, and hook after hook went in. Only pitch darkness drove me home.

8   I do not say that not to have shot the hook is never to have lived, but only that, once having done so, the pleasure it gives is not so easily

forgotten. Every sport offers similar pleasures, the pleasures taken differing by temperament: the canter into the end zone to meet a floating touchdown pass, or the clean, crisp feel of a perfect block or tackle; the long straight drive or the precisely played approach shot to the green; the solid overhead; the pickup on the tricky short hop or the long ball down one of the power alleys. Different sports, different pleasures. But so keen are these pleasures—pleasures of execution, of craft completed—that, along with being unforgettable, they are also worth recapturing in any available way, and the most available way, when reflexes have slowed, when muscle no longer responds so readily to brain, is from the grandstand or, perhaps more often nowadays, from the chair before the television.

Pleasures of the Spectator

9   I have put in days on the bench, but years in my chair before the television set. Recently it has occurred to me that over the years I have heard more hours of talk from the announcer Curt Gowdy than from my own father, who is not a reticent man. I have been thoroughly Schenkeled, Mussbergered, Summeralled, Coselled, DeRogotissed, and Garagiolaed. How many hundreds—thousands?—of hours have I spent watching sports of all sorts, either at parks or stadiums or over television? I am glad I shall never have a precise answer. Yet neither apparently can I get enough. What is the fascination? Why is it that, with the prospect of a game to watch in the evening or on the weekend, the day seems lighter and brighter? What do I get out of it?

10   What I get out of it, according to one fairly prominent view, is an outlet for my violent emotions. Knee-wrenching, rib-cracking, head-busting, this view has it, is what sports are really about, with sports fans being essentially sadists, and cowardly sadists at that, for they take their violence not at firsthand but at second remove. Enthusiasm for sports among Americans is little more than a reflection of the national penchant for violence. Military men talk about game plans; the long touchdown pass is called the bomb. The average pro-football fan, seeing a quarterback writhing on the ground at midfield as a result of the ministrations of Joe Green, Carl Eller, or Lyle Alzado, twitters with glee, finds his ultimate reward, and declares a little holiday in the blackest corner of his heart.

11   But this is a criticism that comes at sports by way of politics. To believe it one has to believe that the history of the United States is chiefly one of rape, expropriation, and aggressive imperialism. To dismiss it, however, one need only know something about sports. Violence is indubitably a part of some sports; in some—hockey is an example—it sometimes comes close to being featured. But in no sport—not even boxing, that most rudimentary of sports—is it the main item, and in many other sports it plays no part at all. A distinction worth insisting on is that between violence and roughness. Roughness, a willingness to mix it up, to take if need be an elbow in the jaw, is part of rebounding in

basketball, yet violence is not. Even in pro football, most maligned of modern American sports, more of roughness than of violence is involved. Roughness raises the stakes, provides the pressure, behind execution. A splendid-because-true phrase has come about in pro football to cover the situation in which a pass receiver, certain that he will be tackled upon the instant he makes his reception, drops a ball he should otherwise have caught easily—the phrase, best delivered in a Southern accent such as Don Meredith's, is "He heard footsteps on that one, Howard." Although a part of the attraction, it is not so much those footsteps that fill the stands and the den chairs on Sunday afternoons as it is those men who elude them: the Lynn Swanns, the Fran Tarkentons, the O. J. Simpsons. The American love of violence theory really will not wash. Dick Butkus did not get us into Vietnam.

12   Many who would not argue that sports reflect American violence nevertheless claim that they imbue one with the competitive spirit. In some who are already amply endowed with it, sports doubtless do tend to refine (or possible brutalize) the desire to win. Yet sports also teach a serious respect for craft. Competition, though it flourishes as always, is in bad odor nowadays; but craft, officially respected, does not flourish greatly outside the boutique.

13   If the love of violence or the competitive urge does not put me in my chair for the countless games I watch, is it, then, nostalgia, a yearning to regain the more glowing moments of adolescence? Many argue that this is precisely so, that American men exist in a state of perpetual immaturity, suspended between boy- and manhood. "The difference between men and boys," says Liberace, "is the price of their toys." (I have paid more than $300 for two half-season tickets to the Chicago Bulls games, parking fees not included.) Such unending enthusiasm for games may have something to do with adolescence, but little, I suspect, with regaining anything whatever. Instead, it has more to do with watching men do regularly and surpassingly what, as an adolescent, one did often bumblingly though with an occasional flash of genius. To have played these games oneself as a boy or a young man helps immeasurably the appreciation that in watching a sport played at professional caliber one is witnessing the extraordinary made to look ordinary. That a game may have no consequence outside itself—no effect on history, on one's own life, on anything, really—does not make it trivial but only makes the enjoyment of it all the purer.

14   The notion that men watch sports to regain their adolescence pictures them sitting in the stands or at home watching a game and, within their psyches, muttering, "There, but for the lack of grace of God, go I." And it is true that a number of contemporary authors who are taken seriously have indeed written about sports with a strong overlay of yearning. In the men's softball games described in the fiction of Philip Roth, center field is a place akin to Arcady. Arcadian, too, is the outfield in Willie Morris's memoir of growing up in the south, *North Toward Home.* In

the first half of *Rabbit Run*, John Updike takes up the life of a man whose days are downhill all the way after hitting his peak as a high-school basketball star—and in the writing Updike himself evinces a nice soft touch of undisguised longing. In *A Fan's Notes*, a book combining yearning and self-disgust in roughly equal measure, Frederick Exley makes plain that he would much prefer to have been born into the skin of Frank Gifford rather than into his own.

15   But most men who are enraptured by sports do not think any such thing. I should like to have Kareem Abdul-Jabbar's sky hook, but not, especially for civilian life, the excessive height that is necessary to its execution. I should like to have Jimmy Connors's ground strokes, but no part of his mind. These are men born with certain gifts, gifts honed by practice and determination, that I, and millions along with me, enjoy seeing on display. But the reality principle is too deeply ingrained, at least in a man of my years, for me to even imagine exchanging places with them. One might as well imagine oneself in the winner's circle at Churchill Downs as the horse.

16   Fantasy is an element in sports when they are played in adolescence—an alley basket becomes the glass backboard at Madison Square Garden, a concrete park district tennis court with grass creeping out of the service line becomes center court at Wimbledon—but fantasy of this kind is hard to come by. Part of this has to do with age; but as large a part has to do with the age in which we live. Sport has always been a business but never more so than currently, and nothing lends itself less to fantasy than business. Reading the sports section has become rather like reading the business section—mergers, trades, salary negotiations, contract disputes, options, and strikes fill the columns. Along with the details of business, those of the psychological and social problems of athletes have come to the fore. The old *Sport* magazine concentrated on play on the field, with only an occasional digressive reference to personal life. ("Yogi likes plenty of pizza in the off-season and spends a lot of his time at his teammate Phil Rizzuto's bowling alley," is a rough facsimile of a sentence from its pages that I recall.) But the magazine in its current version, as well as the now more popular *Sports Illustrated*, expends much space on the private lives of athletes—their divorces, hang-ups, race relations, need for approval, concern for security, potted philosophies—with the result that the grand is made to seem small.

17   On the other side of the ledger, there is a view that finds a shimmering significance in everything having to do with sports. Literary men in general are notoriously to be distrusted on the subject. They dig around everywhere, and can be depended upon to find much treasure where none is buried. Norman Mailer mining metaphysical ore in every jab of Muhammad Ali's, an existential nugget in each of his various and profuse utterances, is a particularly horrendous example. Even the sensible William Carlos Williams was not above this sort of temptation. In a poem entitled "At the Ball Game," we find the lines "It is the Inquisition, the /

Revolution." Dr. Williams could not have been much fun at the ball park.

The Real Thing

18   If enthusiasm for sports has little to do with providing an outlet for violent emotions, regaining adolescence, discovering metaphysical truths, the Inquisition or the Revolution, then what, I ask myself, am I doing past midnight, when I have to be up at 5:30 the next morning, watching on television what will turn out to be a seventeen-inning game between the New York Mets and the St. Louis Cardinals? The conversation coming out of my television set is of a very low grade, even for sports announcing. But even the dreary talk cannot put me off—the rehash of statistics, the advice to youngsters to keep their gloves low when in the field, the thin jokes. Neither the Mets nor the Cards figure to be contenders this year. The only possible effect that this game can have on my life is to make me dog-tired the next day. Yet I cannot pull myself away. I want to know how it is going to end. True, the score will be available in the morning paper. But that is not the same thing. What is going on here?

19   One thing that is going on is the practice of craft of a very high order, which is intrinsically interesting. But something as important is involved, something rarer in contemporary life, the spectacle of which gives enormous satisfaction. To define this satisfaction negatively, it is the absence of fraudulence and fakery. No small item, this, when one stops to think that in nearly every realm of contemporary life fraud and fakery have an established—some would say a preponderant—place. Advertising, politics, business, and journalism are only the most obvious examples. Fraud seems similarly pervasive in modern art: in painters whose reputations rest on press agentry; in writers who write one way and live quite another; in composers who are taken seriously but whose work cannot be seriously listened to. At a time when *image* is one of the most frequently used words in American speech and writing, one does not too often come upon the real thing.

20   Sport may be the toy department of life, but one of its abiding compensations is that, at least on the field, it is the real thing. Much has been done in recent years in the attempt to ruin sport—the ruthlessness of owners, the greed of players, the general exploitation of fans. But even all this cannot destroy it. On the court, down on the field, sport is fraud-free and fakeproof. With a full count, two men on, his team down by one run in the last of the eighth, a batter (as well as a pitcher) is beyond the aid of public relations. At match point at Forest Hills a player's press clippings are of no help. Last year's earnings will not sink a twelve-foot putt on the eighteenth at Augusta. Alan Page, galloping up along a quarterback's blind side, figures to be neglectful of that quarterback's image as a swinger. In all these situations, and hundreds of others, a man either comes through or he doesn't. He is alone out there, naked but for his

ability, which counts for everything. Something there is that is elemental about this, and something greatly satisfying.

21 Another part of the satisfaction to be got from sports—from playing them, but also from watching them being played—derives from their special clarity. Sports offer clarity of a kind sufficient to engage the most serious minds. That the Cambridge mathematician G. H. Hardy closely followed cricket and avidly read cricket scores is not altogether surprising. Numbers in sports are ubiquitous. Scores, standings, averages, times, records—comfort is found in such numbers. ERA, RBIs, FGP, pass completions, turnovers, category upon category of statistics are kept for nearly every aspect of athletic activity. (Why, I recently heard someone ask, are records not kept for catchers throwing out runners attempting to steal? Because, the answer is, often runners steal on pitchers, and so it would be unfair to charge these stolen bases against catchers.) As perhaps in no other sphere, numbers in sports tell one where things stand. No loopholes here, where figures, for once, do not lie. Nowhere else is such specificity of result available.

22 Clarity about character is also available in sports. "You Americans hold to the proposition that it is self-evident that all men are created equal," I not long ago heard an Englishman say, adding, "it had better be self-evident, for no other evidence for it exists." Sport coldly demonstrates physical inequalities—there are the larger, the faster, the stronger, the more graceful athletes—but it also throws up human types who have devised ways to redress these inequalities. One such type is the hustler. In every realm but that of sports the word *hustle* is pejorative, whereas in sports it is approbative. Two of the hustler breed, Pete Rose of the Cincinnati Reds and Jerry Sloan of the Chicago Bulls, are men who supplement reasonably high levels of ability with unreasonably high levels of courage and desire. Other athletes—Joe Morgan and Oscar Robertson come to mind—bring superior athletic intelligence to bear upon their play. And Bill Russell, late of the Boston Celtics, who if the truth be known was not an inherently superior athlete, blended hustle and intelligence with what abilities he did have and through force of character established supremacy.

23 Whence do hustle, intelligence, and character in sports derive, especially since they apparently do not necessarily carry over into life? Joe DiMaggio and Sugar Ray Robinson, two of the most instinctively intelligent and physically elegant athletes, brought little of either of these qualities over into their business or personal activities. Some athletes can do all but one important thing well: Wilt Chamberlain at the free-throw line, for those who recall his misery there, leaves a permanent picture of a mental block in action. Other athletes—Connie Hawkins, Ilie Nastase, Dick Allen—have all the physical gifts in superabundance, yet, because of some insufficiency of character, some searing flaw, never come near to fulfilling their promise. Coaches supply yet another gallery of human types, from the fanatical Vince Lombardi to the comical Casey

Stengel to the measured and aptly named John Wooden. The cast of characters in sport, the variety of situations, the complexity of behavior it puts on display, the overall human exhibit it offers—together these supply an enjoyment akin to that once provided by reading interminably long but inexhaustibly rich nineteenth-century novels.

24   In a wider sense, sport is culture. For many American men it represents a common background, a shared interest. It has a binding power that transcends social class and education. Some years ago I found myself working in the South among men with whom I shared nothing in the way of region, religion, education, politics, or general views; we shared nothing, in fact, but sports, which was enough for us to get along and grow to become friends, in the process showing how superficial all the things that might have kept us apart in fact were. More recently, in Chicago, at a time when race relations were in a particularly jagged state, I recall emerging from an NBA game, in which the Chicago Bulls in overtime beat the Milwaukee Bucks, into a snowy night and an aura of common good feeling that, for a time, submerged the enmity between races; laughing, throwing snowballs, exuberant generally, the crowd leaving the Chicago Stadium that night was not divided by being black and white but unified by being Bull fans. Last year's Boston-Cincinnati World Series, one of the most gratifying in memory, coming hard upon a year of extreme political divisiveness, performed, however briefly, something of the same function. How much better it felt to agree about the mastery of Luis Tiant than to argue about the wretchedness of Richard Nixon.

25   In sports, as in life, character does not much change. I have recently begun to play a game called racquet ball, and I find I would still rather look good than win, which is what I usually do: look good and lose. I beat the rum-dums but go down before quality players. I get compliments in defeat. Men who beat me admire the whip of my strokes, my wrist action, my anticipation, the power I get behind the ball. When this occurs I feel like a woman who is complimented for the shape of her bottom when it is her mind she craves admiration for, though of course she will take what praise she can get.

26   R. H. Tawney, the great historian of religion and capitalism, once remarked that the only progress he could note during the course of his lifetime was in the deportment of dogs. For myself, I would say that the chief progress in the course of my lifetime has been in the quality and variety of athletic gear. Racquets made of metal, aluminum, wood, and fiberglass, balls of different colors, sneakers of all materials and designs, posh warm-up suits, tube socks, sweatbands for the head and wrist in various colors and pipings; only the athletic supporter, the old jockstrap, remains unornamented, but perhaps even now Vera or Peter Max is at the drawing board. In any event, with all this elegant plumage available, it is a nice time to be playing ball again.

27   Sports can be impervious to age. My father-in-law, a man of style, seriousness, and great good humor who died a year ago in his late sixties,

was born in South Bend, Indiana, and in his early manhood left the Catholic Church—two facts that conjoined to give him an intense interest in the fortunes of the teams from Notre Dame. He loved to see them lose. The torch has been passed on. I now love to see Notre Dame lose, and when it does I think of him and remember his smile.

28   When I was a boy I had a neighbor, a man who, after retirement, had a number of strokes. An old man and a young boy, we had in common a love of sports, which, when we met on the street, was our only topic of conversation. He once inspected a new glove of mine, and instructed me to rub it down with neat's-foot oil, place a ball firmly in the pocket, wrap string tightly around the glove, and leave it like that for the winter. I did, and it worked. After his last stroke but one, he seldom left his house. Afternoons he spent in a chair in his bedroom, a blanket over his lap, listening to Cub games over the radio. It was while listening to a ball game that he quietly died. I cannot imagine a better way.

Obsessed with Sport: On the Interpretation of a Fan's Dreams

Questions on Content, Style, and Structure

1. What is Epstein's main purpose in this essay? Where does this purpose become clear?

2. Why does Epstein talk about his youth in the first section of the essay? Why does he describe the afternoon when he mastered the hook shot?

3. Epstein rejects several explanations for the popularity of sports. Summarize these explanations and Epstein's arguments against them.

4. Is Epstein convincing when he says that violence is not a primary part of most sports? Is his distinction between violence and roughness a valid one? Why/why not?

5. Why does Epstein mention the books and writers in paragraph 14? What does "Arcady" refer to?

6. Is Epstein correct when he contends that sport is too much a business now to promote much fantasy on the part of the fans?

7. What is the reason for paragraph 18?

8. What does Epstein mean when he says, "Sport may be the toy department of life, but . . . at least on the field, it is the real thing"?

9. Epstein states several reasons sports are interesting and enjoyable. What are these reasons?

10. What is Epstein's point in paragraph 23 when he refers to nineteenth-century novels?

11. How does Epstein support his claim that sport has a binding power transcending class and education?

12. Is the analogy at the end of paragraph 25 a successful one?
13. Describe and evaluate Epstein's conclusion. Does it fit the essay?

Vocabulary

haberdashery (5)	rudimentary (11)	ubiquitous (21)
intrinsic (6)	maligned (11)	pejorative (22)
reticent (9)	imbue (12)	approbative (22)
penchant (10)	honed (15)	enmity (24)
ministrations (10)	metaphysical (17)	conjoined (27)
expropriation (11)	existential (17)	
indubitably (11)	preponderant (19)	

Suggestions for Writing

1. Write an essay in which you analyze your enjoyment of a particular sport in your role as either a participant or an observer. (You may want to review Epstein's reasons for rejecting several explanations for the popularity of sports. If you agree with one of these explanations, defend your opinion in your essay.)

2. For years many people—especially coaches—have claimed that participation in sports builds character. Others have charged that the overemphasis on sports by parents, coaches, and schools frequently damages young people. Write an essay arguing your position.

3. Write an essay comparing and contrasting the styles of two athletes, two sports announcers, or two brands of a piece of sports equipment.

Sympathy for the Werewolf
Andrew Griffin

Andrew Griffin received his Ph.D. from Harvard in 1969 and is currently an Associate Professor of English at the University of California, Berkeley. He has written articles on Wordsworth, John Stuart Mill, and Mary Shelly's *Frankenstein*. This essay appeared in *University Publishing* in 1979.

Have pity on the Werewolf,
Have sympathy;
For the Werewolf may be someone
Just like you and me.

Have pity on the Werewolf,
Not fear—not hate;
For the Werewolf may be someone
That you've known of late.

The Moray Eel Meets the Holy Modal Rounders *

1   The fact is that we do feel pity for the Werewolf, along with the fear and hate. Monsters frighten us, as they do their movie victims, especially at first sight; but at some point in the course of every classic monster movie we begin to feel sorry for them and, forgetting their victims, to fear for them.

2   In short, we sympathize; we take the monster's side, at least some of the time, and almost always at the end. When it is finally dispatched we feel a great deal of relief, to be sure, but at the same time much sincere regret and guilt. The relief is in any case not the sort of feeling that comes with the simple lifting of a threat: it is the easing of the pressure of our unconscious identification with this dreadful and dangerous being on the sceen, whom we have come to see as in some way "just like you and me." It is this identification that makes us regret the loss of the monster, without whom the world is a poorer place, somehow incomplete. And we have to feel guilty for conniving in its death. The mob of villagers with their torches, the old doctor with his stake seem to be acting for us, yet we are shocked by their brutality, remembering the monster's moments of tenderness.

3   " 'Twas Beauty killed the Beast!" intones Carl Denham, King Kong's captor, always the impresario, dictating tomorrow's headlines to the waiting reporters. But we know better. 'Twasn't Beauty at all but something uncompromising in the human world, a failure of that sympathy for the Werewolf that we have been developing there in our seats—a failure on the part of Denham and his crew, the Army Air Force, and of course civilization itself, represented as usual by images of the metropolis with its skyscrapers and machines. Not that we imagine King Kong could have been saved! We know he can't survive, let alone rule, in New York City. But recognizing this, as the movie forces us to do, we have to reexamine our own relations to the city, "our" world. A part of ourselves clearly belongs to his world: not to Manhattan Island but to Skull Island, where Kong is King indeed.

4   It is obvious what part of ourselves that is. The classic movie monster (excepting Frankenstein's) is all instinct and energy and appetite, especially the latter: so simple and primitive that, for him, love and hate are almost the same thing. Monster movies are, of course, sexually explicit and sexually aggressive; they might almost be said to be about rape. And yet, they remain somehow innocent and presexual—because, I think, the monster is incorrigibly *oral*, seeking to incorporate both what it desires and what it wants to destroy, approaching the world in general through

* from "The Werewolf Song" composed in 1965 by Mike Hurley.

the mouth. Dracula, a fastidious aristocrat, nips and sips; the Wolfman, howling with lust, tears out your throat; King Kong's mighty jaws are capable of masticating and swallowing you whole (at one point he chews up a native). Even the movies' Mr. Hyde, who bites no one to death, has a dandy set of teeth, strong and crude, bared by his habitual lip-twitching simian grin.

5   Surely we are not like that! But we have been—have been all mouth, that is, and have wanted to eat the world—and the movies insist that we still are. Both *The Wolfman* and *Dr. Jekyll and Mr. Hyde* depend on the cinematic trick by which a man becomes a monster before our very eyes: Hyde *is* Jekyll, or a piece of him, and the Wolfman is Lon Chaney, Jr., in many ways an improvement. Dracula's kiss may bring about the same transformation: Mina the good and true struggles *not* to become that narrow but intense "Miss Hyde" within who loves the kiss and would long to return it. King Kong can best be understood, I think, not as Fay Wray's giant lover but as her sexual desire made outward and visible . . . and just as big as she has feared it would be if she ever gave in to it. She has been toying with temptation ever since the first frames of the movie, which show a famished Fay reaching almost experimentally toward an apple in a sidewalk grocery window; on shipboard she flirts with the "Aw, shucks" officer and, at Denham's direction, *acts* the emotion she is soon to experience. When at last Kong takes her in his enormous hand she is literally "in the grip of passion." Her fear now is, quite naturally, that she will be "swallowed up" by this immense feeling, her identity—like Mina Harker's or Lon Chaney's or Dr. Jekyll's—lost in it. But the feeling is still her own, of course: summoned out of the darkness of her inexperience as surely as Kong is called out of the jungle by the annual rituals, brought to the gates of consciousness roaring, demanding to be acknowledged, to have his due.

6   This is what monsters are, this is what monster movies do: they reacquaint us with our own forgotten or forbidden selves, inviting us to recognize and, in imagination, deal with them. They keep alive in us a large and tolerant idea of the human—large enough anyway to include what seems at first inhuman, alien. The fact that monster movies invariably end in another repression makes less difference than one might think at first. For one thing, the viewer always knows the nature of his own silent participation, there in the dark; to watch the movie at all is to accept some responsibility for violence done and passions expressed. Probably, too, this demonstration that outrageous feelings and dangerous appetites *can* be mastered or handled, though at some cost, tends to reassure us, making us not less but more open to our own impulses in the future, soothing exaggerated fears about loss of control and loss of identity.

7   But the fifties changed all this. The classic monster movie is a product of the thirties; sequels and variations dominate the forties. With the coming of the Cold War, however, monsters all but disappear, to be re-

placed by Creatures from this, Beasts from that, and things too fierce to mention. There are exceptions. *Forbidden Planet* (1956) is a monster movie in science fiction clothing, featuring no less than the Freudian id itself on a rampage: Walter Pidgeon's unconscious desires, objectified and magnified enormously through the power of alien technology. The first of the Creatures has a lot of monster in him too. *The Creature from the Black Lagoon* (1954) comes from the dawn of time, roused by scientists incautiously probing its habitat; the plot turns on its inarticulate relations with a pretty girl and, in *Revenge of the Creature* (1955), its rage against mankind and his cities. The Creature is, nevertheless, not a monster. It is, like all its numerous progeny, much farther down the evolutionary scale than the ape-, wolf-, and bat-people of the monster movies (a mammalian genre)—closer to the dinosaurs against whom, in fact, King Kong is really leagued with Fay Wray and ourselves. Though it shadows or mirrors us in important ways (notably its desire for the virgin, stylishly expressed in underwater sequences), it is always clear that it is *not* one of us, nor a part of ourselves, but profoundly alien—almost as alien as the Martians that attack earth in *War of the Worlds* (also 1954).

8   Sympathy for the Creature is by no means impossible, though it would seem to argue a fair degree of alienation or self-loathing to recognize oneself behind those rubber gills. Sympathy with still lower forms of life is out of the question, and it is these low life forms that came to dominate the screen. Hordes, swarms, blobs and slimes, giant insects, sentient plants—these were our bogeys then, images of the fifties' paranoid fear of dangers wholly external and coldly implacable, inexorably encroaching, endangering life-as-we-know-it. It seems reasonable to hold the politics of the period responsible. Certainly the fifties taught us that there was an Enemy pressing against our borders, subverting our institutions, godless and ruthless, to be met with total war. The politics of the day, like the movies, simplified and dehumanized the world, denying relationship, shifting responsibility. Where the monster movies of the thirties showed us similarity in difference, the menace movies of the fifties presented only unlikeness and danger. They told us to look to our weapons, draw the wagons into a circle and stay awake. Their central image is the small community under siege: not (as in *King Kong*) the monster in the city's midst, but almost the reverse—the city surrounded by monsters or, more precisely, by nameless and terrible "things." It is no accident that these films are often set in the desert or the arctic (not to mention imaginary lands still more inhospitable): environments that themselves express the pure inhuman otherness felt to lie just a step beyond the circle of the human, a circle now unnaturally, defensively and anxiously contracted.

9   What this meant for life in the fifties I needn't say. For the movies it meant the end of an era and a genre. Without the play of ambivalent feelings, uneasy alliances made and broken in the course of the film—

without the monster, in short—the viewer's experience is impoverished and his intelligence insulted. If we are only victims, we can only scream—unless, of course, we laugh. In *Attack of the Giant Shrews*, what appear to be Alsatian dogs loosely draped with Spanish moss encircle a house in the bayous. Or take *Night of the Lapis*, with its nocturnes of huge bunnies in a slow-motion romp through a model of a town—an extraordinary but in no way frightening spectacle. Shrews and rabbits? These movies have vanished even from late night TV. They can be made and watched only in a world where absolutely anything might turn on you, a world that doesn't understand itself or what's outside itself—and doesn't want to understand. No wonder that the "things" the fifties feared seem to increase and multiply, spreading and creeping—words that had a special and horrible meaning for this decade (the spread of communism, creeping socialism). No wonder either that the fifties feared itself, felt some loss of contact with itself. *Mutation* and *mind-control*, both insidious forms of usurpation or loss of real identity, play as large a part in the mythology of the decade as do Creatures and Slimes.

10   The best of the menace movies not only exploit this cultural paranoia, they expose it too. Don Siegel's *Invasion of the Body Snatchers* (1956), perhaps the best of the best, shows us an America ironically betrayed by what must be understood as its own dream of the Good Life. In this deadly little parable, a species of alien plant beings (pods) silently infiltrates a small California town, replacing its inhabitants one by one with vegetable simulacra, perfect replicas in every respect—the business of the town continuing, eerily and very meaningfully, as usual. Siegel must have enjoyed confounding the rigid categories of the fifties and overturning its convictions. In *Body Snatchers*, conformity is subversion, the suburban is alien—or, as Siegel plainly suggests, terribly alienating. The implication is, of course, that the one big difference between person and pod is no difference at all; we are all already hollow at the core, pretend people. At the end of the movie a frantic Kevin McCarthy, still human but just one step ahead of the pods, screams "You're next!" at the cars that flash past him on the highway. "I think the world is populated by pods," Siegel has said, "and I wanted to show them."

11   But as this remark itself indicates, Siegel remains true to the fifties formula. The problem, it seems, is still "them," not "us"—even if "them" is your neighborhood automata. The decline of the monster movie and its ethic is best exemplified in a movie actually entitled *Them!* (1954) which opens almost where *Body Snatchers* leaves off. We see a little girl stumbling along a desert road, dirty and disoriented, clutching her doll. What has happened? Where's your mommy and daddy? All the little girl can answer, all her decade ever does answer, is "Them!"

12   They turn out to be, in this instance, giant ants, grown to their present size through atomic accident, invading the human world in search of (mainly) sugar. They make an effective movie, too, as we follow the

desperate search for Their nest, confront Their fierce warriors, and, the battle over, explore Their underground tunnels and chambers, big as a coal mine and much more interesting. The movie ends effectively in the storm drains beneath Los Angeles with the systematic destruction of a second colony (and the rescue of two little boys) by the National Guard.

13   Needless to say, we feel no sympathy for Them. We might wonder, however, why They don't present more of a problem. For despite Their size, They are fairly easy to handle, no tougher than (say) the Japanese dug in on Tarawa. Gas and flamethrowers do the job. Every monster one can think of, although in most cases not nearly so dangerous to life-as-we-know-it, has been more difficult to deal with. Why don't They give more trouble? And why, after the movie is over, don't we give a damn?

14   The answer to both questions is that, oddly enough, there is little at stake. Monster movies dramatize a kind of negotiation with ourselves about what we are; somewhere, a little below the level of conscious thought, the monster is proposed, explored, debated, rejected, as we have already seen. But in a movie like *Them!*, or *The Thing*, or *The Beast from 20,000 Fathoms*, there is no such negotiation, only the defense of an idea of what's human that the movie never questions. Nor, finally, is there much to choose between human and alien. The storm drains of Los Angeles are uncannily well-adapted to the purposes of myrmecoid existence; the ants seem as at home under the city as we are in the ant heap that sprawls above them. And the National Guard, in their uniforms, their shiny helmets, especially with their gas masks on: not only are they indistinguishable from each other, they are hard to tell from the ants. One horde sweeps out another, red ants *vs* black. It seems unlikely that the makers of *Them!* meant to draw our attention to these similarities, but there they are. The implication is, as in *Invasion of the Body Snatchers*, that the supplanting of the human, by ant or pod, would scarcely be noticed by the universe at large.

Sympathy for the Werewolf

Questions on Content, Style, and Structure

1. Why, according to Griffin, do we feel sympathy for such classic monsters as King Kong, Dracula, and the Wolfman?

2. Griffin suggests that classic monster movies of the 1930s and '40s affect their viewers in what ways? Do you agree?

3. Why does Griffin refer to Carl Denham, Fay Wray, Dracula, Wolfman, and other characters?

4. How did the monster movies change in the '50s?

5. Why is it difficult for audiences to identify with typical '50s monsters?

6. What role, according to Griffin, did politics play in changing the monster movie? Who or what was the "Enemy pressing against our borders"?

7. What were the settings for many '50s movies? Why?

8. What did the new menace movies suggest about the decade of the '50s?

9. Why does Griffin discuss in some detail the 1956 movie *Invasion of the Body Snatchers*?

10. How does the movie *Them!* illustrate "the decline of the monster movie and its ethic"?

11. Ultimately, why don't we care about the '50s monsters?

Vocabulary

impresario (3)	mammalian (7)	usurpation (9)
incorrigibly (4)	genre (7)	simulacra (10)
fastidious (4)	sentient (8)	automata (11)
masticating (4)	implacable (8)	myrmecoid (14)
simian (4)	inexorably (8)	supplanting (14)
id (7)	nocturnes (9)	
progeny (7)	insidious (9)	

Suggestions for Writing

1. Write an essay similar to Griffin's comparing/contrasting recent horror movies to those of either the 1930s or 1950s. (If you are not a horror movie fan, substitute westerns, detective stories, disaster films, or some other genre.)

2. If you disagree with Griffin's analysis of 1930s or 1950s monster movies, write an essay in which you argue your own thesis. What *is* the attraction of the classic movie monsters? Do we feel this attraction to all horror movie creatures?

3. Write a movie review of the most frightening movie you have ever seen. In your review try to explain to your readers why you found the story so terrifying.

The Secret Life of Walter Mitty

James Thurber

James Thurber was a famous American humorist who created numerous stories, sketches, cartoons, fables, and essays, often satirizing the relationship between men and women. His books include *My Life and Hard Times* (1933), *Fables for Our Time* (1943), *The Thurber Carnival* (1945), and *Thurber Country* (1953). This story appeared in *My World—and Welcome to It* (1942).

1   "We're going through!" The Commander's voice was like thin ice breaking. He wore his full-dress uniform, with the heavily braided white cap pulled down rakishly over one cold gray eye. "We can't make it, sir. It's spoiling for a hurricane, if you ask me." "I'm not asking you, Lieutenant Berg," said the Commander. "Throw on the power lights! Rev her up to 8,500! We're going through!" The pounding of the cylinders increased; ta-pocketa-pocketa-pocketa-*pocketa-pocketa*. The Commander stared at the ice forming on the pilot window. He walked over and twisted a row of complicated dials. "Switch on No. 8 auxiliary!" he shouted. "Switch on No. 8 auxiliary!" repeated Lieutenant Berg. "Full strength in No. 3 turret!" shouted the Commander. "Full strength in No. 3 turret!" The crew, bending to their various tasks in the huge, hurtling eight-engined Navy hydroplane, looked at each other and grinned. "The Old Man'll get us through," they said to one another. "The Old Man ain't afraid of Hell!". . .

2   "Not so fast! You're driving too fast!" said Mrs. Mitty. "What are you driving so fast for?"

3   "Hmm?" said Walter Mitty. He looked at his wife, in the seat beside him, with shocked astonishment. She seemed grossly unfamiliar, like a strange woman who had yelled at him in a crowd. "You were up to fifty-five," she said. "You know I don't like to go more than forty. You were up to fifty-five." Walter Mitty drove on toward Waterbury in silence, the roaring of the SN202 through the worst storm in twenty years of Navy flying fading in the remote, intimate airways of his mind. "You're tensed up again," said Mrs. Mitty. "It's one of your days. I wish you'd let Dr. Renshaw look you over."

4   Walter Mitty stopped the car in front of the building where his wife went to have her hair done. "Remember to get those overshoes while I'm having my hair done," she said. "I don't need overshoes," said Mitty. She put her mirror back into her bag. "We've been all through that," she said, getting out of the car. "You're not a young man any longer." He raced the engine a little. "Why don't you wear your gloves? Have you lost your

gloves?" Walter Mitty reached in a pocket and brought out the gloves. He put them on, but after she had turned and gone into the building and he had driven on to a red light, he took them off again. "Pick it up, brother," snapped a cop as the light changed, and Mitty hastily pulled on his gloves and lurched ahead. He drove around the streets aimlessly for a time, and then he drove past the hospital on his way to the parking lot.

5   . . . "It's the millionaire banker, Wellington McMillan," said the pretty nurse. "Yes?" said Walter Mitty, removing his gloves slowly. "Who has the case?" "Dr. Renshaw and Dr. Benbow, but there are two specialists here, Dr. Remington from New York and Dr. Pritchard-Mitford from London. He flew over." A door opened down a long, cool corridor and Dr. Renshaw came out. He looked distraught and haggard. "Hello, Mitty," he said. "We're having the devil's own time with McMillan, the millionaire banker and close personal friend of Roosevelt. Obstreosis of the ductal tract.[1] Tertiary. Wish you'd take a look at him." "Glad to," said Mitty.

6   In the operating room there were whispered introductions: "Dr. Remington, Dr. Mitty. Dr. Pritchard-Mitford, Dr. Mitty." "I've read your book on streptothricosis," said Pritchard-Mitford, shaking hands. "A brilliant performance, sir." "Thank you," said Walter Mitty. "Didn't know you were in the states, Mitty," grumbled Remington. "Coals to Newcastle, bringing Mitford and me up here for a tertiary." "You are very kind," said Mitty. A huge, complicated machine, connected to the operating table, with many tubes and wires, began at this moment to go pocketa-pocketa-pocketa. "The new anaesthetizer is giving away!" shouted an interne. "There is no one in the East who knows how to fix it!" "Quiet, man!" said Mitty, in a low, cool voice. He sprang to the machine, which was now going pocketa-pocketa-queep-pocketa-queep. He began fingering delicately a row of glistening dials. "Give me a fountain pen!" he snapped. Someone handed him a fountain pen. He pulled a faulty piston out of the machine and inserted the pen in its place. "That will hold for ten minutes," he said. "Get on with the operation." A nurse hurried over and whispered to Renshaw, and Mitty saw the man turn pale. "Coreopsis has set in,"[2] said Renshaw nervously. "If you would take over, Mitty?" Mitty looked at him and at the craven figure of Benbow, who drank, and at the grave, uncertain faces of the two great specialists. "If you wish," he said. They slipped a white gown on him; he adjusted a mask and drew on thin gloves; nurses handed him shining . . .

7   "Back it up, Mac! Look out for that Buick!" Walter Mitty jammed on the brakes. "Wrong lane, Mac," said the parking-lot attendant, looking at Mitty closely. "Gee. Yeh," muttered Mitty. He began cautiously to back out of the lane marked "Exit Only." "Leave her sit there," said the

[1] Obstreosis is a disease found mainly in pigs and cattle.
[2] Coreopsis is a variety of herb, not a disease.

attendant. "I'll put her away." Mitty got out of the car. "Hey, better leave the key." "Oh," said Mitty, handing the man the ignition key. The attendant vaulted into the car, backed it up with insolent skill, and put it where it belonged.

8   They're so damn cocky, thought Walter Mitty, walking along Main Street; they think they know everything. Once he had tried to take his chains off, outside New Milford, and he had got them wound around the axles. A man had had to come out in a wrecking car and unwind them, a young, grinning garage man. Since then Mrs. Mitty always made him drive to a garage to have the chains taken off. The next time, he thought, I'll wear my right arm in a sling; they won't grin at me then. I'll have my right arm in a sling and they'll see I couldn't possibly take the chains off myself. He kicked at the slush on the sidewalk. "Overshoes," he said to himself, and he began looking for a shoe store.

9   When he came out into the street again, with the overshoes in a box under his arm, Walter Mitty began to wonder what the other thing was his wife had told him to get. She had told him, twice before they set out from their house for Waterbury. In a way he hated these weekly trips to town—he was always getting something wrong. Kleenex, he thought, Squibb's, razor blades? No. Toothpaste, toothbrush, bicarbonate, carborundum, initiative and referendum? He gave it up. But she would remember it. "Where's the what's-its-name?" she would ask. "Don't tell me you forgot the what's-its-name." A newsboy went by shouting something about the Waterbury trial.

10   . . . "Perhaps this will refresh your memory." The District Attorney suddenly thrust a heavy automatic at the quiet figure on the witness stand. "Have you ever seen this before?" Walter Mitty took the gun and examined it expertly. "This is my Webley-Vickers 50.80," he said calmly. An excited buzz ran around the courtroom. The judge rapped for order. "You are a crack shot with any sort of firearms, I believe?" said the District Attorney, insinuatingly. "Objection!" shouted Mitty's attorney. "We have shown that the defendant could not have fired the shot. We have shown that he wore his right arm in a sling on the night of the fourteenth of July." Walter Mitty raised his hand briefly and the bickering attorneys were stilled. "With any known make of gun," he said evenly, "I could have killed Gregory Fitzhurst at three hundred feet *with my left hand.*" Pandemonium broke loose in the courtroom. A woman's scream rose above the bedlam and suddenly a lovely, dark-haired girl was in Walter Mitty's arms. The District Attorney struck at her savagely. Without rising from his chair, Mitty let the man have it on the point of the chin. "You miserable cur!". . .

11   "Puppy biscuit," said Walter Mitty. He stopped walking and the buildings of Waterbury rose up out of the misty courtroom and surrounded him again. A woman who was passing laughed. "He said 'Puppy biscuit,' " she said to her companion. "That man said 'Puppy biscuit' to himself." Walter Mitty hurried on. He went into an A. & P., not the first one he

came to but a smaller one farther up the street. "I want some biscuit for small, young dogs," he said to the clerk. "Any special brand, sir?" The greatest pistol shot in the world thought a moment. "It says 'Puppies Bark for It' on the box," said Walter Mitty.

12   His wife would be through at the hairdresser's in fifteen minutes, Mitty saw in looking at his watch, unless they had trouble drying it; sometimes they had trouble drying it. She didn't like to get to the hotel first; she would want him to be there waiting for her as usual. He found a big leather chair in the lobby, facing a window, and he put the overshoes and the puppy biscuit on the floor beside it. He picked up an old copy of *Liberty* and sank down into the chair. "Can Germany Conquer the World through the Air?" Walter Mitty looked at the pictures of bombing planes and of ruined streets.

13   . . . "The cannonading has got the wind up in young Raleigh, sir," said the sergeant. Captain Mitty looked up at him through tousled hair. "Get him to bed," he said wearily, "with the others. I'll fly alone." "But you can't sir," said the sergeant anxiously. "It takes two men to handle that bomber and the Archies are pounding hell out of the air. Von Richtman's circus is between here and Saulier." "Somebody's got to get that ammunition dump," said Mitty. "I'm going over. Spot of brandy?" He poured a drink for the sergeant and one for himself. War thundered and whined around the dugout and battered at the door. There was a rending of wood and splinters flew through the room. "A bit of a near thing," said Captain Mitty carelessly. "The box barrage is closing in," said the sergeant. "We only live once, sergeant," said Mitty, with his faint, fleeting smile. "Or do we?" He poured another brandy and tossed it off. "I never see a man could hold his brandy like you, sir," said the sergeant. "Begging your pardon, sir." Captain Mitty stood up and strapped on his huge Webley-Vickers automatic. "It's forty kilometers through hell, sir," said the sergeant. Mitty finished one last brandy. "After all," he said softly, "what isn't?" The pounding of the cannon increased; there was the rat-tat-tatting of machine guns, and from somewhere came the menacing pocketa-pocketa-pocketa of the new flame-throwers. Walter Mitty walked to the door of the dugout humming "Auprès de Ma Blonde." He turned and waved to the sergeant. "Cheerio!" he said. . . .

14   Something struck his shoulder. "I've been looking all over this hotel for you," said Mrs. Mitty. "Why do you have to hide in this old chair? How did you expect me to find you?" "Things close in," said Walter Mitty vaguely. "What?" Mrs. Mitty said. "Did you get the what's-its-name? The puppy biscuit? What's in that box?" "Overshoes," said Mitty. "Couldn't you have put them on in the store?" "I was thinking," said Walter Mitty. "Does it ever occur to you that I am sometimes thinking?" She looked at him. "I'm going to take your temperature when I get you home," she said.

15   They went out through the revolving doors that made a faintly derisive

whistling sound when you pushed them. It was two blocks to the parking lot. At the drugstore on the corner she said, "Wait here for me. I forgot something. I won't be a minute. She was more than a minute. Walter Mitty lighted a cigarette. It began to rain, rain with sleet in it. He stood up against the wall of the drugstore, smoking. . . . He put his shoulders back and his heels together. "To hell with the handkerchief," said Walter Mitty scornfully. He took one last drag on his cigarette and snapped it away. Then, with that faint, fleeting smile playing about his lips, he faced the firing squad; erect and motionless, proud and disdainful, Walter Mitty the Undefeated, inscrutable to the last.

The Secret Life of Walter Mitty

Questions on Content, Style, and Structure

1. What kind of daydreams does Mitty have? Why?
2. What evidence is there that Mitty is dominated by people other than his wife?
3. What are the probable sources of Mitty's fantasies? What kinds of clichés do you see?
4. Is this story meant to be funny or tragic? Defend your answer.
5. How does each fantasy arise?
6. What pieces of misinformation does Mitty incorporate into his fantasies?
7. In what way is Mitty "Undefeated, inscrutable to the last"?

Vocabulary

turret (1)	tertiary (5)	derisive (15)
distraught (5)	carborundum (9)	disdainful (15)
haggard (5)	insinuatingly (10)	inscrutable (15)

Suggestions for Writing

1. Write an essay describing and analyzing your favorite fantasy.
2. Select a character from history and imagine being that person for one day. Write an essay telling why you chose the person and time you did.
3. Write a humorous story describing the fantasies of a struggling college student, an aspiring politician, or a second-rate actor.

A Proposal to Abolish Grading
Paul Goodman

Paul Goodman received his Ph.D. from the University of Chicago and taught in several universities. He is the author of numerous stories, essays, and books on a variety of subjects, including adolescent psychology, politics, education, and literature. This essay is an excerpt from *Compulsory Mis-Education* (1964).

1   Let half a dozen of the prestigious Universities—Chicago, Stanford, the Ivy League—abolish grading, and use testing only and entirely for pedagogic purposes as teachers see fit.

2   Anyone who knows the frantic temper of the present schools will understand the transvaluation of values that would be effected by this modest innovation. For most of the students, the competitive grade has come to be the essence. The naive teacher points to the beauty of the subject and the ingenuity of the research; the shrewd student asks if he is responsible for that on the final exam.

3   Let me at once dispose of an objection whose unanimity is quite fascinating. I think that the great majority of professors agree that grading hinders teaching and creates a bad spirit, going as far as cheating and plagiarizing. I have before me the collection of essays, *Examining in Harvard College*, and this is the consensus. It is uniformly asserted, however, that the grading is inevitable; for how else will the graduate schools, the foundations, the corporations *know* whom to accept, reward, hire? How will the talent scouts know whom to tap?

4   By testing the applicants, of course, according to the specific task-requirements of the inducting institution, just as applicants for the Civil Service or for licenses in medicine, law, and architecture are tested. Why should Harvard professors do the testing *for* corporations and graduate-schools?

5   The objection is ludicrous. Dean Whitla, of the Harvard Office of Tests, points out that the scholastic-aptitude and achievement tests used for *admission* to Harvard are a super-excellent index for all-around Harvard performance, better than high-school grades or particular Harvard course-grades. Presumably, these college-entrance tests are tailored for what Harvard and similar institutions want. By the same logic, would not an employer do far better to apply his own job-aptitude test rather than to rely on the vagaries of Harvard section-men. Indeed, I doubt that many employers bother to look at such grades; they are more likely to be interested merely in the fact of a Harvard diploma, whatever that connotes to them. The grades have most of their weight with the grad-

uate schools—here, as elsewhere, the system runs mainly for its own sake.

6   It is really necessary to remind our academics of the ancient history of Examination. In the medieval university, the whole point of the gruelling trial of the candidate was whether or not to accept him as a peer. His disputation and lecture for the Master's was just that, a master-piece to enter the guild. It was not to make comparative evaluations. It was not to weed out and select for an extra-mural licensor or employer. It was certainly not to pit one young fellow against another in an ugly competition. My philosophic impression is that the medievals thought they knew what a good job of work was and that we are competitive because we do not know. But the more status is achieved by largely irrelevant competitive evaluation, the less will we ever know.

7   (Of course, our American examinations never did have this purely guild orientation, just as our faculties have rarely had absolute autonomy; the examining was to satisfy Overseers, Elders, distant Regents— and they as paternal superiors have always doted on giving grades, rather than accepting peers. But I submit that this set-up itself makes it impossible for the student to *become* a master, to *have* grown up, and to commence on his own. He will always be making A or B for some overseer. And in the present atmosphere, he will always be climbing on his friend's neck.)

8   Perhaps the chief objectors to abolishing grading would be the students and their parents. The parents should be simply disregarded; their anxiety has done enough damage already. For the students, it seems to me that a primary duty of the university is to deprive them of their props, their dependence on extrinsic valuation and motivation, and to force them to confront the difficult enterprise itself and finally lose themselves in it.

9   A miserable effect of grading is to nullify the various uses of testing. Testing, for both student and teacher, is a means of structuring, and also of finding out what is blank or wrong and what has been assimilated and can be taken for granted. Review—including high-pressure review—is a means of bringing together the fragments, so that there are flashes of synoptic insight.

10   There are several good reasons for testing, and kinds of tests. But if the aim is to discover weakness, what is the point of down-grading and punishing it, and thereby inviting the student to conceal his weakness, by faking and bulling, if not cheating? The natural conclusion of synthesis is the insight itself, not a grade for having had it. For the important purpose of placement, if one can establish in the student the belief that one is testing *not* to grade and make invidious comparisons but for his own advantage, the student should normally seek his own level, where he is challenged and yet capable, rather than trying to get by. If the student dares to accept himself as he is, a teacher's grade is a crude instrument compared with a student's self-awareness. But it is rare in our universities that students are encouraged to notice objectively their

vast confusion. Unlike Socrates, our teachers rely on power-drives rather than shame and ingenuous idealism.

11 Many students are lazy, so teachers try to goad or threaten them by grading. In the long run this must do more harm than good. Laziness is a character-defense. It may be a way of avoiding learning, in order to protect the conceit that one is already perfect (deeper, the despair that one *never* can). It may be a way of avoiding just the risk of failing and being down-graded. Sometimes it is a way of politely saying, "I won't." But since it is the authoritarian grown-up demands that that have created such attitudes in the first place, why repeat the trauma? There comes a time when we must treat people as adult, laziness and all. It is one thing courageously to fire a do-nothing out of your class; it is quite another thing to evaluate him with a lordly F.

12 Most important of all, it is often obvious that balking in doing the work, especially among bright young people who get to great universities, means exactly what it says: The work does not suit me, not this subject, or not at this time, or not in this school, or not in school altogether. The student might not be bookish; he might be school-tired; perhaps his development ought now to take another direction. Yet unfortunately, if such a student is intelligent and is not sure of himself, he *can* be bullied into passing, and this obscures everything. My hunch is that I am describing a common situation. What a grim waste of young life and teacherly effort! Such a student will retain nothing of what he has "passed" in. Sometimes he must get mononucleosis to tell his story and be believed.

13 And ironically, the converse is also probably commonly true. A student flunks and is mechanically weeded out, who is really ready and eager to learn in a scholastic setting, but he has not quite caught on. A good teacher can recognize the situation, but the computer wreaks its will.

A Proposal to Abolish Grading

Questions on Content, Style, and Structure

1. What is Goodman's thesis?
2. Why do most teachers think grading is necessary?
3. What is Goodman's answer to the problem of grading?
4. What was the point of the candidate's examination in the medieval university? Does Goodman's description of this exam conflict with his claim that "it was not to weed out"?
5. Who might be the chief objectors to abolishing grading? Does Goodman effectively answer each group?
6. What are the purposes of testing?

7. In the last sentence of paragraph 11, Goodman contrasts two actions; are these actions as different as he maintains?

8. What is Goodman's attitude toward students who feel "the work does not suit me"?

9. Does Goodman offer a clear plan to replace grading? Support your answer.

10. Evaluate the effectiveness of Goodman's essay. Does he offer enough detail and support to make his argument convincing?

Vocabulary

pedagogic (1)
transvaluation (2)
innovation (2)
ingenuity (2)

ludicrous (5)
connotes (5)
disputation (6)
guild (6)

doted (7)
extrinsic (8)
assimilated (9)
synoptic (9)
invidious (10)

Suggestions for Writing

1. Write an essay in which you agree or disagree with Goodman's thesis. If you or any of your friends have ever taken a pass-fail or self-paced course, you may want to refer to that experience as part of your argument.

2. Read Suzanne Britt Jordan's essay " 'I Wants to Go to the Prose' " on pp. 138–140. Write an essay comparing/contrasting the opinions, prose styles, and effectiveness of those two authors.

3. Write an essay analyzing the causes of your worst or best performance in any academic course you've taken.

University Days
James Thurber

James Thurber was a famous American humorist who created numerous stories, sketches, cartoons, fables, and essays, often satirizing the relationships between men and women. His books include *My World—and Welcome to It* (1942), *Fables for Our Time* (1943), *The Thurber Carnival* (1945), and *Thurber Country* (1953). This essay was included in *My Life and Hard Times* (1933).

1 I passed all the other courses that I took at my university, but I could never pass botany. This was because all botany students had to spend several hours a week in a laboratory looking through a microscope at

plant cells, and I could never see through a microscope. I never once saw a cell through a microscope. This used to enrage my instructor. He would wander around the laboratory pleased with the progress all the students were making in drawing the involved and, so I am told, interesting structure of flower cells, until he came to me. I would just be standing there. "I can't see anything," I would say. He would begin patiently enough, explaining how anybody can see through a microscope, but he would always end up in a fury, claiming that I could *too* see through a microscope but just pretended that I couldn't. "It takes away from the beauty of flowers anyway," I used to tell him. "We are not concerned with beauty in this course," he would say. "We are concerned solely with what I may call the *mechanics* of flars." "Well," I'd say, "I can't see anything." "Try it just once again," he'd say, and I would put my eye to the microscope and see nothing at all, except now and again, a nebulous milky substance—a phenomenon of maladjustment. You were supposed to see a vivid, restless clockwork of sharply defined plant cells. "I see what looks like a lot of milk," I would tell him. This, he claimed, was the result of my not having adjusted the microscope properly; so he would readjust it for me, or rather, for himself. And I would look again and see milk.

2   I finally took a deferred pass, as they called it, and waited a year and tried again. (You had to pass one of the biological sciences or you couldn't graduate.) The professor had come back from vacation brown as a berry, bright-eyed, and eager to explain cell-structure again to his classes. "Well," he said to me, cheerily, when we met in the first laboratory hour of the semester, "we're going to see cells this time, aren't we?" "Yes, sir," I said. Students to right of me and to left of me and in front of me were seeing cells; what's more, they were quietly drawing pictures of them in their notebooks. Of course, I didn't see anything.

3   "We'll try it," the professor said to me, grimly, "with every adjustment of the microscope known to man. As God is my witness, I'll arrange this glass so that you see cells through it or I'll give up teaching. In twenty-two years of botany, I—" He cut off abruptly, for he was beginning to quiver all over, like Lionel Barrymore, and he genuinely wished to hold onto his temper; his scenes with me had taken a great deal out of him.

4   So we tried it with every adjustment of the microscope known to man. With only one of them did I see anything but blackness or the familiar lacteal opacity, and that time I saw, to my pleasure and amazement, a variegated constellation of flecks, specks, and dots. These I hastily drew. The instructor, noting my activity, came back from an adjoining desk, a smile on his lips and his eyebrows high in hope. He looked at my cell drawing. "What's that?" he demanded, with a hint of a squeal in his voice. "That's what I saw," I said. "You didn't, you didn't, you *did*n't!" he screamed, losing control of his temper instantly, and he bent over and squinted into the microscope. His head snapped up. "That's your eye!" he shouted. "You've fixed the lens so that it reflects! You've drawn your eye!"

5   Another course that I didn't like, but somehow managed to pass, was economics. I went to that class straight from the botany class, which didn't help me any in understanding either subject. I used to get them mixed up. But not as mixed up as another student in my economics class who came there direct from a physics laboratory. He was a tackle on the football team, named Bolenciecwcz. At that time Ohio State University had one of the best football teams in the country, and Bolenciecwcz was one of its outstanding stars. In order to be eligible to play it was necessary for him to keep up in his studies, a very difficult matter, for while he was not dumber than an ox he was not any smarter. Most of his professors were lenient and helped him along. None gave him more hints, in answering questions, or asked him simpler ones than the economics professor, a thin, timid man named Bassum. One day when we were on the subject of transportation and distribution, it came Bolenciecwcz's turn to answer a question. "Name one means of transportation," the professor said to him. No light came into the big tackle's eyes. "Just any means of transportation," said the professor. Bolenciecwcz sat staring at him. "That is," pursued the professor, "any medium, agency, or method of going from one place to another." Bolenciecwcz had the look of a man who is being led into a trap. "You may choose among steam, horse-drawn, or electrically propelled vehicles," said the instructor. "I might suggest the one which we commonly take in making long journeys across land." There was a profound silence in which everybody stirred uneasily, including Bolenciecwcz and Mr. Bassum. Mr. Bassum abruptly broke this silence in an amazing manner. "Choo-choo-choo," he said, in a low voice, and turned instantly scarlet. He glanced appealingly around the room. All of us, of course, shared Mr. Bassum's desire that Bolenciecwcz should stay abreast of the class in economics, for the Illinois game, one of the hardest and most important of the season, was only a week off. "Toot, toot, too-toooooooot!" some student with a deep voice moaned, and we all looked encouragingly at Bolenciecwcz. Somebody else gave a fine imitation of a locomotive letting off steam. Mr. Bassum himself rounded off the little show. "Ding, dong, ding, dong," he said, hopefully. Bolenciecwcz was staring at the floor now, trying to think, his great brow furrowed, his huge hands rubbing together, his face red.

6   "How did you come to college this year, Mr. Bolenciecwcz?" asked the professor. "*Chuf*fa chuffa, *chuf*fa chuffa."

7   "M'father sent me," said the football player.

8   "What on?" asked Bassum.

9   "I git an 'lowance," said the tackle, in a low, husky voice, obviously embarrassed.

10   "No, no," said Bassum. "Name a means of transportation. What did you *ride* here on?"

11   "Train," said Bolenciecwcz.

12   "Quite right," said the professor. "Now, Mr. Nugent, will you tell us—"

13   If I went through anguish in botany and economics—for different reasons—gymnasium work was even worse. I don't even like to think about it. They wouldn't let you play games or join in the exercises with your glasses on and I couldn't see with mine off. I bumped into professors, horizontal bars, agricultural students, and swinging iron rings. Not being able to see, I could take it but I couldn't dish it out. Also, in order to pass gymnasium (and you had to pass it to graduate) you had to learn to swim if you didn't know how. I didn't like the swimming pool, I didn't like swimming, and I didn't like the swimming instructor, and after all these years I still don't. I never swam but I passed my gym work anyway, by having another student give my gymnasium number (978) and swim across the pool in my place. He was a quiet, amiable blonde youth, number 473, and he would have seen through a microscope for me if we could have got away with it, but we couldn't get away with it. Another thing I didn't like about gymnasium work was that they made you strip the day you registered. It is impossible for me to be happy when I am stripped and being asked a lot of questions. Still, I did better than a lanky agricultural student who was cross-examined just before I was. They asked each student what college he was in—that is, whether Arts, Engineering, Commerce, or Agriculture. "What college are you in?" the instructor snapped at the youth in front of me. "Ohio State University," he said promptly.

14   It wasn't that agricultural student but it was another a whole lot like him who decided to take up journalism, possibly on the ground that when farming went to hell he could fall back on newspaper work. He didn't realize, of course, that that would be very much like falling back full-length on a kit of carpenter's tools. Haskins didn't seem cut out for journalism, being too embarrassed to talk to anybody and unable to use a typewriter, but the editor of the college paper assigned him to the cow barns, the sheep house, the horse pavilion, and the animal husbandry department generally. This was a genuinely big "beat," for it took up five times as much ground and got ten times as great a legislative appropriation as the College of Liberal Arts. The agricultural student knew animals, but nevertheless his stories were dull and colorlessly written. He took all afternoon on each of them, because he had to hunt for each letter on the typewriter. Once in a while he had to ask somebody to help him hunt. "C" and "L," in particular, were hard letters for him to find. His editor finally got pretty much annoyed at the farmer-journalist because his pieces were so uninteresting. "See here, Haskins," he snapped at him one day, "why is it we never have anything hot from you on the horse pavilion? Here we have two hundred head of horses on this campus—more than any other university in the Western Conference except Purdue—and yet you never get any real lowdown on them. Now shoot over to the horse barns and dig up something lively." Haskins shambled out and came back in about an hour; he said he had something. "Well, start it off snappily," said the editor. "Something people will read." Has-

kins set to work and in a couple of hours brought a sheet of typewritten paper to the desk; it was a two-hundred-word story about some disease that had broken out among the horses. Its opening sentence was simple but arresting. It read: "Who has noticed the sores on the tops of the horses in the animal husbandry building?"

15   Ohio State was a land grant university and therefore two years of military drill was compulsory. We drilled with old Springfield rifles and studied the tactics of the Civil War even though the World War was going on at the time. At 11 o'clock each morning thousands of freshmen and sophomores used to deploy over the campus, moodily creeping up on the old chemistry building. It was good training for the kind of warfare that was waged at Shiloh but it had no connection with what was going on in Europe. Some people used to think there was German money behind it, but they didn't dare say so or they would have been thrown in jail as German spies. It was a period of muddy thought and marked, I believe, the decline of higher education in the Middle West.

16   As a soldier I was never good at all. Most of the cadets were glumly indifferent soldiers, but I was no good at all. Once General Littlefield, who was commandant of the cadet corps, popped up in front of me during regimental drill and snapped, "You are the main trouble with this university!" I think he meant that my type was the main trouble with the university but he may have meant me individually. I was mediocre at drill, certainly—that is, until my senior year. By that time I had drilled longer than anybody else in the Western Conference, having failed at military at the end of each preceding year so that I had to do it all over again. I was the only senior still in uniform. The uniform which, when new, had made me look like an interurban railway conductor, now that it had become faded and too tight, made me look like Bert Williams in his bell-boy act. This had a definitely bad effect on my morale. Even so, I had become by sheer practise little short of wonderful at squad manoeuvres.

17   One day General Littlefield picked our company out of the whole regiment and tried to get it mixed up by putting it through one movement after another as fast as we could execute them: squads right, squads left, squads on right into line, squads right about, squads left front into line, etc. In about three minutes one hundred and nine men were marching in one direction and I was marching away from them at an angle of forty-five degrees, all alone. "Company, halt!" shouted General Littlefield. "That man is the only man who has it right!" I was made a corporal for my achievement.

18   The next day General Littlefield summoned me to his office. He was swatting flies when I went in. I was silent and he was silent too, for a long time. I don't think he remembered me or why he had sent for me, but he didn't want to admit it. He swatted some more flies, keeping his eyes on them narrowly before he let go with the swatter. "Button up your coat!" he snapped. Looking back on it now I can see that he meant

me although he was looking at a fly, but I just stood there. Another fly came to rest on a paper in front of the general and began rubbing its hind legs together. The general lifted the swatter cautiously. I moved restlessly and the fly flew away. "You startled him!" barked General Littlefield, looking at me severely. I said I was sorry. "That won't help the situation!" snapped the general, with cold military logic. I didn't see what I could do except offer to chase some more flies toward his desk, but I didn't say anything. He stared out the window at the faraway figures of co-eds crossing the campus toward the library. Finally, he told me I could go. So I went. He either didn't know which cadet I was or else he forgot what he wanted to see me about. It may have been that he wished to apologize for having called me the main trouble with the university; or maybe he had decided to compliment me on my brilliant drilling of the day before and then at the last minute decided not to. I don't know. I don't think about it much any more.

University Days

Questions on Content, Style, and Structure

1. What is Thurber's point in telling these tales from his college days? Is this point stated in the essay?
2. What does Thurber finally see through his microscope?
3. How does the story of Bolenciecwcz fit a common stereotype?
4. What does the story of number 473 tell you about Thurber's attitude toward some university requirements?
5. The stories of Bolenciecwcz, the agricultural student, and the young journalist illustrate what about some of Thurber's college classmates?
6. What is the source of humor in the story about the military drill?
7. What is the point of Thurber's meeting with the general?
8. Does this essay have a conclusion?
9. Identify Thurber's methods of transition from anecdote to anecdote.
10. Characterize the tone of this essay.

Vocabulary

nebulous (1)
maladjustment (1)
deferred (2)
lacteal (4)
opacity (4)
indifferent (16)
mediocre (16)

Suggestions for Writing

1. Summarize your attitude toward high school (or college, so far) by presenting at least three stories that illustrate your opinion.

2. Write a paragraph in which you tell the funniest incident you've witnessed in one of your college classes.

3. Select a university or high school requirement you think is unfair or unnecessary. Write an essay arguing for its modification or removal.

"I Wants to Go to the Prose"
Suzanne Britt Jordan

Suzanne Britt Jordan taught English at North Carolina State University at Raleigh from 1976–1979. She is currently a free-lance writer whose articles have appeared in a variety of magazines and newspapers. This essay was originally published in the "My Turn" column of *Newsweek* in 1977.

1 I'm tired—and have been for quite a while. In fact, I think I can pinpoint the exact minute at which I first felt the weariness begin. I had been teaching for three years at a community college. I had, for quite a while, overlooked ignorance, dismissed arrogance, championed fairness, emphasized motivation, boosted egos and tolerated laziness. I was, in short, the classic modern educator.

2 One day a student, Marylou Simmons, dropped by my office. She had not completed a single assignment and had missed perhaps 50 per cent of her classes. Her writing, what little I saw of it, was illogical, grammatically incorrect and sloppy. "Can I help you, Marylou?" I said cheerily, ever the understanding and forgiving teacher. Her lip began to tremble; her eyes grew teary. It seemed she had been having trouble with her boyfriend. "I'm sorry, but what can *I* do?" I asked. Suddenly all business, Marylou said, "Since I've been so unhappy, I thought you might want to just give me a D or an Incomplete on the course." She smiled encouragingly, even confidently. That's when the weariness set in, the moment at which I turned into a flaming conservative in matters educational. Whatever Marylou's troubles, I suddenly saw that I was not the cause, nor was I about to be the solution.

Namby-pamby Courses

3 When I read about declining SAT scores, the "functional illiteracy" of our students, the namby-pamby courses, the army of child psychologists, reading aides, educational liaisons, starry-eyed administrators and bungling fools who people our school systems, my heart sinks. Public schools

abide mediocre students; put 18-year-olds, who can't decide what to wear in the morning, into independent study programs; excuse every absence under the sun, and counsel, counsel, counsel. A youngster in my own school system got into a knife fight and was expelled—for one week. I noticed in the paper that bus drivers regularly see riders smoking marijuana and drinking wine on the bus at, for God's sake, 8 in the morning. I could go on, but the public knows well enough the effects of a system of education gone awry.

4   Consider for a moment what caused the mess. A few years ago people began demanding their rights. Fair enough. They wanted equal education under the law. I'm for it. Social consciousness was born. Right on. Now, enter the big wrong turn, the one that sent our schools into never-never land. We suddenly, naïvely, believed that by offering equal opportunities we could (1) make everybody happy, (2) make everybody well-adjusted, (3) forgive everybody who failed, and (4) expect gratitude to boot. When students were surly, uncooperative, whiny and apathetic, educators decided they themselves didn't know how to teach. So they made it easier on the poor, disadvantaged victims of broken homes, the misfits, the unloved. Well and good. But the catch to such lofty theories is evident. Poverty, ignorance and just plain orneriness will always abound. We look for every reason in the world for the declining test scores of our children, except for stupidity and laziness.

A Curmudgeon Speaks

5   I'm perfectly aware that I sound like an old curmudgeon and it frightens me more than it offends you. But I have accepted what educators can't seem to face. The function of schools, their first and primary obligation, is not to probe tender psyches, to feed and clothe the homeless, nor to be the papa and mama a kid never had. The job is to teach.

6   The teacher's job is to know his subject, inside out, backward, forward and every which way. Nothing unnerves a student more than to have a teacher who doesn't know his or her stuff. Incompetence they cannot abide. Neither can I.

7   Before educators lost their way and tried to diversify by getting into the business of molding human beings, a teacher was, ideally, someone who knew a certain body of information and conveyed it. Period. Remember crochety old Miss Dinwiddie, who could recite 40 lines of the *Aeneid* at a clip? Picture Mr. Wassleheimer, who could give a zero to a cheating student without pausing in his lecture on frog dissection. Every student knew that it wasn't wise to mess around with a teacher who had the subject down cold. They were the teachers we once despised and later admired.

8   I want them back, those fearsome, awe-inspiring experts. I want them back because they knew what a school was for and didn't waste any time getting on with the task at hand. They were hard, even at times unjust,

but when they were through, we knew those multiplication tables blind-folded with both trembling hands tied behind our backs.

9   Before the schoolmasters and the administrators change, they will have to shake off the guilt, the simpering, apologetic smiles and the Freudian theories. Which is crueler? Flunking a kid who has flunked or passing a kid who has flunked? Which teaches more about the realities of life? Which, in fact, shows more respect for the child as a human being?

10   Just today I talked to a big blond bruiser of a football player who wants to learn the basics of grammar. I didn't tell him it was too late. You see, he was a very, very good football player, so good that he never failed a course in high school. He had written on a weekly theme, "I wants to go to the prose and come fames." He may become a pro, may even become famous, but he will probably never read a good book, write a coherent letter or read a story to his children. I will, however, flunk him if he does not learn the material in the course. My job means too much to me to sacrifice my standards and turn soft. Suppose that every time my student played football badly, the coach said it was "just a game." Suppose the coach allowed him to drink booze, stay up all night, eat poorly and play sloppily. My student would be summarily dismissed from the team or the team would lose the game. So it goes with academic courses.

Life Is Real

11   The young people are interested, I think, in taking their knocks, just as adults must take theirs. Students deserve a fair chance, and, failing to take advantage of that chance, a straightforward dismissal. It has been said that government must guarantee equal opportunity, not equal re-sults. I like that. Through the theoretical fog that has clouded our per-ceptions and blanketed our minds, we know what is equitable and right. Mother put it another way. She always said, "Life is real; life is earnest." Incidentally, she taught me Latin and never gave me air in a jug. I had to breathe on my own. So do we all.

"I Wants to Go to the Prose"

Questions on Content, Style, and Structure

1   How does Jordan introduce her essay? What is her purpose in telling the story of Marylou?

2. What, according to Jordan, are some of the signs of "a system of education gone awry"?

3. In Jordan's opinion, what are the causes of our poor educational system?

4. Why does Jordan include the first sentence in paragraph 5?

5. What is Jordan's conception of a good teacher? How does she illustrate her opinion?

6. What is the purpose of the story of the football player in paragraph 10? Is it effective? Why/why not?

7. What does Jordan mean when she refers to her mother never giving her "air in a jug"? Why does she end on this reference?

8. Characterize the tone of this essay. Is it effective for all audiences? Why/why not?

9. Consider Jordan's use of sentence variety. Why, for example, does she include such short sentences as "Fair enough," "I'm for it," "Right on," "Well and good" (all in paragraph 4)?

10. What was Jordan's purpose in writing this essay? Did she succeed?

Vocabulary

arrogance (1)	apathetic (4)
liaisons (3)	orneriness (4)
mediocre (3)	curmudgeon (5)
surly (4)	crochety (7)
whiny (4)	

Suggestions for Writing

1. Write an essay in which you agree or disagree with Jordan's stance on education.

2. Use one of the following statements to lead you to an essay topic:

"Public schools abide mediocre students; put 18-year-olds, who can't decide what to wear in the morning, into independent study programs. . . ."

"They were hard, even at times unjust, but when they were through, we knew those multiplication tables blindfolded with both trembling hands tied behind our backs."

"Students deserve a fair chance, and, failing to take advantage of that chance, a straightforward dismissal."

3. Write an essay characterizing your favorite or least favorite teacher, or write an essay describing the most "namby-pamby" course you ever took.

Away with Big-Time Athletics
Roger M. Williams

Roger M. Williams has been published in *Time* and in *Sports Illustrated* and has been an editor for *Saturday Review*. This essay first appeared in *Saturday Review* in 1976.

1   At their mid-January annual meeting, members of the National Collegiate Athletic Association were locked in anguished discussion over twin threats to big-time college athletic programs: rapidly rising costs and federal regulations forcing the allocation of some funds to women's competition. The members ignored, as they always have, the basic issue concerning intercollegiate athletics. That is the need to overhaul the entire bloated, hypocritical athletic system and return athletics to a sensible place in the educational process.

2   A complete overhaul of the athletic programs, not the fiscal repair now being attempted by the NCAA, is what is necessary. For decades now big-time football, and to a lesser degree basketball, have commanded absurdly high priorities at our colleges and universities. Football stands at the center of the big-time system, both symbolically and financially; the income from football has long supported other, less glamorous sports.

3   Many American universities are known more for the teams they field than for the education they impart. Each year they pour hundreds of thousands of dollars apiece into athletic programs whose success is measured in games won and dollars earned—standards that bear no relation to the business of education and offer nothing to the vast majority of students.

4   The waste of resources is not the only lamentable result of the overemphasis of intercollegiate athletics. The skewing of values is at least as damaging. Everyone involved in the big-time system—players, coaches, alumni and other boosters, school officials, trustees, even legislators—is persuaded that a good football team is a mark of the real worth of an educational institution. Some of the most successful coaches elevate that bizarre notion to a sort of philosophy. Woody Hayes of Ohio State has said that the most important part of a young man's college education is the football he plays. Jim Kehoe, athletic director at the University of Maryland, has said of the games played by Maryland: "You do anything to win. I believe completely, totally, and absolutely in winning."

5   Anyone doubtful of the broad psychic satisfaction provided by winning teams need only observe who it is that shouts, "We're number one!" It is seldom the players and only sometimes other students. The hard core of team boosters is composed of middle-aged men—mainly alumni but also legions of lawyers, doctors, and businessmen with no tangible connection to the school.

6   In the South, where football mania rides at a shrill and steady peak, winning seems to offer a special reward: an opportunity to claim the parity with other regions that has been so conspicuously lacking in more important areas of endeavor. In Alabama in the late sixties, when Coach Bear Bryant was fielding the first of his remarkable series of national championship teams, both Bear and team were the objects of outright public adulation: that is, *white* public adulation. White Alabamians, re-acting to the assaults on George Wallace* and other bastions of segrega-tion, took a grim, almost vengeful pride in "their" team. During those years, when I covered the South as a reporter, one could hardly meet a white Alabamian who didn't talk football or display, on an office or den wall, a picture of Bryant and the Crimson Tide squad.

7   The disease of bigtime-ism seems to run rampant in provincial places where there is little else to do or cheer for: Tuscaloosa and Knoxville, Columbus and Lincoln, Norman and Fayetteville. But everywhere, al-ways, it feeds on a need to win—not just win a fair share of games but win almost all of them, and surely all of the "big" ones.

8   At the University of Tennessee last fall, coach Bill Battle nearly lost his job because the Volunteers won a mere seven out of twelve games. Never mind that Battle's Tennessee teams had previously amassed a five-year record of forty-six victories, twelve defeats, and two ties and had been to a bowl in each of those years. Although Battle was eventually rehired, he received no public support from a university administration which seemed to agree with the fanatics that, outstanding as his record was, it was not good enough.

9   Everyone knows something about the excess of recruiting high-school players and something about the other trappings of the big-time system: the athletic dormitory and training table, where the "jocks" or "animals" are segregated in the interests of conformity and control, the "brain coaches" hired to keep athletes from flunking out of school; the full scholarships ("grants in aid"), worth several thousand dollars apiece, that big-time schools can give to 243 athletes each year. (Conference regula-tions restrict the size of football traveling squads to about sixty, while the NCAA permits ninety-five players to be on football scholarships. This means that some three dozen football players at each big-time school are getting what's called a full ride without earning it.)

10   What a few people realize is that these are only the visible workings of a system that feeds on higher education and diverts it from its true purposes. The solution, therefore, is not to deliver slaps on the wrist to the most zealous recruiters, as the NCAA often does, or to make modest reductions in the permissible number of athletic scholarships, as it did last year. The solution is to banish big-time athletics from American colleges and universities.

11   Specifically, we should:

12   1. Eliminate all scholarships awarded on the basis of athletic ability

*George Wallace was governor of Alabama (1963–1966, 1971–1974, 1975–1978).

and those given to athletes in financial need. Every school should form its teams from a student body drawn there to pursue academic interests.

13   2. Eliminate athletic dormitories and training tables, which keep athletes out of the mainstream of college life and further their image as hired guns. Also eliminate special tutoring, which is a preferential treatment of athletes, and "red shirting," the practice of keeping players in school an additional year in the hope that they'll improve enough to make the varsity.

14   3. Cut drastically the size and the cost of the coaching staffs. Football staffs at Division I schools typically number twelve or fourteen, so that they are larger than those employed by professional teams. With practice squads numbering eighty or fifty, the present staff size creates a "teacher-pupil" ratio that permits far more individualized instruction on the playing field than in the classroom. The salaries paid to assistant coaches should be spent to hire additional faculty members. The salaries of head coaches, who in some states earn more than the governor, should be reduced to a point where no head coach is paid more than a full professor.

15   4. Work to eliminate all recruiting of high-school athletes. It has produced horrendous cases of misrepresentation, illegal payments, and trauma for the young man involved.

16   The worst of the abuses is the athletic scholarship, because it is central to all the others. If members of a college team are not principally athletes, there is no need to lure them to the school by offering special treatment and platoons of coaches. They should be students to whom football or basketball is the season's major extracurricular activity.

17   What will happen if these changes are made? The games will go on. In fact, they may well be more like real games than the present clashes between hired, supertrained, and sometimes brutalized gladiators. Will the caliber of play suffer? Of course, but every school will be producing the same lower caliber. Given a certain proficiency, which the best of any random selection of student-athletes always possesses, the games will be as competitive and as exciting for spectators as they are today. Is a 70-yard run by a nonscholarship halfback less exciting than the same run by Bear Bryant's best pro prospect? For spectators who crave top athletic performance, it is available from a myriad of professional teams. We need not demand it of students.

18   Certainly, the counter-argument runs, alumni and other influential supporters would not stand for such changes. There would indeed be ill feeling among—and diminished contributions from—old grads who think of their alma mater primarily as a football team. Let them stew in their own pot of distorted values. Those legislators whose goodwill toward a state university depends on winning seasons and free tickets can stew with them. A serious institution is well rid of such "supporters." They may discover the pleasures of a game played enthusiastically by moderately skilled students who are not in effect paid performers.

19   Will athletic-program revenues drop? They undoubtedly will, at least

for a while; not many people will pay seven dollars to see games of admittedly lower quality, nor will the TV networks pay fancy fees for the right to televise them. The fans and the networks will eventually return, because these will be the only college games available. And think of the financial savings, as the costs of the typical big-time athletic program drop by hundreds of thousands of dollars a year. If a revenue gap persists, let it be made up out of general funds. The glee club, the intramural athletic program, and innumerable other student activities do not pay for themselves. Why should intercollegiate athletics have to do so?

20   Supporters of big-time programs often say piously that, thanks to those programs, many young men get a college education who otherwise would have no chance for one. That is true. But there are even more young men, of academic rather than athletic promise, who deserve whatever scholarship money is available. If somebody has to pay an athlete's way to college, let it be the professional teams that need the training that college competition provides.

21   The president of a good Southern university once told me privately that he would like to hire outright a football team to represent his school and let the educational process proceed. George Hanford of the College Entrance Examination Board, who has made a study of intercollegiate athletics, would keep the present system but legitimize the preparation of players for professional sports. Hanford would have a college teach athletes such skills as selecting a business agent and would permit student-athletes to play now and return later to do the academic work required for a degree.

22   While Hanford's suggested changes would remove the mask of hypocrisy from big-time college athletic programs, they would not solve the fundamental problem: the intrusions the programs make on the legitimate functions and goals of an educational institution. For institutions with a conscience, this problem has been persistently vexing. Vanderbilt University football coach Art Guepe summed it up years ago, when he characterized Vanderbilt's dilemma as "trying to be Harvard five days a week and Alabama on Saturday."

23   Because of pressures from alumni and others who exalt the role of football, Vanderbilt is still attempting to resolve this dilemma; and it is still failing. Now it is time for all the Vanderbilts and all the Alabamas to try to be Harvard whenever they can and Small-Time State on Saturday.

Away with Big-Time Athletics

Questions on Content, Style, and Structure

1. What is Williams' thesis?
2. What are the main reasons behind his argument?

3. Why does Williams quote Jim Kehoe?

4. Why, according to Williams, are the South and other provincial places especially susceptible to "the disease of bigtime-ism"?

5. What in the past has been the solution to the excesses of big-time athletics?

6. What is Williams' solution? How is this solution presented to the reader?

7. In Williams' opinion, what is the worst abuse in college athletics?

8. What tactic does Williams take in paragraphs 18–20? Is it effective?

9. Why does Williams refer to the college president, George Hanford, and to coach Art Guepe in paragraphs 21 and 22?

10. Describe the pattern of organization of Williams' essay. What parts can you identify?

11. Evaluate Williams' argument in terms of its strengths and weaknesses. Is he persuasive?

Vocabulary

anguished (1)   adulation (6)   preferential (11)
lamentable (4)   bastions (6)   myriad (13)
tangible (5)   rampant (7)   exalt (19)
parity (6)   zealous (10)

Suggestions for Writing

1. Write an essay in which you argue against Williams' thesis and/or any part of his solution.

2. Write an essay in which you suggest a major change in some policy at your college. Consider using Williams' pattern of organization as your model.

3. Investigate the athletic program at your school; then write an essay explaining your attitude toward this program. What changes, if any, would you make?

How to Make People Smaller Than They Are
Norman Cousins

Norman Cousins was the editor of *Saturday Review* for over thirty-five years (1940–71 and 1973–77). His many books include *The Improbable Triumvirate* (1972), *The Celebration of Life* (1974), and *The Quest for Immortality* (1974). This essay was published as an editorial in *Saturday Review* in 1978.

1   Three months ago in this space we wrote about the costly retreat from the humanities on all the levels of American education. Since that time, we have had occasion to visit a number of campuses and have been troubled to find that the general situation is even more serious than we had thought. It has become apparent to us that one of the biggest problems confronting American education today is the increasing vocationalization of our colleges and universities. Throughout the country, schools are under pressure to become job-training centers and employment agencies.

2   The pressure comes mainly from two sources. One is the growing determination of many citizens to reduce taxes—understandable and even commendable in itself, but irrational and irresponsible when connected to the reduction or dismantling of vital public services. The second source of pressure comes from parents and students who tend to scorn courses of study that do not teach people how to become attractive to employers in a rapidly tightening job market.

3   It is absurd to believe that the development of skills does not also require the systematic development of the human mind. Education is being measured more by the size of the benefits the individual can extract from society than by the extent to which the individual can come into possession of his or her full powers. The result is that the life-giving juices are in danger of being drained out of education.

4   Emphasis on "practicalities" is being characterized by the subordination of words to numbers. History is seen not as essential experience to be transmitted to new generations, but as abstractions that carry dank odors. Art is regarded as something that calls for indulgence or patronage and that has no place among the practical realities. Political science is viewed more as a specialized subject for people who want to go into politics than as an opportunity for citizens to develop a knowledgeable relationship with the systems by which human societies are governed. Finally, literature and philosophy are assigned the role of add-ons—intellectual adornments that have nothing to do with "genuine" education.

5   Instead of trying to shrink the liberal arts, the American people ought

to be putting pressure on colleges and universities to increase the ratio of the humanities to the sciences. Most serious studies of medical-school curricula in recent years have called attention to the stark gaps in the liberal education of medical students. The experts agree that the schools shouldn't leave it up to students to close those gaps.

6   We must not make it appear, however, that nothing is being done. In the past decade, the National Endowment for the Humanities has been a prime mover in infusing the liberal arts into medical education and other specialized schools. During this past year alone, NEH has given 108 grants to medical schools and research organizations in the areas of ethics and human values. Some medical schools, like the one at Pennsylvania State University, have led the way in both the number and the depth of courses offered in the humanities. Penn State has been especially innovative in weaving literature and philosophy into the full medical course of study. It is ironical that the pressure against the humanities should be manifesting itself at precisely the time when so many medical schools are at long last moving in this direction.

7   The irony of the emphasis being placed on careers is that nothing is more valuable for anyone who has had a professional or vocational education than to be able to deal with abstractions or complexities, or to feel comfortable with subtleties of thought or language, or to think sequentially. The doctor who knows only disease is at a disadvantage alongside the doctor who knows at least as much about people as he does about pathological organisms. The lawyer who argues in court from a narrow legal base is no match for the lawyer who can connect legal precedents to historical experience and who employs wide-ranging intellectual resources. The business executive whose competence in general management is bolstered by an artistic ability to deal with people is of prime value to his company. For the technologist, the engineering of consent can be just as important as the engineering of moving parts. In all these respects, the liberal arts have much to offer. Just in terms of career preparation, therefore, a student is shortchanging himself by shortcutting the humanities.

8   But even if it could be demonstrated that the humanities contribute nothing directly to a job, they would still be an essential part of the educational equipment of any person who wants to come to terms with life. The humanities would be expendable only if human beings didn't have to make decisions that affect their lives and the lives of others; if the human past never existed or had nothing to tell us about the present; if thought processes were irrelevant to the achievement of purpose; if creativity was beyond the human mind and had nothing to do with the joy of living; if human relationships were random aspects of life; if human beings never had to cope with panic or pain, or if they never had to anticipate the connection between cause and effect; if all the mysteries

of mind and nature were fully plumbed; and if no special demands arose from the accident of being born a human being instead of a hen or a hog.

9   Finally, there would be good reason to eliminate the humanities if a free society were not absolutely dependent on a functioning citizenry. If the main purpose of a university is job training, then the underlying philosophy of our government has little meaning. The debates that went into the making of American society concerned not just institutions or governing principles but the capacity of humans to sustain those institutions. Whatever the disagreements were over other issues at the American Constitutional Convention, the fundamental question sensed by everyone, a question that lay over the entire assembly, was whether the people themselves would understand what it meant to hold the ultimate power of society, and whether they had enough of a sense of history and destiny to know where they had been and where they ought to be going.

10   Jefferson was prouder of having been the founder of the University of Virginia than of having been President of the United States. He knew that the educated and developed mind was the best assurance that a political system could be made to work—a system based on the informed consent of the governed. If this idea fails, then all the saved tax dollars in the world will not be enough to prevent the nation from turning on itself.

How to Make People Smaller Than They Are

Questions on Content, Style, and Structure

1. What problem does Cousins present in paragraph 1?
2. What is his attitude toward this problem? What danger does he see?
3. What are the sources of this problem?
4. What is the purpose of paragraph 4?
5. What action does Cousins advocate?
6. What irony does Cousins point out in paragraph 6? Why is this paragraph included in this essay?
7. What is the topic sentence in paragraph 7? How is the rest of the paragraph developed? Is the paragraph effective?
8. What is the purpose of the last sentence in paragraph 7?
9. Summarize Cousins' main arguments for studying the humanities.
10. Describe the construction of the second sentence in paragraph 8. Why does Cousins use one long sentence instead of a series of shorter ones?
11. What is the relationship between government and education?
12. Why does Cousins refer to Jefferson in paragraph 10?

13. How does Cousins conclude his essay? Is it an effective ending?
14. Overall, how persuasive is Cousins' argument?

Vocabulary

vocationalization (1)   infusing (6)   pathological (7)
dismantling (2)   innovative (6)   bolstered (7)
dank (4)   subtleties (7)   plumbed (8)
indulgence (4)   sequentially (7)

Suggestions for Writing

1. Write an essay in which you defend the "increasing vocationalization of our colleges."
2. Write an essay in which you criticize or defend the requirements for the college degree in your major.
3. Interview premed, business, and liberal arts advisors on your campus. Write an essay comparing/contrasting their views on the role of humanities in their students' education.

When I Heard the Learn'd Astronomer
Walt Whitman

Walt Whitman was a nineteenth-century American poet whose free-verse poems broke with conventional style and subject matter. Some of his most famous poems, including "Song of Myself," "Crossing Brooklyn Ferry," and "Passage to India," extol the virtues of the common people and stress their unity with a universal oversoul. This poem was published in 1865.

When I heard the learn'd astronomer;
When the proofs, the figures, were ranged in columns before me;
When I was shown the charts and the diagrams, to add, divide, and
    measure them;
4 When I, sitting, heard the astronomer, where he lectured with much
    applause in the lecture-room,
How soon, unaccountable, I became tired and sick;
Till rising and gliding out, I wander'd off by myself,
In the mystical moist night-air, and from time to time,
8 Look'd up in perfect silence at the stars.

When I Heard the Learn'd Astronomer

Questions on Content, Style, and Structure

1. Who is the speaker of this poem?
2. In lines 1–4, where is the speaker? What is he/she listening to?
3. How does the speaker react to the lecture?
4. How do lines 5–8 differ in content from lines 1–4?
5. Why does the speaker stare at the stars?
6. Why do lines 1–4 contain repetition?
7. Why did the poet make lines 3 and 4 longer than the lines that follow them?
8. Characterize the sounds in "rising and gliding," "mystical moist," "time to time," and "silence at the stars." Why are these sounds included in lines 6–8? Why are there no similar groupings in lines 1–4?
9. Does this poem have a set rhythm or rhyme scheme?
10. How is this poem an example of development by contrast?

Vocabulary

ranged (l. 2)
unaccountable (l. 5)

Suggestions for Writing

1. Write an essay contrasting your reactions to an experience you first heard or read about and the actual event as you participated in it. (For example, was your first date or first day at college what you thought it would be?)

2. Write an essay in which you describe an interest you developed after hearing about the subject in a class.

3. Write an essay in which you compare/contrast two attitudes towards a particular class or teacher.

Section 5

Life Confronts Death

38 Who Saw Murder Didn't Call the Police
Martin Gansburg

Martin Gansburg has been a reporter and editor for *The New York Times* since 1942 and has also written for such magazines as *Diplomat*, *Catholic Digest*, and *Facts*. This news story was published in *The New York Times* in 1964, shortly after the murder of Kitty Genovese.

1   For more than half an hour 38 respectable, law-abiding citizens in Queens watched a killer stalk and stab a woman in three separate attacks in Kew Gardens.

2   Twice the sound of their voices and the sudden glow of their bedroom lights interrupted him and frightened him off. Each time he returned, sought her out and stabbed her again. Not one person telephoned the police during the assault; one witness called after the woman was dead.

3   That was two weeks ago today. But Assistant Chief Inspector Frederick M. Lussen, in charge of the borough's detectives and a veteran of 25 years of homicide investigations, is still shocked.

4   He can give a matter-of-fact recitation of many murders. But the Kew Gardens slaying baffles him—not because it is a murder, but because the "good people" failed to call the police.

5   "As we have reconstructed the crime," he said, "the assailant had three chances to kill this woman during a 35-minute period. He returned twice to complete the job. If we had been called when he first attacked, the woman might not be dead now."

6   This is what the police say happened beginning at 3:20 A.M. in the staid, middle-class, tree-lined Austin Street area:

7   Twenty-eight-year-old Catherine Genovese, who was called Kitty by almost everyone in the neighborhood, was returning home from her job as manager of a bar in Hollis. She parked her red Fiat in a lot adjacent to the Kew Gardens Long Island Rail Road Station, facing Mowbray Place. Like many residents of the neighborhood, she had parked there day after day since her arrival from Connecticut a year ago, although the railroad frowns on the practice.

8   She turned off the lights of her car, locked the door and started to walk the 100 feet to the entrance of her apartment at 82–70 Austin Street, which is in a Tudor building, with stores on the first floor and apartments on the second.

9   The entrance to the apartment is in the rear of the building because the front is rented to retail stores. At night the quiet neighborhood is shrouded in the slumbering darkness that marks most residential areas.

10   Miss Genovese noticed a man at the far end of the lot, near a seven-story apartment house at 82–40 Austin Street. She halted. Then, ner-

vously, she headed up Austin Street toward Lefferts Boulevard, where there is a call box to the 102nd Police Precinct in nearby Richmond Hill.

"He Stabbed Me"

11 She got as far as a street light in front of a bookstore before the man grabbed her. She screamed. Lights went on in the 10-story apartment house at 82–67 Austin Street, which faces the bookstore. Windows slid open and voices punctuated the early-morning stillness.

12 Miss Genovese screamed: "Oh, my God, he stabbed me! Please help me! Please help me!"

13 From one of the upper windows in the apartment house, a man called down: "Let that girl alone!"

14 The assailant looked up at him, shrugged and walked down Austin Street toward a white sedan parked a short distance away. Miss Genovese struggled to her feet.

15 Lights went out. The killer returned to Miss Genovese, now trying to make her way around the side of the building by the parking lot to get to her apartment. The assailant stabbed her again.

16 "I'm dying!" she shrieked. "I'm dying!"

A City Bus Passed

17 Windows were opened again, and lights went on in many apartments. The assailant got into his car and drove away. Miss Genovese staggered to her feet. A city bus, Q-10, the Lefferts Boulevard line to Kennedy International Airport, passed. It was 3:35 A.M.

18 The assailant returned. By then, Miss Genovese had crawled to the back of the building, where the freshly painted brown doors to the apartment house held out hope of safety. The killer tried the first door; she wasn't there. At the second door, 82–62 Austin Street, he saw her slumped on the floor at the foot of the stairs. He stabbed her a third time—fatally.

19 It was 3:50 by the time the police received their first call, from a man who was a neighbor of Miss Genovese. In two minutes they were at the scene. The neighbor, a 70-year-old woman and another woman were the only persons on the street. Nobody else came forward.

20 The man explained that he had called the police after much deliberation. He had phoned a friend in Nassau County for advice and then he had crossed the roof of the building to the apartment of the elderly woman to get her to make the call.

21 "I didn't want to get involved," he sheepishly told the police.

Suspect Is Arrested

22 Six days later, the police arrested Winston Moseley, a 29-year-old business-machine operator, and charged him with homicide. Moseley had no previous record. He is married, has two children and owns a home at

133-19 Sutter Avenue, South Ozone Park, Queens. On Wednesday, a court committed him to Kings County Hospital for psychiatric observation.

23   When questioned by the police, Moseley also said that he had slain Mrs. Annie May Johnson, 24, of 146-12 133d Avenue, Jamaica, on Feb. 29 and Barbara Kralik, 15, of 174-17 140th Avenue, Springfield Gardens, last July. In the Kralik case, the police are holding Alvin L. Mitchell, who is said to have confessed that slaying.

24   The police stressed how simple it would have been to have gotten in touch with them. "A phone call," said one of the detectives, "would have done it." The police may be reached by dialing "0" for operator or SPring 7-3100. . . .

25   Today witnesses from the neighborhood, which is made up of one-family homes in the $35,000 to $60,000 range with the exception of the two apartment houses near the railroad station, find it difficult to explain why they didn't call the police. . . .

26   A housewife, knowingly if quite casually, said, "We thought it was a lover's quarrel." A husband and wife both said, "Frankly, we were afraid." They seemed aware of the fact that events might have been different. A distraught woman, wiping her hands in her apron, said, "I didn't want my husband to get involved."

27   One couple, now willing to talk about that night, said they heard the first screams. The husband looked thoughtfully at the bookstore where the killer first grabbed Miss Genovese.

28   "We went to the window to see what was happening," he said, "but the light from our bedroom made it difficult to see the street." The wife, still apprehensive, added: "I put out the light and we were able to see better."

29   Asked why they hadn't called the police, she shrugged and replied: "I don't know."

30   A man peeked out from a slight opening in the doorway to his apartment and rattled off an account of the killer's second attack. Why hadn't he called the police at the time? "I was tired," he said without emotion. "I went back to bed."

31   It was 4:25 A.M. when the ambulance arrived to take the body of Miss Genovese. It drove off. "Then," a solemn police detective said, "the people came out."

38 Who Saw Murder Didn't Call the Police

Questions on Content, Style, and Structure

1. This article originally appeared in a newspaper, *The New York Times*. In what ways do paragraphs in newspaper stories differ from paragraphs in essays?

2. Describe the effect of the first paragraph; how does it attract the reader's attention?

3. What is the function of the first five paragraphs? of paragraph 6? What happens between the first five paragraphs and the rest of the story?

4. Why does Gansberg put quotation marks around "good people" in paragraph 4?

5. Evaluate Gansberg's use of objective reporting. Is he always objective?

6. What transition devices are used to move the story along? Cite some examples.

7. Analyze Gansberg's use of dialogue. How effective is it? Why?

8. How does Gansberg realistically recreate the scene of the murder?

9. In addition to reporting a news story about murder, what was Gansberg's purpose in writing this article?

10. Would Gansberg's point have been more persuasive had he written an argumentative essay rather than this narrative? Why/why not?

11. Characterize the tone throughout the article. Is it appropriate? Why/why not?

12. Evaluate the conclusion of the article. Why did Gansberg choose the words of the detective for his ending?

Vocabulary

borough (4)   shrouded (9)
recitation (4)   deliberation (20)
baffles (4)   distraught (26)
staid (6)   apprehensive (28)
adjacent (7)

Suggestions for Writing

1. Write a narrative, using an event from your experience, to illustrate people's lack of involvement with others.

2. Write an editorial based on the Kitty Genovese incident.

3. Write an essay detailing the precautions one should take to avoid becoming the victim of an attacker.

To Bid the World Farewell
Jessica Mitford

Jessica Mitford was born in England but is now an American citizen. She has written many articles and books, including *Daughters and Rebels* (1960), *The Trial of Dr. Spock* (1969), *Kind and Usual Punishment* (1973), *A Fine Old Conflict* (1977), and *Poison Penmanship* (1979). This essay is a part of her best-selling exposé *The American Way of Death* (1963).

1   Embalming is indeed a most extraordinary procedure, and one must wonder at the docility of Americans who each year pay hundreds of millions of dollars for its perpetuation, blissfully ignorant of what it is all about, what is done, how it is done. Not one in ten thousand has any idea of what actually takes place. Books on the subject are extremely hard to come by. They are not to be found in most libraries or bookshops.

2   In an era when huge television audiences watch surgical operations in the comfort of their living rooms, when, thanks to the animated cartoon, the geography of the digestive system has become familiar territory even to the nursery school set, in a land where the satisfaction of curiosity about almost all matters is a national pastime, the secrecy surrounding embalming can, surely, hardly be attributed to the inherent gruesomeness of the subject. Custom in this regard has within this century suffered a complete reversal. In the early days of American embalming, when it was performed in the home of the deceased, it was almost mandatory for some relative to stay by the embalmer's side and witness the procedure. Today, family members who might wish to be in attendance would certainly be dissuaded by the funeral director. All others, except apprentices, are excluded by law from the preparation room.

3   A close look at what does actually take place may explain in large measure the undertaker's intractable reticence concerning a procedure that has become his major *raison d'être*. Is it possible he fears that public information about embalming might lead patrons to wonder if they really want this service? If the funeral men are loath to discuss the subject outside the trade, the reader may, understandably, be equally loath to go on reading at this point. For those who have the stomach for it, let us part the formaldehyde curtain. . . .

4   The body is first laid out in the undertaker's morgue—or rather, Mr. Jones is reposing in the preparation room—to be readied to bid the world farewell.

5   The preparation room in any of the better funeral establishments has the tiled and sterile look of a surgery, and indeed the embalmer-restorative artist who does his chores there is beginning to adopt the term "dermasurgeon" (appropriately corrupted by some mortician-writ-

ers as "demisurgeon") to describe his calling. His equipment, consisting of scalpels, scissors, augers, forceps, clamps, needles, pumps, tubes, bowls and basins, is crudely imitative of the surgeon's as is his technique, acquired in a nine- or twelve-month post-high-school course in an embalming school. He is supplied by an advanced chemical industry with a bewildering array of fluids, sprays, pastes, oils, powders, creams, to fix or soften tissue, shrink or distend it as needed, dry it here, restore the moisture there. There are cosmetics, waxes and paints to fill and cover features, even plaster of Paris to replace entire limbs. There are ingenious aids to prop and stabilize the cadaver: a Vari-Pose Head Rest, the Edwards Arm and Hand Positioner, the Repose Block (to support the shoulders during the embalming), and the Throop Foot Positioner, which resembles an old-fashioned stocks.

6   Mr. John H. Eckels, president of the Eckels College of Mortuary Science, thus describes the first part of the embalming procedure: "In the hands of a skilled practitioner, this work may be done in a comparatively short time and without mutilating the body other than by slight incision—so slight that it scarcely would cause serious inconvenience if made upon a living person. It is necessary to remove the blood, and doing this not only helps in the disinfecting, but removes the principal cause of disfigurements due to discoloration."

7   Another textbook discusses the all-important time element: "The earlier this is done, the better, for every hour that elapses between death and embalming will add to the problems and complications encountered...." Just how soon should one get going on the embalming? The author tells us, "On the basis of such scanty information made available to this profession through its rudimentary and haphazard system of technical research, we must conclude that the best results are to be obtained if the subject is embalmed before life is completely extinct—that is, before cellular death has occurred. In the average case, this would mean within an hour after somatic death." For those who feel that there is something a little rudimentary, not to say haphazard, about this advice, a comforting thought is offered by another writer. Speaking of fears entertained in early days of premature burial, he points out, "One of the effects of embalming by chemical injection, however, has been to dispel fears of live burial." How true; once the blood is removed, chances of live burial are indeed remote.

8   To return to Mr. Jones, the blood is drained out through the veins and replaced by embalming fluid pumped in through the arteries. As noted in *The Principles and Practices of Embalming*, "every operator has a favorite injection and drainage point—a fact which becomes a handicap only if he fails or refuses to forsake his favorites when conditions demand it." Typical favorites are the carotid artery, femoral artery, jugular vein, subclavian vein. There are various choices of embalming fluid. If Flextone is used, it will produce a "mild flexible rigidity. The skin retains a velvety softness, the tissues are rubbery and pliable. Ideal for women and

children." It may be blended with B. and G. Products Company's Lyf-Lyk tint, which is guaranteed to reproduce "nature's own skin texture ... the velvety appearance of living tissue." Suntone comes in three separate tints: Suntan; Special Cosmetic Tint, a pink shade "especially indicated for young female subjects"; and Regular Cosmetic Tint, moderately pink.

9   About three to six gallons of a dyed and perfumed solution of formaldehyde, glycerin, borax, phenol, alcohol and water is soon circulating through Mr. Jones, whose mouth has been sewn together with a "needle directed upward between the upper lip and gum and brought out through the left nostril," with the corners raised slightly "for a more pleasant expression." If he should be bucktoothed, his teeth are cleaned with Bon Ami and coated with colorless nail polish. His eyes, meanwhile, are closed with flesh-tinted eye caps and eye cement.

10   The next step is to have at Mr. Jones with a thing called a trocar. This is a long, hollow needle attached to a tube. It is jabbed into the abdomen, poked around the entrails and chest cavity, the contents of which are pumped out and replaced with "cavity fluid." This done, and the hole in the abdomen sewn up, Mr. Jones's face is heavily creamed (to protect the skin from burns which may be caused by leakage of the chemicals), and he is covered with a sheet and left unmolested for a while. But not for long—there is more, much more, in store for him. He has been embalmed, but not yet restored, and the best time to start the restorative work is eight to ten hours after embalming, when the tissues have become firm and dry.

11   The object of all this attention to the corpse, it must be remembered, is to make it presentable for viewing in an attitude of healthy repose. "Our customs require the presentation of our dead in the semblance of normality ... unmarred by the ravages of illness, disease or mutilation," says Mr. J. Sheridan Mayer in his *Restorative Art*. This is rather a large order since few people die in the full bloom of health, unravaged by illness and unmarked by some disfigurement. The funeral industry is equal to the challenge: "In some cases the gruesome appearance of a mutilated or disease-ridden subject may be quite discouraging. The task of restoration may seem impossible and shake the confidence of the embalmer. This is the time for intestinal fortitude and determination. Once the formative work is begun and affected tissues are cleaned or removed, all doubts of success vanish. It is surprising and gratifying to discover the results which may be obtained."

12   The embalmer, having allowed an appropriate interval to elapse, returns to the attack, but now he brings into play the skill and equipment of sculptor and cosmetician. Is a hand missing? Casting one in plaster of Paris is a simple matter. "For replacement purposes, only a cast of the back of the hand is necessary; this is within the ability of the average operator and is quite adequate." If a lip or two, a nose or an ear should be missing, the embalmer has at hand a variety of restorative waxes with

which to model replacements. Pores and skin texture are simulated by stippling with a little brush, and over this cosmetics are laid on. Head off? Decapitation cases are rather routinely handled. Ragged edges are trimmed, and head joined to torso with a series of splints, wires and sutures. It is a good idea to have a little something at the neck—a scarf or high collar—when time for viewing comes. Swollen mouth? Cut out tissue as needed from inside the lips. If too much is removed, the surface contour can easily be restored by padding with cotton. Swollen necks and cheeks are reduced by removing tissue through vertical incisions made down each side of the neck. "When the deceased is casketed, the pillow will hide the suture incisions . . . as an extra precaution against leakage, the suture may be painted with liquid sealer."

13   The opposite condition is more likely to be present itself—that of emaciation. His hypodermic syringe now loaded with massage cream, the embalmer seeks out and fills the hollowed and sunken areas by injection. In this procedure the backs of the hands and fingers and the under-chin area should not be neglected.

14   Positioning the lips is a problem that recurrently challenges the ingenuity of the embalmer. Closed too tightly, they tend to give a stern, even disapproving expression. Ideally, embalmers feel, the lips should give the impression of being ever so slightly parted, the upper lip protruding slightly for a more youthful appearance. This takes some engineering, however, as the lips tend to drift apart. Lip drift can sometimes be remedied by pushing one or two straight pins through the inner margin of the lower lip and then inserting them between the two front upper teeth. If Mr. Jones happens to have no teeth, the pins can just as easily be anchored in his Armstrong Face Former and Denture Replacer. Another method to maintain lip closure is to dislocate the lower jaw, which is then held in its new position by a wire run through holes which have been drilled through the upper and lower jaws at the midline. As the French are fond of saying, *il faut souffrir pour être belle.* *

15   If Mr. Jones has died of jaundice, the embalming fluid will very likely turn him green. Does this deter the embalmer? Not if he has intestinal fortitude. Masking pastes and cosmetics are heavily laid on, burial garments and casket interiors are color-correlated with particular care, and Jones is displayed beneath rose-colored lights. Friends will say, "How *well* he looks." Death by carbon monoxide, on the other hand, can be rather a good thing from the embalmer's viewpoint: "One advantage is the fact that this type of discoloration is an exaggerated form of a natural pink coloration." This is nice because the healthy glow is already present and needs but little attention.

16   The patching and filling completed, Mr. Jones is now shaved, washed and dressed. Cream-based cosmetic, available in pink, flesh, suntan, brunette and blond, is applied to his hands and face, his hair is shampooed

* "One must suffer in order to be beautiful."

and combed (and, in the case of Mrs. Jones, set), his hands manicured. For the horny-handed son of toil special care must be taken; cream should be applied to removed ingrained grime, and the nails cleaned. "If he were not in the habit of having them manicured in life, trimming and shaping is advised for better appearance—never questioned by kin."

17   Jones is now ready for casketing (this is the present participle of the verb "to casket"). In this operation his right shoulder should be depressed slightly "to turn the body a bit to the right and soften the appearance of lying flat on his back." Positioning the hands is a matter of importance, and special rubber positioning blocks may be used. The hands should be cupped slightly for a more lifelike, relaxed appearance. Proper placement of the body requires a delicate sense of balance. It should lie as high as possible in the casket, yet not so high that the lid, when lowered, will hit the nose. On the other hand, we are cautioned, placing the body too low "creates the impression that the body is in a box."

18   Jones is next wheeled into the appointed slumber room where a few last touches may be added—his favorite pipe placed in his hand or, if he was a great reader, a book propped into position. (In the case of little Master Jones a Teddy bear may be clutched.) Here he will hold open house for a few days, visiting hours 10 A.M. to 9 P.M.

To Bid the World Farewell

Questions on Content, Style, and Structure

1. By studying the first three paragraphs, summarize both Mitford's reason for explaining the embalming process and her attitude toward undertakers who wish to keep their patrons uninformed about this procedure.

2. Mitford's essay is developed by *process analysis*; that is, it explains what steps must be taken to complete an operation or procedure. Process essays may be identified as either *directional* or *informative*. A directional process tells the reader how to do or make something; an informative process describes the steps by which someone other than the reader does or makes something, or how something was done or made in the past. Is Mitford's essay a directional or informative process analysis?

3. Does this process flow smoothly from step to step? Identify the transition devices connecting the paragraphs.

4. Does Mitford use enough specific details to help you visualize each step as it occurs? Point out examples of details which create vivid descriptions by appealing to your sense of sight, smell, or touch.

5. How does the technique of using the hypothetical "Mr. Jones" make the explanation of the process more effective? Why didn't Mitford simply refer to "the corpse" or "a body" throughout her essay?

6. What is Mitford's general attitude toward this procedure? the overall tone of the essay? Study Mitford's choice of words and then identify the tone in each of the following passages:

> "The next step is to have at Mr. Jones with a thing called a trocar." (10)
>
> "The embalmer, having allowed an appropriate interval to elapse, returns to the attack. . . ." (12)
>
> "Friends will say, 'How *well* he looks.' " (15)
>
> "On the other hand, we are cautioned, placing the body too low 'creates the impression that the body is in a box.' " (17)
>
> "Here he will hold open house for a few days, visiting hours 10 A.M. to 9 P.M." (18)

What other words and passages reveal Mitford's attitude and tone?

7. Why does Mitford repeatedly quote various undertakers and textbooks on the embalming and restorative process (" 'needle directed upward between the upper lip and gum and brought out through the left nostril' ")? Why is the quote in paragraph 7 that begins, ' 'On the basis of such scanty information made available to this profession through its rudimentary and haphazard system of technical research . . .' " particularly effective in emphasizing Mitford's attitude toward the funeral industry?

8. What does Mitford gain by quoting euphemisms (dandified terms replacing more offensive words) used by the funeral business, such as "dermasurgeon," "Repose Block," and "slumber room"?

9. What are the connotations of the words "jabbed," "poked," and "left unmolested" in paragraph 10? What effect is Mitford trying to produce with the series of questions (such as "Head off?") in paragraph 12?

10. Evaluate Mitford's last sentence. Does it successfully sum up the author's attitude and conclude the essay?

Vocabulary

docility (1)	*raison d'être* (3)	dispel (7)
inherent (2)	ingenious (5)	pliable (8)
intractable (3)	cadaver (5)	semblance (11)
reticence (3)	somatic (7)	stippling (12)

Suggestions for Writing

1. By supplying information about the embalming process, did Mitford change your attitude toward this procedure or toward the funeral industry? Should we subject our dead to this process? Are there advantages Mitford fails to mention? Write an essay defending your position.

2. Consider other American customs, such as the traditional wedding or the celebration of Christmas. Are there any rituals you disapprove of? If so, write an essay explaining your criticisms, making your case as detailed and vivid as Mitford's.

3. Write a process essay in which you leave step-by-step instructions for carrying out your own funeral. Detail the location, music, speakers, and events so that the appropriate mood will be set.

The Discus Thrower
Richard Selzer

Richard Selzer teaches surgery at Yale Medical School and has contributed both stories and essays to a number of magazines. He has published a collection of short stories, *Rituals of Surgery* (1974), and a collection of essays, *Mortal Lessons* (1977), many of which concern his life in medicine. This essay was published in *Harper's* in 1977.

1   I spy on my patients. Ought not a doctor to observe his patients by any means and from any stance, that he might the more fully assemble evidence? So I stand in the doorways of hospital rooms and gaze. Oh, it is not all that furtive an act. Those in bed need only look up to discover me. But they never do.

2   From the doorway of Room 542 the man in the bed seems deeply tanned. Blue eyes and close-cropped white hair give him the appearance of vigor and good health. But I know that his skin is not brown from the sun. It is rusted, rather, in the last stage of containing the vile repose within. And the blue eyes are frosted, looking inward like the windows of a snowbound cottage. This man is blind. This man is also legless— the right leg missing from midthigh down, the left from just below the knee. It gives him the look of a bonsai, roots and branches pruned into the dwarfed facsimile of a great tree.

3   Propped on pillows, he cups his right thigh in both hands. Now and then he shakes his head as though acknowledging the intensity of his suffering. In all of this he makes no sound. Is he mute as well as blind?

4   The room in which he dwells is empty of all possessions—no get-well cards, small, private caches of food, day-old flowers, slippers, all the usual kickshaws of the sickroom. There is only the bed, a chair, a nightstand, and a tray on wheels that can be swung across his lap for meals.

5   "What time is it?" he asks.

6   "Three o'clock."

7   "Morning or afternoon?"

8   "Afternoon."

9   He is silent. There is nothing else he wants to know.

10   "How are you?" I say.

11   "Who is it?" he asks.

12   "It's the doctor. How do you feel?"

13   He does not answer right away.

14   "Feel?" he says.

15   "I hope you feel better," I say.

16   I press the button at the side of the bed.

17   "Down you go," I say.

18   "Yes, down," he says.

19   He falls back upon the bed awkwardly. His stumps, unweighted by legs and feet, rise in the air, presenting themselves. I unwrap the bandages from the stumps, and begin to cut away the black scabs and the dead, glazed fat with scissors and forceps. A shard of white bone comes loose. I pick it away. I wash the wounds with disinfectant and redress the stumps. All this while, he does not speak. What is he thinking behind those lids that do not blink? Is he remembering a time when he was whole? Does he dream of feet? Of when his body was not a rotting log?

20   He lies solid and inert. In spite of everything, he remains impressive, as though he were a sailor standing athwart a slanting deck.

21   "Anything more I can do for you?" I ask.

22   For a long moment he is silent.

23   "Yes," he says at last and without the least irony. "You can bring me a pair of shoes."

24   In the corridor, the head nurse is waiting for me.

25   "We have to do something about him," she says. "Every morning he orders scrambled eggs for breakfast, and, instead of eating them, he picks up the plate and throws it against the wall."

26   "Throws his plate?"

27   "Nasty. That's what he is. No wonder his family doesn't come to visit. They probably can't stand him any more than we can."

28   She is waiting for me to do something.

29   "Well?"

30   "We'll see," I say.

31   The next morning I am waiting in the corridor when the kitchen delivers his breakfast. I watch the aide place the tray on the stand and swing it across his lap. She presses the button to raise the head of the bed. Then she leaves.

32   In time the man reaches to find the rim of the tray, then on to find the dome of the covered dish. He lifts off the cover and places it on the stand. He fingers across the plate until he probes the eggs. He lifts the plate in both hands, sets it on the palm of his right hand, centers it, balances it. He hefts it up and down slightly, getting the feel of it. Abruptly, he draws back his right arm as far as he can.

33   There is the crack of the plate breaking against the wall at the foot of his bed and the small wet sound of the scrambled eggs dropping to the floor.

34   And then he laughs. It is a sound you have never heard. It is something new under the sun. It could cure cancer.

35   Out in the corridor, the eyes of the head nurse narrow.

36   "Laughed, did he?"

37   She writes something down on her clipboard.

38   A second aide arrives, brings a second breakfast tray, puts it on the nightstand, out of his reach. She looks over at me shaking her head and making her mouth go. I see that we are to be accomplices.

39   "I've got to feed you," she says to the man.

40   "Oh, no you don't," the man says.

41   "Oh, yes I do," the aide says, "after the way you just did. Nurse says so."

42   "Get me my shoes," the man says.

43   "Here's oatmeal," the aide says. "Open." And she touches the spoon to his lower lip.

44   "I ordered scrambled eggs," says the man.

45   "That's right," the aide says.

46   I step forward.

47   "Is there anything I can do?" I say.

48   "Who are you?" the man asks.

49   In the evening I go once more to that ward to make my rounds. The head nurse reports to me that Room 542 is deceased. She has discovered this quite by accident, she says. No, there had been no sound. Nothing. It's a blessing, she says.

50   I go into his room, a spy looking for secrets. He is still there in his bed. His face is relaxed, grave, dignified. After a while, I turn to leave. My gaze sweeps the wall at the foot of the bed, and I see the place where it has been repeatedly washed, where the wall looks very clean and very white.

The Discus Thrower

Questions on Content, Style, and Structure

1. How does Selzer establish the story's point of view?

2. Why does the patient throw his eggs on the wall each day? Why does he laugh?

3. Why does the patient repeatedly call for his shoes?

4. What is Selzer's attitude toward his patient? How do you know? What is the attitude of the head nurse?

5. What is Selzer's point in telling this story? Why doesn't he "do something" about the patient, as the nurse wants?

6. Why does Selzer use dialogue in some places rather than description?

7. What is the tone of this essay? Study the sentences in the essay. What effect does their length and construction have on the general tone?

8. Point out several examples of metaphor and simile. What does each of these add to the essay's effectiveness?

9. Why does Selzer end his essay by referring to the clean wall? Is it an effective conclusion? Why/why not?

10. Selzer's subtitle for this essay was "Do Not Go Gentle," a reference to "Do Not Go Gentle into that Good Night," a poem by Dylan Thomas. Find a copy of the poem and discover why Selzer selected his subtitle.

Vocabulary

furtive (1)   kickshaws (4)
vile (2)   shard (19)
repose (2)   inert (20)
facsimile (2)   athwart (20)
caches (4)   irony (23)

Suggestions for Writing

1. If you knew you had only a few months (or days) to live, how would you spend your time? Be specific in your essay.

2. Consider the death of a person you have known. Write an essay describing one way this death has affected you or your attitude toward dying.

3. Write a research paper on hospices for the terminally ill. If there is one in your area, investigate the services it offers.

The Right to Die
Norman Cousins

Norman Cousins served as editor of *Saturday Review* for over thirty-five years (1940–71 and 1973–77). His many books include *The Improbable Triumvirate* (1972), *The Celebration of Life* (1974), and *The Quest for Immortality* (1974). This essay was published as an editorial in *Saturday Review* in 1975.

1 The world of religion and philosophy was shocked recently when Henry P. Van Dusen and his wife ended their lives by their own hands. Dr. Van Dusen had been president of Union Theological Seminary; for more than

a quarter-century he had been one of the luminous names in Protestant theology. He enjoyed world status as a spiritual leader. News of the self-inflicted death of the Van Dusens, therefore, was profoundly disturbing to all those who attach a moral stigma to suicide and regard it as a violation of God's laws.

2   Dr. Van Dusen had anticipated this reaction. He and his wife left behind a letter that may have historic significance. It was very brief, but the essential point it made is now being widely discussed by theologians and could represent the beginning of a reconsideration of traditional religious attitudes toward self-inflicted death. The letter raised a moral issue: does an individual have the obligation to go on living even when the beauty and meaning and power of life are gone?

3   Henry and Elizabeth Van Dusen had lived full lives. In recent years, they had become increasingly ill, requiring almost continual medical care. Their infirmities were worsening, and they realized they would soon become completely dependent for even the most elementary needs and functions. Under these circumstances, little dignity would have been left in life. They didn't like the idea of taking up space in a world with too many mouths and too little food. They believed it was a misuse of medical science to keep them technically alive.

4   They therefore believed they had the right to decide when to die. In making that decision, they weren't turning against life as the highest value; what they were turning against was the notion that there were no circumstances under which life should be discontinued.

5   An important aspect of human uniqueness is the power of free will. In his books and lectures, Dr. Van Dusen frequently spoke about the exercise of this uniqueness. The fact that he used his free will to prevent life from becoming a caricature of itself was completely in character. In their letter, the Van Dusens sought to convince family and friends that they were not acting solely out of despair or pain.

6   The use of free will to put an end to one's life finds no sanction in the theology to which Pitney Van Dusen was committed. Suicide symbolizes discontinuity; religion symbolizes continuity, represented at its quintessence by the concept of the immortal soul. Human logic finds it almost impossible to come to terms with the concept of nonexistence. In religion, the human mind finds a larger dimension and is relieved of the ordeal of a confrontation with non-existence.

7   Even without respect to religion, the idea of suicide has been abhorrent throughout history. Some societies have imposed severe penalties on the families of suicides in the hope that the individual who sees no reason to continue his existence may be deterred by the stigma his self-destruction would inflict on loved ones. Other societies have enacted laws prohibiting suicide on the grounds that it is murder. The enforcement of such laws, of course, has been an exercise in futility.

8   Customs and attitudes, like individuals themselves, are largely shaped by the surrounding environment. In today's world, life can be prolonged by science far beyond meaning or sensibility. Under these circumstances,

individuals who feel they have nothing more to give to life, or to receive from it, need not be applauded, but they can be spared our condemnation.

9   The general reaction to suicide is bound to change as people come to understand that it may be a denial, not an assertion, of moral or religious ethics to allow life to be extended without regard to decency or pride. What moral or religious purpose is celebrated by the annihilation of the human spirit in the triumphant act of keeping the body alive? Why are so many people more readily appalled by an unnatural form of dying than by an unnatural form of living?

10   "Nowadays," the Van Dusens wrote in their last letter, "it is difficult to die. We feel that this way we are taking will become more usual and acceptable as the years pass.

11   "Of course, the thought of our children and our grandchildren makes us sad, but we still feel that this is the best way and the right way to go. We are both increasingly weak and unwell and who would want to die in a nursing home?

12   "We are not afraid to die. . . ."

13   Pitney Van Dusen was admired and respected in life. He can be admired and respected in death. "Suicide," said Goethe, "is an incident in human life which, however much disputed and discussed, demands the sympathy of every man, and in every age must be dealt with anew."

14   Death is not the greatest loss in life. The greatest loss is what dies inside us while we live. The unbearable tragedy is to live without dignity or sensitivity.

The Right to Die

Questions on Content, Style, and Structure

1. Why was it so shocking that the Van Dusens committed suicide?
2. What moral issue did the Van Dusens' letter raise?
3. What is Cousins' attitude toward suicide? Where does this attitude become clear?
4. How does Cousins use the Van Dusens to support his view on suicide?
5. How has suicide been regarded throughout history?
6. What change in attitude toward suicide does Cousins foresee? Why?
7. What does Cousins gain by quoting from the Van Dusens' letter?
8. Why does Cousins quote the philosopher Goethe?
9. According to Cousins, what is the "greatest loss in life"?
10. Evaluate Cousins' diction. Why, for example, does he use such phrases as "technically alive" (paragraph 3) and "prevent life from becoming a caricature of itself" (paragraph 5)?

Vocabulary

luminous (1)	sanction (6)	sensibility (8)
stigma (1)	continuity (6)	annihilation (9)
infirmities (3)	quintessence (6)	appalled (9)
caricature (5)	abhorrent (7)	

Suggestions for Writing

1. Do you agree that suicidal people should not be restrained? Write an essay defending your position.

2. Most colleges have a suicide prevention or mental health center of some kind. Contact your center and write an essay on the services they offer. Do you agree with their attitude toward suicidal people?

3. Write an essay in support of or in opposition to Cousins' statement that "Death is not the greatest loss in life."

A Hanging
George Orwell

George Orwell is the pseudonym of Eric Blair, well-known British novelist and essayist. Two of his most popular books are *Animal Farm* (1945), a political satire, and *1984* (1949), a novel depicting life in a totalitarian society under the watchful eye of "Big Brother." This narrative is included in *Shooting an Elephant and Other Essays* (1950).

1   It was in Burma, a sodden morning of the rains. A sickly light, like yellow tinfoil, was slanting over the high walls into the jail yard. We were waiting outside the condemned cells, a row of sheds fronted with double bars, like small animal cages. Each cell measured about ten feet by ten and was quite bare within except for a plank bed and a pot for drinking water. In some of them brown silent men were squatting at the inner bars, with their blankets draped around them. These were the condemned men, due to be hanged within the next week or two.

2   One prisoner had been brought out of his cell. He was a Hindu, a puny wisp of a man, with a shaven head and vague liquid eyes. He had a thick, sprouting moustache, absurdly too big for his body, rather like the moustache of a comic man on the films. Six tall Indian warders[1] were guarding

---

[1] *Warder* is the British word for a prison guard.

him and getting him ready for the gallows. Two of them stood by with rifles and fixed bayonets, while the others handcuffed him, passed a chain through his handcuffs and fixed it to their belts, and lashed his arms tight to his sides. They crowded very close about him, with their hands always on him in a careful, caressing grip, as though all the while feeling him to make sure he was there. It was like men handling a fish which is still alive and may jump back into the water. But he stood quite unresisting, yielding his arms limply to the ropes, as though he hardly noticed what was happening.

3   Eight o'clock struck and a bugle call, desolately thin in the wet air, floated from the distant barracks. The superintendent of the jail, who was standing apart from the rest of us, moodily prodding the gravel with his stick, raised his head at the sound. He was an army doctor, with a grey toothbrush moustache and a gruff voice. "For God's sake hurry up, Francis," he said irritably. "The man ought to have been dead by this time. Aren't you ready yet?"

4   Francis, the head jailer, a fat Dravidian in a white drill suit and gold spectacles, waved his black hand. "Yes sir, yes sir," he bubbled. "All iss satisfactorily prepared. The hangman iss waiting. We shall proceed."

"Well, quick march, then. The prisoners can't get their breakfast till this job's over."

5   We set out for the gallows. Two warders marched on either side of the prisoner, with their rifles at the slope; two others marched close against him, gripping him by arm and shoulder, as though at once pushing and supporting him. The rest of us, magistrates and the like, followed behind. Suddenly, when we had gone ten yards, the procession stopped short without any order or warning. A dreadful thing had happened—a dog, come goodness knows whence, had appeared in the yard. It came bounding among us with a loud volley of barks, and leapt round us wagging its whole body, wild with glee at finding so many human beings together. It was a large woolly dog, half Airedale, half pariah. For a moment it pranced round us, and then, before anyone could stop it, it had made a dash for the prisoner and, jumping up, tried to lick his face. Everyone stood aghast, too taken aback even to grab at the dog.

6   "Who let that bloody brute in here?" said the superintendent angrily. "Catch it, someone!"

7   A warder, detached from the escort, charged clumsily after the dog, but it danced and gambolled just out of his reach, taking everything as part of the game. A young Eurasian jailer picked up a handful of gravel and tried to stone the dog away, but it dodged the stones and came after us again. Its yaps echoed from the jail walls. The prisoner, in the grasp of the two warders, looked on incuriously, as though this was another formality of the hanging. It was several minutes before someone managed to catch the dog. Then we put my handkerchief through its collar and moved off once more, with the dog still straining and whimpering.

8   It was about forty yards to the gallows. I watched the bare brown back of the prisoner marching in front of me. He walked clumsily with his bound arms, but quite steadily, with that bobbing gait of the Indian who never straightens his knees. At each step his muscles slid neatly into place, the lock of hair on his scalp danced up and down, his feet printed themselves on the wet gravel. And once, in spite of the men who gripped him by each shoulder, he stepped slightly aside to avoid a puddle on the path.

9   It is curious, but till that moment I had never realized what it means to destroy a healthy, conscious man. When I saw the prisoner step aside to avoid the puddle I saw the mystery, the unspeakable wrongness, of cutting a life short when it is in full tide. This man was not dying, he was alive just as we are alive. All the organs of his body were working—bowels digesting food, skin renewing itself, nails growing, tissues forming—all toiling away in solemn foolery. His nails would still be growing when he stood on the drop, when he was falling through the air with a tenth-of-a-second to live. His eyes saw the yellow gravel and the grey walls, and his brain still remembered, foresaw, reasoned—reasoned even about puddles. He and we were a party of men walking together, seeing, hearing, feeling, understanding the same world; and in two minutes, with a sudden snap, one of us would be gone—one mind less, one world less.

10   The gallows stood in a small yard, separate from the main grounds of the prison, and overgrown with tall prickly weeds. It was a brick erection like three sides of a shed, with planking on top, and above that two beams and a crossbar with the rope dangling. The hangman, a grey-haired convict in the white uniform of the prison, was waiting beside his machine. He greeted us with a servile crouch as we entered. At a word from Francis the two warders, gripping the prisoner more closely than ever, half led half pushed him to the gallows and helped him clumsily up the ladder. Then the hangman climbed up and fixed the rope round the prisoner's neck.

11   We stood waiting, five yards away. The warders had formed in a rough circle round the gallows. And then, when the noose was fixed, the prisoner began crying out to his god. It was a high, reiterated cry of "Ram! Ram! Ram! Ram!" not urgent and fearful like a prayer or cry for help, but steady, rhythmical, almost like the tolling of a bell. The dog answered the sound with a whine. The hangman, still standing on the gallows, produced a small cotton bag like a flour bag and drew it down over the prisoner's face. But the sound, muffled by the cloth, still persisted, over and over again: "Ram! Ram! Ram! Ram! Ram!"

12   The hangman climbed down and stood ready, holding the lever. Minutes seemed to pass. The steady, muffled crying from the prisoner went on and on. "Ram! Ram! Ram!" never faltering for an instant. The superintendent, his head on his chest, was slowly poking the ground with his stick; perhaps he was counting the cries, allowing the prisoner a fixed

number—fifty, perhaps, or a hundred. Everyone had changed color. The Indians had gone grey like bad coffee, and one or two of the bayonets were wavering. We looked at the lashed, hooded man on the drop, and listened to his cries—each cry another second of life; the same thought was in all our minds: oh, kill him quickly, get it over, stop that abominable noise!

13   Suddenly the superintendent made up his mind. Throwing up his head he made a swift motion with his stick. "Chalo!" he shouted almost fiercely.

14   There was a clanking noise, and then dead silence. The prisoner had vanished, and the rope was twisting on itself. I let go of the dog, and it galloped immediately to the back of the gallows; but when it got there it stopped short, barked, and then retreated into a corner of the yard, where it stood among the weeds, looking timorously out at us. We went round the gallows to inspect the prisoner's body. He was dangling with his toes pointed straight downwards, very slowly revolving, as dead as a stone.

15   The superintendent reached out with his stick and poked the bare brown body; it oscillated slightly. "*He's* all right," said the superintendent. He backed out from under the gallows, and blew out a deep breath. The moody look had gone out of his face quite suddenly. He glanced at his wrist-watch. "Eight minutes past eight. Well, that's all for this morning, thank God."

16   The warders unfixed bayonets and marched away. The dog, sobered and conscious of having misbehaved itself, slipped after them. We walked out of the gallows yard, past the condemned cells with their waiting prisoners, into the big central yard of the prison. The convicts, under the command of warders armed with lathis[2], were already receiving their breakfast. They squatted in long rows, each man holding a tin pannikin[3], while two warders with buckets marched round ladling out rice; it seemed quite a homely, jolly scene, after the hanging. An enormous relief had come upon us now that the job was done. One felt an impulse to sing, to break into a run, to snigger. All at once everyone began chattering gaily.

17   The Eurasian boy walking beside me nodded towards the way we had come, with a knowing smile: "Do you know, sir, our friend (he meant the dead man) when he heard his appeal had been dismissed, he pissed on the floor of his cell. From fright. Kindly take one of my cigarettes, sir. Do you not admire my new silver case, sir? From the boxwalah, two rupees eight annas. Classy European style."

18   Several people laughed—at what, nobody seemed certain.

19   Francis was walking by the superintendent, talking garrulously: "Well, sir, all hass passed off with the utmost satisfactoriness. It was all finished—flick! like that. It iss not always so—oah, no! I have known cases

---

[2] *Lathis* is the Anglo-Indian word for a heavy pole or stick often used as a club by police.
[3] A *pannikin* is a small pan.

where the doctor wass obliged to go beneath the gallows and pull the prissoner's legs to ensure decease. Most disagreeable!"

20   "Wriggling about, eh? That's bad," said the superintendent.

21   "Ach, sir, it iss worse when they become refractory! One man, I recall, clung to the bars of hiss cage when we went to take him out. You will scarcely credit, sir, that it took six warders to dislodge him, three pulling at each leg. We reasoned with him. 'My dear fellow,' we said, 'think of all the pain and trouble you are causing to us!' But no, he would not listen! Ach, he wass very troublesome!"

22   I found that I was laughing quite loudly. Everyone was laughing. Even the superintendent grinned in a tolerant way. "You'd better all come out and have a drink," he said quite genially. "I've got a bottle of whisky in the car. We could do with it."

23   We went through the big double gates of the prison into the road. "Pulling at his legs!" exclaimed a Burmese magistrate suddenly, and burst into a loud chuckling. We all began laughing again. At that moment Francis' anecdote seemed extraordinarily funny. We all had a drink together, native and European alike, quite amicably. The dead man was a hundred yards away.

A Hanging

Questions on Content, Style, and Structure

1. What is the point of view in this essay?
2. In paragraph 1 how does Orwell set the mood for this hanging?
3. What is the attitude of the Indian guards toward the prisoner?
4. Why does Orwell include the description of the dog throughout the story?
5. Why does Orwell mention that the prisoner avoided a rain puddle? What thoughts does this small event cause Orwell to have?
6. Contrast Orwell's attitude toward the hanging to that of the superintendent.
7. Why does everyone, including Orwell, laugh at Francis' story?
8. How does Orwell build tension while he moves the story forward?
9. How does Orwell make the scene and its participants vivid to the reader?
10. Point out examples of figurative language you think are especially effective and tell why.
11. Note the use of dialogue; what does it add to the story?
12. How successful is Orwell's conclusion?
13. In this narrative Orwell "shows" rather than "tells." Would an argumentative essay voicing his opinion on capital punishment have been as effective? Why/why not?

Vocabulary

sodden (1)	servile (10)	garrulously (19)
desolately (3)	reiterated (11)	refractory (21)
pariah (5)	timorously (14)	genially (22)
aghast (5)	oscillated (15)	anecdote (23)
gambolled (7)	homely (16)	amicably (23)
incuriously (7)	snigger (16)	

Suggestions for Writing

1. Narrate an event that illustrates one of your strong moral beliefs. Try to make your story as vivid as Orwell's.

2. Some opponents of capital punishment claim that only the poor receive the death penalty while middle- and upper-class criminals receive less severe sentences. Research this claim and other arguments for and against capital punishment; write an essay arguing your side of the controversy.

3. Write an essay analyzing Orwell's use of figurative language and vivid detail. (You may find it helpful to read Orwell's essay "Politics and the English Language" on pages 339–350; does Orwell follow his own advice?)

The Death of the Ball Turret Gunner*
Randall Jarrell

Randall Jarrell was a twentieth-century American poet, critic, and teacher. Volumes of his poetry include *Blood for a Stranger* (1942), *Losses* (1948), and *The Lost World* (1965); criticism is collected in *Poetry and the Age* (1953), *A Sad Heart at the Supermarket* (1962), and *The Third Book of Criticism* (1971). This poem was published in 1945.

From my mother's sleep I fell into the State
And I hunched in its belly till my wet fur froze.
Six miles from earth, loosed from its dream of life,
I woke to black flak and the nightmare fighters.
When I died they washed me out of the turret with a hose.

* "A ball turret was a plexiglass sphere set into the belly of a B–17 or B–42 and inhabited by two .50 caliber machine-guns and one man, a short small man. When this gunner tracked with his machine-guns a fighter attacking his bomber from below, he revolved with the turret; hunched upside-down in his little sphere, he looked like the fetus in the womb. The fighters which attacked him were armed with cannon firing explosive shells. The hose was a steam hose."—Jarrell's note.

The Death of the Ball Turret Gunner

Questions on Content, Style, and Structure

1. Who is speaking in this poem?
2. How did the speaker "fall" into the State? What is meant by "my mother's sleep"?
3. What is the "belly" of the State?
4. Why does the speaker say he woke from "a dream of life"? How are images of sleep and wakefulness being used in this poem?
5. Who is the "they" of the last line?
6. What is the tone of this poem?
7. What is the attitude of the speaker toward death? toward war?
8. Why might have Jarrell chosen to make his poem only five lines long?

Vocabulary

hunched (l. 2)
flak (l. 4)

Suggestions for Writing

1. Many people oppose the idea of a peace-time draft; others argue that an all-volunteer military is an inadequate defense for our country. Write an essay presenting your opinion of this controversy.
2. Read some other war poems, such as Richard Eberhart's "The Fury of Aerial Bombardment," Thomas Hardy's "Channel Firing," Wilfred Owen's "Dulce et Decorum Est," or e. e. cummings' "i sing of olaf glad and big." Select one of these poems and write an essay comparing its attitude toward war to that expressed in "The Death of the Ball Turret Gunner."
3. Imagine that the United States has suddenly entered another war and you have received your draft notice to report in one week. Write an essay describing your reactions and how you would spend the week.

A Good Man Is Hard to Find
Flannery O'Connor

Flannery O'Connor lived almost all of her thirty-nine years in her native Georgia; her many stories and two novels (*Wise Blood*, 1952, and *The Violent Bear It Away*, 1960) reflect her strong southern Catholic heritage as well as her fascination with grotesque characters. This story lends its title to a collection published in 1955.

1   The grandmother didn't want to go to Florida. She wanted to visit some of her connections in east Tennessee and she was seizing at every chance to change Bailey's mind. Bailey was the son she lived with, her only boy. He was sitting on the edge of his chair at the table, bent over the orange sports section of the *Journal*. "Now look here, Bailey," she said, "see here, read this," and she stood with one hand on her thin hip and the other rattling the newspaper at his bald head. "Here this fellow that calls himself The Misfit is aloose from the Federal Pen and headed toward Florida and you read here what it says he did to these people. Just you read it. I wouldn't take my children in any direction with a criminal like that aloose in it. I couldn't answer to my conscience if I did."

2   Bailey didn't look up from his reading so she wheeled around then and faced the children's mother, a young woman in slacks, whose face was as broad and innocent as a cabbage and was tied around with a green head-kerchief that had two points on the top like rabbit's ears. She was sitting on the sofa, feeding the baby his apricots out of a jar. "The children have been to Florida before," the old lady said. "You all ought to take them somewhere else for a change so they would see different parts of the world and be broad. They never have been to east Tennessee."

3   The children's mother didn't seem to hear her but the eight-year-old boy, John Wesley, a stocky child with glasses, said, "If you don't want to go to Florida, why dontcha stay at home?" He and the little girl, June Star, were reading the funny papers on the floor.

4   "She wouldn't stay at home to be queen for a day," June Star said without raising her yellow head.

5   "Yes and what would you do if this fellow, The Misfit, caught you?" the grandmother asked.

6   "I'd smack his face," John Wesley said.

7   "She wouldn't stay at home for a million bucks," June Star said. "Afraid she'd miss something. She has to go everywhere we go."

8   "All right, Miss," the grandmother said. "Just remember that the next time you want me to curl your hair."

9   June Star said her hair was naturally curly.

10   The next morning the grandmother was the first one in the car, ready to go. She had her big black valise that looked like the head of a hippopotamus in one corner, and underneath it she was hiding a basket with Pitty Sing, the cat, in it. She didn't intend for the cat to be left alone in the house for three days because he would miss her too much and she was afraid he might brush against one of the gas burners and accidentally asphyxiate himself. Her son, Bailey, didn't like to arrive at a motel with a cat.

11   She sat in the middle of the back seat with John Wesley and June Star on either side of her. Bailey and the children's mother and the baby sat in front and they left Atlanta at eight forty-five with the mileage on the car at 55890. The grandmother wrote this down because she thought it would be interesting to say how many miles they had been when they got back. It took them twenty minutes to reach the outskirts of the city.

12   The old lady settled herself comfortably, removing her white cotton gloves and putting them up with her purse on the shelf in front of the back window. The children's mother still had on slacks and still had her head tied up in a green kerchief, but the grandmother had on a navy blue straw sailor hat with a bunch of white violets on the brim and a navy blue dress with a small white dot in the print. Her collars and cuffs were white organdy trimmed with lace and at her neckline she had pinned a purple spray of cloth violets containing a sachet. In case of an accident, anyone seeing her dead on the highway would know at once that she was a lady.

13   She said she thought it was going to be a good day for driving, neither too hot nor too cold, and she cautioned Bailey that the speed limit was fifty-five miles an hour and that the patrolmen hid themselves behind billboards and small clumps of trees and sped out after you before you had a chance to slow down. She pointed out interesting details of the scenery: Stone Mountain; the blue granite that in some places came up to both sides of the highway; the brilliant red clay banks slightly streaked with purple; and the various crops that made rows of green lace-work on the ground. The trees were full of silver-white sunlight and the meanest of them sparkled. The children were reading comic magazines and their mother had gone back to sleep.

14   "Let's go through Georgia fast so we won't have to look at it much," John Wesley said.

15   "If I were a little boy," said the grandmother, "I wouldn't talk about my native state that way. Tennessee has the mountains and Georgia has the hills."

16   "Tennessee is just a hillbilly dumping ground," John Wesley said, "and Georgia is a lousy state too."

17   "You said it," June Star said.

18   "In my time," said the grandmother, folding her thin veined fingers, "children were more respectful of their native states and their parents

and everything else. People did right then. Oh look at the cute little pickaninny!" she said and pointed to a Negro child standing in the door of a shack. "Wouldn't that make a picture, now?" she asked and they all turned and looked at the little Negro out of the back window. He waved.

19   "He didn't have any britches on," June Star said.

20   "He probably didn't have any," the grandmother explained. "Little niggers in the country don't have things like we do. If I could paint, I'd paint that picture," she said.

21   The children exchanged comic books.

22   The grandmother offered to hold the baby and the children's mother passed him over the front seat to her. She set him on her knee and bounced him and told him about the things they were passing. She rolled her eyes and screwed up her mouth and stuck her leathery thin face into his smooth bland one. Occasionally he gave her a far-away smile. They passed a large cotton field with five or six graves fenced in the middle of it, like a small island. "Look at the graveyard!" the grandmother said, pointing it out. "That was the old family burying ground. That belonged to the plantation."

23   "Where's the plantation?" John Wesley asked.

24   "Gone With the Wind," said the grandmother. "Ha. Ha."

25   When the children finished all the comic books they had brought, they opened the lunch and ate it. The grandmother ate a peanut butter sandwich and an olive and would not let the children throw the box and the paper napkins out the window. When there was nothing else to do they played a game by choosing a cloud and making the other two guess what shape it suggested. John Wesley took one the shape of a cow and June Star guessed a cow and John Wesley said, no, an automobile, and June Star said he didn't play fair, and they began to slap each other over the grandmother.

26   The grandmother said she would tell them a story if they would keep quiet. When she told a story, she rolled her eyes and waved her head and was very dramatic. She said once when she was a maiden lady she had been courted by a Mr. Edgar Atkins Teagarden from Jasper, Georgia. She said he was a very good-looking man and a gentleman and that he brought her a watermelon every Saturday afternoon with his initials cut in it, E. A. T. Well, one Saturday, she said, Mr. Teagarden brought the watermelon and there was nobody at home and he left it on the front porch and returned in his buggy to Jasper, but she never got the watermelon, she said, because a nigger boy ate it when he saw the initials, E. A. T.! This story tickled John Wesley's funny bone and he giggled and giggled but June Star didn't think it was any good. She said she wouldn't marry a man that just brought her a watermelon on Saturday. The grandmother said she would have done well to marry Mr. Teagarden because he was a gentleman and had bought Coca-Cola stock when it first came out and that he had died only a few years ago, a very wealthy man.

27   They stopped at The Tower for barbecued sandwiches. The Tower was

a part stucco and part wood filling station and dance hall set in a clearing outside of Timothy. A fat man named Red Sammy Butts ran it and there were signs stuck here and there on the building and for miles up and down the highway saying, TRY RED SAMMY'S FAMOUS BARBECUE. NONE LIKE FAMOUS RED SAMMY'S! RED SAM! THE FAT BOY WITH THE HAPPY LAUGH. A VETERAN! RED SAMMY'S YOUR MAN!

28   Red Sammy was lying on the bare ground outside The Tower with his head under a truck while a gray monkey about a foot high, chained to a small chinaberry tree, chattered nearby. The monkey sprang back into the tree and got on the highest limb as soon as he saw the children jump out of the car and run toward him.

29   Inside, The Tower was a long dark room with a counter at one end and tables at the other and dancing space in the middle. They all sat down at a board table next to the nickelodeon and Red Sam's wife, a tall burnt-brown woman with hair and eyes lighter than her skin, came and took their order. The children's mother put a dime in the machine and played "The Tennessee Waltz," and the grandmother said that tune always made her want to dance. She asked Bailey if he would like to dance but he only glared at her. He didn't have a naturally sunny disposition like she did and trips made him nervous. The grandmother's brown eyes were very bright. She swayed her head from side to side and pretended she was dancing in her chair. June Star said play something she could tap to so the children's mother put in another dime and played a fast number and June Star stepped out onto the dance floor and did her tap routine.

30   "Ain't she cute?" Red Sam's wife said, leaning over the counter. "Would you like to come be my little girl?"

31   "No I certainly wouldn't," June Star said. "I wouldn't live in a broken-down place like this for a million bucks!" and she ran back to the table.

32   "Ain't she cute?" the woman repeated, stretching her mouth politely.

33   "Aren't you ashamed?" hissed the grandmother.

34   Red Sam came in and told his wife to quit lounging on the counter and hurry up with these people's order. His khaki trousers reached just to his hip bones and his stomach hung over them like a sack of meal swaying under his shirt. He came over and sat down at a table nearby and let out a combination sigh and yodel. "You can't win," he said. "You can't win," and he wiped his sweating red face off with a gray handkerchief. "These days you don't know who to trust," he said. "Ain't that the truth?"

35   "People are certainly not nice like they used to be," said the grandmother.

36   "Two fellers come in here last week," Red Sammy said, "driving a Chrysler. It was a old beat-up car but it was a good one and these boys looked all right to me. Said they worked at the mill and you know I let them fellers charge the gas they bought? Now why did I do that?"

37   "Because you're a good man!" the grandmother said at once.

38   "Yes'm, I suppose so," Red Sam said as if he were struck with this answer.

39   His wife brought the orders, carrying the five plates all at once without a tray, two in each hand and one balanced on her arm. "It isn't a soul in this green world of God's that you can trust," she said. "And I don't count nobody out of that, not nobody," she repeated, looking at Red Sammy.

40   "Did you read about that criminal, The Misfit, that's escaped?" asked the grandmother.

41   "I wouldn't be a bit surprised if he didn't attact this place right here," said the woman. "If he hears about it being here, I wouldn't be none surprised to see him. If he hears it's two cent in the cash register, I wouldn't be a tall surprised if he . . ."

42   "That'll do," Red Sam said. "Go bring these people their Co'-Colas," and the woman went off to get the rest of the order.

43   "A good man is hard to find," Red Sammy said. "Everything is getting terrible. I remember the day you could go off and leave your screen door unlatched. Not no more."

44   He and the grandmother discussed better times. The old lady said that in her opinion Europe was entirely to blame for the way things were now. She said the way Europe acted you would think we were made of money and Red Sam said it was no use talking about it, she was exactly right. The children ran outside into the white sunlight and looked at the monkey in the lacy chinaberry tree. He was busy catching fleas on himself and biting each one carefully between his teeth as if it were a delicacy.

45   They drove off again into the hot afternoon. The grandmother took cat naps and woke up every few minutes with her own snoring. Outside of Toombsboro she woke up and recalled an old plantation that she had visited in this neighborhood once when she was a young lady. She said the house had six white columns across the front and that there was an avenue of oaks leading up to it and two little wooden trellis arbors on either side in front where you sat down with your suitor after a stroll in the garden. She recalled exactly which road to turn off to get to it. She knew that Bailey would not be willing to lose any time looking at an old house, but the more she talked about it, the more she wanted to see it once again and find out if the little twin arbors were still standing. "There was a secret panel in this house," she said craftily, not telling the truth but wishing that she were, "and the story went that all the family silver was hidden in it when Sherman came through but it was never found . . ."

46   "Hey!" John Wesley said. "Let's go see it! We'll find it! We'll poke all the woodwork and find it! Who lives there? Where do you turn off at? Hey Pop, can't we turn off there?"

47   "We never have seen a house with a secret panel!" June Star shrieked. "Let's go to the house with the secret panel! Hey Pop, can't we go see the house with the secret panel!"

48   "It's not far from here, I know," the grandmother said. "It wouldn't take over twenty minutes."

49   Bailey was looking straight ahead. His jaw was as rigid as a horseshoe. "No," he said.

50   The children began to yell and scream that they wanted to see the house with the secret panel. John Wesley kicked the back of the front seat and June Star hung over her mother's shoulder and whined desperately into her ear that they never had any fun even on their vacation, that they could never do what THEY wanted to do. The baby began to scream and John Wesley kicked the back of the seat so hard that his father could feel the blows in his kidney.

51   "All right!" he shouted and drew the car to a stop at the side of the road. "Will you all shut up? Will you all just shut up for one second? If you don't shut up, we won't go anywhere."

52   "It would be very educational for them," the grandmother murmured.

53   "All right," Bailey said, "but get this: this is the only time we're going to stop for anything like this. This is the one and only time."

54   "The dirt road that you have to turn down is about a mile back," the grandmother directed. "I marked it when we passed."

55   "A dirt road," Bailey groaned.

56   After they had turned around and were headed toward the dirt road, the grandmother recalled other points about the house, the beautiful glass over the front doorway and the candle-lamp in the hall. John Wesley said that the secret panel was probably in the fireplace.

57   "You can't go inside this house," Bailey said. "You don't know who lives there."

58   "While you all talk to the people in front, I'll run around behind and get in a window," John Wesley suggested.

59   "We'll all stay in the car," his mother said.

60   They turned onto the dirt road and the car raced roughly along in a swirl of pink dust. The grandmother recalled the times when there were no paved roads and thirty miles was a day's journey. The dirt road was hilly and there were sudden washes in it and sharp curves on dangerous embankments. All at once they would be on a hill, looking down over the blue tops of trees for miles around, then the next minute, they would be in a red depression with the dust-coated trees looking down on them.

61   "This place had better turn up in a minute," Bailey said, "or I'm going to turn around."

62   The road looked as if no one had traveled on it in months.

63   "It's not much farther," the grandmother said and just as she said it, a horrible thought came to her. The thought was so embarrassing that she turned red in the face and her eyes dilated and her feet jumped up, upsetting her valise in the corner. The instant the valise moved, the newspaper top she had over the basket under it rose with a snarl and Pitty Sing, the cat, sprang onto Bailey's shoulder.

64   The children were thrown to the floor and their mother, clutching the

baby, was thrown out the door onto the ground; the old lady was thrown into the front seat. The car turned over once and landed right-side-up in a gulch off the side of the road. Bailey remained in the driver's seat with the cat—gray-striped with a broad white face and an orange nose—clinging to his neck like a caterpillar.

65   As soon as the children saw they could move their arms and legs, they scrambled out of the car, shouting, "We've had an ACCIDENT!" The grandmother was curled up under the dashboard, hoping she was injured so that Bailey's wrath would not come down on her all at once. The horrible thought she had had before the accident was that the house she had remembered so vividly was not in Georgia but in Tennessee.

66   Bailey removed the cat from his neck with both hands and flung it out the window against the side of a pine tree. Then he got out of the car and started looking for the children's mother. She was sitting against the side of the red gutted ditch, holding the screaming baby, but she only had a cut down her face and a broken shoulder. "We've had an ACCIDENT!" the children screamed in a frenzy of delight.

67   "But nobody's killed," June Star said with disappointment as the grandmother limped out of the car, her hat still pinned to her head but the broken front brim standing up at a jaunty angle and the violet spray hanging off the side. They all sat down in the ditch, except the children, to recover from the shock. They were all shaking.

68   "Maybe a car will come along," said the children's mother hoarsely.

69   "I believe I have injured an organ," said the grandmother, pressing her side, but no one answered her. Bailey's teeth were clattering. He had on a yellow sport shirt with bright blue parrots designed in it and his face was as yellow as the shirt. The grandmother decided that she would not mention that the house was in Tennessee.

70   The road was about ten feet above and they could see only the tops of the trees on the other side of it. Behind the ditch they were sitting in there were more woods, tall and dark and deep. In a few minutes they saw a car some distance away on top of a hill, coming slowly as if the occupants were watching them. The grandmother stood up and waved both arms dramatically to attract their attention. The car continued to come on slowly, disappeared around a bend and appeared again, moving even slower, on top of the hill they had gone over. It was a big black battered hearse-like automobile. There were three men in it.

71   It came to a stop just over them and for some minutes, the driver looked down with a steady expressionless gaze to where they were sitting, and didn't speak. Then he turned his head and muttered something to the other two and they got out. One was a fat boy in black trousers and a red sweat shirt with a silver stallion embossed on the front of it. He moved around on the right side of them and stood staring, his mouth partly open in a kind of loose grin. The other had on khaki pants and a blue striped coat and a gray hat pulled down very low, hiding most of his face. He came around slowly on the left side. Neither spoke.

72   The driver got out of the car and stood by the side of it, looking down at them. He was an older man than the other two. His hair was just beginning to gray and he wore silver-rimmed spectacles that gave him a scholarly look. He had a long creased face and didn't have on any shirt or undershirt. He had on blue jeans that were too tight for him and was holding a black hat and a gun. The two boys also had guns.

73   "We've had an ACCIDENT!" the children screamed.

74   The grandmother had the peculiar feeling that the bespectacled man was someone she knew. His face was as familiar to her as if she had known him all her life but she could not recall who he was. He moved away from the car and began to come down the embankment, placing his feet carefully so that he wouldn't slip. He had on tan and white shoes and no socks, and his ankles were red and thin. "Good afternoon," he said. "I see you all had you a little spill."

75   "We turned over twice!" said the grandmother.

76   "Oncet," he corrected. "We seen it happen. Try their car and see will it run, Hiram," he said quietly to the boy with the gray hat.

77   "What you got that gun for?" John Wesley asked. "Whatcha gonna do with that gun?"

78   "Lady," the man said to the children's mother, "would you mind calling them children to sit down by you? Children make me nervous. I want all you all to sit down right together there where you're at."

79   "What are you telling US what to do for?" June Star asked.

80   Behind them the line of woods gaped like a dark open mouth. "Come here," said their mother.

81   "Look here now," Bailey began suddenly, "we're in a predicament! We're in . . ."

82   The grandmother shrieked. She scrambled to her feet and stood staring. "You're The Misfit!" she said. "I recognized you at once!"

83   "Yes'm," the man said, smiling slightly as if he were pleased in spite of himself to be known, "but it would have been better for all of you, lady, if you hadn't of reckernized me."

84   Bailey turned his head sharply and said something to his mother that shocked even the children. The old lady began to cry and The Misfit reddened.

85   "Lady," he said, "don't you get upset. Sometimes a man says things he don't mean. I don't reckon he meant to talk to you thataway."

86   "You wouldn't shoot a lady, would you?" the grandmother said and removed a clean handkerchief from her cuff and began to slap at her eyes with it.

87   The Misfit pointed the toe of his shoe into the ground and made a little hole and then covered it up again. "I would hate to have to," he said.

88   "Listen," the grandmother almost screamed, "I know you're a good man. You don't look a bit like you have common blood. I know you must come from nice people!"

89   "Yes mam," he said, "finest people in the world." When he smiled he showed a row of strong white teeth. "God never made a finer woman than my mother and my daddy's heart was pure gold," he said. The boy with the red sweat shirt had come around behind them and was standing with his gun at his hip. The Misfit squatted down on the ground. "Watch them children, Bobby Lee," he said. "You know they make me nervous." He looked at the six of them huddled together in front of him and he seemed to be embarrassed as if he couldn't think of anything to say. "Ain't a cloud in the sky," he remarked, looking up at it. "Don't see no sun but don't see no cloud neither."

90   "Yes, it's a beautiful day," said the grandmother. "Listen," she said, "you shouldn't call yourself The Misfit because I know you're a good man at heart. I can just look at you and tell."

91   "Hush!" Bailey yelled. "Hush! Everybody shut up and let me handle this!" He was squatting in the position of a runner about to sprint forward but he didn't move.

92   "I pre-chate that, lady," The Misfit said and drew a little circle in the ground with the butt of his gun.

93   "It'll take a half a hour to fix this here car," Hiram called, looking over the raised hood of it.

94   "Well, first you and Bobby Lee get him and that little boy to step over yonder with you," The Misfit said, pointing to Bailey and John Wesley. "The boys want to ast you something," he said to Bailey. "Would you mind stepping back in them woods there with them?"

95   "Listen," Bailey began, "we're in a terrible predicament! Nobody realizes what this is," and his voice cracked. His eyes were as blue and intense as the parrots in his shirt and he remained perfectly still.

96   The grandmother reached up to adjust her hat brim as if she were going to the woods with him but it came off in her hand. She stood staring at it and after a second she let it fall on the ground. Hiram pulled Bailey up by the arm as if he were assisting an old man. John Wesley caught hold of his father's hand and Bobby Lee followed. They went off toward the woods and just as they reached the dark edge, Bailey turned and supporting himself against a gray naked pine trunk, he shouted, "I'll be back in a minute, Mamma, wait on me!"

97   "Come back this instant!" his mother shrilled but they all disappeared into the woods.

98   "Bailey Boy!" the grandmother called in a tragic voice but she found she was looking at The Misfit squatting on the ground in front of her. "I just know you're a good man," she said desperately. "You're not a bit common!"

99   "Nome, I ain't a good man," The Mistfit said after a second as if he had considered her statement carefully, "but I ain't the worst in the world neither. My daddy said I was a different breed of dog from my brothers and sisters. 'You know,' Daddy said, 'it's some that can live their whole life out without asking about it and it's others has to know

why it is, and this boy is one of the latters. He's going to be into every-thing!' " He put on his black hat and looked up suddenly and then away deep into the woods as if he were embarrassed again. "I'm sorry I don't have on a shirt before you ladies," he said, hunching his shoulders slightly. "We buried our clothes that we had on when we escaped and we're just making do until we can get better. We borrowed these from some folks we met," he explained.

100   "That's perfectly all right," the grandmother said. "Maybe Bailey has an extra shirt in his suitcase."

101   "I'll look and see terrectly," The Misfit said.

102   "Where are they taking him?" the children's mother screamed.

103   "Daddy was a card himself," The Misfit said. "You couldn't put any-thing over on him. He never got in trouble with the Authorities though. Just had the knack of handling them."

104   "You could be honest too if you'd only try," said the grandmother. "Think how wonderful it would be to settle down and live a comfortable life and not have to think about somebody chasing you all the time."

105   The Misfit kept scratching in the ground with the butt of his gun as if he were thinking about it. "Yes'm, somebody is always after you," he murmured.

106   The grandmother noticed how thin his shoulder blades were just be-hind his hat because she was standing up looking down on him. "Do you ever pray?" she asked.

107   He shook his head. All she saw was the black hat wiggle between his shoulder blades. "Nome," he said.

108   There was a pistol shot from the woods, followed closely by another. Then silence. The old lady's head jerked around. She could hear the wind move through the tree tops like a long satisfied insuck of breath. "Bailey Boy!" she called.

109   "I was a gospel singer for a while," The Misfit said. "I been most everything. Been in the arm service, both land and sea, at home and abroad, been twict married, been an undertaker, been with the railroads, plowed Mother Earth, been in a tornado, seen a man burnt alive oncet," and he looked up at the children's mother and the little girl who were sitting close together, their faces white and their eyes glassy; "I even seen a woman flogged," he said.

110   "Pray, pray," the grandmother began, "pray, pray . . ."

111   "I never was a bad boy that I remember of," The Misfit said in an almost dreamy voice, "but somewheres along the line I done something wrong and got sent to the penitentiary. I was buried alive," and he looked up and held her attention to him by a steady stare.

112   "That's when you should have started to pray," she said. "What did you do to get sent to the penitentiary that first time?"

113   "Turn to the right, it was a wall," The Misfit said, looking up again at the cloudless sky. "Turn to the left, it was a wall. Look up it was a ceiling, look down it was a floor. I forget what I done, lady. I set there

and set there, trying to remember what it was I done and I ain't recalled it to this day. Oncet in a while, I would think it was coming to me, but it never come."

114   "Maybe they put you in by mistake," the old lady said vaguely.

115   "Nome," he said. "It wasn't no mistake. They had the papers on me."

116   "You must have stolen something," she said.

117   The Misfit sneered slightly. "Nobody had nothing I wanted," he said. "It was a head-doctor at the penitentiary said what I had done was kill my daddy but I known that for a lie. My daddy died in nineteen ought nineteen of the epidemic flu and I never had a thing to do with it. He was buried in the Mount Hopewell Baptist churchyard and you can go there and see for yourself."

118   "If you would pray," the old lady said, "Jesus would help you."

119   "That's right," The Misfit said.

120   "Well then, why don't you pray?" she asked trembling with delight suddenly.

121   "I don't want no hep," he said. "I'm doing all right by myself."

122   Bobby Lee and Hiram came ambling back from the woods. Bobby Lee was dragging a yellow shirt with bright blue parrots in it.

123   "Thow me that shirt, Bobby Lee," The Misfit said. The shirt came flying at him and landed on his shoulder and he put it on. The grandmother couldn't name what the shirt reminded her of. "No, lady," The Misfit said while he was buttoning it up, "I found out the crime don't matter. You can do one thing or you can do another, kill a man or take a tire off his car, because sooner or later you're going to forget what it was you done and just be punished for it."

124   The children's mother had begun to make heaving noises as if she couldn't get her breath. "Lady," he asked, "would you and that little girl like to step off yonder with Bobby Lee and Hiram and join your husband?"

125   "Yes, thank you," the mother said faintly. Her left arm dangled helplessly and she was holding the baby, who had gone to sleep, in the other. "Hep that lady up, Hiram," The Misfit said as she struggled to climb out of the ditch, "and Bobby Lee, you hold onto that little girl's hand."

126   "I don't want to hold hands with him," June Star said. "He reminds me of a pig."

127   The fat boy blushed and laughed and caught her by the arm and pulled her off into the woods after Hiram and her mother.

128   Alone with The Misfit, the grandmother found that she had lost her voice. There was not a cloud in the sky nor any sun. There was nothing around her but woods. She wanted to tell him that he must pray. She opened and closed her mouth several times before anything came out. Finally she found herself saying, "Jesus. Jesus," meaning, Jesus will help you, but the way she was saying it, it sounded as if she might be cursing.

129   "Yes'm," The Misfit said as if he agreed. "Jesus thown everything off

balance. It was the same case with Him as with me except He hadn't committed any crime and they could prove I had committed one because they had the papers on me. Of course," he said, "they never shown me my papers. That's why I sign myself now. I said long ago, you get you a signature and sign everything you do and keep a copy of it. Then you'll know what you done and you can hold up the crime to the punishment and see do they match and in the end you'll have something to prove you ain't been treated right. I call myself The Misfit," he said, "because I can't make what all I done wrong fit what all I gone through in punishment."

130   There was a piercing scream from the woods, followed closely by a pistol report. "Does it seem right to you, lady, that one is punished a heap and another ain't punished at all?"

131   "Jesus!" the old lady cried. "You've got good blood! I know you wouldn't shoot a lady! I know you come from nice people! Pray! Jesus, you ought not to shoot a lady. I'll give you all the money I've got!"

132   "Lady," The Misfit said, looking beyond her far into the woods, "there never was a body that give the undertaker a tip."

133   There were two more pistol reports and the grandmother raised her head like a parched old turkey hen crying for water and called, "Bailey Boy, Bailey Boy!" as if her heart would break.

134   "Jesus was the only One that ever raised the dead," The Misfit continued, "and He shouldn't have done it. He thown everything off balance. If He did what He said, then it's nothing for you to do but thow away everything and follow Him, and if He didn't, then it's nothing for you to do but enjoy the few minutes you got left the best way you can—by killing somebody or burning down his house or doing some other meanness to him. No pleasure but meanness," he said and his voice had become almost a snarl.

135   "Maybe He didn't raise the dead," the old lady mumbled, not knowing what she was saying and feeling so dizzy that she sank down in the ditch with her legs twisted under her.

136   "I wasn't there so I can't say He didn't," The Misfit said. "I wisht I had of been there," he said, hitting the ground with his fist. "It ain't right I wasn't there because if I had of been there I would of known. Listen lady," he said in a high voice, "if I had of been there I would of known and I wouldn't be like I am now." His voice seemed about to crack and the grandmother's head cleared for an instant. She saw the man's face twisted close to her own as if he were going to cry and she murmured, "Why you're one of my babies. You're one of my own children!" She reached out and touched him on the shoulder. The Misfit sprang back as if a snake had bitten him and shot her three times through the chest. Then he put his gun down on the ground and took off his glasses and began to clean them.

137   Hiram and Bobby Lee returned from the woods and stood over the

ditch, looking down at the grandmother who half sat and half lay in a puddle of blood with her legs crossed under her like a child's and her face smiling up at the cloudless sky.

138   Without his glasses, The Misfit's eyes were red-rimmed and pale and defenseless-looking. "Take her off and thow her where you thown the others," he said, picking up the cat that was rubbing itself against his leg.

139   "She was a talker, wasn't she?" Bobby Lee said, sliding down the ditch with a yodel.

140   "She would of been a good woman," The Misfit said, "if it had been somebody there to shoot her every minute of her life."

141   "Some fun!" Bobby Lee said.

142   "Shut up, Bobby Lee," The Misfit said. "It's no real pleasure in life."

A Good Man is Hard to Find

Questions on Content, Style, and Structure

1. How do the grandmother's clothes and her comments to her family as they travel reveal her character? How does she see herself?

2. What does her story about Mr. Teagarden and her conversations with Red Sammy reveal about her definition of "good people"? Who is a "good man" to the grandmother?

3. What do her comments about the past reveal about her view of reality?

4. What hints do we get that the grandmother is not always honest?

5. What examples of foreshadowing appear in the story?

6. Characterize The Misfit and the way he speaks to the grandmother and her daughter-in-law. Who better fits grandmother's idea of a gentleman, Bailey or The Misfit? How is The Misfit's behavior ironic?

7. List the ways the grandmother tries to flatter and pacify The Misfit.

8. How does the grandmother's advice to The Misfit on religion change as the story progresses? What does this change suggest about the depth of her religious beliefs?

9. Summarize The Misfit's philosophy of life. What does he mean when he says, " 'Jesus thown everything off balance' "? Why does he call himself The Misfit?

10. Why does the grandmother reach out to touch The Misfit? Does she have a revelation of some kind? If so, what?

11. Is there anything symbolic about the description of the grandmother's body? If so, what?

12. The Misfit says that he doesn't need any help, that he's doing " 'all right by myself.' " What indication do we have at the story's end that this claim is not true?

13. What does The Misfit mean when he says of the grandmother, " 'She would of been a good woman . . . if it had been somebody there to shoot her every minute of her life' "? How does this story comment on the spiritual condition of our times?

Vocabulary

wheeled (2)
valise (10)
asphyxiate (10)
meanest ("the meanest of [the trees] sparkled") (13)
stucco (27)

nickelodeon (29)
disposition (29)
trellis (45)
parched (133)

Suggestions for Writing

1. Write an essay analyzing the use of setting as a foreshadowing device in this story.
2. Select one or two of the minor characters and write an essay explaining their functions in this story.
3. Write an essay showing how O'Connor uses clothing and physical descriptions to comment upon her characters and their actions.

I Like Colonel Sanders
Ralph Keyes

Ralph Keyes is the author of *Is There Life After High School?* (1976). He has been a frequent contributor to the "My Turn" column in *Newsweek*, where this essay first appeared in 1973.

1   Plastic America is easy to knock. There are so many targets, and such vulnerable ones—Colonel Sander's smiling visage, the tinsel and glitter of shopping centers, our bumper-sticker clichés, and the identical rows of laundermat washing machines stretching coast to coast.

2   John Kenneth Galbraith[1] thinks this car-dominated society has produced "the world's most hideous architecture"—in service stations, hot-dog stands and pizza parlors. The Harvard professor is sure that in time we'll recognize the need to set minimum esthetic standards for such locales, because they tend to be "designed by architects whose sole motivation is to be completely hideous."

3   That's nonsense. Car-oriented buildings aren't meant to be hideous. They're meant to be seen. Esthetics count little at 70 mph; the object of the exercise is that Colonel Sanders's smile can be seen miles away, and McDonald's golden arches.

4   Casual pot-shooting at the setting of mass commerce misses far more than it hits. Helping the country to look more like Harvard won't necessarily make it more humane. To knock plastic is to ignore the extent to which form follows function, the subtle ways that even garish parts of our culture serve genuine human needs.

5   Take laundermats. At a glance these are just ugly rows of washing machines and driers, complemented by a few cheap chairs littered with yesterday's newspaper. Yet laundermats are also community centers, one of the few places in urban/suburban America where people can hang out without being hassled. Transients meet over Tide in the laundermat, kids gather there after school and singles engage in laundermating, having discovered that washing clothes together is a good way to get acquainted. Psychiatrist Donald Muhich has spent time observing the groups of women who gather regularly in some laundermats, as they once did at streamside, and says the interaction he's seen constitutes "leaderless group therapy." The year before last a judge held an arraignment in the laundermat of a small Kentucky town. It was the closest thing to a public building in the town.

[1] John Kenneth Galbraith is a well-known economist, historian, and writer.

6   Shopping centers serve a similar function, particularly in the social void of our suburbs. While working for a Long Island newspaper, I once spent a week hanging around a big regional center, thinking to expose the materialistic corruption of kids who congregate there. What I found was a mixed-up but friendly group of people who huddled in the warmth of the covered mall and welcomed me into their community. That shopping center, like other enclosed, climate-controlled malls, was the most tranquil and pleasant environment I'd ever found within suburbia. Like a town square of old, it provided the opportunity to promenade among the familiar faces of those living within. What I had overlooked was that these big, carnival-like centers are one of the few suburban environments where automobiles can't intrude, where one can walk without dodging bumpers or protecting one's ears from the roar of engines.

7   Shopping centers, like so much of plastic America, are a response to the omnipresence of cars in our lives. Bumper stickers are another response, an amusing if harmless triviality, and more. Since we now drive by each other as we once walked, today's bumper stickers must carry a heavy load:

> Messages on the bulletin board—BOY SCOUT FAIR, MAY 8
> Rolling graffiti—NIXON IS ROSEMARY'S BABY
> Political commentary—DON'T BLAME ME, I VOTED FOR MCGOVERN[2]
> Dialogue—HAVE A NICE DAY—POW'S NEVER HAVE A NICE DAY
> Reaching out—WAVE, I'M LONELY
> IF YOU LIKE ME, GRIN

8   In particular, bumper stickers have become a way we identify ourselves. Take something like HAPPINESS IS A GOOD SCRUM. Two drivers pass with that message on their bumpers, know they both play rugby, wave to each other and grin, feel a little warmth and a common pursuit: community.

9   The search for community is what really underlies so many of our cultural forms, in obscure, distorted, sometimes ludicrous ways that reflect our uprootedness and longing for a more predictable environment. This is what Galbraith and all the other high culture critics don't account for in their outrage at our increasingly uniform garishness, those grotesque multicolor plastic configurations big enough to be seen from a speeding car.

10   One in five of us will change address every year and will look, in the process, for comforting points of reference. When crossing the country from Long Island to San Diego, I found it reassuring to know that despite all our divisions, something was gluing this nation together—A&W root beer. When we moved into a little frame house in Pacific Beach, 7-Eleven's huge red-and-green sign up the street was a comfort. This was to be our friendly neighborhood store, just as it had been in Westbury. Even the kids outside seemed familiar, gathered on their banana-seat

[2] George McGovern was defeated by Richard Nixon in the 1972 presidential race.

bikes. And even though I knew very little else about San Diego, I did know exactly where 7-Eleven's magazines were shelved, where the milk was stored and the names of their Slurpees.

11   It's for reasons such as these that I've come to enjoy bumper-stickered conversation, the friendly pageantry of shopping centers, the trust that can be built over dirty underwear in a laundermat and the familiarity of my friendly corner franchises. This may not be my optimum environment, but so long as I'm dependent on a car, and expect to move now and then, I don't want anyone tinkering with the outside plastic settings that serve us so well in that process.

12   Even our most garish social structures meet some human needs, needs no longer being met by the hallowed walls of another time. Until those human needs, those functions of plastic America, are served better in other ways, please don't mess with the forms that are helping me stay afloat. I like Colonel Sanders. He's been a smiling friend to me on the road. Until this society does better with real human substitutes, I don't want anyone tinkering with that friendly old grandfather of mine.

I Like Colonel Sanders

Questions on Content, Style, and Structure

1. Why does Keyes begin his essay with reference to the economist John Kenneth Galbraith?
2. According to Keyes, what search underlies so many of our cultural forms today?
3. What are the causes of this search?
4. What is the purpose of paragraph 5 on laundermats?
5. How does Keyes characterize shopping centers? To what are they compared? What is Keyes' point in making that comparison?
6. What purposes do bumper stickers serve?
7. Why does Keyes tell the reader about his move to California?
8. How does Keyes conclude his essay? Is it an effective ending?
9. Is the title of this essay a good choice? Why/why not?
10. Evaluate Keyes' causal analysis essay. Overall, is it convincing? Support your answer.

Vocabulary

vulnerable (1)	arraignment (5)
visage (1)	omnipresence (7)
esthetic (2)	ludicrous (9)
hideous (2)	optimum (11)
garish (4)	hallowed (12)

Suggestions for Writing

1. Write an essay in which you disagree with Keyes about the causes of "plastic America."

2. Some critics of architecture claim that ugly, harsh structures promote antisocial behavior and that softer, attractive buildings encourage positive behavior. Consider such buildings as dorms, high schools, and prisons; then write an essay agreeing or disagreeing that "hard" or "soft" architecture affects people's attitudes.

3. Write a description of a public place, such as a laundermat, bus station, post office, or shopping mall. Select vivid details that communicate the scene's dominant impression.

Two Ways of Viewing the River
Samuel Clemens

Samuel Clemens, whose pen name was Mark Twain, is regarded as one of America's most outstanding writers. Well known for his humorous stories and books, Twain was also a pioneer of fictional realism and local color. His most famous novel, *The Adventures of Huckleberry Finn* (1884), is often hailed as a masterpiece. This selection is from the autobiographical book *Life on the Mississippi* (1883), which recounts Clemens' job as a riverboat pilot.

1   Now when I had mastered the language of this water and had come to know every trifling feature that bordered the great river as familiarly as I knew the letters of the alphabet, I had made a valuable acquisition. But I had lost something, too. I had lost something which could never be restored to me while I lived. All the grace, the beauty, the poetry, had gone out of the majestic river! I still kept in mind a certain wonderful sunset which I witnessed when steamboating was new to me. A broad expanse of the river was turned to blood; in the middle distance the red hue brightened into gold, through which a solitary log came floating, black and conspicuous; in one place a long, slanting mark lay sparkling upon the water; in another the surface was broken by boiling, tumbling rings, that were as many-tinted as an opal; where the ruddy flush was faintest, was a smooth spot that was covered with graceful circles and radiating lines, ever so delicately traced; the shore on our left was densely wooded and the somber shadow that fell from this forest was broken in one place by a long, ruffled trail that shone like silver; and high above

the forest wall a clean-stemmed dead tree waved a single leafy bough that glowed like a flame in the unobstructed splendor that was flowing from the sun. There were graceful curves, reflected images, woody heights, soft distances, and over the whole scene, far and near, the dissolving lights drifted steadily, enriching it every passing moment with new marvels of coloring.

2   I stood like one bewitched. I drank it in, in a speechless rapture. The world was new to me and I had never seen anything like this at home. But as I have said, a day came when I began to cease from noting the glories and the charms which the moon and the sun and the twilight wrought upon the river's face; another day came when I ceased altogether to note them. Then, if that sunset scene had been repeated, I should have looked upon it without rapture, and should have commented upon it inwardly after this fashion: "This sun means that we are going to have wind to-morrow; that floating log means that the river is rising, small thanks to it; that slanting mark on the water refers to a bluff reef which is going to kill somebody's steamboat one of these nights, if it keeps on stretching out like that; those tumbling 'boils' show a dissolving bar and a changing channel there; the lines and circles in the slick water over yonder are a warning that that troublesome place is shoaling up dangerously; that silver streak in the shadow of the forest is the 'break' from a new snag and he has located himself in the very best place he could have found to fish for steamboats; that tall dead tree, with a single living branch, is not going to last long, and then how is a body ever going to get through this blind place at night without the friendly old landmark?"

3   No, the romance and beauty were all gone from the river. All the value any feature of it had for me now was the amount of usefulness it could furnish toward compassing the safe piloting of a steamboat. Since those days, I have pitied doctors from my heart. What does the lovely flush in a beauty's cheek mean to a doctor but a "break" that ripples above some deadly disease? Are not all her visible charms sown thick with what are to him the signs and symbols of hidden decay? Does he ever see her beauty at all, or doesn't he simply view her professionally and comment upon her unwholesome condition all to himself? And doesn't he sometimes wonder whether he has gained most or lost most by learning his trade?

Two Ways of Viewing the River

Questions on Content, Style, and Structure

1. What is Clemens contrasting in this essay? Identify his thesis.
2. What organizational pattern does he choose? Is his contrast clearly presented?

3. How does Clemens make a smooth transition to his second view of the river?

4. Why does Clemens refer to doctors in paragraph 3?

5. What is the purpose of the questions in paragraph 3? Why is the last question especially important?

6. Characterize the language Clemens uses in his description in paragraph 1. Is his diction appropriate?

7. Point out several examples of similes in paragraph 1; what do they add to the description of the sunset?

8. How does the language in the description in paragraph 2 differ from the diction in paragraph 1? What aspect of the river is emphasized there?

9. Identify an example of personification in paragraph 2. Why did Clemens add it to his description?

10. Describe the tone of this essay. Does it ever shift?

Vocabulary

trifling (1)	ruddy (1)
acquisition (1)	wrought (2)
conspicuous (1)	compassing (3)

Suggestions for Writing

1. Write an essay in which you contrast a first view of an object or scene to a later, less romantic view of the same object or scene.

2. Write an essay in which you, like Clemens, explain how you have gained or lost by mastering a trade or skill.

3. Describe a scene whose beauty also conceals its danger.

Seeing
Annie Dillard

Annie Dillard is an American writer, teacher, and observer of nature, who has lived in the Roanoke Valley of Virginia and on an island in Puget Sound. She has written a collection of poems, *Tickets for a Prayer Wheel* (1974), and two books of nonfiction, *Holy the Firm* (1977) and *Pilgrim at Tinker Creek* (1974), which won the Pulitzer Prize. This essay is from that prize-winning book.

1   I chanced on a wonderful book by Marius von Senden, called *Space and Sight*. When Western surgeons discovered how to perform safe cataract

operations, they ranged across Europe and America operating on dozens of men and women of all ages who had been blinded by cataracts since birth. Von Senden collected accounts of such cases; the histories are fascinating. Many doctors had tested their patients' sense perceptions and ideas of space both before and after the operations. The vast majority of patients, of both sexes and all ages, had, in von Senden's opinion, no idea of space whatsoever. Form, distance, and size were so many meaningless syllables. A patient "had no idea of depth, confusing it with roundness." Before the operation a doctor would give a blind patient a cube and a sphere; the patient would tongue it or feel it with his hands, and name it correctly. After the operation the doctor would show the same objects to the patient without letting him touch them; now he had no clue whatsoever what he was seeing. One patient called lemonade "square" because it pricked on his tongue as a square shape pricked on the touch of his hands. Of another postoperative patient, the doctor writes, "I have found in her no notion of size, for example, not even within the narrow limits which she might have encompassed with the aid of touch. Thus when I asked her to show me how big her mother was, she did not stretch out her hands, but set her two index-fingers a few inches apart." Other doctors reported their patients' own statements to similar effect. "The room he was in . . . he knew to be but part of the house, yet he could not conceive that the whole house could look bigger"; "Those who are blind from birth . . . have no real conception of height or distance. A house that is a mile away is thought of as nearby, but requiring the taking of a lot of steps. . . . The elevator that whizzes him up and down gives no more sense of vertical distance than does the train of horizontal."

2   For the newly sighted, vision is pure sensation unencumbered by meaning: "The girl went through the experience that we all go through and forget, the moment we are born. She saw, but it did not mean anything but a lot of different kinds of brightness." Again, "I asked the patient what he could see; he answered that he saw an extensive field of light, in which everything appeared dull, confused, and in motion. He could not distinguish objects." Another patient saw "nothing but a confusion of forms and colours." When a newly sighted girl saw photographs and paintings, she asked, " 'Why do they put those dark marks all over them?' 'Those aren't dark marks,' her mother explained, 'those are shadows. That is one of the ways the eye knows that things have shape. If it were not for shadows many things would look flat.' 'Well, that's how things do look,' Joan answered. 'Everything looks flat with dark patches.' "

3   But it is the patients' concepts of space that are most revealing. One patient, according to his doctor, "practiced his vision in a strange fashion; thus he takes off one of his boots, throws it some way off in front of him, and then attempts to gauge the distance at which it lies; he takes a few steps towards the boot and tries to grasp it; on failing to reach it, he moves on a step or two and gropes for the boot until he finally gets hold

of it." "But even at this stage, after three weeks' experience of seeing," von Senden goes on, " 'space,' as he conceives it, ends with visual space, i.e. with colour-patches that happen to bound his view. He does not yet have the notion that a larger object (a chair) can mask a smaller one (a dog), or that the latter can still be present even though it is not directly seen."

4   In general the newly sighted see the world as a dazzle of color-patches. They are pleased by the sensation of color, and learn quickly to name the colors, but the rest of seeing is tormentingly difficult. Soon after his operation a patient "generally bumps into one of these colour-patches and observes them to be substantial, since they resist him as tactual objects do. In walking about it also strikes him—or can if he pays attention—that he is continually passing in between the colours he sees, that he can go past a visual object, that a part of it then steadily disappears from view; and that in spite of this, however he twists and turns—whether entering the room from the door, for example, or returning back to it—he always has a visual space in front of him. Thus he gradually comes to realize that there is also a space behind him, which he does not see."

5   The mental effort involved in these reasonings proves overwhelming for many patients. It oppresses them to realize, if they ever do at all, the tremendous size of the world, which they had previously conceived of as something touchingly manageable. It oppresses them to realize that they have been visible to people all along, perhaps unattractively so, without their knowledge or consent. A disheartening number of them refuse to use their new vision, continuing to go over objects with their tongues, and lapsing into apathy and despair. "The child can see, but will not make use of his sight. Only when pressed can he with difficulty be brought to look at objects in his neighbourhood; but more than a foot away it is impossible to bestir him to the necessary effort." Of a twenty-one-year-old girl, the doctor relates, "Her unfortunate father, who had hoped for so much from this operation, wrote that his daughter carefully shuts her eyes whenever she wishes to go about the house, especially when she comes to a staircase, and that she is never happier or more at ease than when, by closing her eyelids, she relapses into her former state of total blindness." A fifteen-year-old boy, who was also in love with a girl at the asylum for the blind, finally blurted out, "No, really, I can't stand it any more; I want to be sent back to the asylum again. If things aren't altered, I'll tear my eyes out."

6   Some do learn to see, especially the young ones. But it changes their lives. One doctor comments on "the rapid and complete loss of that striking and wonderful serenity which is characteristic only of those who have never yet seen." A blind man who learns to see is ashamed of his old habits. He dresses up, grooms himself, and tries to make a good impression. While he was blind he was indifferent to objects unless they

were edible; now, "a sifting of values sets in . . . his thoughts and wishes are mightily stirred and some few of the patients are thereby led into dissimulation, envy, theft and fraud."

7   On the other hand, many newly sighted people speak well of the world, and teach us how dull is our own vision. To one patient, a human hand, unrecognized, is "something bright and then holes." Shown a bunch of grapes, a boy calls out, "It is dark, blue and shiny . . . . It isn't smooth, it has bumps and hollows." A little girl visits a garden. "She is greatly astonished, and can scarcely be persuaded to answer, stands speechless in front of the tree, which she only names on taking hold of it, and then as 'the tree with the lights in it.' " Some delight in their sight and give themselves over to the visual world. Of a patient just after her bandages were removed, her doctor writes, "The first things to attract her attention were her own hands; she looked at them very closely, moved them repeatedly to and fro, bent and stretched the fingers, and seemed greatly astonished at the sight." One girl was eager to tell her blind friend that "men do not really look like trees at all," and astounded to discover that her every visitor had an utterly different face. Finally, a twenty-two-year-old girl was dazzled by the world's brightness and kept her eyes shut for two weeks. When at the end of that time she opened her eyes again, she did not recognize any objects, but, "the more she now directed her gaze upon everything about her, the more it could be seen how an expression of gratification and astonishment overspread her features; she repeatedly exclaimed: 'Oh God! How beautiful!' "

8   I saw color-patches for weeks after I read this wonderful book. It was summer; the peaches were ripe in the valley orchards. When I woke in the morning, color-patches wrapped round my eyes, intricately, leaving not one unfilled spot. All day long I walked among shifting color-patches that parted before me like the Red Sea and closed again in silence, transfigured, wherever I looked back. Some patches swelled and loomed, while others vanished utterly, and dark marks flitted at random over the whole dazzling sweep. But I couldn't sustain the illusion of flatness. I've been around for too long. Form is condemned to an eternal danse macabre with meaning: I couldn't unpeach the peaches. Nor can I remember ever having seen without understanding; the color-patches of infancy are lost. My brain then must have been smooth as any balloon. I'm told I reached for the moon; many babies do. But the color-patches of infancy swelled as meaning filled them; they arrayed themselves in solemn ranks down distance which unrolled and stretched before me like a plain. The moon rocketed away. I live now in a world of shadows that shape and distance color, a world where space makes a kind of terrible sense. What gnosticism is this, and what physics? The fluttering patch I saw in my nursery window—silver and green and shape-shifting blue—is gone; a row of Lombardy poplars takes its place, mute, across the distant lawn. That

humming oblong creature pale as light that stole along the walls of my room at night, stretching exhilaratingly around the corners, is gone, too, gone the night I ate of the bittersweet fruit, put two and two together and puckered forever my brain. Martin Buber[1] tells this tale: "Rabbi Mendel once boasted to his teacher Rabbi Elimelekh that evenings he saw the angel who rolls away the light before the darkness, and mornings the angel who rolls away the darkness before the light. 'Yes,' said Rabbi Elimelekh, 'in my youth I saw that too. Later on you don't see these things any more.' "

9   Why didn't someone hand those newly sighted people paints and brushes from the start, when they still didn't know what anything was? Then maybe as we all could see color-patches too, the world unraveled from reason, Eden before Adam gave names. The scales would drop from my eyes; I'd see trees like men walking; I'd run down the road against all orders, hallooing and leaping.

10   Seeing is of course very much a matter of verbalization. Unless I call my attention to what passes before my eyes, I simply won't see it. It is, as Ruskin[2] says, "not merely unnoticed, but in the full, clear sense of the word, unseen." My eyes alone can't solve analogy tests using figures, the ones which show, with increasing elaborations, a big square, then a small square in a big square, then a big triangle, and expect me to find a small triangle in a big triangle. I have to say the words, describe what I'm seeing. If Tinker Mountain erupted, I'd be likely to notice. But if I want to notice the lesser cataclysms of valley life, I have to maintain in my head a running description of the present. It's not that I'm observant; it's just that I talk too much. Otherwise, especially in a strange place, I'll never know what's happening. Like a blind man at the ball game, I need a radio.

11   When I see this way I analyze and pry. I hurl over logs and roll away stones; I study the bank a square foot at a time, probing and tilting my head. Some days when a mist covers the mountains, when the muskrats won't show and the microscope's mirror shatters, I want to climb up the blank blue dome as a man would storm the inside of a circus tent, wildly, dangling, and with a steel knife claw a rent in the top, peep, and, if I must, fall.

12   But there is another kind of seeing that involves a letting go. When I see this way I sway transfixed and emptied. The difference between the two ways of seeing is the difference between walking with and without a camera. When I walk with a camera I walk from shot to shot, reading the light on a calibrated meter. When I walk without a camera, my own shutter opens, and the moment's light prints on my own silver gut. When I see this second way I am above all an unscrupulous observer.

[1] Martin Buber was a social philosopher and author who taught at Hebrew University in Jerusalem.
[2] John Ruskin was the leading Victorian critic of art and also an important social critic.

13   It was sunny one evening last summer at Tinker Creek; the sun was low in the sky, upstream. I was sitting on the sycamore log bridge with the sunset at my back, watching the shiners the size of minnows who were feeding over the muddy sand in skittery schools. Again and again, one fish, then another, turned for a split second across the current and flash! the sun shot out from its silver side. I couldn't watch for it. It was always just happening somewhere else, and it drew my vision just as it disappeared: flash, like a sudden dazzle of the thinnest blade, a sparking over a dun and olive ground at chance intervals from every direction. The I noticed white specks, some sort of pale petals, small, floating from under my feet on the creek's surface, very slow and steady. So I blurred my eyes and gazed towards the brim of my hat and saw a new world. I saw the pale white circles roll up, roll up, like the world's turning, mute and perfect, and I saw the linear flashes, gleaming silver, like stars being born at random down a rolling scroll of time. Something broke and something opened. I filled up like a new wineskin. I breathed an air like light; I saw a light like water. I was the lip of a fountain the creek filled forever; I was ether, the leaf in the zephyr; I was flesh-flake, feather, bone.

14   When I see this way I see truly. As Thoreau[3] says, I return to my senses. I am the man who watches the baseball game in silence in an empty stadium. I see the game purely; I'm abstracted and dazed. When it's all over and the white-suited players lope off the green field to their shadowed dugouts, I leap to my feet; I cheer and cheer.

15   But I can't go out and try to see this way. I'll fail, I'll go mad. All I can do is try to gag the commentator, to hush the noise of useless interior babble that keeps me from seeing just as surely as a newspaper dangled before my eyes. The effort is really a discipline requiring a lifetime of dedicated struggle; it marks the literature of saints and monks of every order East and West, under every rule and no rule, discalced and shod. The world's spiritual geniuses seem to discover universally that the mind's muddy river, this ceaseless flow of trivia and trash, cannot be dammed, and that trying to dam it is a waste of effort that might lead to madness. Instead you must allow the muddy river to flow unheeded in the dim channels of consciousness; you raise your sights; you look along it, mildly, acknowledging its presence without interest and gazing beyond it into the realm of the real where subjects and objects act and rest purely, without utterance. "Launch into the deep," says Jacques Ellul[4], "and you shall see."

16   The secret of seeing is, then, the pearl of great price. If I thought he could teach me to find it and keep it forever I would stagger barefoot across a hundred deserts after any lunatic at all. But although the pearl may be found, it may not be sought. The literature of illumination reveals this above all: although it comes to those who wait for it, it is always,

[3] Henry David Thoreau was a nineteenth-century American poet, essayist, and naturalist.
[4] Jacques Ellul is the author of eight books on religion and on our technological society.

even to the most practiced and adept, a gift and a total surprise. I return from one walk knowing where the killdeer nests in the field by the creek and the hour the laurel blooms. I return from the same walk a day later scarcely knowing my own name. Litanies hum in my ears; my tongue flaps in my mouth Ailinon, alleluia! I cannot cause light; the most I can do is try to put myself in the path of its beam. It is possible, in deep space, to sail on solar wind. Light, be it particle or wave, has force: you rig a giant sail and go. The secret of seeing is to sail on solar wind. Hone and spread your spirit till you yourself are a sail, whetted, translucent, broadside to the merest puff.

17   When her doctor took her bandages off and led her into the garden, the girl who was no longer blind saw "the tree with the lights in it." It was for this tree I searched through the peach orchards of summer, in the forests of fall and down winter and spring for years. Then one day I was walking along Tinker Creek thinking of nothing at all and I saw the tree with the lights in it. I saw the backyard cedar where the mourning doves roost charged and transfigured, each cell buzzing with flame. I stood on the grass with the lights in it, grass that was wholly fire, utterly focused and utterly dreamed. It was less like seeing than like being for the first time seen, knocked breathless by a powerful glance. The flood of fire abated, but I'm still spending the power. Gradually the lights went out in the cedar, the colors died, the cells unflamed and disappeared. I was still ringing. I had been my whole life a bell, and never knew it until at that moment I was lifted and struck. I have since only very rarely seen the tree with the lights in it. The vision comes and goes, mostly goes, but I live for it, for the moment when the mountains open and a new light roars in spate through the crack, and the mountains slam.

Seeing

Questions on Content, Style, and Structure

1. Why does Dillard begin her essay with a discussion of the newly sighted patients described in *Space and Sight*?

2. How does reading *Space and Sight* affect Dillard's sight for several weeks?

3. Why can't Dillard maintain the point of view she acquires after reading the book? What does she mean by "I couldn't unpeach the peaches" (paragraph 8)?

4. Why, in paragraph 8, does Dillard refer to her infancy? to the story of the two rabbis?

5. How is seeing "a matter of verbalization"? How is it a matter of "letting go"?

6. Identify several of the similes and metaphors Dillard uses to describe herself in paragraphs 12 through 14. How do they clarify her meaning?

7. What, according to Dillard, is the "secret of seeing"? What image does she use to explain this secret?

8. Why does Dillard conclude by describing the tree she has searched for all summer? Where is this tree? What does this tree represent to her?

9. What does Dillard mean when, in her last sentence, she says she lives for the moment when the mountains open, light roars, and the mountains slam?

10. Briefly characterize the diction and tone of this selection. Support your answers with reference to specific passages in the essay.

11. In one or two sentences, tell what you think is Dillard's purpose in writing this essay.

Vocabulary

unencumbered (2)
tactual (4)
disheartening (5)
intricately (8)
gnosticism (8)
cataclysms (10)

unscrupulous (12)
zephyr (13)
discalced (15)
litanies (16)
spate (17)

Suggestions for Writing

1. Write an essay describing a familiar scene that you have only recently "seen" for the first time.

2. Write an impressionistic description of a favorite outdoor spot. Explain both the appearance of the place and the atmosphere or mood it presents. Try to avoid clichés.

3. Write an objective description of a common object. Include as many details regarding its size, shape, color, texture, taste, and so forth as possible.

Once More to the Lake (August 1941)
E. B. White

Elwyn Brooks White was an editor and writer for *The New Yorker* and a columnist for *Harper's Magazine.* He is well known for his essays, collected in volumes including *One Man's Meat* (1943), *The Second Tree from the Corner* (1954), and *The Points of My Compass* (1962), and for his children's books, *Charlotte's Web* (1952) and *Stuart Little* (1945). This essay, written in 1941, originally appeared in *Harper's.*

1   One summer, along about 1904, my father rented a camp on a lake in Maine and took us all there for the month of August. We all got ringworm from some kittens and had to rub Pond's Extract on our arms and legs night and morning, and my father rolled over in a canoe with all his clothes on; but outside of that the vacation was a success and from then on none of us ever thought there was any place in the world like that lake in Maine. We returned summer after summer—always on August 1st for one month. I have since become a salt-water man, but sometimes in summer there are days when the restlessness of the tides and the fearful cold of the sea water and the incessant wind which blows across the afternoon and into the evening make me wish for the placidity of a lake in the woods. A few weeks ago this feeling got so strong I bought myself a couple of bass hooks and a spinner and returned to the lake where we used to go, for a week's fishing and to revisit old haunts.

2   I took along my son, who had never had any fresh water up his nose and who had seen lily pads only from train windows. On the journey over to the lake I began to wonder what it would be like. I wondered how time would have marred this unique, this holy spot—the coves and streams, the hills that the sun set behind, the camps and the paths behind the camps. I was sure the tarred road would have found it out and I wondered in what other ways it would be desolated. It is strange how much you can remember about places like that once you allow your mind to return into the grooves which lead back. You remember one thing, and that suddenly reminds you of another thing. I guess I remembered clearest of all the early mornings, when the lake was cool and motionless, remembered how the bedroom smelled of the lumber it was made of and of the wet woods whose scent entered through the screen. The partitions in the camp were thin and did not extend clear to the top of the rooms, and as I was always the first up I would dress softly so as not to wake the others, and sneak out into the sweet outdoors and start out in the canoe, keeping close along the shore in the long shadows of the pines. I remembered being very careful never to rub my paddle against the gunwale for fear of disturbing the stillness of the cathedral.

3   The lake had never been what you would call a wild lake. There were cottages sprinkled around the shores, and it was in farming country although the shores of the lake were quite heavily wooded. Some of the cottages were owned by nearby farmers, and you would live at the shore and eat your meals at the farmhouse. That's what our family did. But although it wasn't wild, it was a fairly large and undisturbed lake and there were places in it which, to a child at least, seemed infinitely remote and primeval.

4   I was right about the tar: it led to within half a mile of the shore. But when I got back there, with my boy, and we settled into a camp near a farmhouse and into the kind of summertime I had known, I could tell that it was going to be pretty much the same as it had been before—I knew it, lying in bed the first morning, smelling the bedroom, and hearing the boy sneak quietly out and go off along the shore in a boat. I began to sustain the illusion that he was I, and therefore by simple transposition, that I was my father. This sensation persisted, kept cropping up all the time we were there. It was not an entirely new feeling, but in this setting it grew much stronger. I seemed to be living a dual existence. I would be in the middle of some simple act, I would be picking up a bait box or laying down a table fork, or I would be saying something, and suddenly it would be not I but my father who was saying the words or making the gesture. It gave me a creepy sensation.

5   We went fishing the first morning. I felt the same damp moss covering the worms in the bait can, and saw the dragonfly alight on the tip of my rod as it hovered a few inches from the surface of the water. It was the arrival of this fly that convinced me beyond any doubt that everything was as it always had been, that the years were a mirage and there had been no years. The small waves were the same, chucking the rowboat under the chin as we fished at anchor, and the boat was the same boat, the same color green and the ribs broken in the same places, and under the floor-boards the same fresh-water leavings and débris—the dead helgramite,* the wisps of moss, the rusty discarded fishhook, the dried blood from yesterday's catch. We stared silently at the tips of our rods, at the dragonflies that came and went. I lowered the tip of mine into the water, tentatively, pensively dislodging the fly, which darted two feet away, poised, darted two feet back, and came to rest again a little farther up the rod. There had been no years between the ducking of this dragonfly and other one—the one that was part of memory. I looked at the boy, who was silently watching his fly, and it was my hands that held his rod, my eyes watching. I felt dizzy and didn't know which rod I was at the end of.

6   We caught two bass, hauling them in briskly as though they were mackerel, pulling them over the side of the boat in a businesslike manner

* A helgramite is an insect sometimes used for bait.

without any landing net, and stunning them with a blow on the back of the head. When we got back for a swim before lunch, the lake was exactly where we had left it, the same number of inches from the dock, and there was only the merest suggestion of a breeze. This seemed an utterly enchanted sea, this lake you could leave to its own devices for a few hours and come back to, and find that it had not stirred, this constant and trustworthy body of water. In the shallows, the dark, water-soaked sticks and twigs, smooth and old, were undulating in clusters on the bottom against the clean ribbed sand, and the track of the mussel was plain. A school of minnows swam by, each minnow with its small individual shadow, doubling the attendance, so clear and sharp in the sunlight. Some of the other campers were in swimming, along the shore, one of them with a cake of soap, and the water felt thin and clear and unsubstantial. Over the years there had been this person with the cake of soap, this cultist, and here he was. There had been no years.

7   Up to the farmhouse to dinner through the teeming, dusty field, the road under our sneakers was only a two-track road. The middle track was missing, the one with the marks of the hooves and the splotches of dried, flaky manure. There had always been three tracks to choose from in choosing which track to walk in; now the choice was narrowed down to two. For a moment I missed terribly the middle alternative. But the way led past the tennis court, and something about the way it lay there in the sun reassured me; the tape had loosened along the backline, the alleys were green with plantains and other weeds, and the net (installed in June and removed in September) sagged in the dry noon, and the whole place steamed with mid-day heat and hunger and emptiness. There was a choice of pie for dessert, and one was blueberry and one was apple, and the waitresses were the same country girls, there having been no passage of time, only the illusion of it as in a dropped curtain—the waitresses were still fifteen; their hair had been washed, that was the only difference—they had been to the movies and seen the pretty girls with the clean hair.

8   Summertime, oh summertime, pattern of life indelible, the fade-proof lake, the woods unshatterable, the pasture with the sweetfern and the juniper forever and ever, summer without end; this was the background, and the life along the shore was the design, the cottages with their innocent and tranquil design, their tiny docks with the flagpole and the American flag floating against the white clouds in the blue sky, the little paths over the roots of the trees leading from camp to camp and the paths leading back to the outhouses and the can of lime for sprinkling, and at the souvenir counters at the store the miniature birch-bark canoes and the post cards that showed things looking a little better than they looked. This was the American family at play, escaping the city heat, wondering whether the newcomers in the camp at the head of the cove were "common" or "nice," wondering whether it was true that the people who drove up for Sunday dinner at the farmhouse were turned away because there wasn't enough chicken.

9   It seemed to me, as I kept remembering all this, that those times and those summers had been infinitely precious and worth saving. There had been jollity and peace and goodness. The arriving (at the beginning of August) had been so big a business in itself, at the railway station the farm wagon drawn up, the first smell of the pine-laden air, the first glimpse of the smiling farmer, and the great importance of the trunks and your father's enormous authority in such matters, and the feel of the wagon under you for a long ten-mile haul, and at the top of the last long hill catching the first view of the lake after eleven months of not seeing this cherished body of water. The shouts and cries of the other campers when they saw you, and the trunks to be unpacked, to give up their rich burden. (Arriving was less exciting nowadays, when you sneaked up in your car and parked it under a tree near the camp and took out the bags and in five minutes it was all over, no fuss, no loud wonderful fuss about trunks.)

10   Peace and goodness and jollity. The only thing that was wrong now, really, was the sound of the place, an unfamiliar nervous sound of the outboard motors. This was the note that jarred, the one thing that would sometimes break the illusion and set the years moving. In those other summertimes all motors were inboard; and when they were at a little distance, the noise they made was a sedative, an ingredient of summer sleep. They were one-cylinder and two-cylinder engines, and some were make-and-break and some were jump-spark, but they all made a sleepy sound across the lake. The one-lungers throbbed and fluttered, and the twin-cylinder ones purred and purred, and that was a quiet sound too. But now the campers all had outboards. In the daytime, in the hot mornings, these motors made a petulant, irritable sound; at night, in the still evening when the afterglow lit the water, they whined about one's ears like mosquitoes. My boy loved our rented outboard, and his great desire was to achieve singlehanded mastery over it, and authority, and he soon learned the trick of choking it a little (but not too much), and the adjustment of the needle valve. Watching him I would remember the things you could do with the old one-cylinder engine with the heavy flywheel, how you could have it eating out of your hand if you got really close to it spiritually. Motor boats in those days didn't have clutches, and you would make a landing by shutting off the motor at the proper time and coasting in with a dead rudder. But there was a way of reversing them, if you learned the trick, by cutting the switch and putting it on again exactly on the final dying revolution of the flywheel, so that it would kick back against compression and begin reversing. Approaching a dock in a strong following breeze, it was difficult to slow up sufficiently by the ordinary coasting method, and if a boy felt he had complete mastery over his motor, he was tempted to keep it running beyond its time and then reverse it a few feet from the dock. It took a cool nerve, because if you threw the switch a twentieth of a second too soon you would catch the flywheel when it still had speed enough to go up past center, and the boat would leap ahead, charging bull-fashion at the dock.

11   We had a good week at the camp. The bass were biting well and the sun shone endlessly, day after day. We would be tired at night and lie down in the accumulated heat of the little bedrooms after the long hot day and the breeze would stir almost imperceptibly outside and the smell of the swamp drift in through the rusty screens. Sleep would come easily and in the morning the red squirrel would be on the roof, tapping out his gay routine. I kept remembering everything, lying in bed in the mornings—the small steamboat that had a long rounded stern like the lip of a Ubangi, and how quietly she ran on the moonlight sails, when the older boys played their mandolins and the girls sang and we ate doughnuts dipped in sugar, and how sweet the music was on the water in the shining night, and what it had felt like to think about girls then. After breakfast we would go up to the store and the things were in the same place—the minnows in a bottle, the plugs and spinners disarranged and pawed over by the youngsters from the boys' camp, the fig newtons and the Beeman's gum. Outside, the road was tarred and cars stood in front of the store. Inside, all was just as it had always been, except there was more Coca-Cola and not so much Moxie and root beer and birch beer and sarsaparilla. We would walk out with a bottle of pop apiece and sometimes the pop would backfire up our noses and hurt. We explored the streams, quietly, where the turtles slid off the sunny logs and dug their way into the soft bottom; and we lay on the town wharf and fed worms to the tame bass. Everywhere we went I had trouble making out which was I, the one walking at my side, the one walking in my pants.

12   One afternoon while we were there at that lake a thunderstorm came up. It was like the revival of an old melodrama that I had seen long ago with childish awe. The second-act climax of the drama of the electrical disturbance over a lake in America had not changed in any important respect. This was the big scene, still the big scene. The whole thing was so familiar, the first feeling of oppression and heat and a general air around camp of not wanting to go very far away. In midafternoon (it was all the same) a curious darkening of the sky, and a lull in everything that had made life tick; and then the way the boats suddenly swung the other way at their moorings with the coming of a breeze out of the new quarter, and the premonitory rumble. Then the kettle drum, then the snare, then the bass drum and cymbals, then crackling light against the dark, and the gods grinning and licking their chops in the hills. Afterward the calm, the rain steadily rustling in the calm lake, the return of light and hope and spirits, and the campers running out in joy and relief to go swimming in the rain, their bright cries perpetuating the deathless joke about how they were getting simply drenched, and the children screaming with delight at the new sensation of bathing in the rain, and the joke about getting drenched linking the generations in a strong indestructible chain. And the comedian who waded in carrying an umbrella.

13   When the others went swimming my son said he was going in too. He

pulled his dripping trunks from the line where they had hung all through the shower, and wrung them out. Languidly, and with no thought of going in, I watched him, his hard little body, skinny and bare, saw him wince slightly as he pulled up around his vitals the small, soggy, icy garment. As he buckled the swollen belt suddenly my groin felt the chill of death.

Once More to the Lake (August 1941)

Questions on Content, Style, and Structure

1. How does White introduce this essay? Why?
2. What gives White a "creepy sensation"?
3. What things about the lake have remained unchanged from White's boyhood?
4. What things around the lake have changed? What is the one jarring note that "set the years moving"?
5. What is the effect of the first sentence in paragraph 8? sentence 3 in paragraph 9?
6. Evaluate White's use of specific sensory detail in his descriptions of the lake and the surrounding area. Support your answer with examples.
7. In what ways is this essay ordered and unified?
8. What images are used in paragraph 12 to depict the thunderstorm?
9. Why does White feel "the chill of death" as he watches his son put on his wet swimsuit? What is the relationship between this final comment and White's recurring feeling that he is his father?
10. This narrative is primarily developed by what expository strategy?

Vocabulary

incessant (1)	unsubstantial (6)
placidity (1)	indelible (8)
desolated (2)	imperceptibly (11)
primeval (3)	mandolins (11)
undulating (6)	languidly (13)

Suggestions for Writing

1. If you have returned to your home town since you've been at college, write an essay comparing the way you see some familiar place (your room, high school, local hangout, etc.) now to the way you used to see it.
2. Write an essay describing a vacation of your childhood that was full

of "jollity and peace and goodness." What made this particular vacation so special? Remember to use enough details to recreate the experience clearly for the reader.

3. Describe the worst vacation you ever had, again using vivid details to make your reader experience the trip with you.

Will Our World Survive?
John J. McKetta

John J. McKetta is currently a professor of chemical engineering at the University of Texas at Austin. He has published over 378 articles and has written or collaborated on seventeen books. He also served as the first chairman of the National Energy Policy Committee under President Nixon and was chairman of the Committee on National Air Quality Management from 1970–75. This selection was originally a speech delivered to the American Trucking Association in 1970; since that time it has appeared in numerous publications.

1   There is an entire spectrum from zero to infinity, of views and actions on almost any problem.

2   Let's take the pollution problem, for example. We all know there are still some companies and cities who put toxic gases and liquids into our air and streams. It's almost unbelievable that many of our large cities still discharge raw sewage, or only partially treated sewage into our streams. Both industry and the cities should be stopped immediately from these flagrant violations. On the other extreme, we have those people who wish to have distilled water in the streams and zero particulates in the atmosphere. These are impossible concentrations and could not be attained even if we had no people on this earth. The answer, obviously, is somewhere between these two extremes.

3   We're all deeply concerned about reports of the destruction of our environment as a result of technological recklessness, overpopulation, and the lack of consideration to the preservation of nature. As chairman of the National Air Quality Management Committee, I have to read great amounts of technical literature in this area. I've turned up a lot of information that I'd like to share with you.

Is Our Oxygen Really Disappearing?

4   My first surprise concerns the air we breathe. You have been reading that we are seriously depleting the oxygen in the atmosphere and replacing it with toxic substances such as carbon monoxide.

5   We've always been taught that oxygen in our atmosphere is supplied by green plants using the process of photosynthesis. We know that plants take in carbon dioxide and through activation by sunlight, combine CO_2 with water to make starches and cellulose, and give off oxygen. In this way the whole chain of plant and animal life is sustained by energy from the sun. When the vegetable or animal materials thus produced are eaten, burned, or allowed to decay, they combine with oxygen and return to the carbon dioxide and water from whence they came. We all know this. Then, what is the surprise?

6   Surprise number one is that most of the oxygen in the atmosphere doesn't come from photosynthesis. The evidence is now overwhelming that photosynthesis is just inadequate to have produced the amount of oxygen that is present in our atmosphere. The amount of oxygen produced by photosynthesis is just exactly enough to convert the plant tissue back to the carbon dioxide and water from which it came. The net gain in oxygen due to photosynthesis is extremely small. The oxygen in the atmosphere had to come from another source. The most likely possibility involves the photodissociation of water vapor in the upper atmosphere by high energy rays from the sun and by cosmic rays.

7   This means that the supply of oxygen in the atmosphere is virtually unlimited. It is not threatened by man's activities in any significant way. If all the organic material on earth were oxidized, it would reduce the atmospheric concentration of oxygen by less than 1 per cent. We can forget the depletion of oxygen in the atmosphere and get on with the solution of more serious problems.

Will Carbon Monoxide Kill Us All?

8   As you know, the most toxic component of automobile exhaust is carbon monoxide. Each year man adds 270 million tons of carbon monoxide to the atmosphere. Most of this comes from automobiles. People are concerned about the accumulation of this toxic material because they know that it has a life in dry air of about three years. Monitoring stations on land and sea have been measuring the carbon monoxide content of the atmosphere.

9   Since there are nine times more automobiles in the northern hemisphere than in the southern hemisphere it is expected that the northern hemisphere will have a much higher concentration of atmospheric carbon monoxide. The true measurements show, however, that there is no difference in CO amounts between the hemispheres and that the overall concentration in the air is not increasing at all. In fact, they've found higher concentrations of CO over the Atlantic and Pacific oceans than over land.

10   Early in 1971 scientists at the Stanford Research Institute in Palo Alto disclosed that they had done some experiments in smog chambers containing soil. They reported that carbon monoxide rapidly disappeared from the chamber. After sterilizing the soil they found that the carbon monoxide did not disappear. They quickly identified that organisms were

responsible for CO disappearance. These organisms, on a world-wide basis, are using all of the 270 million tons of the CO made by man for their own metabolism, thus enriching the soils of the forest and the fields.

11   This does not say carbon monoxide is any less toxic. It does say that, in spite of man's activities, carbon monoxide will never build up in the atmosphere to a dangerous level except on a localized basis. To put things in perspective, let me point out that the average concentration of CO in Austin, Texas, is about 1.5 parts per million. In downtown Houston, in heavy traffic, it sometimes builds up to 15 or 20 p.p.m. In Los Angeles it gets to be as high as 35 p.p.m. In parking garages and tunnels it is sometimes 50 p.p.m.

12   Here lies surprise number two for you—do you know that the CO content of cigarette smoke is as high as 42,000 p.p.m.? The CO concentration in practically any smoke-filled room grossly exceeds the safety standards we allow in our laboratories. Of course, 35 to 50 p.p.m. CO should not be ignored but there are so many of us who subject ourselves to CO concentrations voluntarily (and involuntarily) that are greater than those of our worse polluted cities, including those in the Holland Tunnel in New York, without any catastrophic effects. It is not at all unusual for CO concentrations to reach 100–200 p.p.m. range in poorly ventilated, smoke-filled rooms. Incidentally, if a heavy smoker spends several hours without smoking in highly polluted city air containing 35 p.p.m. of CO concentration, the concentration of CO in his blood will actually decrease. In the broad expanse of our natural air, CO levels are totally safe for human beings. We all know that we should not start our automobiles in closed unventilated garages.

Will Oxides of Nitrogen Choke Us to Death?

13   One cannot help but be extremely impressed by the various research efforts on the part of petroleum, automotive, and chemical companies to remove oxides of nitrogen from the products of combustion in the tail pipe gas of our automobiles. You've read about the brilliant work of Dr. Haagen-Smit that showed that the oxides of nitrogen play a critical role in the chain reaction of photochemical smog formation in Los Angeles. Oxides of nitrogen are definitely problems in places where temperature inversions trap the air.

14   But we've all known for many years that nature also produces oxides of nitrogen.

15   The number three surprise (and shock) is that most of the oxides of nitrogen come from nature. If we consider only nitric oxide and nitrogen dioxide, the best estimates are 97 per cent is natural and only 3 per cent is man-made. If we also consider nitrous oxide and amines, then it turns out that 99 plus per cent is natural and less than 1 per cent is man-made.

16   The significance of this is that even if we are 100 per cent successful in our removal of the oxides of nitrogen from combustion bases, we will still have more than 99 per cent left in the atmosphere which is produced by nature.

Did Lake Erie Really Succumb?

17   We've all read for some time that Lake Erie is dead. It's true that the beaches are no longer safe in the Cleveland area and the oxygen content at the bottom of the lake is decreasing. This is called eutrophication. The blame has been placed on phosphates as the cause of this situation. Housewives were urged to curb the use of phosphate detergents. In fact, for several years phosphate detergents were taken off the market. There's been a change in law since scientific evidence proved that the phosphate detergents were not the only culprits and never should have been removed from the market in the first place.

18   Some studies show clearly that the cause of the eutrophication of Lake Erie has not been properly defined. This evidence suggests that if we totally stopped using phosphate detergents it would have no effect whatever on the eutrophication of Lake Erie. Many experiments have now been carried out that bring surprise number four—that it is the organic carbon content from sewage that is using up the oxygen in the lake and not the phosphates in the detergents. One must be extremely careful in these studies since the most recent report by Dr. D. W. Shindler states that phosphorus is the culprit rather than the organic carbon. But the reason that the Cleveland area beaches are not swimmable is that the coliform bacterial count is too high, not that there is too much detergent in the water.

19   Enlarged and improved sewage treatment facilities by Detroit, Toledo, Sandusky, and Cleveland will be required to correct this situation. Our garbage disposal units do far more to pollute Lake Erie than do the phosphate detergents. If we put in the proper sewage treatment facilities, the lake will sparkle blue again in a very few years.

20   Incidentally, we've all heard that Lake Superior is so much larger, cleaner, and nicer than Lake Erie. It's kind of strange then to learn that in 1972 and 1973 more tons of commercial fish were taken from Lake Erie than were taken from Lake Superior.

Is DDT Really Our Deadly Foe?

21   DDT and other chlorinated compounds are supposedly endangering the lives of mankind and eliminating some bird species by the thinning of the egg shells of birds. There is a big question mark as to whether or not this is true. Even if it is true, it's quite possible that the desirable properties of DDT so greatly outnumber the undesirable ones that it might prove to be a serious mistake to ban entirely this remarkable chemical.

22   Many of you have heard of Dr. Norman E. Borlaug, the Nobel Peace Prize winner. He is opposed to the banning of DDT. Obviously he is a competent scientist. He won the Nobel prize because he was able to develop a new strain of wheat that can double the food production per acre anywhere in the world that it is grown.

23   Dr. Borlaug said, "If DDT is banned in the United States, I have wasted my life's work. I have dedicated myself to finding better methods of feeding the world's starving population. Without DDT and other important agricultural chemicals, our goals are simply unattainable."

24   DDT has had a miraculous impact on arresting insect borne diseases and increasing grain production from fields once ravaged by insects. According to the World Health Organization, malaria fatalities alone dropped from 4 million a year in the 1930s to less than 1 million per year in 1968. Other insect borne diseases, such as encephalitis, yellow fever, and typhus fever, showed similar declines.

25   Surprise number five is that it has been estimated that 100 million human beings who would have died of these afflictions are alive today because of DDT. Incidentally, recent tests indicate that the thinning of bird egg shells may have been caused by mercury compounds rather than DDT. . . .

26   Many people feel that mankind is the one responsible for the disappearance of animal species. The abundance of evidence indicates that he has very little to do with it. About 50 species are expected to disappear during this century. It is also true that 50 species became extinct last century and 50 species the century before that and so on.

27   Dr. T. H. Jukes of the University of California points out that about 100 million species of plant and animal life have become extinct since life began on this planet, about 3 billion years ago. Animals come and animals disappear. This is the essence of evolution as Mr. Darwin pointed out many years ago. Mankind is a relatively recent visitor here.

28   Surprise number six is that one of man's failures is that he has not been successful in eliminating a single insect species—in spite of his all-out war on certain undesirable ones in recent years.

Is Mankind the Real Polluter?

29   Here's the seventh surprise! The late Dr. William Pecora reported that all of man's air pollution during his thousands of years of life on earth does not equal the amount of particulate and noxious gases from just three volcanoes (Krakatoa, near Java—1883; Mt. Katmai, Alaska—1912; Hekla, Iceland—1947).

30   Dr. Pecora pointed out that nature's pure water is not so pure after all. Here are a few examples:

   1. The natural springs feeding the Arkansas and Red Rivers carry approximately 17 tons of salt per minute.
   2. The Lemonade Springs in New Mexico carry approximately 900 pounds

H_2SO_4 per million pounds of water. (This is more than ten times the acid concentration in coal mine discharges.)

3. The Mississippi River carries over 2 million tons of natural sediment into the Gulf of Mexico each day.

4. The Paria River of Arizona and Utah carries as much as 500 times more natural sediment per unit volume than the Mississippi River. The Mississippi sediment concentration ranges from 100 to 1,000 mg. per liter. The Paria River concentration has been measured as high as 780,000 mg. per liter during 1973.

Should We Go Back to the Good Old Days?

31   Dr. Isaac Asimov admonishes us not to believe the trash about the happy lives that people once had before all this nasty industrialization came along. There was no such thing. One of his neighbors once asked him, "What has all these 2,000 years of development of industry and civilization done for us? Wouldn't we have been happier in 100 B.C.?" Dr. Asimov said, "No, chances are 97 out of 100 that, if you were not a poor slave, you'd be a poor farmer, living at bare subsistence level."

32   When people think of ancient times, they think of themselves as members of aristocracy. They are never slaves, never peasants, but that's what most of them would be.

33   My wife once said to me, "If we lived a hundred years ago we'd have no trouble getting servants." I said, "If we'd lived 150 years ago, we'd be the servants."

34   Let's consider what life was really like in America just 150 years ago. For one thing, we didn't have to worry about pollution very long—because life was very brief. Life expectancy of males was about 38 years. The work week was 72 hours. The women's lot was even worse. They worked 98 hours a week scrubbing floors, making clothes by hand, bringing in fire wood, cooking in heavy iron pots, fighting off insects without pesticides. Most of the clothes were rags by present day standards. There were no fresh vegetables in winter. Vitamin deficiency diseases were prevalent. Homes were cold in winter and sweltering in the summer.

35   Epidemics were expected yearly and chances were high that they would carry off some members of the immediate family. If you think the water pollution is bad now, it was deadly then. In 1793 one person in every five in the city of Philadelphia died in a single epidemic of typhoid as a result of polluted water. Many people of that time never heard a symphony orchestra or traveled more than 20 miles from their birthplace during their entire lifetime. Many informed people do not want to return to the "paradise" of 150 years ago. Perhaps the simple life was not so simple.

Are Nuclear Plants Latter Day Witches?

36   Dr. A. Letcher Jones points out that in every age we have people practicing witchcraft in one form or another. We all think the people of New

England were irrational in accusing certain women of being witches without evidence to prove it.

37   Suppose someone accused you of being a witch? How could you prove you were not? It is impossible to prove unless you can give evidence. It is precisely this same witchcraft practice that is being used to deter the construction of nuclear power plants. The opponents are saying these plants are witches and it is up to the builders and owners to prove they are not. The scientific evidence is that nuclear power plants constructed to date are the cleanest and least polluting devices for generating electricity so far developed by man. We need electricity to maintain the standard of living we have reached, but to the extreme environmentalists we are witches. We should be burned at the stake.

38   We hear the same accusations about lead compounds from the gasoline engine. Our Environmental Protection Agency has no evidence that there has ever been a single case of death, or even illness, from lead in the air coming from burning of gasoline, but they still insist we remove the lead from gasoline.

39   To the EPA we are witches. They have no evidence—no proof—we are pronounced guilty! And yet you know gasoline needs some additives to prevent engine knocks. If we don't use tetraethyl-lead we'll have to use aromatic compounds. Some aromatics are carcinogenic. We know that! The use of unleaded gasoline also can use up to 12 per cent more crude oil. (Incidentally, the real reason for removing lead from gasoline was because it was suspected that lead poisoned the catalyst in the emission control unit. Now we have some evidence that it isn't the lead but ethylene bromide which is the poisoner.)

Is There Real Hope for Our Survival?

40   From what we read and hear it would seem we are on the edge of impending doom. A scientific evaluation of the evidence does not support this conclusion. Of course we have many undesirable problems attributed to technological activities. The solution of these problems will require a technical understanding of their nature, not through emotion. They cannot be solved unless properly identified, which will require more technically trained people—not less.

41   Thomas Jefferson said if the public is properly informed, the people will make wise decisions. The public has not been getting all of the facts on matters relating to ecology. This is the reason some of us are speaking out on this subject today—as technical people and as citizens.

42   In summary, let me state we are not on the brink of ecological disaster. Our O_2 is not disappearing. There will be no build up of poisonous CO. The waters can be made pure again by adequate sewage treatment plants. The disappearance of species is natural. A large percentage of pollution is natural pollution and would be here whether or not man was on this

earth. We cannot solve our real problems unless we attack them on the basis of what we know rather than what we don't know. Let us use our knowledge and not our fears to solve the real problems of our environment.

Will Our World Survive?

Questions on Content, Style, and Structure

1. Is McKetta's evaluation of our environmental problems optimistic or pessimistic?

2. How does McKetta establish his authority early in the essay?

3. Summarize McKetta's general attitude toward industrialists, on one hand, and those he calls "extreme environmentalists" on the other. Support your answer with specific reference to the essay. (Would you be surprised to know that this essay was reprinted and distributed by the Peabody Coal Company?)

4. What two unifying devices does McKetta use to tie his points together?

5. Why, according to McKetta, can we stop worrying about the depletion of oxygen?

6. Why does McKetta mention cigarettes in his discussion of smog? Is his point convincing?

7. Why does McKetta quote Dr. Norman E. Borlaug and other scientists throughout his essay?

8. Evaluate the logic of paragraphs 26 through 28. Considering such animals as the whales, do you see any problems in the argument that "animals come and animals disappear"?

9. How does McKetta make vivid his picture of life 150 years ago?

10. Is McKetta's analogy between witch hunters and critics of nuclear power a persuasive one? Explain your answer.

11. How does McKetta conclude his essay?

12. Summarize McKetta's "surprises." Do you agree with him on all his points?

Vocabulary

spectrum (1)	culprits (17)
toxic (2)	sediment (30)
flagrant (2)	admonishes (31)
depletion (7)	impending (40)
component (8)	

Suggestions for Writing

1. If you disagree with McKetta on some point (such as use of DDT or nuclear energy), write an essay arguing your position.

2. Write an essay that describes a local environmental problem and suggests a solution.

3. Write an essay evaluating McKetta's essay; point out the strengths and weaknesses of his argument.

The Road Not Taken
Robert Frost

Robert Frost was a twentieth-century poet whose poems frequently focus on the characters, events, and scenes of New England. Three of his many volumes of poetry won Pulitzer Prizes: *New Hampshire* (1923), *Collected Poems* (1930), and *A Further Range* (1936). Frost taught at Amherst College, Dartmouth, Yale, and Harvard, and was one of the founders of the Bread Loaf School of English in Vermont. This poem was published in 1916.

1 Two roads diverged in a yellow wood,
  And sorry I could not travel both
  And be one traveler, long I stood
  And looked down one as far as I could
  To where it bent in the undergrowth;

6 Then took the other, as just as fair,
  And having perhaps the better claim,
  Because it was grassy and wanted wear;
  Though as for that the passing there
  Had worn them really about the same,

11 And both that morning equally lay
  In leaves no step had trodden black.
  Oh, I kept the first for another day!
  Yet knowing how way leads on to way,
  I doubted if I should ever come back.

16 I shall be telling this with a sigh
    Somewhere ages and ages hence:
    Two roads diverged in a wood, and I—
    I took the one less traveled by,
    And that has made all the difference.

The Road Not Taken

Questions on Content, Style, and Structure

1. In this poem the speaker was faced with what decision? What was his choice?
2. How do the roads differ? What is similar about them?
3. What does the speaker mean when he says, "Yet knowing how way leads on to way,/I doubted if I should ever come back" (lines 14–15)?
4. Why does the speaker think he will be telling about his decision in the future with a sigh?
5. Paraphrase the last three lines of the poem.
6. How does Frost use the story of two roads as a metaphor?

Vocabulary

diverged (l. 1)
trodden (l. 12)

Suggestions for Writing

1. Write an essay explaining how choosing a less popular plan of action has made a difference in your life.
2. Write an essay explaining a decision you now regret.
3. Write an essay using some scene in nature as a metaphor for an important event in your life.

The Open Window
"Saki" (H. H. Munro)

Hector Hugh Munro was a journalist and short story writer who wrote
under the pseudonym "Saki." His collections of stories include
Reginald (1904), *Reginald in Russia* (1910), *The Chronicles Clovis*
(1911), and *Beasts and Superbeasts* (1914). This story is collected in
The Short Stories of Saki, published in 1930.

1   "My aunt will be down presently, Mr. Nuttel," said a very self-possessed
young lady of fifteen; "in the meantime you must try and put up with
me."

2   Framton Nuttel endeavoured to say the correct something which
should duly flatter the niece of the moment without unduly discounting
the aunt that was to come. Privately he doubted more than ever whether
these formal visits on a succession of total strangers would do much
towards helping the nerve cure which he was supposed to be undergoing.

3   "I know how it will be," his sister had said when he was preparing to
migrate to this rural retreat; "you will bury yourself down there and not
speak to a living soul, and your nerves will be worse than ever from
moping. I shall just give you letters of introduction to all the people I
know there. Some of them, as far as I can remember, were quite nice."

4   Framton wondered whether Mrs. Sappleton, the lady to whom he was
presenting one of the letters of introduction, came into the nice division.

5   "Do you know many of the people round here?" asked the niece, when
she judged that they had had sufficient silent communion.

6   "Hardly a soul," said Framton, "My sister was staying here, at the
rectory, you know, some four years ago, and she gave me letters of introduction to some of the people here."

7   He made the last statement in a tone of distinct regret.

8   "Then you know practically nothing about my aunt?" pursued the
self-possessed young lady.

9   "Only her name and address," admitted the caller. He was wondering
whether Mrs. Sappleton was in the married or widowed state. An un-
definable something about the room seemed to suggest masculine habi-
tation.

10   "Her great tragedy happened just three years ago," said the child; "that
would be since your sister's time."

11   "Her tragedy?" asked Framton; somehow in this restful country spot
tragedies seemed out of place.

12   "You may wonder why we keep that window wide open on an October
afternoon," said the niece, indicating a large French window that opened
on to a lawn.

13   "It is quite warm for the time of the year," said Framton; "but has that window got anything to do with the tragedy?"

14   "Out through that window, three years ago to a day, her husband and her two young brothers went off for their day's shooting. They never came back. In crossing the moor to their favourite snipe-shooting ground they were all three engulfed in a treacherous piece of bog. It had been that dreadful wet summer, you know, and places that were safe in other years gave way suddenly without warning. Their bodies were never recovered. That was the dreadful part of it." Here the child's voice lost its self-possessed note and became falteringly human. "Poor aunt always thinks that they will come back some day, they and the little brown spaniel that was lost with them, and walk in at that window just as they used to do. That is why the window is kept open every evening till it is quite dusk. Poor dear aunt, she has often told me how they went out, her husband with his white waterproof coat over his arm, and Ronnie, her youngest brother, singing, 'Bertie, why do you bound?' as he always did to tease her, because she said it got on her nerves. Do you know, sometimes on still, quiet evenings like this, I almost get a creepy feeling that they will all walk in through that window—"

15   She broke off with a little shudder. It was a relief to Framton when the aunt bustled into the room with a whirl of apologies for being late in making her appearance.

16   "I hope Vera has been amusing you?" she said.

17   "She has been very interesting," said Framton.

18   "I hope you don't mind the open window," said Mrs. Sappleton briskly; "my husband and brothers will be home directly from shooting, and they always come in this way. They've been out for snipe in the marshes today, so they'll make a fine mess over my poor carpets. So like you menfolk, isn't it?"

19   She rattled on cheerfully about the shooting and the scarcity of birds, and the prospects for duck in the winter. To Framton it was all purely horrible. He made a desperate but only partially successful effort to turn the talk on to a less ghastly topic; he was conscious that his hostess was giving him only a fragment of her attention, and her eyes were constantly straying past him to the open window and the lawn beyond. It was certainly an unfortunate coincidence that he should have paid his visit on this tragic anniversary.

20   "The doctors agree in ordering me complete rest, an absence of mental excitement, and avoidance of anything in the nature of violent physical exercise," announced Framton, who laboured under the tolerably widespread delusion that total strangers and chance acquaintances are hungry for the least detail of one's ailments and infirmities, their cause and cure. "On the matter of diet they are not so much in agreement," he continued.

21   "No?" said Mrs. Sappleton, in a voice which only replaced a yawn at the last moment. Then she suddenly brightened into alert attention— but not to what Framton was saying.

22   "Here they are at last!" she cried. "Just in time for tea, and don't they look as if they were muddy up to the eyes!"

23   Framton shivered slightly and turned towards the niece with a look intended to convey sympathetic comprehension. The child was staring out through the open window with dazed horror in her eyes. In a chill shock of nameless fear Framton swung round in his seat and looked in the same direction.

24   In the deepening twilight three figures were walking across the lawn towards the window; they all carried guns under their arms, and one of them was additionally burdened with a white coat hung over his shoulders. A tired brown spaniel kept close at their heels. Noiselessly they neared the house, and then a hoarse young voice chanted out of the dusk: "I said, Bertie, why do you bound?"

25   Framton grabbed wildly at his stick and hat; the hall-door, the gravel-drive, and the front gate were dimly noted stages in his headlong retreat. A cyclist coming along the road had to run into the hedge to avoid imminent collision.

26   "Here we are, my dear," said the bearer of the white mackintosh, coming in through the window; "fairly muddy, but most of it's dry. Who was that who bolted out as we came up?"

27   "A most extraordinary man, a Mr. Nuttel," said Mrs. Sappleton; "could only talk about his illnesses, and dashed off without a word of good-bye or apology when you arrived. One would think he had seen a ghost."

28   "I expect it was the spaniel," said the niece calmly; "he told me he had a horror of dogs. He was once hunted into a cemetery somewhere on the banks of the Ganges by a pack of pariah dogs, and had to spend the night in a newly dug grave with the creatures snarling and grinning and foaming just above him. Enough to make any one lose their nerve."

29   Romance at short notice was her speciality.

The Open Window

Questions on Content, Style, and Structure

1. Why does Nuttel bolt so suddenly from the house?
2. What is Vera's special talent? What does Munro mean by "romance" in the last line of the story?
3. What hints are we given early in the story that Vera is an exceptional girl?
4. Why is Nuttel a perfect victim for Vera's "speciality"?
5. Describe Vera's performance when she tells Nuttel of the hunting trip and when she sees the men return. Why is she convincing?

6. What does the setting (time and place) add to Vera's story?

7. How does Munro make this story humorous rather than tragic?

8. How does Munro build up to the twist in the last sentence? Why didn't he tell the reader about Vera's speciality earlier in the story?

9. How does Vera's story about Nuttel's fear of dogs add to your understanding of her character?

Vocabulary

duly (2)	ghastly (19)
moping (3)	mackintosh (26)
falteringly (14)	pariah (28)

Suggestions for Writing

1. Write an essay analyzing Munro's ability to create lively characters in such a brief story.

2. Write an essay elaborating on your answer to question 6. Consider the many details Munro gives regarding the time of day, season, weather, house, and location of the house.

3. Write a brief analysis of Mrs. Sappleton's function in this story. Why is her character necessary?

On Decriminalization
Robert M. Hutchins

Robert M. Hutchins was a lawyer, scholar, and educator. President and
then chancellor of the University of Chicago, he also wrote several
books on education and served as chairman of the *Encyclopædia
Britannica*. This essay first appeared in 1971 in *The Center Magazine*,
following a conference on crime control held by the Center for the
Study of Democratic Institutions. Hutchins was chairman of that
organization.

1   At the Center's Conference on Crime Control Legislation James V. Bennett, former director of the United States Bureau of Prisons, estimated
the cost of modernizing the penal institutions of the country at eighteen
billion dollars. Nobody thought this figure was too high. Many of those
present thought it was too low. Whatever the correct figure is, it is a
fraction of what it would take to get a modern penal system, for Mr.
Bennett was talking only about modernizing buildings. The cost of a
well-trained staff in numbers and quality adequate to administer an en-
lightened program running from conviction through probation and parole
would be many billions. More important, it would demand much intelligence, courage, and patience.

2   The same is true of every department of criminal justice. We need
more and better judges, more and better prosecutors, more and better
public defenders, more and better police, more and better probation officers and parole boards, and all these groups need more and better facilities. Of course, what they need most of all is more and better ideas.

3   The demand for more personnel and more facilities would diminish
if the President[1], instead of ranting, would take up the one good idea he
has in this field and educate the country to understand and accept it.
This is the idea of "decriminalization," which became a sort of central
theme of the conference at the Center and which the President referred
to in a speech on March 11. As far as I can recall, it received unanimous
support. Even Carl Rauh, of the Department of Justice, endorsed it. The
reservations expressed about it had to do with details.

4   On the main point there was general agreement, and that was that
offenses that did not damage the person or property of others, where
there was no victim and no complainant, should as far as possible be
taken out of the system of criminal justice.

5   This would remove from the scope of the criminal law people for
whom that law can do nothing and who are now the principal burden

[1] President Richard Nixon

upon it. Narcotics addicts and alcoholics cannot be helped by terms in the penitentiary. What they need is medical treatment. It was said at the Center's conference that sixty percent at least of all serious crime is drug-related and that alcoholics account for more than fifty percent of the arrests in the country. Although all statistics on crime are unreliable, these figures suggest what would happen if narcotics addicts and alcoholics were regarded as patients rather than criminals.

6   Some eight to ten million people in this country are said to be using marijuana in open violation of the law. In some states an enormous part of the apparatus of criminal justice is dedicated to detecting and convicting these people and to getting them locked up. If no convincing evidence can be offered that marijuana is more harmful than alcohol or tobacco, the possession and use of marijuana should be legalized. It should follow that the sale of marijuana would be legal as well.

7   The criminal law cannot stop the traffic in "hard" drugs. As Troy Duster pointed out at the Center's conference, the profits in the business are so large that dealers caught and jailed are immediately replaced. If criminal penalties were removed and the whole business were regulated or owned by government, if something like the British system were introduced, the resources now wasted in tracking down those involved in the drug business could be devoted to the invention of practical solutions to the problem.

8   Some form of gambling is legal everywhere. Some states have gone so far as to set up state owned gambling institutions. If all restrictions on gambling were removed, the strain it places on the system of criminal justice would be relieved. The hazards to civil liberties would be reduced. The only argument advanced for "no-knock" and wiretapping where "national security" is not involved is that in drug and gambling cases these procedures are necessary to obtain and preserve evidence. If there were no drug or gambling cases nobody would have the face to advocate these procedures.

9   Drugs turn out to be, too, an important argument for preventive detention: the addict out on bail must engage in crime in order to support his habit. Taking addicts out of the criminal system would minimize the demand to lock up people in order to protect the public from them.

10   Every reader can make his own list of those acts, now called criminal, which should be considered candidates for "decriminalization." Many readers may differ with some of the examples I have used. This is not material. The point is that the idea should be accepted and as many acts covered by it as possible as soon as possible.

11   Where there is a social problem with which the system of criminal justice is now vainly trying to deal, we do not solve the problem by removing it from the scope of the criminal law. We merely abandon a wasteful and futile attempt to cope with it. The problem remains. Attempts to take mentally ill persons out of the reach of the criminal law

have been a dubious advantage to them. Most students of the subject agree that a mentally ill defendant in a criminal case is better off, in those jurisdictions which have civil commitment, if his illness is not referred to during his trial. If he is sent to the penitentiary, he has at least some idea when he will get out. If he is civilly committed he may be detained for years and in the meantime get little more or better treatment than he would have in prison.

12   Civil commitment was thought to be a great step forward when it was introduced. The reason that a noble, humanitarian effort has failed to produce better results is the same as that which must be given for the failure of the system of criminal justice. We as a people do not care to put the necessary intellectual and financial resources into the job. We are therefore an easy prey for snake-oil salesmen who tell us that if we will only stop "coddling criminals" we shall be secure.

13   *Newsweek* quotes Joe Olgiati, who runs a work-training program for probationers in New York, as saying, "If you were to eliminate all cops, judges, parole officers, and courts, it would have a highly negligible effect on crime in the streets. In fact, it might even be better. You wouldn't just be trying to repair what we have now."

14   The thought does cross one's mind as one listens to the horrors recited in a conference on crime control that it might be better if no criminal were ever caught. Everybody who is involved with the criminal law seems to be worse because of his contact with it. For example, the fifty-two percent of the jail population who are being detained pending trial must be more dangerous to society as a result of this experience than they were before.

15   Yet we cannot dispense with the criminal law. Although we know very little about deterrence, it seems probable that the prospect of punishment does dissuade some people from the commission of some crimes. We should try to make the system of criminal justice work as swiftly, surely, and fairly as we can. As Ramsey Clark[2] said at the Center's conference, safety and freedom are not incompatible; the thing to do is to enlarge both. Law and Order, in the modern interpretation of this slogan, will give us neither.

[2] Ramsey Clark is a former U.S. Attorney General.

On Decriminalization

Questions on Content, Style, and Structure

1. Why does Hutchins begin his essay by referring to James V. Bennett's speech?

2. What does Hutchins mean by "decriminalization"? In general, what sort of offenses should be decriminalized?

3. What are the advantages of decriminalization?

4. For what specific crimes does Hutchins suggest decriminalization? Are his arguments convincing?

5. How would the decriminalization of gambling reduce a threat to civil liberties?

6. Why isn't civil commitment for social problems a better alternative to decriminalization?

7. Point out at least two examples of Hutchins' use of authorities to support his ideas. Is his use effective?

8. How often does Hutchins use statistics in his argument? Where do his figures come from?

9. Why, according to Hutchins, won't stiff jail sentences make us safe and secure?

10. Hutchins ends his essay with a commonly used technique—what is it?

11. Overall, how persuasive is Hutchins' argument?

Vocabulary

ranting (3)   detained (11)
complainant (4)   humanitarian (12)
futile (11)   deterrence (15)
dubious (11)   incompatible (15)
jurisdictions (11)

Suggestions for Writing

1. If you disagree with Hutchins, write an essay arguing your point of view; if you agree, select some other criminal act he did not mention, such as prostitution, and argue for its decriminalization.

2. Write a research paper that illustrates or refutes Hutchins' statement that "everybody who is involved with criminal law seems to be worse because of his contact with it."

3. In paragraph 7, Hutchins refers to the British system of regulating "hard" drugs. After researching this system, write an essay comparing and contrasting it to our methods of handling the problem. In your opinion, which system is the more effective?

The Gay Mystique
Peter Fisher

Peter Fisher is the author of *Prescription for National Health Insurance* (1972) and coauthor of *Special Teachers—Special Boys* (1979). This selection is an excerpt from *The Gay Mystique: The Myth and Reality of Male Homosexuality* (1972), his book on the homosexual experience

1 There are some straight people who use many of the various offensive slang terms for homosexuals without realizing they are put-downs. Embarrassment about homosexuality is still so common that some people cannot bring themselves to use the word "homosexual"—they find it distastefully clinical. Instead they will refer to homos, queers, queens, fairies, faggots, pansies, and—where gay women are concerned—dykes and lezzies, not really realizing that gay people find these terms insulting and demeaning.

2 Some people who would never dream of referring to blacks as niggers or Jews as kikes will use derogatory terms for gay people casually. Some don't realize this is in poor taste; others don't think it matters.

3 People who use "nigger" usually will have the sense not to do so in front of black people. It's not difficult to maintain this minimum courtesy, because there is seldom any problem in identifying blacks. But most gay people are invisible, and straights are often unaware that some of their friends are gay. Gay people who are still in the closet often hear people whom they consider friends refer to homosexuals as queers and faggots or tell antihomosexual jokes. This experience is hardly likely to make a gay person feel that he will be well received if he ceases to be secretive about his homosexuality.

Coming Out

4 Many gay people find the idea of coming out quite terrifying. Aside from the difficulties they can expect to have with their families, they fear that their straight friends will turn against them and no longer want to have anything to do with them. If somebody is a real friend, an admission of homosexuality won't change his or her feelings in the slightest, but many gay people find it difficult to put this to the test.

5 When gay people tell straight friends they are gay, various stock responses are encountered over and over. "But you don't look gay"—as though all homosexuals could be expected to look alike. Some straight people will say that they would have preferred not to know. After all, if the person was able to keep his homosexuality a secret so successfully,

why make such a big issue of it now? Nobody really wants to know. The emotional cost of a secret life is enormous.

6   Another common response is "I'm sorry" or "What a shame." After all, some people will say, everyone has his problems, and you just have to learn to live with them. But not many homosexuals enjoy being treated as though they were handicapped or emotionally crippled.

7   The situation is an awkward one. Given the fact that a friend may have felt it necessary to hide his homosexuality for years, it is hard to know how to respond to it in positive terms when it is finally revealed. About the only thing you can say is "Right on!"

8   Once a gay person has made his homosexuality known, even his most sympathetic friends may find it difficult to treat him as he would like to be treated. Who knows how homosexuals like to be treated anyway?

9   It's a lot easier to figure out how gay people do *not* like to be treated, for this requires only a little common sense.

10   The homosexual who has left the closet does not want to be treated like an invalid with an unmentionable disease—he does not want to be treated like a tragic victim of circumstances beyond his control. Things can be bad enough for gay people in our society so that they would prefer not to be constantly reminded of how bad they are, no matter how sympathetic the intentions. It is too easy for a sympathetic attitude to come across as patronizing or condescending. Besides, after a while gay people get thoroughly tired of talking about the problems they encounter as gay people.

11   Straight people sometimes wonder how they should introduce a gay friend to other acquaintances. Do you say that he is gay, and thereby make an issue out of it, or do you avoid mentioning it, thereby creating an impression that his homosexuality is an embarrassment to you? The best thing for a straight person in this position to do is to ask his gay friend what he would prefer. Most gay people see no point in making an issue about the matter with every stranger they meet. They have told their friends about their homosexuality because their friends are important to them. Unless there is some particular reason for introducing someone as a gay friend, what difference does it make?

The "Good" Homosexual

12   The problem most frequently encountered by gay people who have left the closet is being expected to be on "good" behavior. The "good" homosexual is the gay equivalent of an Uncle Tom. He is supposed to be serious and reticent about his homosexuality. If it comes up as a topic of discussion, he is expected to deal with it in intellectual rather than emotional terms, speak in a sociological vein about the many problems faced by homosexuals. He should be understanding about the hostility he encounters from many straights—after all, they really can't help it,

you know, they were brought up that way and they don't know any better. He should never reveal the measure of the anger he sometimes feels.

13   The "good" homosexual is a heterosexual homosexual. He may wear a sign around his neck stating "I am a homosexual," but he should look, act, think, and feel no differently than a straight person would. He should not be an embarrassment. His straight friends should never have to feel uncomfortable about introducing him to people whose respect they want to keep. He should be a tribute to their liberalism, not to their unconventionality.

14   Actually, the "good" homosexual should not even really be a heterosexual homosexual. Heterosexuals are all too open about their sexuality, and the "good" homosexual should avoid giving any hint that he has a sex life. He must be sexually neutral.

15   The "good" homosexual does not mention the affairs he has from time to time or the men he is seeing. If he falls in love, he does not make others uncomfortable by trying to share his joy with them. If an affair comes to a sudden end, he does not embarrass his straight friends by telling them of his unhappiness. He should not mention having sex with other men, because most straight people find the whole idea distasteful. If he has a lover, the two of them should behave like gentlemen—straight gentlemen—in front of other people. This is particularly noticeable when it comes to displays of affection.

Reactions of Families

16   My lover Marc and I found this to be the case the first time we visited my family as a couple. It had taken a good deal of courage for my parents to even invite us together in the first place. They were anything but pleased about my homosexuality, and it was difficult for them to be confronted with living proof of that homosexuality in the form of my lover. It was an awkward situation for all of us, and yet a vital step in attempting to understand one another better.

17   We sat around having a drink and chatting. Without thinking anything of it, I rested my arm on Marc's shoulder while we talked. Later, my parents told me privately that it had made them very uncomfortable to watch us "making love" right before their eyes. Making love? The same thing happened when we visited Marc's relatives. He happened to put his hand on my knee and was later told how embarrassing it had been to watch us "making out and petting."

18   I could understand and sympathize with our families' reactions. In straight society, men are not supposed to touch. Nor are they supposed to be homosexuals.

19   Many straight people will say "Right on" when it's a matter of leaving the closet, admitting that we are gay, and being ourselves after years of

hiding and secrecy. But when we try to really be ourselves, live full and happy lives, search for love, and enjoy it when we find it—they tell us we are going too far. It is all right for us to be homosexuals in name, but we must leave our love in the closet.

20   This is too much to ask.

The Gay Mystique

Questions on Content, Style, and Structure

1. How does Fisher want people to respond to homosexuals?
2. Fisher compares calling homosexuals names to what other kind of tasteless behavior?
3. What, according to Fisher, are the most common responses to someone who has revealed his or her homosexuality?
4. What does Fisher mean when he says, "The 'good' homosexual is the gay equivalent of an Uncle Tom"?
5. How does Fisher clarify his definition of the so-called "good" homosexual?
6. How are "good" homosexuals different from heterosexuals regarding sexuality?
7. What is the tone of paragraphs 13–15? Is this tone effective or damaging to Fisher's point?
8. Why does Fisher tell the reader about the visits to his and Marc's relatives?
9. How does Fisher play on the phrase "to come out of the closet" in his conclusion?
10. Why is the last line of the essay in a paragraph by itself?

Vocabulary

clinical (1)   condescending (10)
derogatory (2)   reticent (12)
patronizing (10)

Suggestions for Writing

1. Do you think reactions to homosexuality have improved since this selection was written in 1972? Write an essay supporting your opinion with illustrations from your own experience and/or from your research.
2. Suppose at your high school a teacher with an impressive record declares his or her homosexuality. Should the school board renew his or

her contract? Write a letter to the board persuading them to rehire or fire the teacher.

3. Gay student groups sometimes have a difficult time being recognized as legitimate campus organizations entitled to use school facilities for meetings and social gatherings. Investigate the history of gay rights on your campus and write a report on your findings.

Irrational Behavior or Evangelical Zeal?
Michael Mewshaw

Michael Mewshaw is an associate professor of English at the University of Texas at Austin and the author of six books, including *The Toll* (1974), *Land Without Shadow* (1979), and *Life for Death* (1980). This essay was partially the result of research Mewshaw did for his novel *Earthly Bread* (1976), which told the story of a "Jesus freak" kidnapped by a professional deprogrammer; the essay was published in *The Chronicle of Higher Education* in 1976.

1   As the radio ads have announced—to the accompaniment of spooky music, shrieks, and the burble of green pea soup—*The Exorcist* is back. But one wonders whether it ever went away. Judging by the recent spate of books and movies dealing with demonic possession, it seems to have spawned clones and provided a self-replenishing resource for publishing and film companies.

2   This phenomenon, odd as it is, would deserve no more than a footnote in a pop-culture thesis if it weren't for the fact that grotesque parodies of exorcism are performed whenever pentecostal Christians, Moon people, and Hare Krishna chanters are kidnapped, confined for days with little food and sleep, and badgered into recanting their beliefs.

3   Euphemistically called "deprogramming," the process amounts to little more than a methodical and sometimes violent attempt to exorcise not Satan, but unpopular, misunderstood, or inarticulate notions about God.

4   During the last four years as I researched, wrote, and published a novel concerning this subject, I ran into very few people—except for direct participants—who had much substantive knowledge about deprogramming. Although most victims of these systematized efforts at brainwashing are college or graduate students, or members of the free-floating communities that congregate around universities, my academic col-

leagues were either oblivious to the situation or else felt that evangelical Christianity wasn't intellectually respectable and therefore its *dévotés* deserved whatever they got. At the start, I myself was ill-informed, and, though a practicing Catholic, I scarcely qualified as a pentecostal or charismatic believer. Yet driven by curiosity and convinced of the basic decency of the "born-again" Christians in my classes, I decided to take a closer look at the problem.

5   What I learned surprised and dismayed me. Much as I might disagree with the theology of certain evangelical groups, they struck me as no more deluded or neurotic than others on campus. Yet from parents I repeatedly heard the same justification of deprogrammings. They claimed their children were misguided, distressingly inclined to give away money, incapable of making mature decisions, maybe even demented. In cases where the "children" turned out to be college graduates in their 20's and 30's and sometimes mothers and fathers themselves, the charges grew more dramatic. The "kids," I was told, had been abducted, hypnotized, or—shades of Patty Hearst—forced into joining a cult which then held them captive against their will.

6   Just recently a distraught mother confronted me and tearfully asked what I would do if my own son had joined a religious group and would no longer communicate with me. Wouldn't I consider kidnapping him and trying to talk sense to him? It was only after I had sympathized with her that she revealed that her son was 26, a Phi Beta Kappa graduate of Notre Dame, and a former student at the Sorbonne. I suggested that since he sounded like a gifted, responsible boy she should perhaps try to understand and accept his decision. Our conversation was then broken off by hysterical sobs and her accusation that I didn't know what I was talking about.

7   The woman may have been right; I may be wrong. But I must say I never encountered any of the irrational, robot-like zealots I heard about, and, to my knowledge, none of the sensational allegations against unorthodox religious groups has ever stood up in court.

8   Gradually I've come to believe the problem may be semantic as much as anything else. For example, what parents call propaganda and coercion the religious groups invariably call evangelical zeal. After all, don't Catholics and Protestants also send out missionaries? What the parents see as irrational behavior the groups say is ritualized devotion. Don't most religions encourage ideas and rites that strike outsiders as bizarre, if not insane? What the parents interpret as extortion or embezzlement the groups view as voluntary charity. Don't all organized churches accept—and in some instances demand—contributions?

9   Yet, while parents have failed to prove their charges, they have managed to convince a crucial segment of the media and the public that their children are in danger. Thus young people continue to be captured, imprisoned, and physically and emotionally abused because of their beliefs. Civil libertarians have shown no great eagerness to get involved, and

some local police forces have admitted that they actually encouraged and assisted deprogrammers. There have been a few cuts and bruises, broken bones, and chipped teeth. Fortunately no one has been killed or maimed so far, but substantial damage has been done to our constitutional guarantees of religious freedom.

10   All of this prompts questions about America's commitment to the First Amendment and to human rights in general. While the country retains its capacity for selective indignation, it often appears to relinquish one old liberty for each new one it wins. For instance, recent court rulings have affirmed the right of adolescent girls, regardless of age, to undergo abortions without parental approval. Yet both by their decisions and by their refusal to hear certain cases, the courts have suggested that the same young girl who has gained complete control over her body might have to accept familial interference with her soul. And this interference won't necessarily end when she reaches 21. Even marriage offers no sanctuary, for many people have paid to have their spouses kidnapped and deprogrammed.

11   Frequently I have been asked questions by students and young people who have been harassed because of their theology, their dress, and their behavior. Why have "born-again" Christians been singled out? Why aren't dope dealers or pornographers kidnapped and deprogrammed? How would the public respond if a Protestant pulled his son out of a seminary and kept him incommunicado until he gave up his vocation? What would the Vatican do if a Catholic dragged his daughter from a convent? How would the Black Muslims react if their congregation was picked off one by one? Would Jews consider it just if Reform members grabbed Orthodox believers and put them through a crude form of behavior modification?

12   These questions, I think, deserve careful consideration—and honest answers. As a country committed to the separation of church and state and to freedom of worship, we may not always approve of what others believe or the way they express their beliefs, but we have no moral or legal right to intervene except in the most extreme circumstances. It would be a shame . . . if America was not mature and wise enough to insist upon that religious liberty that was one of its founding principles and is still one of its greatest claims to international respect.

Irrational Behavior or Evangelical Zeal?

Questions on Content, Style, and Structure

1. What is Mewshaw's attitude toward deprogramming?
2. Why does Mewshaw begin his essay with reference to *The Exorcist* and other pop culture treatments of exorcism? Is this an effective introduction to his subject?

3. How does paragraph 4 help set up the tone of this essay?
4. What does Mewshaw gain by writing in the first person?
5. On what does Mewshaw base his understanding of deprogramming?
6. Why does Mewshaw tell about his conversation with the distraught mother?
7. What does Mewshaw mean when he says the problem "may be semantic"?
8. Point out the analogy in paragraph 10; is this analogy convincing?
9. What is the purpose of the series of questions in paragraph 11? Do they succeed?
10. How does Mewshaw end his essay? Is this an appropriate conclusion?
11. Overall, how persuasive is Mewshaw's argument? Would he convince parents who have hired a deprogrammer to change their minds? Why or why not?

Vocabulary

spate (1)	recanting (2)	distraught (6)
parodies (2)	euphemistically (3)	zealots (7)
exorcism (2)	evangelical (4)	semantic (8)
pentecostal (2)	charismatic (4)	incommunicado (11)

Suggestions for Writing

1. Do you agree with Mewshaw that regarding a person's religious choice "we have no moral or legal right to intervene except in the most extreme circumstances"? What might constitute "extreme circumstances"? Write an essay defending your views.
2. Write an essay in which you try to explain the reasons people join cults or nontraditional religious groups. Why do you think such groups are more popular now than fifty years ago?
3. If you or someone you know has ever been a member of a nontraditional spiritual group, write an essay describing and evaluating the experience.

When Lawyers Help Villains
Steven Brill

Steven Brill is a graduate of the Yale Law School, a former assistant to John Lindsay during his years as mayor of New York, and the author of *The Teamsters* (1978). He frequently writes articles on law and politics for a variety of popular magazines; this essay, published in 1978, was one of a series of articles Brill wrote as a regular columnist and contributing editor for *Esquire.*

1   Leroy "Nicky" Barnes is one-hundred-percent villain. Recently he was convicted in federal court in New York of masterminding one of the city's largest heroin-dealer networks. A millionaire who spent lavishly on cars, homes and furs with the profits he made from delivering heroin to the veins of the men, women and children of Harlem, Barnes had been called Mr. Untouchable because his lawyers had in the past gotten him off when he faced charges of murder, gun possession, heroin dealing and bribery.

2   Barnes's lawyer is a young former assistant district attorney named David Breitbart. He has handled Barnes's court fights since 1973. Sources close to this most recent case claim that Barnes gave Breitbart a million dollars in cash to split between himself and lawyers working for Barnes's codefendants. Armed with that tip and curious to meet the man who'd argued with a straight face that his client was an innocent man framed by the government, I went to see Breitbart soon after the trial.

3   Breitbart's office is in a run-down building at Broadway and Canal Street. There Breitbart adamantly denied the story of the million-dollar fee, saying only that "Barnes paid me well."

4   "*If* you believed Barnes really was a top heroin dealer," I asked, "and he was supplying, even helping to hook, children on the stuff, would you have any qualms about working for him?" "Not at all," Breitbart shot back. "I don't care what he's done. . . . A criminal lawyer is an advocate. . . . If a man's got the price, I'll try his case and do everything I can to get him off. And I do a great job of it. . . ." Would there ever be a case he wouldn't take? "Well, I suppose if they found a Nazi who'd killed millions of Jews and put him on trial here, I'd have problems taking his case. But, you know, most of us are whores, and I guess if they offered me enough money for it I'd take it. . . ."

5   What's great about Nicky Barnes and David Breitbart is that they sharpen an issue about lawyers and lawyering that otherwise tends to be much fuzzier. For several days after the interview with Breitbart, I talked about it with several lawyer friends who work at prestigious New York

firms. All seemed to have the same reaction—that Breitbart is a detestable type, hardly a credit to the bar.

6 But Breitbart isn't really much different from other lawyers. Give him some nicely tailored wools to replace his double knits, a hundred-lawyer office in a classy skyscraper, an Ivy League diploma and some skill at editing what he says to reporters, and he could be any of my lawyer friends who snickered at him, or, for that matter, any of the nation's respected attorneys who, for the right price, will take on clients engaged in all kinds of antisocial activities.

7 For example, there's Thomas Sullivan, a longtime criminal lawyer and a partner in the Chicago firm of Jenner & Block. In early 1975, Sullivan was the lead lawyer defending several organized-crime figures charged with defrauding the Teamsters' $1.6 billion Central States Pension Fund. His clients were accused of using a Teamster pension-fund loan to take over a small manufacturer, then siphoning off the loaned money from the company until it went bankrupt.

8 The jury found them not guilty. One reason was that one of two star witnesses was shotgunned to death several weeks before the trial. (The F.B.I. later found that the title to a getaway car used by the murderers was under a phony name but had been notarized by a secretary who worked for Sullivan's client.) Another reason for the verdict was Tom Sullivan. He was brilliant. Trial rules didn't allow the prosecution to mention the past organized-crime activities of any of the defendants, and Sullivan got the jury to accept the proposition that these were innocent entrepreneurs whose dream of manufacturing plastic pails had failed.

9 Today, Sullivan is the United States attorney for the Northern District of Illinois, which includes Chicago. President Carter appointed him last year. No reservations were expressed by the Senate committee that voted on his nomination or by the press about his role in the Teamster-Mafia case or in cases where he had defended other alleged pension-fund embezzlers and corrupt government officials.

10 That's the way it should be. Sullivan has an unblemished reputation as an honest lawyer and a decent guy who has been involved in a number of bar-related civic activities. Carter's decision to replace Sullivan's Republican-appointed predecessor, like his more recent dismissal of the U.S. attorney in Philadelphia, was not based on merit. But the choice of Sullivan as a replacement was. He was a good lawyer willing to cut his income to about a fourth of what it had been in order to enter public service.

11 Sullivan has resolved conflict-of-interest problems by removing himself from involvement in any case concerning former clients of his, or his old law firm. With this restriction invoked, his side switching—common among prosecutors and defense lawyers—becomes a plus. Who's better qualified to win cases for the government than a man who has beaten it so many times in the past?

12   On the other hand, isn't there something we should dislike about men like Thomas Sullivan or David Breitbart, whose ethical compasses, or lack thereof, allow them to make lots of money defending mobsters or heroin dealers?

13   Few lawyers see it that way. In broad terms, the lawyers' Code of Professional Responsibility entitles the impeccably evil Nicky Barnes to the best lawyer he can buy. It allows—in fact, encourages—lawyers to be vigorous advocates of their clients' cases regardless of what they personally believe about their clients' guilt or goodness (as long as they don't knowingly present perjured evidence).

14   There's good logic in these standards. If lawyers refused to represent clients because they felt they were guilty, many defendants wouldn't be able to find good lawyers and we'd have replaced a jury-trial system that puts the burden of proof on the government with one in which an accused person's fate is decided by the first-impression judgments of lawyers. Also, if lawyers were scared away from defending unpopular clients or people involved in unpopular issues, unpopular *innocent* people (the targets of a Joe McCarthy-type witch-hunt[1], for instance) would suffer.

15   Most lawyers aren't as free of qualms as Breitbart in taking clients. Sullivan, for example, says he'd never defend a heroin dealer.

16   Still, these personal hesitations rarely interfere with the general willingness of lawyers to take any clients with cases falling within the bounds of their practices. The reason Breitbart sharpens this issue so nicely is not just that he apparently has none of these hang-ups but also that his practice is in a particularly unseemly field. He forces us to consider the most troubling consequence of the principle that lawyers shouldn't allow distaste for a client or an issue to dissuade them from taking a case and that lawyers who do take such cases should not be identified negatively with their clients for doing so—namely, that this often allows people like Barnes to go free. But there just isn't a better way to preserve a rule of law that resolves most civil disputes peaceably and does much to make sure that the government can't cut corners to put one of us in jail.

17   But look where that leaves lawyers. It makes them amoral automatons. At a time when so many other pillars of our social and economic establishment, spurred by the Watergate and the corporate-bribery disclosures, are reassessing the ethical consequences of their conduct, lawyers have immunity from the new morality. They're in the unique, if not enviable, position of holding themselves out as hired guns, allowed by their own code to be above the moral implications of their work because, as Breitbart puts it, "it's our tough advocacy that keeps the system honest."

[1] Joseph McCarthy was a U. S. Senator from Wisconsin in the 1950s who led a nationwide search for Communists and other "un-American" citizens. His irresponsible accusations resulted in a variety of "blacklists" that ruined the careers of thousands of innocent people.

18   Faced with the Breitbart lawyer-amorality question, one Wall Street lawyer suggested that if we give lawyers a free pass on worrying about the moral consequences of what they do for a particular client, then maybe we should try to take something in return by asking them to do a set amount of noncompensated work for charitable or public-interest groups. Requiring such *pro bono*[2] work, or even defining what qualifies as such, has obvious practical pitfalls. Even so, many lawyers already do some charitable work. But if lawyers are going to lessen the growing public distrust and resentment of their profession, it would seem that they'd want to do something in a concrete, organized way to show that they're more than the "whores" Breitbart thinks they are.

[2] *Pro bono publico* means "for the public good."

When Lawyers Help Villains

Questions on Content, Style, and Structure

1. For what is Brill arguing? Does he have a clear thesis statement?
2. Why does Brill begin his essay by describing Nicky Barnes and his "detestable" lawyer? What issue do they "sharpen"?
3. What is Brill's reason for introducing Tom Sullivan?
4. What is the purpose of paragraph 12?
5. According to Brill, how do most lawyers feel about defending clients who may be guilty?
6. What are Brill's two main arguments supporting his point of view?
7. What specific example does Brill offer to illustrate his second argument? Is this example explained sufficiently?
8. According to Brill, what ethical problem do lawyers face?
9. What response to this problem is suggested in Brill's conclusion?
10. Overall, how persuasive is Brill? Did he organize his essay in the most effective way?

Vocabulary

adamantly (3)	entrepreneurs (8)	amoral (17)
qualms (4)	invoked (11)	automatons (17)
advocate (4)	impeccably (13)	noncompensated (18)
detestable (5)	unseemly (16)	

Suggestions for Writing

1. Write an essay evaluating Brill's essay. Illustrate both the strengths and weaknesses you see.

2. Write an editorial criticizing or defending some controversial aspect of our legal system, such as plea bargaining, the temporary insanity plea, or wiretapping to obtain evidence.

3. Research a famous trial of the past or present in which a lawyer defended a "villain" or an unpopular client. Use this case to defend or attack Brill's thesis.

On Cloning a Human Being
Lewis Thomas

Lewis Thomas is a noted physician and writer who contributes articles to both medical journals and popular scientific magazines such as *Discovery*. Currently chancellor of the Memorial Sloan-Kettering Cancer Center in Manhattan, Thomas is the author of two collections of essays, *The Lives of a Cell* (1974), which won the National Book Award, and *The Medusa and the Snail* (1979). This essay originally appeared in *The New England Journal of Medicine* in 1974.

1   It is now theoretically possible to recreate an identical creature from any animal or plant, from the DNA contained in the nucleus of any somatic cell[1]. A single plant root-tip cell can be teased and seduced into conceiving a perfect copy of the whole plant; a frog's intestinal epithelial cell possesses the complete instructions needed for a new, same frog. If the technology were further advanced, you could do this with a human being, and there are now startled predictions all over the place that this will in fact be done, someday, in order to provide a version of immortality for carefully selected, especially valuable people.

2   The cloning of humans is on most of the lists of things to worry about from Science, along with behavior control, genetic engineering, transplanted heads, computer poetry, and the unrestrained growth of plastic flowers.

3   Cloning is the most dismaying of prospects, mandating as it does the elimination of sex with only a metaphoric elimination of death as compensation. It is almost no comfort to know that one's cloned, identical

[1] Somatic cells make up tissues and organs.

surrogate lives on, especially when the living will very likely involve edging one's real, now aging self off to the side, sooner or later. It is hard to imagine anything like filial affection or respect for a single, unmated nucleus; harder still to think of one's new, self-generated self as anything but an absolute, desolate orphan. Not to mention the complex interpersonal relationship involved in raising one's self from infancy, teaching the language, enforcing discipline, instilling good manners, and the like. How would you feel if you became an incorrigible juvenile delinquent by proxy, at the age of fifty-five?

4   The public questions are obvious. Who is to be selected, and on what qualifications? How to handle the risks of misused technology, such as self-determined cloning by the rich and powerful but socially objectionable, or the cloning by governments of dumb, docile masses for the world's work? What will be the effect on all the uncloned rest of us of human sameness? After all, we've accustomed ourselves through hundreds of millennia to the continual exhilaration of uniqueness; each of us is totally different, in a fundamental sense, from all the other four billion. Selfness is an essential fact of life. The thought of human nonselfness, precise sameness, is terrifying, when you think about it.

5   Well, don't think about it, because it isn't a probable possibility, not even as a long shot for the distant future, in my opinion. I agree that you might clone some people who would look amazingly like their parental cell donors, but the odds are that they'd be almost as different as you or me, and certainly more different than any of today's identical twins.

6   The time required for the experiment is only one of the problems, but a formidable one. Suppose you wanted to clone a prominent, spectacularly successful diplomat, to look after the Middle East problems of the distant future. You'd have to catch him and persuade him, probably not very hard to do, and extirpate a cell. But then you'd have to wait for him to grow up through embryonic life and then for at least forty years more, and you'd have to be sure all observers remained patient and unmeddlesome through his unpromising, ambiguous childhood and adolescence.

7   Moreover, you'd have to be sure of recreating his environment, perhaps down to the last detail. "Environment" is a word which really means people, so you'd have to do a lot more cloning than just the diplomat himself.

8   This is a very important part of the cloning problem, largely overlooked in our excitement about the cloned individual himself. You don't have to agree all the way with B. F. Skinner[2] to acknowledge that the environment does make a difference, and when you examine what we really mean by the word "environment" it comes down to other human beings. We use euphemisms and jargon for this, like "social forces,"

---

[2] B. F. Skinner is an American psychologist and author who stressed the importance of environment in experiments on behavior modification.

"cultural influences," even Skinner's "verbal community," but what is meant is the dense crowd of nearby people who talk to, listen to, smile or frown at, give to, withhold from, nudge, push, caress, or flail out at the individual. No matter what the genome[3] says, these people have a lot to do with shaping a character. Indeed, if all you had was the genome, and no people around, you'd grow a sort of vertebrate plant, nothing more.

9   So, to start with, you will undoubtedly need to clone the parents. No question about this. This means the diplomat is out, even in theory, since you couldn't have gotten cells from both his parents at the time when he was himself just recognizable as an early social treasure. You'd have to limit the list of clones to people already certified as sufficiently valuable for the effort, with both parents still alive. The parents would need cloning and, for consistency, their parents as well. I suppose you'd also need the usual informed-consent forms, filled out and signed, not easy to get if I know parents, even harder for grandparents.

10   But this is only the beginning. It is the whole family that really influences the way a person turns out, not just the parents, according to current psychiatric thinking. Clone the family.

11   Then what? The way each member of the family develops has already been determined by the environment set around him, and this environment is more people, people outside the family, schoolmates, acquaintances, lovers, enemies, car-pool partners, even, in special circumstances, peculiar strangers across the aisle on the subway. Find them, and clone them.

12   But there is no end to the protocol. Each of the outer contacts has his own surrounding family, and his and their outer contacts. Clone them all.

13   To do the thing properly, with any hope of ending up with a genuine duplicate of a single person, you really have no choice. You must clone the world, no less.

14   We are not ready for an experiment of this size, nor, I should think, are we willing. For one thing, it would mean replacing today's world by an entirely identical world to follow immediately, and this means no new, natural spontaneous, random, chancy children. No children at all, except for the manufactured doubles of those now on the scene. Plus all those identical adults, including all of today's politicians, all seen double. It is too much to contemplate.

15   Moreover, when the whole experiment is finally finished, fifty years or so from now, how could you get a responsible scientific reading on the outcome? Somewhere in there would be the original clonee, probably lost and overworked, now well into middle age, but everyone around him would be precise duplicates of today's everyone. It would be today's same

---

[3] A genome is one set of chromosomes with the genes they contain.

world, filled to overflowing with duplicates of today's people and their same, duplicated problems, probably all resentful at having had to go through our whole thing all over, sore enough at the clone to make endless trouble for him, if they found him.

16   And obviously, if the whole thing were done precisely right, they would still be casting about for ways to solve the problem of universal dissatisfaction, and sooner or later they'd surely begin to look around at each other, wondering who should be cloned for his special value to society, to get us out of all this. And so it would go, in regular cycles, perhaps forever.

17   I once lived through a period when I wondered what Hell could be like, and I stretched my imagination to try to think of a perpetual sort of damnation. I have to confess, I never thought of anything like this.

18   I have an alternative suggestion, if you're looking for a way out. Set cloning aside, and don't try it. Instead, go in the other direction. Look for ways to get mutations more quickly, new variety, different songs. Fiddle around, if you must fiddle, but never with ways to keep things the same, no matter who, not even yourself. Heaven, somewhere ahead, has got to be a change.

On Cloning a Human Being

Questions on Content, Style, and Structure

1. Satire is a form of humor that holds human vices and follies up to ridicule. What folly is Thomas satirizing? Is his satire gentle or harsh?

2. What statements early in the essay suggest that Thomas is not entirely serious in his discussion of cloning?

3. What problems of selection will cloning pose?

4. If clones of humans can be produced, why isn't Thomas worried about the possibility of "precise sameness"?

5. What is the role of environment in shaping a clone?

6. What joke does Thomas make about parents in paragraph 9?

7. What, according to Thomas, would be the fate of the original clonee? How does his description add to the humor of this essay?

8. Why would the cloning procedure turn into a "perpetual sort of damnation"?

9. What alterative to cloning does Thomas suggest in his last paragraph?

10. What change in tone occurs in the last paragraph? Why?

Vocabulary

dismaying (3) incorrigible (3) extirpate (6)
mandating (3) proxy (3) flail (8)
surrogate (3) docile (4) protocol (12)
filial (3) millennia (4) contemplate (14)

Suggestions for Writing

1. Write an essay in which you identify and take a stand on some of the "moral" problems involved in cloning human beings. Are there any situations in which you would find cloning acceptable?

2. In the past two years several so-called "test-tube babies" have been born; these children are the results of *in vitro* fertilization, a process by which an egg removed from the mother is fertilized in a petri dish and then replanted in the mother's uterus. Some people consider this process an unfortunate step in the direction of cloning and genetic manipulation and have tried to instigate legislation prohibiting its use in this country. Research this controversy and write an essay explaining your views.

3. Try writing a satire. Select some current belief or issue and expose its ridiculousness.

The Mother
Gwendolyn Brooks

Gwendolyn Brooks is an American poet who won the Pulitzer Prize in 1950 for *Annie Allen*. Some of her other books of poetry include *A Street In Bronzeville* (1945), *Bronzeville Boys and Girls* (1956), and *The Bear Eaters* (1960). This poem first appeared in *The World of Gwendolyn Brooks* (1945).

Abortions will not let you forget.
You remember the children you got that you did not get,
The damp small pulps with a little or with no hair,
The singers and workers that never handled the air.
5 You will never neglect or beat
Them, or silence or buy with a sweet.
You will never wind up the sucking-thumb
Or scuttle off ghosts that come.
You will never leave them, controlling your luscious sigh,

10   Return for a snack of them, with gobbling mother-eye.

I have heard in the voices of the wind the voices of my
   dim killed children.
I have contracted. I have eased
My dim dears at the breasts they could never suck.
I have said, Sweets, if I sinned, if I seized
15   Your luck
And your lives from your unfinished reach,
If I stole your births and your names,
Your straight baby tears and your games,
Your stilted or lovely loves, your tumults, your marriages, aches,
   and your deaths,
20   If I poisoned the beginnings of your breaths,
Believe that even in my deliberateness I was not deliberate.
Though why should I whine,
Whine that the crime was other than mine?—
Since anyhow you are dead.
25   Or rather, or instead,
You were never made.
But that too, I am afraid,
Is faulty: oh, what shall I say, how is the truth to be said?
You were born, you had body, you died.
30   It is just that you never giggled or planned or cried.

Believe me, I loved you all.
Believe me, I knew you, though faintly, and I loved, I loved you
33   All.

The Mother

Questions on Content, Style, and Structure

1. Try to characterize the person speaking in this poem. Is she old or young? Does she have living children? Does she like children?
2. Why is the first stanza addressed to "you"?
3. Why is the second stanza written in the first person "I"? Why did the poet change from "you" to "I" between stanzas?
4. Explain the metaphor in line 10.
5. What does the speaker mean when she says, "even in my deliberateness I was not deliberate"? Is she making excuses for herself?
6. What is the rhyme scheme of this poem? Is it consistent?

7. What is the effect of repetition in the last three lines? of the one-word concluding line?

8. Describe the tone of the speaker's comments. Does she sentimentalize motherhood?

9. Is the speaker convincing when she says she loved her aborted children? Why/why not?

10. What is the speaker trying to say to the reader about aborted children? Is the poem effective?

Vocabulary

luscious (l. 9)
stilted (l. 19)
tumults (l. 19)

Suggestions for Writing

1. Write an essay arguing either that the Brooks poem is a powerful statement or that it is, in fact, a "whine."

2. Arguments for and against abortion can be highly emotional or extremely technical. Find an essay, editorial, or article that takes a clear stand on the issue and write an essay analyzing the tone and word choice. How does the author's diction help convey or undercut the argument?

3. Should a girl under eighteen be allowed to have an abortion without the consent or notification of her parents? Write an essay arguing your opinion.

August 2026: There Will Come Soft Rains
Ray Bradbury

Ray Bradbury is a well-known science fiction writer; two of his books, *Fahrenheit 451* (1953) and *The Illustrated Man* (1951), have been made into movies. Some of his other books include *Switch on the Night* (1955), *Something Wicked This Way Comes* (1962), *The Machinery of Joy* (1963), and *Tomorrow Midnight* (1966). This story was part of *The Martian Chronicles* (1950).

1   In the living room the voice-clock sang, *Tick-tock, seven o'clock, time to get up, time to get up, seven o'clock!* as if it were afraid that nobody would. The morning house lay empty. The clock ticked on, repeating

and repeating its sounds into the emptiness. *Seven-nine, breakfast time, seven-nine!*

2   In the kitchen the breakfast stove gave a hissing sigh and ejected from its warm interior eight pieces of perfectly browned toast, eight eggs sunnyside up, sixteen slices of bacon, two coffees, and two cool glasses of milk.

3   "Today is August 4, 2026," said a second voice from the kitchen ceiling, "in the city of Allendale, California." It repeated the date three times for memory's sake. "Today is Mr. Featherstone's birthday. Today is the anniversary of Tilita's marriage. Insurance is payable, as are the water, gas, and light bills."

4   Somewhere in the walls, relays clicked, memory tapes glided under electric eyes.

5   *Eight-one, tick-tock, eight-one o'clock, off to school, off to work, run, run, eight-one!* But no doors slammed, no carpets took the soft tread of rubber heels. It was raining outside. The weather box on the front door sang quietly: "Rain, rain, go away; rubbers, raincoats for today . . ." And the rain tapped on the empty house, echoing.

6   Outside, the garage chimed and lifted its door to reveal the waiting car. After a long wait the door swung down again.

7   At eight-thirty the eggs were shriveled and the toast was like stone. An aluminum wedge scraped them into the sink, where hot water whirled them down a metal throat which digested and flushed them away to the distant sea. The dirty dishes were dropped into a hot washer and emerged twinkling dry.

8   *Nine-fifteen,* sang the clock, *time to clean.*

9   Out of warrens in the wall, tiny robot mice darted. The rooms were acrawl with the small cleaning animals, all rubber and metal. They thudded against chairs, whirling their mustached runners, kneading the rug nap, sucking gently at hidden dust. Then, like mysterious invaders, they popped into their burrows. Their pink electric eyes faded. The house was clean.

10   *Ten o'clock.* The sun came out from behind the rain. The house stood alone in a city of rubble and ashes. This was the one house left standing. At night the ruined city gave off a radioactive glow which could be seen for miles.

11   *Ten-fifteen.* The garden sprinklers whirled up in golden founts, filling the soft morning air with scatterings of brightness. The water pelted windowpanes, running down the charred west side where the house had been burned evenly free of its white paint. The entire west face of the house was black, save for five places. Here the silhouette in paint of a man mowing a lawn. Here, as in a photograph, a woman bent to pick flowers. Still farther over, their images burned on wood in one titanic instant, a small boy, hands flung into the air; higher up, the image of a thrown ball, and opposite him a girl, hands raised to catch a ball which never came down.

12   The five spots of paint—the man, the woman, the children, the ball—remained. The rest was a thin charcoaled layer.

13   The gentle sprinkler rain filled the garden with falling light.

14   Until this day, how well the house had kept its peace. How carefully it had inquired, "Who goes there? What's the password?" and, getting no answer from lonely foxes and whining cats, it had shut up its windows and drawn shades in an oldmaidenly preoccupation with self-protection which bordered on a mechanical paranoia.

15   It quivered at each sound, the house did. If a sparrow brushed a window, the shade snapped up. The bird, startled, flew off! No, not even a bird must touch the house!

16   The house was an altar with ten thousand attendants, big, small, servicing, attending, in choirs. But the gods had gone away, and the ritual of the religion continued senselessly, uselessly.

17   *Twelve noon.*

18   A dog whined, shivering, on the front porch.

19   The front door recognized the dog voice and opened. The dog, once huge and fleshy, but now gone to bone and covered with sores, moved in and through the house, tracking mud. Behind it whirred angry mice, angry at having to pick up mud, angry at inconvenience.

20   For not a leaf fragment blew under the door but what the wall panels flipped open and the copper scrap rats flashed swiftly out. The offending dust, hair, or paper, seized in miniature steel jaws, was raced back to the burrows. There, down tubes which fed into the cellar, it was dropped into the sighing vent of an incinerator which sat like evil Baal in a dark corner.

21   The dog ran upstairs, hysterically yelping to each door, at last realizing, as the house realized, that only silence was here.

22   It sniffed the air and scratched the kitchen door. Behind the door, the stove was making pancakes which filled the house with a rich baked odor and the scent of maple syrup.

23   The dog frothed at the mouth, lying at the door, sniffing, its eyes turned to fire. It ran wildly in circles, biting at its tail, spun in a frenzy, and died. It lay in the parlor for an hour.

24   *Two o'clock,* sang a voice.

25   Delicately sensing decay at last, the regiments of mice hummed out as softly as blown gray leaves in an electrical wind.

26   *Two-fifteen.*

27   The dog was gone.

28   In the cellar, the incinerator glowed suddenly and a whirl of sparks leaped up the chimney.

29   *Two thirty-five.*

30   Bridge tables sprouted from patio walls. Playing cards fluttered onto pads in a shower of pips. Martinis manifested on an oaken bench with egg-salad sandwiches. Music played.

31   But the tables were silent and the cards untouched.

32   At four o'clock the tables folded like great butterflies back through the paneled walls.

33   *Four-thirty.*
34   The nursery walls glowed.
35   Animals took shape: yellow giraffes, blue lions, pink antelopes, lilac panthers cavorting in crystal substance. The walls were glass. They looked out upon color and fantasy. Hidden films clocked through well-oiled sprockets, and the walls lived. The nursery floor was woven to resemble a crisp, cereal meadow. Over this ran aluminum roaches and iron crickets, and in the hot still air butterflies of delicate red tissue wavered among the sharp aroma of animal spoors! There was the sound like a great matted yellow hive of bees within a dark bellows, the lazy bumble of a purring lion. And there was the patter of okapi feet and the murmur of a fresh jungle rain, like other hoofs, falling upon the summer-starched grass. Now the walls dissolved into distances of parched weed, mile on mile, and warm endless sky. The animals drew away into thorn brakes and water holes.
36   It was the children's hour.

37   *Five o'clock.* The bath filled with clear hot water.
38   *Six, seven, eight o'clock.* The dinner dishes manipulated like magic tricks, and in the study a *click.* In the metal stand opposite the hearth where a fire now blazed up warmly, a cigar popped out, half an inch of soft gray ash on it, smoking, waiting.
39   *Nine o'clock.* The beds warmed their hidden circuits, for nights were cool here.
40   *Nine-five.* A voice spoke from the study ceiling:
41   "Mrs. McClellan, which poem would you like this evening?"
42   The house was silent.
43   The voice said at last, "Since you express no preference, I shall select a poem at random." Quiet music rose to back the voice. "Sara Teasdale. As I recall, your favorite. . . .

"There will come soft rains and the smell of the ground,
And swallows circling with their shimmering sound;

And frogs in the pools singing at night,
And wild plum trees in tremulous white;

Robins will wear their feathery fire,
Whistling their whims on a low fence-wire;

And not one will know of the war, not one
Will care at last when it is done.

Not one would mind, neither bird nor tree,
If mankind perished utterly;

And Spring herself, when she woke at dawn
Would scarcely know that we were gone."

44   The fire burned on the stone hearth and the cigar fell away into a mound of quiet ash on its tray. The empty chairs faced each other between the silent walls, and the music played.

45   At ten o'clock the house began to die.

46   The wind blew. A falling tree bough crashed through the kitchen window. Cleaning solvent, bottled, shattered over the stove. The room was ablaze in an instant!

47   "Fire!" screamed a voice. The house lights flashed, water pumps shot water from the ceilings. But the solvent spread on the linoleum, licking, eating, under the kitchen door, while the voices took it up in chorus: "Fire, fire, fire!"

48   The house tried to save itself. Doors sprang tightly shut, but the windows were broken by the heat and the wind blew and sucked upon the fire.

49   The house gave ground as the fire in ten billion angry sparks moved with flaming ease from room to room and then up the stairs. While scurrying water rats squeaked from the walls, pistoled their water, and ran for more. And the wall sprays let down showers of mechanical rain.

50   But too late. Somewhere, sighing, a pump shrugged to a stop. The quenching rain ceased. The reserve water supply which had filled baths and washed dishes for many quiet days was gone.

51   The fire crackled up the stairs. It fed upon Picassos and Matisses in the upper halls, like delicacies, baking off the oily flesh, tenderly crisping the canvases into black shavings.

52   Now the fire lay in beds, stood in windows, changed the colors of drapes!

53   And then, reinforcements.

54   From attic trapdoors, blind robot faces peered down with faucet mouths gushing green chemical.

55   The fire backed off, as even an elephant must at the sight of a dead snake. Now there were twenty snakes whipping over the floor, killing the fire with a clear cold venom of green froth.

56   But the fire was clever. It had sent flames outside the house, up through the attic to the pumps there. An explosion! The attic brain which directed the pumps was shattered into bronze shrapnel on the beams.

57   The fire rushed back into every closet and felt of the clothes hung there.

58   The house shuddered, oak bone on bone, its bared skeleton cringing from the heat, its wire, its nerves revealed as if a surgeon had torn the skin off to let the red veins and capillaries quiver in the scalded air. Help, help! Fire! Run, run! Heat snapped mirrors like the brittle winter ice. And the voices wailed Fire, fire, run, run, like a tragic nursery rhyme, a dozen voices, high, low, like children dying in a forest, alone, alone. And the voices fading as the wires popped their sheathings like hot chestnuts. One, two, three, four, five voices died.

59   In the nursery the jungle burned. Blue lions roared, purple giraffes bounded off. The panthers ran in circles, changing color, and ten million animals, running before the fire, vanished off toward a distant steaming river. . . .

60   Ten more voices died. In the last instant under the fire avalanche, other choruses, oblivious, could be heard announcing the time, playing music, cutting the lawn by remote-control mower, or setting an umbrella frantically out and in, the slamming and opening front door, a thousand things happening, like a clock shop when each clock strikes the hour insanely before or after the other, a scene of maniac confusion, yet unity; singing, screaming, a few last cleaning mice darting bravely out to carry the horrid ashes away! and one voice, with sublime disregard for the situation, read poetry aloud in the fiery study, until all the film spools burned, until all the wires withered and the circuits cracked.

61   The fire burst the house and let it slam flat down, puffing out skirts of spark and smoke.

62   In the kitchen, an instant before the rain of fire and timber, the stove could be seen making breakfasts at a psychopathic rate, ten dozen eggs, six loaves of toast, twenty dozen bacon strips, which, eaten by fire, started the stove working again, hysterically hissing!

63   The crash. The attic smashing into kitchen and parlor. The parlor into cellar, cellar into sub-cellar. Deep freeze, armchair, film tapes, circuits, beds, and all like skeletons thrown in a cluttered mound deep under.

64   Smoke and silence. A great quantity of smoke.

65   Dawn showed faintly in the east. Among the ruins, one wall stood alone. Within the wall, a last voice said, over and over again and again, even as the sun rose to shine upon the heaped rubble and steam:

66   "Today is August 5, 2026, today is August 5, 2026, today is . . ."

August 2026: There Will Come Soft Rains

Questions on Content, Style, and Structure

1. In this story what has happened to the city of Allendale, California? to the McClellan family?

2. What device does Bradbury use to unify the events in this story?

3. Briefly describe life in the McClellan house before August 4, 2026. What sort of life was it?

4. What is ironic about the house's activities before the fire?

5. Point out places where Bradbury personifies the house. Why does he present the house this way?

6. How is the fire characterized? Why?

7. Find several other examples of figurative language. What do these add to the story?

8. Study the sentence structure in paragraphs 58–63. How does Bradbury communicate a sense of chaos during the fire?

9. Why is the Teasdale poem an especially ironic choice for August 4?

10. How does the ending add to the overall tone of the story?

11. In a few sentences state what you think Bradbury's purpose was in writing this story. What effect is he trying to have on the reader? Does he succeed?

Vocabulary

warrens (9)   wavered (35)
nap (9)   spoors (35)
founts (11)   okapi (35)
cavorting (35)   sublime (60)
cereal (35)   psychopathic (62)

Suggestions for Writing

1. Write an essay in which you explain and illustrate Bradbury's uses of irony or his uses of personification.

2. Write an essay arguing for or against the ban of certain types of nuclear weapons.

3. Bradbury's story shows a house of the future full of gadgets. Write an essay in which you defend or criticize the role of technology in modern life. Are we becoming unnecessarily dependent on any of our technological aids?

Section 8

Scenes of the Past

To Make Them Stand in Fear
Kenneth M. Stampp

Kenneth M. Stampp is a professor of history at the University of
California at Berkeley. His books include *And the War Came* (1950),
The Era of Reconstruction (1956), and *The Peculiar Institution.* (1956),
a study of pre-Civil War slavery, from which this selection is taken.

1   A wise master did not take seriously the belief that Negroes were natural-
born slaves. He knew better. He knew that Negroes freshly imported
from Africa had to be broken in to bondage; that each succeeding generation had to be carefully trained. This was no easy task, for the bonds-
man rarely submitted willingly. Moreover, he rarely submitted completely. In most cases there was no end to the need for control—at least
not until old age reduced the slave to a condition of helplessness.

2   Masters revealed the qualities they sought to develop in slaves when
they singled out certain ones for special commendation. A small Mississippi planter mourned the death of his "faithful and dearly beloved servant" Jack: "Since I have owned him he has been true to me in all
respects. He was an obedient trusty servant. . . . I never knew him to
steal nor lie and he ever set a moral and industrious example to those
around him. . . . I shall ever cherish his memory." A Louisiana sugar
planter lost a "very valuable Boy" through an accident: "His life was a
very great one. I have always found him willing and obedient and never
knew him to fail to do anything he was put to do." These were "ideal"
slaves, the models slaveholders had in mind as they trained and governed
their workers.

3   How might this ideal be approached? The first step, advised those who
wrote discourses on the management of slaves, was to establish and
maintain strict discipline. An Arkansas master suggested the adoption
of the "Army Regulations as to the discipline in Forts." "They must obey
at all times, and under all circumstances, cheerfully and with alacrity,"
affirmed a Virginia slaveholder. "It greatly impairs the happiness of a
negro, to be allowed to cultivate an insubordinate temper. Unconditional
submission is the only footing upon which slavery should be placed. It
is precisely similar to the attitude of a minor to his parent, or a soldier
to his general." A South Carolinian limned a perfect relationship between
a slave and his master: "that the slave should know that his master is
to govern absolutely, and he is to obey implicitly. That he is never for
a moment to exercise either his will or judgment in opposition to a
positive order."

4   The second step was to implant in the bondsmen themselves a con-

sciousness of personal inferiority. They had "to know and keep their places," to "feel the difference between master and slave," to understand that bondage was their natural status. They had to feel that African ancestry tainted them, that their color was a badge of degradation. In the country they were to show respect for even their master's nonslaveholding neighbors; in the towns they were to give way on the streets to the most wretched white man. The line between the races must never be crossed, for familiarity caused slaves to forget their lowly station and to become "impudent."

5   Frederick Douglass[1] explained that a slave might commit the offense of impudence in various ways: "in the tone of an answer; in answering at all; in not answering; in the expression of countenance; in the motion of the head; in the gait, manner and bearing of the slave." Any of these acts, in some subtle way, might indicate the absence of proper subordination. "In a well regulated community," wrote a Texan, "a negro takes off his hat in addressing a white man. . . . Where this is not enforced, we may always look for impudent and rebellious negroes."

6   The third step in the training of slaves was to awe them with a sense of their master's enormous power. The only principle upon which slavery could be maintained, reported a group of Charlestonians, was the "principle of fear." In his defense of slavery James H. Hammond admitted that this, unfortunately, was true but put the responsibility upon the abolitionists. Antislavery agitation had forced masters to strengthen their authority: "We have to rely more and more on the power of fear. . . . We are determined to continue masters, and to do so we have to draw the rein tighter and tighter day by day to be assured that we hold them in complete check." A North Carolina mistress, after subduing a troublesome domestic, realized that it was essential "to make them stand in fear"!

7   In this the slaveholders had considerable success. Frederick Douglass believed that most slaves stood "in awe" of white men; few could free themselves altogether from the notion that their masters were "invested with a sort of sacredness." Olmsted[2] saw a small white girl stop a slave on the road and boldly order him to return to his plantation. The slave fearfully obeyed her command. A visitor in Mississippi claimed that a master, armed only with a whip or cane, could throw himself among a score of bondsmen and cause them to "flee with terror." He accomplished this by the "peculiar tone of authority" with which he spoke. "Fear, awe, and obedience . . . are interwoven into the very nature of the slave."

[1] Frederick Douglass escaped from slavery to become an abolitionist leader and ultimately U.S. ambassador to Haiti.
[2] Frederick L. Olmsted, designer of New York City's Central Park, wrote a series of books on his travels through the South: *A Journey in the Seaboard States* (1856), *A Journey Through Texas* (1857), *A Journey in the Back Country* (1860), and *Journeys and Explorations in the Cotton Kingdom* (1861).

8   The fourth step was to persuade the bondsmen to take an interest in the master's enterprise and to accept his standards of good conduct. A South Carolina planter explained: "The master should make it his business to show his slaves, that the advancement of his individual interest, is at the same time an advancement of theirs. Once they feel this, it will require but little compulsion to make them act as it becomes them." Though slaveholders induced only a few chattels to respond to this appeal, these few were useful examples for others.

9   The final step was to impress Negroes with their helplessness, to create in them "a habit of perfect dependence" upon their masters. Many believed it dangerous to train slaves to be skilled artisans in the towns, because they tended to become self-reliant. Some thought it equally dangerous to hire them to factory owners. In the Richmond tobacco factories they were alarmingly independent and "insolent." A Virginian was dismayed to find that his bondsmen, while working at an iron furnace, "got a habit of roaming about and *taking care of themselves.*" Permitting them to hire their own time produced even worse results. "No higher evidence can be furnished of its baneful effects," wrote a Charlestonian, "than the unwillingness it produces in the slave, to return to the regular life and domestic control of the master."

10   A spirit of independence was less likely to develop among slaves kept on the land, where most of them became accustomed to having their master provide their basic needs, and where they might be taught that they were unfit to look out for themselves. Slaves then directed their energies to the attainment of mere "temporary ease and enjoyment." "Their masters," Olmsted believed, "calculated on it in them—do not wish to cure it—and by constant practice encourage it."

11   Here, then, was the way to produce the perfect slave: accustom him to rigid discipline, demand from him unconditional submission, impress upon him his innate inferiority, develop in him a paralyzing fear of white men, train him to adopt the master's code of good behavior, and instill in him a sense of complete dependence. This, at least, was the goal.

12   But the goal was seldom reached. Every master knew that the average slave was only an imperfect copy of the model. He knew that some bondsmen yielded only to superior power—and yielded reluctantly. This complicated his problem of control.

To Make Them Stand in Fear

Questions on Content, Style, and Structure

1. How does Stampp introduce his essay?
2. What is Stampp's thesis?

3. By what strategy is this essay primarily developed?

4. Briefly list the steps Stampp explains. Are these steps in a logical order or could they have been ordered a different way?

5. Which steps proved most successful? Overall, were the masters successful?

6. What is Stampp's main technique for explaining each step?

7. Why does the author use so much quoted material in his explanation? Is this use effective? Why or why not?

8. Identify the transition devices that link paragraphs 2–9. Do the paragraphs flow smoothly?

9. Study paragraphs 11–12. Describe and evaluate Stampp's conclusion.

10. Analyze the tone of this selection. Is the tone appropriate? Why/why not?

Vocabulary

commendation (2)   implicity (3)   chattels (8)
discourses (3)   degradation (4)   insolent (9)
alacrity (3)   impudent (4)   baneful (9)
limned (3)   countenance (5)

Suggestions for Writing

1. If you have ever been involved in a racially tense incident, write an essay describing the situation. Analyze the causes and effects of the event and explain in your essay what the incident taught you.

2. Read Maya Angelou's essay "Graduation" on pages 20–29. Compare and contrast the attitudes of the slave owners as presented in this essay to the assumptions underlying Donleavy's speech. Do any similarities exist? Write an essay explaining your findings.

3. Many blacks fought vigorously against their slavery. Research a nineteenth-century black leader such as Nat Turner, Harriet Tubman, or Frederick Douglass and write an essay describing his or her most important contributions in the fight against bondage.

The Role of the Undesirables
Eric Hoffer

Eric Hoffer has worked as a migrant field hand, a gold miner, a
longshoreman, a teacher, and a writer. His books include *The
Passionate State of Mind* (1955), *First Things, Last Things* (1971), and
Reflections on the Human Condition (1973). This is an excerpt from
The True Believer, published in 1951.

1   In the winter of 1934, I spent several weeks in a federal transient camp
in California. These camps were originally established by Governor
Rolph in the early days of the Depression to care for the single homeless
unemployed of the state. In 1934 the federal government took charge of
the camps for a time, and it was then that I first heard of them.

2   How I happened to get into one of the camps is soon told. Like thousands of migrant agricultural workers in California I then followed the
crops from one part of the state to the other. Early in 1934 I arrived in
the town of El Centro, in the Imperial Valley. I had been given a free ride
on a truck from San Diego, and it was midnight when the truck driver
dropped me on the outskirts of El Centro. I spread my bedroll by the side
of the road and went to sleep. I had hardly dozed off when the rattle of
a motorcycle drilled itself into my head and a policeman was bending
over me saying, "Roll up, Mister." It looked as though I was in for something; it happened now and then that the police got overzealous and
rounded up the freight trains. But this time the cop had no such thought.
He said, "Better go over to the federal shelter and get yourself a bed and
maybe some breakfast." He directed me to the place.

3   I found a large hall, obviously a former garage, dimly lit, and packed
with cots. A concert of heavy breathing shook the thick air. In a small
office near the door, I was registered by a middle-aged clerk. He informed
me that this was the "receiving shelter" where I would get one night's
lodging and breakfast. The meal was served in the camp nearby. Those
who wished to stay on, he said, had to enroll in the camp. He then gave
me three blankets and excused himself for not having a vacant cot. I
spread the blankets on the cement floor and went to sleep.

4   I awoke with dawn amid a chorus of coughing, throat-clearing, the
sound of running water, and the intermittent flushing of toilets in the
back of the hall. There were about fifty of us, of all colors and ages, all
of us more or less ragged and soiled. The clerk handed out tickets for
breakfast, and we filed out to the camp located several blocks away, near
the railroad tracks.

5   From the outside the camp looked like a cross between a factory and

a prison. A high fence of wire enclosed it, and inside were three large sheds and a huge boiler topped by a pillar of black smoke. Men in blue shirts and dungarees were strolling across the sandy yard. A ship's bell in front of one of the buildings announced breakfast. The regular camp members—there was a long line of them—ate first. Then we filed in through the gate, handing our tickets to the guard.

6   It was a good, plentiful meal. After breakfast our crowd dispersed. I heard some say that the camps in the northern part of the state were better, that they were going to catch a northbound freight. I decided to try this camp in El Centro.

7   My motives in enrolling were not crystal clear. I wanted to clean up. There were shower baths in the camp and wash tubs and plenty of soap. Of course I could have bathed and washed my clothes in one of the irrigation ditches, but here in the camp I had a chance to rest, get the wrinkles out of my belly, and clean up at leisure. In short, it was the easiest way out.

8   A brief interview at the camp office and a physical examination were all the formalities for enrollment.

9   There were some two hundred men in the camp. They were the kind I had worked and traveled with for years. I even saw familiar faces—men I had worked with in orchards and fields. Yet my predominant feeling was one of strangeness. It was my first experience of life in intimate contact with a crowd. For it is one thing to work and travel with a gang, and quite another thing to eat, sleep, and spend the greater part of the day cheek by jowl with two hundred men.

10   I found myself speculating on a variety of subjects: the reasons for their chronic bellyaching and beefing—it was more a ritual than the expression of a grievance; the amazing orderliness of the men; the comic seriousness with which they took their games of cards, checkers, and dominoes; the weird manner of reasoning one overheard now and then. Why, I kept wondering, were these men within the enclosure of a federal transient camp? Were they people temporarily hard up? Would jobs solve all their difficulties? Were we indeed like the people outside?

11   Up to then I was not aware of being one of a specific species of humanity. I had considered myself simply a human being—not particularly good or bad, and on the whole harmless. The people I worked and traveled with I knew as Americans and Mexicans, whites and Negroes, Northerners and Southerners, etc. It did not occur to me that we were a group possessed of peculiar traits, and that there was something—innate or acquired—in our make-up which made us adopt a particular mode of existence.

12   It was a slight thing that started me on a new track.

13   I got to talking to a mild-looking, elderly fellow. I liked his soft speech and pleasant manner. We swapped trivial experiences. Then he suggested a game of checkers. As we started to arrange the pieces on the board, I was startled by the sight of his crippled right hand. I had not noticed it

before. Half of it was chopped off lengthwise, so that the horny stump with its three fingers looked like a hen's leg. I was mortified that I had not noticed the hand until he dangled it, so to speak, before my eyes. It was, perhaps, to bolster my shaken confidence in my powers of observation that I now began paying close attention to the hands of the people around me. The result was astounding. It seemed that every other man had had his hand mangled. There was a man with one arm. Some men limped. One young, good-looking fellow had a wooden leg. It was as though the majority of the men had escaped the snapping teeth of a machine and left part of themselves behind.

14 It was, I knew, an exaggerated impression. But I began counting the cripples as the men lined up in the yard at mealtime. I found thirty (out of two hundred) crippled either in arms or legs. I immediately sensed where the counting would land me. The simile preceded the statistical deduction: we in the camp were a human junk pile.

15 I began evaluating my fellow tramps as human material, and for the first time in my life I became face-conscious. There were some good faces, particularly among the young. Several of the middle-aged and the old looked healthy and well preserved. But the damaged and decayed faces were in the majority. I saw faces that were wrinkled, or bloated, or raw as the surface of a peeled plum. Some of the noses were purple and swollen, some broken, some pitted with enlarged pores. There were many toothless mouths (I counted seventy-eight). I noticed eyes that were blurred, faded, opaque, or bloodshot. I was struck by the fact that the old men, even the very old, showed their age mainly in the face. Their bodies were still slender and erect. One little man over sixty years of age looked a mere boy when seen from behind. The shriveled face joined to a boyish body made a startling sight.

16 My diffidence had now vanished. I was getting to know everybody in the camp. They were a friendly and talkative lot. Before many weeks I knew some essential fact about practically everyone.

17 And I was continually counting. Of the two hundred men in the camp there were approximately as follows:

Cripples	30
Confirmed drunkards	60
Old men (55 and over)	50
Youths under twenty	10
Men with chronic diseases, heart, asthma, TB	12
Mildly insane	4
Constitutionally lazy	6
Fugitives from justice	4
Apparently normal	70

(The numbers do not tally up to two hundred since some of the men were counted twice or even thrice—as cripples and old, or as old and confirmed drunks, etc.)

18   In other words: less than half the camp inmates (seventy normal, plus ten youths) were unemployed workers whose difficulties would be at an end once jobs were available. The rest (60 per cent) had handicaps in addition to unemployment.

19   I also counted fifty war veterans, and eighty skilled workers representing sixteen trades. All the men (including those with chronic diseases) were able to work. The one-armed man was a wizard with the shovel.

20   I did not attempt any definite measurement of character and intelligence. But it seemed to me that the intelligence of the men in the camp was certainly not below the average. And as to character, I found much forbearance and genuine good humor. I never came across one instance of real viciousness. Yet, on the whole, one would hardly say that these men were possessed of strong characters. Resistance, whether to one's appetites or to the ways of the world, is a chief factor in the shaping of character; and the average tramp is, more or less, a slave of his few appetites. He generally takes the easiest way out.

21   The connection between our make-up and our mode of existence as migrant workers presented itself now with some clarity.

22   The majority of us were incapable of holding on to a steady job. We lacked self-discipline and the ability to endure monotonous, leaden hours. We were probably misfits from the very beginning. Our contact with a steady job was not unlike a collision. Some of us were maimed, some got frightened and ran away, and some took to drink. We inevitably drifted in the direction of least resistance—the open road. The life of a migrant worker is varied and demands only a minimum of self-discipline. We were now in one of the drainage ditches of ordered society. We could not keep a footing in the ranks of respectability and were washed into the slough of our present existence.

23   Yet, I mused, there must be in this world a task with an appeal so strong that were we to have a taste of it we would hold on and be rid for good of our restlessness.

24   My stay in the camp lasted about four weeks. Then I found a haying job not far from town, and finally, in April, when the hot winds began blowing, I shouldered my bedroll and took the highway to San Bernardino.

25   It was the next morning, after I had got a lift to Indio by truck, that a new idea began to take hold of me. The highway out of Indio leads through waving date groves, fragrant grapefruit orchards, and lush alfalfa fields; then, abruptly, passes into a desert of white sand. The sharp line between garden and desert is very striking. The turning of white sand into garden seemed to me an act of magic. This, I thought, was a job one would jump at—even the men in the transient camps. They had the skill and ability of the average American. But their energies, I felt, could be quickened only by a task that was spectacular, that had in it something

of the miraculous. The pioneer task of making the desert flower would certainly fill the bill.

26   Tramps as pioneers? It seemed absurd. Every man and child in California knows that the pioneers had been giants, men of boundless courage and indomitable spirit. However, as I strode on across the white sand, I kept mulling the idea over.

27   Who were the pioneers? Who were the men who left their homes and went into the wilderness? A man rarely leaves a soft spot and goes deliberately in search of hardship and privation. People become attached to the places they live in; they drive roots. A change of habitat is a painful act of uprooting. A man who has made good and has a standing in his community stays put. The successful businessmen, farmers, and workers usually stayed where they were. Who then left for the wilderness and the unknown? Obviously those who had not made good: men who went broke or never amounted to much; men who though possessed of abilities were too impulsive to stand the daily grind; men who were slaves of their appetites—drunkards, gamblers, and woman-chasers; outcasts—fugitives from justice and ex-jailbirds. There were no doubt some who went in search of health—men suffering with TB, asthma, heart trouble. Finally there was a sprinkling of young and middle-aged in search of adventure.

28   All these people craved change, some probably actuated by the naive belief that a change in place brings with it a change in luck. Many wanted to go to a place where they were not known and there make a new beginning. Certainly they did not go out deliberately in search of hard work and suffering. If in the end they shouldered enormous tasks, endured unspeakable hardships, and accomplished the impossible, it was because they had to. They became men of action on the run. They acquired strength and skill in the inescapable struggle for existence. It was a question of do or die. And once they tasted the joy of achievement, they craved for more.

29   Clearly the same types of people which now swelled the ranks of migratory workers and tramps had probably in former times made up the bulk of the pioneers. As a group the pioneers were probably as unlike the present-day "native sons"—their descendants—as one could well imagine. Indeed, were there to be today a new influx of typical pioneers, twin brothers of the forty-niners only in a modern garb, the citizens of California would consider it a menace to health, wealth, and morals.

30   With few exceptions, this seems to be the case in the settlement of all new countries. Ex-convicts were the vanguard in the settling of Australia. Exiles and convicts settled Siberia. In this country, a large portion of our earlier and later settlers were failures, fugitives, and felons. The exceptions seemed to be those who were motivated by religious fervor, such as the Pilgrim Fathers and the Mormons.

31   Although quite logical, this train of thought seemed to me then a

wonderful joke. In my exhilaration I was eating up the road in long strides, and I reached the oasis of Elim in what seemed almost no time. A passing empty truck picked me up just then and we thundered through Banning and Beaumont, all the way to Riverside. From there I walked the seven miles to San Bernardino.

32   Somehow, this discovery of a family likeness between tramps and pioneers took a firm hold on my mind. For years afterward it kept intertwining itself with a mass of observations which on the face of them had no relation to either tramps or pioneers. And it moved me to speculate on subjects in which, up to then, I had no real interest, and of which I knew very little.

33   I talked with several old-timers—one of them over eighty and a native son—in Sacramento, Placerville, Auburn, and Fresno. It was not easy, at first, to obtain the information I was after. I could not make my questions specific enough. "What kind of people were the early settlers and miners?" I asked. They were a hard-working, tough lot, I was told. They drank, fought, gambled, and wenched. They were big-hearted, grasping, profane, and God-fearing. They wallowed in luxury, or lived on next to nothing with equal ease. They were the salt of the earth.

34   Still it was not clear what manner of people they were.

35   If I asked what they looked like, I was told of whiskers, broadbrimmed hats, high boots, shirts of many colors, sun-tanned faces, horny hands. Finally I asked: "What group of people in present-day California most closely resembles the pioneers?" The answer, usually after some hesitation, was invariably the same: "The Okies[1] and the fruit tramps."

36   I tried to evaluate the tramps as potential pioneers by watching them in action. I saw them fell timber, clear firebreaks, build rock walls, put up barracks, build dams and roads, handle steam shovels, bulldozers, tractors, and concrete mixers. I saw them put in a hard day's work after a night of steady drinking. They sweated and growled, but they did the work. I saw tramps elevated to positions of authority as foremen and superintendents. Then I could notice a remarkable physical transformation: a seamed face gradually smoothed out and the skin showed a healthy hue; an indifferent mouth became firm and expressive; dull eyes cleared and brightened; voices actually changed; there was even an apparent increase in stature. In almost no time these promoted tramps looked as if they had been on top all their lives. Yet sooner or later I would meet up with them again in a railroad yard, on some skid row, or in the fields—tramps again. It was usually the same story: they got drunk or lost their temper and were fired, or they got fed up with the steady job and quit. Usually, when a tramp becomes a foreman, he is careful in

[1] The name "Okies" was indiscriminately applied to the thousands of farmers who left Oklahoma, Texas, and Arkansas after the drought and dust storms of the early 1930s to become migratory workers in California.

his treatment of the tramps under him; he knows the day of reckoning is never far off.

37   In short, it was not difficult to visualize the tramps as pioneers. I reflected that if they were to find themselves in a singlehanded life-and-death struggle with nature, they would undoubtedly display persistence. For the pressure of responsibility and the heat of battle steel a character. The inadaptable would perish, and those who survived would be the equal of the successful pioneers.

38   I also considered the few instances of pioneering engineered from above—that is to say, by settlers possessed of lavish means, who were classed with the best where they came from. In these instances, it seemed to me, the resulting social structure was inevitably precarious. For pioneering deluxe usually results in a plantation society, made up of large landowners and peon labor, either native or imported. Very often there is a racial cleavage between the two. The colonizing activities of the Teutonic barons in the Baltic, the Hungarian nobles in Transylvania, the English in Ireland, the planters in our South, and present-day plantation societies in Kenya and other British and Dutch colonies are cases in point. Whatever their merits, they are characterized by poor adaptability. They are likely eventually to be broken up either by a peon revolution or by an influx of typical pioneers—who are usually of the same race or nation as the landowners. The adjustment is not necessarily implemented by war. Even our old South, had it not been for the complication of secession, might eventually have attained stability without war: namely, by the activity of its own poor whites or by influx of the indigent from other states.

39   There is in us a tendency to judge a race, a nation, or an organization by its least worthy members. The tendency is manifestly perverse and unfair; yet it has some justification. For the quality and destiny of a nation is determined to a considerable extent by the nature and potentialities of its inferior elements. The inert mass of a nation is in its middle section. The industrious, decent, well-to-do, and satisfied middle classes—whether in cities or on the land—are worked upon and shaped by minorities at both extremes: the best and the worst.

40   The superior individual, whether in politics, business, industry, science, literature, or religion, undoubtedly plays a major role in the shaping of a nation. But so do the individuals at the other extreme: the poor, the outcasts, the misfits, and those who are in the grip of some overpowering passion. The importance of these inferior elements as formative factors lies in the readiness with which they are swayed in any direction. This peculiarity is due to their inclination to take risks ("not giving a damn") and their propensity for united action. They crave to merge their drab, wasted lives into something grand and complete. Thus they are the first and most fervent adherents of new religions, political upheavals, patriotic hysteria, gangs, and mass rushes to new lands.

41   And the quality of a nation—its innermost worth—is made manifest by its dregs as they rise to the top: by how brave they are, how humane, how orderly, how skilled, how generous, how independent or servile; by the bounds they will not transgress in their dealings with man's soul, with truth, and with honor.

42   The average American of today bristles with indignation when he is told that this country was built, largely, by hordes of undesirables from Europe. Yet, far from being derogatory, this statement, if true, should be a cause for rejoicing, should fortify our pride in the stock from which we have sprung.

43   This vast continent with its towns, farms, factories, dams, aqueducts, docks, railroads, highways, powerhouses, schools, and parks is the hand-iwork of common folk from the Old World, where for centuries men of their kind had been as beasts of burden, the property of the masters—kings, nobles, and priests,—and with no will and aspirations of their own. When on rare occasions one of the lowly had reached the top in Europe he had kept the pattern intact and, if anything, tightened the screws. The stuffy little corporal from Corsica[2] harnessed the lusty forces released by the French Revolution to a gilded state coach, and could think of nothing grander than mixing his blood with that of the Hapsburg masters and establishing a new dynasty. In our day a bricklayer in Italy,[3] a house painter in Germany,[4] and a shoemaker's son in Russia[5] have made them-selves masters of their nations; what they did was to re-establish and reinforce the old pattern.

44   Only here, in America, were the common folk of the Old World given a chance to show what they could do on their own, without a master to push and order them about. History contrived an earth-shaking joke when it lifted by the nape of the neck lowly peasants, shopkeepers, la-borers, paupers, jailbirds, and drunks from the midst of Europe, dumped them on a vast, virgin continent and said: "Go to it; it is yours!"

45   And the lowly were not awed by the magnitude of the task. A hunger for action, pent up for centuries, found an outlet. They went to it with ax, pick, shovel, plow, and rifle; on foot, on horse, in wagons, and on flatboats. They went to it praying, howling, singing, brawling, drinking, and fighting. Make way for the people! This is how I read the statement that this country was built by hordes of undesirables from the Old World.

46   Small wonder that we in this country have a deeply ingrained faith in human regeneration. We believe that, given a chance, even the degraded and the apparently worthless are capable of constructive work and great deeds. It is a faith founded on experience, not on some idealistic theory. And no matter what some anthropologists, sociologists, and geneticists may tell us, we shall go on believing that man, unlike other forms of life,

[2] Napoleon
[3] Mussolini
[4] Hitler
[5] Stalin

is not a captive of his past—of his heredity and habits—but is possessed of infinite plasticity, and his potentialities for good and for evil are never wholly exhausted.

The Role of the Undesirables

Questions on Content, Style, and Structure

1. How did Hoffer arrive at his understanding of the American pioneers? To whom does he compare them?

2. What, according to Hoffer, is the "role of the undesirables" in shaping a nation?

3. How were the American "common folk" different from those in Europe?

4. Why does Hoffer take so long to come to his main point? Is the essay's organization an effective one? Why/why not?

5. Why does Hoffer write his essay in first person?

6. Why does Hoffer catalogue the men in the federal relief camp?

7. What were the motivations of the pioneers?

8. How are the tramps and pioneers similar? Are these similarities presented convincingly?

9. Point out some examples of Hoffer's frequent use of sentences containing a series of words or phrases. What is the effect of this kind of sentence structure?

10. Point out some of Hoffer's similes and metaphors. What do they add to his essay?

11. Evaluate Hoffer's concluding paragraph. What does he mean when he refers to the "infinite plasticity" of Americans?

Vocabulary

transient (1)	precarious (38)
intermittent (4)	indigent (38)
diffidence (16)	propensity (40)
privation (27)	servile (41)
wenched (33)	transgress (41)
inadaptable (37)	derogatory (42)

Suggestions for Writing

1. Write an essay in which you support or refute Hoffer's statement that "given a chance, even the degraded and the apparently worthless are capable of constructive work and great deeds."

2. Write a research paper describing some well-known aspect of the Great Depression such as the "Hoovervilles," the Works Progress Administration, or the exodus of the Dust Bowl farmers. (At some point you might wish to read *The Grapes of Wrath* by John Steinbeck, regarded by many as the best novel on the plight of the Okies.)

3. Write a research paper describing the condition of migrant workers today. Has there been much improvement in the last fifty years?

Arrival at Auschwitz
Viktor E. Frankl

Viktor E. Frankl is an Austrian psychiatrist who has taught at the University of Vienna, Harvard, and Southern Methodist University. Some of his books include *From Death-Camp to Existentialism* (1967) and *The Will to Meaning* (1969). This selection is an excerpt from *Man's Search for Meaning*, published in 1962.

1   Fifteen hundred persons had been traveling by train for several days and nights: there were eighty people in each coach. All had to lie on top of their luggage, the few remnants of their personal possessions. The carriages were so full that only the top parts of the windows were free to let in the gray of dawn. Everyone expected the train to head for some munitions factory, in which we would be employed as forced labor. We did not know whether we were still in Silesia or already in Poland. The engine's whistle had an uncanny sound, like a cry for help sent out in commiseration for the unhappy load which it was destined to lead into perdition. Then the train shunted, obviously nearing a main station. Suddenly a cry broke from the ranks of the anxious passengers, "There is a sign, Auschwitz!" Everyone's heart missed a beat at that moment. Auschwitz—the very name stood for all that was horrible: gas chambers, crematoriums, massacres. Slowly, almost hesitatingly, the train moved on as if it wanted to spare its passengers the dreadful realization as long as possible: Auschwitz!

2   With the progressive dawn, the outlines of an immense camp became visible: long stretches of several rows of barbed wire fences; watch towers; search lights; and long columns of ragged human figures, gray in the grayness of dawn, trekking along the straight desolate roads, to what destination we did not know. There were isolated shouts and whistles of command. We did not know their meaning. My imagination led me to see gallows with people dangling on them. I was horrified, but this

was just as well, because step by step we had to become accustomed to a terrible and immense horror.

3   Eventually we moved into the station. The initial silence was interrupted by shouted commands. We were to hear those rough, shrill tones from then on, over and over again in all the camps. Their sound was almost like the last cry of a victim, and yet there was a difference. It had a rasping hoarseness, as if it came from the throat of a man who had to keep shouting like that, a man who was being murdered again and again. The carriage doors were flung open and a small detachment of prisoners stormed inside. They wore striped uniforms, their heads were shaved, but they looked well fed. They spoke in every possible European tongue, and all with a certain amount of humor, which sounded grotesque under the circumstances. Like a drowning man clutching a straw, my inborn optimism (which has often controlled my feelings even in the most desperate situations) clung to this thought: These prisoners look quite well, they seem to be in good spirits and even laugh. Who knows? I might manage to share their favorable position.

4   In psychiatry there is a certain condition known as "delusion of reprieve." The condemned man, immediately before his execution, gets the illusion that he might be reprieved at the very last moment. We, too, clung to shreds of hope and believed to the last moment that it would not be so bad. Just the sight of the red cheeks and round faces of those prisoners was a great encouragement. Little did we know then that they formed a specially chosen elite, who for years had been the receiving squad for new transports as they rolled into the station day after day. They took charge of the new arrivals and their luggage, including scarce items and smuggled jewelry. Auschwitz must have been a strange spot in this Europe of the last years of the war. There must have been unique treasures of gold and silver, platinum and diamonds, not only in the huge storehouses but also in the hands of the SS.*

5   Fifteen hundred captives were cooped up in a shed built to accommodate probably two hundred at the most. We were cold and hungry and there was not enough room for everyone to squat on the bare ground, let alone to lie down. One five-ounce piece of bread was our only food in four days. Yet I heard the senior prisoners in charge of the shed bargain with one member of the receiving party about a tie-pin made of platinum and diamonds. Most of the profits would eventually be traded for liquor—schnapps. I do not remember any more just how many thousands of marks were needed to purchase the quantity of schnapps required for a "gay evening," but I do know that those long-term prisoners needed schnapps. Under such conditions, who could blame them for trying to dope themselves? There was another group of prisoners who got liquor supplied in almost unlimited quantities by the SS: these were the men

* The SS (*Schutzstaffel*) was Hitler's sadistic security force; the men were chosen for their physique and for their blind dedication to Nazi goals.

who were employed in the gas chambers and crematoriums, and who knew very well that one day they would be relieved by a new shift of men, and that they would have to leave their enforced role of executioner and become victims themselves.

6   Nearly everyone in our transport lived under the illusion that he would be reprieved, that everything would yet be well. We did not realize the meaning behind the scene that was to follow presently. We were told to leave our luggage in the train and to fall into two lines—women on one side, men on the other—in order to file past a senior SS officer. Surprisingly enough, I had the courage to hide my haversack under my coat. My line filed past the officer, man by man. I realized that it would be dangerous if the officer spotted my bag. He would at least knock me down; I knew that from previous experience. Instinctively, I straightened on approaching the officer, so that he would not notice my heavy load. Then I was face to face with him. He was a tall man who looked slim and fit in his spotless uniform. What a contrast to us, who were untidy and grimy after our long journey! He had assumed an attitude of careless ease, supporting his right elbow with his left hand. His right hand was lifted, and with the forefinger of that hand he pointed very leisurely to the right or to the left. None of us had the slightest idea of the sinister meaning behind that little movement of a man's finger, pointing now to the right and now to the left, but far more frequently to the left.

7   It was my turn. Somebody whispered to me that to be sent to the right side would mean work, the way to the left being for the sick and those incapable of work, who would be sent to a special camp. I just waited for things to take their course, the first of many such times to come. My haversack weighed me down a bit to the left, but I made an effort to walk upright. The SS man looked me over, appeared to hesitate, then put both his hands on my shoulders. I tried very hard to look smart, and he turned my shoulders very slowly until I faced right, and I moved over to that side.

8   The significance of the finger game was explained to us in the evening. It was the first selection, the first verdict made on our existence or nonexistence. For the great majority of our transport, about 90 per cent, it meant death. Their sentence was carried out within the next few hours. Those who were sent to the left were marched from the station straight to the crematorium. This building, as I was told by someone who worked there, had the word "bath" written over its doors in several European languages. On entering, each prisoner was handed a piece of soap, and then—but mercifully I do not need to describe the events which followed. Many accounts have been written about this horror.

9   We who were saved, the minority of our transport, found out the truth in the evening. I inquired from prisoners who had been there for some time where my colleague and friend P—— had been sent.

10   "Was he sent to the left side?"

11   "Yes," I replied.

12   "Then you can see him there," I was told.

13   "Where?" A hand pointed to the chimney a few hundred yards off, which was sending a column of flame up into the gray sky of Poland. It dissolved into a sinister cloud of smoke.

14   "That's where your friend is, floating up to Heaven," was the answer. But I still did not understand until the truth was explained to me in plain words.

15   But I am telling things out of their turn. From a psychological point of view, we had a long, long way in front of us from the break of that dawn at the station until our first night's rest at the camp.

16   Escorted by SS guards with loaded guns, we were made to run from the station, past electrically charged barbed wire, through the camp, to the cleansing station; for those of us who had passed the first selection, this was a real bath. Again our illusion of reprieve found confirmation. The SS men seemed almost charming. Soon we found out their reason. They were nice to us as long as they saw watches on our wrists and could persuade us in well-meaning tones to hand them over. Would we not have to hand over all our possessions anyway, and why should not that relatively nice person have the watch? Maybe one day he would do one a good turn.

17   We waited in a shed which seemed to be the anteroom to the disinfecting chamber. SS men appeared and spread out blankets into which we had to throw all our possessions, all our watches and jewelry. There were still naïve prisoners among us who asked, to the amusement of the more seasoned ones who were there as helpers, if they could not keep a wedding ring, a medal or a good-luck piece. No one could yet grasp the fact that everything would be taken away.

18   I tried to take one of the old prisoners into my confidence. Approaching him furtively, I pointed to the roll of paper in the inner pocket of my coat and said. "Look, this is the manuscript of a scientific book. I know what you will say; that I should be grateful to escape with my life, that that should be all I can expect of fate. But I cannot help myself. I must keep this manuscript at all costs; it contains my life's work. Do you understand that?"

19   Yes, he was beginning to understand. A grin spread slowly over his face, first piteous, then more amused, mocking, insulting, until he bellowed one word at me in answer to my question, a word that was ever present in the vocabulary of the camp inmates: "Shit!" At that moment I saw the plain truth and did what marked the culminating point of the first phase of my psychological reaction: I struck out my whole former life.

20   Suddenly there was a stir among my fellow travelers, who had been standing about with pale, frightened faces, helplessly debating. Again we heard the hoarsely shouted commands. We were driven with blows into

the immediate anteroom of the bath. There we assembled around an SS man who waited until we had all arrived. Then he said, "I will give you two minutes, and I shall time you by my watch. In these two minutes you will get fully undressed and drop everything on the floor where you are standing. You will take nothing with you except your shoes, your belt or suspenders, and possibly a truss. I am starting to count—now!"

21   With unthinkable haste, people tore off their clothes. As the time grew shorter, they became increasingly nervous and pulled clumsily at their underwear, belts and shoelaces. Then we heard the first sounds of whipping; leather straps beating down on naked bodies.

22   Next we were herded into another room to be shaved: not only our heads were shorn, but not a hair was left on our entire bodies. Then on to the showers, where we lined up again. We hardly recognized each other; but with great relief some people noted that real water dripped from the sprays.

23   While we were waiting for the shower, our nakedness was brought home to us: we really had nothing now except our bare bodies—even minus hair; all we possessed, literally, was our naked existence. What else remained for us as a material link with our former lives? For me there were my glasses and my belt; the latter I had to exchange later on for a piece of bread. There was an extra bit of excitement in store for the owners of trusses. In the evening the senior prisoner in charge of our hut welcomed us with a speech in which he gave us his word of honor that he would hang, personally, "from that beam"—he pointed to it—any person who had sewn money or precious stones into his truss. Proudly he explained that as a senior inhabitant the camp laws entitled him to do so.

24   Where our shoes were concerned, matters were not so simple. Although we were supposed to keep them, those who had fairly decent pairs had to give them up after all and were given in exchange shoes that did not fit. In for real trouble were those prisoners who had followed the apparently well-meant advice (given in the anteroom) of the senior prisoners and had shortened their jackboots by cutting the tops off, then smearing soap on the cut edges to hide the sabotage. The SS men seemed to have waited for just that. All suspected of this crime had to go into a small adjoining room. After a time we again heard the lashings of the strap, and the screams of tortured men. This time it lasted for quite a while.

25   Thus the illusions some of us still held were destroyed one by one, and then, quite unexpectedly, most of us were overcome by a grim sense of humor. We knew that we had nothing to lose except our so ridiculously naked lives. When the showers started to run, we all tried very hard to make fun, both about ourselves and about each other. After all, real water did flow from the sprays!

26   Apart from that strange kind of humor, another sensation seized us:

curiosity. I have experienced this kind of curiosity before, as a fundamental reaction toward certain strange circumstances. When my life was
once endangered by a climbing accident, I felt only one sensation at the
critical moment: curiosity, curiosity as to whether I should come out of
it alive or with a fractured skull or some other injuries.

27   Cold curiosity predominated even in Auschwitz, somehow detaching
the mind from its surroundings, which came to be regarded with a kind
of objectivity. At that time one cultivated this state of mind as a means
of protection. We were anxious to know what would happen next; and
what would be the consequence, for example, of our standing in the open
air, in the chill of late autumn, stark naked, and still wet from the showers. In the next few days our curiosity evolved into surprise; surprise that
we did not catch cold.

28   There were many similar surprises in store for new arrivals. The medical men among us learned first of all: "Textbooks tell lies!" Somewhere
it is said that man cannot exist without sleep for more than a stated
number of hours. Quite wrong! I had been convinced that there were
certain things I just could not do: I could not sleep without this or I could
not live with that or the other. The first night in Auschwitz we slept in
beds which were constructed in tiers. On each tier (measuring about six-
and-a-half to eight feet) slept nine men, directly on the boards. Two
blankets were shared by each nine men. We could, of course, lie only on
our sides, crowded and huddled against each other, which had some advantages because of the bitter cold. Though it was forbidden to take shoes
up to the bunks, some people did use them secretly as pillows in spite
of the fact that they were caked with mud. Otherwise one's head had to
rest on the crook of an almost dislocated arm. And yet sleep came and
brought oblivion and relief from pain for a few hours.

29   I would like to mention a few similar surprises on how much we could
endure: we were unable to clean our teeth, and yet, in spite of that and
a severe vitamin deficiency, we had healthier gums than ever before. We
had to wear the same shirts for half a year, until they had lost all appearance of being shirts. For days we were unable to wash, even partially,
because of frozen water pipes, and yet the sores and abrasions on hands
which were dirty from work in the soil did not suppurate (that is, unless
there was frostbite). Or for instance, a light sleeper, who used to be disturbed by the slightest noise in the next room, now found himself lying
pressed against a comrade who snored loudly a few inches from his ear
and yet slept quite soundly through the noise.

30   If someone now asked of us the truth of Dostoevski's statement that
flatly defines man as a being who can get used to anything, we would
reply, "Yes, a man can get used to anything, but do not ask us how." But
our psychological investigations have not taken us that far yet; neither
had we prisoners reached that point. We were still in the first phase of
our psychological reactions.

Arrival at Auschwitz

Questions on Content, Style, and Structure

1. From whose point of view is this narrative written? Is the point of view effective? Why/why not?

2. In paragraphs 1–3, why is there so much description of sounds? Point out some examples of Frankl's use of simile in these paragraphs.

3. What is the "delusion of reprieve"? Why does Frankl refer to it several times?

4. In what kind of time sequence does Frankl tell this story? Is the time sequence consistent throughout? If not, does the break interfere with the narrative?

5. What was the meaning of the SS officer's "finger game"?

6. Why does the experienced prisoner insult Frankl when he tells him of his manuscript? Why does Frankl include this incident?

7. Why are the men grateful for the "real water" in the showers?

8. What role does curiosity play for Frankl during this time?

9. How does Frankl demonstrate the men's ability to endure?

10. Much of any narrative's strength lies in its author's ability to recreate people and places. Evaluate Frankl's descriptions, citing examples to support your answer.

11. What is Frankl's purpose in telling of his experience? Why does he refer to the "first phase of our psychological reactions" several times in the essay?

Vocabulary

munitions (1)
uncanny (1)
commiseration (1)
perdition (1)

shunted (1)
crematoriums (1)
haversack (6)
anteroom (17)

furtively (18)
culminating (19)
truss (23)
tier (28)
suppurate (29)

Suggestions for Writing

1. Write an essay describing an experience that destroyed your illusions one by one.

2. Write an essay explaining *Kristallnacht* (Night of Broken Glass) or describing the resistance of the Warsaw ghetto.

3. After researching the subject, write an essay analyzing Hitler's uses of propaganda.

That Day at Hiroshima
Alexander H. Leighton

Alexander H. Leighton is professor of psychiatry and preventive medicine at Dalhousie University in Nova Scotia. His books include *Human Relations in a Changing World* (1949), *Approaches to Cross-Cultural Psychiatry* (1965), and *Changing Perspectives on Mental Illness* (1969). This essay was first published in *Atlantic Monthly* in 1946.

I

1 We approached Hiroshima a little after daybreak on a winter day, driving in a jeep below a leaden sky and in the face of a cold, wet wind. On either side of the road, black flat fields were turning green under winter wheat. Here and there peasants worked, swinging spades or grubbing in mud and water with blue hands. Some in black split-toed shoes left tracks like cloven hoofs. To the north, looming close over the level land, mountains thrust heavy summits of pine darkly against the overcast. To the south and far away, the bay lay in dull brightness under fitful rain.

2 "Hiroshima," said the driver, a GI from a Kansas farm, who had been through the city many times, "don't look no different from any other bombed town. You soon get used to it. You'll see little old mud walls right in the middle of town that wasn't knocked down. They been exaggerating about that bomb."

3 Within a few miles the fields along the road were replaced by houses and shops that looked worn and dull yet intact. On the road itself people straggled to work, some on bicycles, most of them on foot—tattered and bandy-legged old men, girls with red cheeks and bright eyes, ancient women under towering bundles, middle-aged men looking stiff in Western business suits. In one place there were several Koreans together, the women easily distinguished from the Japanese by their white blouses and the full skirts that swung as they strode. At a bus stop a crowd stood waiting in a line long enough to fill a train. Half a mile farther on we passed the bus, small, battered, and gray, standing half obliterated by the cloud of smoke that came from the charcoal burner at the back while the driver stood working at its machinery.

4 Children of all ages waved, laughed, and shouted at us as had the children in other parts of Japan.

5 "Haro-goodabye! Haro-goodabye!"

6 "Jeepu! Jeeeepu!"

7 Like the children of Hamelin to the piper, they came rushing, at the

sound of our approach, from doorways and alleyways and from behind houses, to line up by the road and cheer. One little fellow of about six threw himself into the air, his little body twisting and feet kicking in a fit of glee.

8   The adults gazed at us with solemn eyes or looked straight ahead. They were more subdued than those I had seen elsewhere in Japan. The children seemed different, possessed by some common animation denied their elders—an animation which impelled them toward the occupation forces, toward the strong and the new.

9   Presently a two-story trade school appeared, with boards instead of window glass, and then a factory in the same condition. Soon there were shops and houses all along the way with windows missing. A house came into view with its roof pressed down, tiles scattered, and walls bulging outward. A shop with no front, like an open mouth, showed its contents, public and private, clear to the rear window.

10   The road turned to the Ota River, where the tide was running out and boats lay heaved over on the beach. A bridge ended suddenly like a head-less neck. Now every house and shop was damaged and lay with only one end or a corner standing.

11   Then all the buildings ceased and we came as if from a forest out on a plain, as if from tumult into silence. Imagine a city dump with its smells of wet ashes, mold, and things rotting, but one that runs from your feet almost to the limits of vision. As is often the case with level and desolate places on the earth, the sky seemed close above it. The predominant colors were red and yellow, crumbles of stone, bricks, red earth, and rust. Low walls made rectangles that marked where houses had stood, like sites of prehistoric villages. Here and there in the middle distance, a few large buildings stood about, buttes in the rubble of the plain.

12   "You see them?" said the driver, as if it were a triumph for his side. "The bomb didn't knock *them* down."

13   Running like ruler lines through the waste were black roads surprisingly dotted with people, some on foot and some in carts of all sizes drawn by man, woman, horse, or cow. Clothing was old and tattered and of every combination from full European to full Japanese. People looked as if they had grabbed what they could from a rummage sale.

14   Occasionally, blending like protective coloration with the rubble were shacks built out of fragments of boards and iron. Around them were vegetable gardens, for the most part full of *daikon*, Japanese radish. A few more pretentious sheds were going up, shining bright yellow with new boards.

15   We slowed down to go around a piece of cornice that lay partly across the road like a glacial boulder, and from somewhere in a band of children who cheered and called to us came the gift of a tangerine that landed on the floor of the jeep. Wondering at them, I picked it up and put it in my pocket.

16   When crossing a bridge, we could see down through the swiftly running water to the stones and shells on the bottom. This clearness gave a feeling of odd contrast to the disorder of the land. We passed a number of trees burned black but still holding up some leafless branches as if in perpetual winter.

17   The drive ended at a large building that was still standing, a former bank, now a police headquarters, where I had an appointment with the chief to arrange for office space and guides. The driver said, as he got out, "This is it."

II

18   One hears it said that, after all, Japanese cities were really a collection of tinderboxes, while American urban centers are made of stronger stuff. In Hiroshima there were many buildings of types common in the United States and some, prepared against earthquakes, far stronger. The engineers of the U.S. Strategic Bombing Survey concluded from their examination that "the overwhelming bulk of buildings in American cities would not stand up against an atomic bomb bursting at a mile or a mile and a half from them." To this must be added the realization that the bomb dropped at Hiroshima will be considered primitive by future standards.

19   The bank building which housed the police headquarters was a well-made structure of stone, three stories high. Through an imposing entrance my interpreter and I went past tall and solid metal doors that were bent inward like cardboard and no longer usable. The lobby was large and high, but dark because it had no window glass and the openings were boarded to keep out the wind. Through poor light there loomed the white face of a clock up on one wall, its hands pointing to 8:10—the time it had stopped on August 6.

20   In the years when that clock had been going, Hiroshima had been a city, at first unknown to Europe and America, then a source of immigrants to the United States, and finally an enemy port. It lay on a delta between the seven mouths of the Ota and was traversed by canals and an ancient highway that connected Kyoto in the east with Shimonoseki in the west. Close around the city stood mountains covered with red pine, while before it stretched the bay, indented with headlands and spread with islands, in places narrow and steep like a fjord. In shallows near the shore, rows of poles stood as if in a bean patch, set in the sea to anchor oysters and to catch edible seaweed passing in the tide. In deeper water, fishing boats with hawkish prows and planked with red pine were tending nets. A few fishermen used cormorants* to make their catch.

21   Hiroshima had expanses of park, residences, gardens, orange and persimmon trees. Since there had been much traveling back and forth by

---

*Cormorants are voracious seabirds often used in eastern Asia for catching fish.

relatives of immigrants to California, the influence of the United States was marked. On main streets there were movies and restaurants with façades that would have fitted into shopping districts of Bakersfield or San Diego.

22   But Hiroshima was also ancient. Its feudal castle raised a five-story keep that could be seen a long distance over the level land of the delta. There were three large temples and many smaller ones and the tombs of the Asano family and of the wife and son of the leader of the Forty-seven Ronin, Oishi-Yoshio. There were also Christian churches, whose bells mingled with the temple gongs and the honking of auto horns and the rattling of trolleys.

23   The people of the city had earned their living by buying and selling farm produce and fish, by making mountain pines into boats for the fishing fleet of the Inland Sea, by meat packing, rubber processing, and oil refining, by making textiles from the cocoons of wild silkworms, by brewing rice and grape wine, by manufacturing paper umbrellas, needles, *tabi* socks, small arms, metal castings, and by working in utilities and services such as electricity, transportation, schools, and hospitals.

24   During the war there was an increase of industrialization, and plants grew up, chiefly in the outskirts.

25   There was a famous gay district with little streets along which a person walking in the night could hear laughter, the twang of the *shamisen*, and geishas singing.

26   The university had been an active cultural center but also stressed athletics, particularly swimming. There were sometimes mass aquatic exercises when hundreds of students would swim for miles, strung out in the bay in a long line with boats attending.

27   Although not a fortified town, Hiroshima was a major military command station, supply depot, and staging area because of its protected position and because of Ujina Harbor with access to the Pacific, the Sea of Japan, and the East China Sea. More than a third of the city's land was taken up with military installations, and from the harbor troopships left for Korea, Manchuria, China, and the southern regions. However, toward the end of hostilities, most of the shipping had ceased because of sinkings in the Inland Sea.

28   The population of Hiroshima was given as well over 300,000 before the war, but this was reduced by evacuation, before the atomic bomb fell, probably to about 245,000. It is still not certain how many the bomb killed, but the best estimate is from 70,000 to 80,000.

III

29   About seven o'clock on the morning of August 6 there was an air-raid warning and three planes were reported in the vicinity. No one was much disturbed. For a long time B-29's flying over in small numbers had been

a common sight. At some future date, Hiroshima might suffer an incendiary raid from masses of planes such as had devastated other Japanese cities. With this possibility in mind there had been evacuations, and firebreaks were being prepared. But on this particular morning there could be no disaster from just three planes.

30 By 7:30 the "all clear" had sounded and people were thinking again of the day's plans, looking forward to their affairs and engagements of the morning and afternoon. The castle keep stood in the sun. Children bathed in the river. Farmers labored in the fields and fishermen on the water. City stores and factories got under way with their businesses.

31 In the heart of the city near the buildings of the Prefectural Government and at the intersection of the business streets, everybody had stopped and stood in a crowd gazing up at three parachutes floating down through the blue air.

32 The bomb exploded several hundred feet above their heads.

33 The people for miles around Hiroshima, in the fields, in the mountains, and on the bay, saw a light that was brilliant even in the sun, and felt heat. A countrywoman was going out to her farm when suddenly, "I saw a light reflected on the mountain and then a streak just like lightning came."

34 A town official was crossing a bridge on his bicycle about ten miles from the heart of the city when he felt the right side of his face seared, and thinking that he had sunstroke, he jumped to the ground.

35 A woman who was washing dishes noticed that she felt "very warm on the side of my face next to the wall. I looked out the window toward the city and saw something like a sun in bright color."

36 At a slower pace, after the flash, came the sound of the explosion, which some people have no recollection of hearing, while others described it as an earth-shaking roar, like thunder or a big wind. A black smoky mass, lit up with color, ascended into the sky and impressed beholders with its beauty. Red, gold, blue, orange, and many other shades mingled with the black.

37 Nearer to the city and at its edges, the explosion made a more direct and individual impact on people. Almost everyone thought that an ordinary bomb had landed very close to him, and only later realized the extent of the damage.

38 A man who was oiling the machinery in a factory saw the lights go out and thought that something must be wrong with the electricity. "But when the roof started crumbling down, I was in a daze, wondering what was happening. Then I noticed my hands and feet were bleeding. I don't know how I hurt myself."

39 Another, who was putting points on needles, was knocked unconscious, and when he came to, found "all my surroundings burned to the ground and flames raging here and there. I ran home for my family without knowing I was burned around my head. When I arrived home, our

house was devastated and destroyed by flames. I ran to the neighbors and inquired about my family and learned that they had all been taken to safety across the river."

40   An invalid who was drinking tea said, "The tin roof sidings came swirling into my room and everything was black. Rubble and glass and everything you can think of was blasted into my house."

41   Said a woman, "I was in the back of the house doing the washing. All of a sudden, the bomb exploded. My clothes were burned off and I received burns on my legs, arms, and back. The skin was just hanging loose. The first thing I did was run in the air-raid shelter and lie there exhausted. Then I thought of my baby in the house and ran back to it. The whole house was knocked down and was burning. My mother and father came crawling out of the debris, their faces and arms just black. I heard the baby crying, and crawled in and dug it out from under the burning embers. It was pretty badly burned. My mother carried it to the shelter."

42   In the heart of the city death prevailed and few were left to tell us about it. That part of the picture has to be reconstructed, as in archeology, from the remains.

43   The crowd that stood gazing upward at the parachutes went down withered and black, like a burned-out patch of weeds. Flames shot out of the castle keep. Trolleys bulging with passengers stopped, and all died at once, leaving burned figures still standing supporting each other and fingers fused to the straps. The military at their barracks and officers were wiped out. So too were factories full of workers, including students from schools, volunteers from neighboring towns working on the fire-breaks, children scavenging for wood, the Mayor's staff, and the units for air-raid precaution, fire, welfare, and relief. The larger war industries, since they were on the fringe of the city, were for the most part not seriously damaged. Most of the personnel in the Prefectural Government offices were killed, though the Governor himself happened to be in Tokyo. In hospitals and clinics, patients, doctors, and nurses all died together, as did the priests and pastors of the temples and churches. Of 1780 nurses, 1654 were killed, and 90 per cent of the doctors in Hiroshima were casualties.

44   People who were in buildings that sheltered them from the instantaneous effects that accompanied the flash were moments later decapitated or cut to ribbons by flying glass. Others were crushed as walls and floors gave way even in buildings that maintained their outer shells erect. In the thousands of houses that fell, people were pinned below the wreckage, not killed in many cases, but held there till the fire that swept the city caught up with them and put an end to their screams.

45   A police chief said that he was in his back yard when the bomb went off. He was knocked down and a concrete wall fell over him, but he was able to dig himself out and go at once toward the police station in the

bank. "When I arrived at the office, I found ten policemen, some severely wounded. These were evacuated to a place of safety where they could get aid. We tried to clean up the glass from the windows, but fire was spreading and a hot southerly wind was blowing. We used a hose with water from a hydrant and also formed a bucket brigade. At noon the water in the hydrants gave out, but in this building we were lucky because we could pump water from a well. We carried buckets up from the basement to the roof and threw water down over the building. People on the road were fainting from the heat and we threw water on them too and carried them into the one room in the building that had not been affected by the bomb. We applied oil and ointment to those who had burns.

46   "About 1:00 P.M. we began to apply first aid to the people outside, since the fire seemed under control as far as this building was concerned. A doctor came to help. He himself was wounded in one leg. By night this place was covered by a mass of people. One doctor applied all the first aid."

47   A doctor who was at a military hospital outside Hiroshima said that about an hour after the bomb went off, "many, many people came rushing to my clinic. They were rushing in all directions of the compass from the city. Many were stretcher cases. Some had their hair burned off, were injured in the back, had broken legs, arms, and thighs. The majority of the cases were those injured from glass; many had glass imbedded in the body. Next to the glass injuries, the most frequent were those who had their faces and hands burned, and also the chest and back. Most of the people arrived barefooted; many had their clothes burned off. Women were wearing men's clothing and men were wearing women's. They had put on anything they could pick up along the way.

48   "On the first day about 250 came, who were so injured they had to stay in the hospital, and we also attended about 500 others. Of all of these about 100 died."

49   A talkative man in a newspaper office said that the most severely burned people looked like red shrimps. Some had "skin which still burned sagging from the face and body with a reddish-white skin underneath showing."

50   A reporter who was outside the city at the time of the explosion, but came in immediately afterward, noticed among the dead a mother with a baby held tightly in her arms. He saw several women running around nude, red from burns, and without hair. Many people climbed into water tanks kept for putting out fires and there died. "The most pathetic cases were the small children looking for their parents. There was one child of about eleven with a four-year-old on his back, looking, looking for his mother in vain."

51   Shortly after the bomb fell, there was a high wind, or "fire storm" engendered by the heat, that tore up trees and, whirling over the river, made waterspouts. In some areas rain fell.

52   The severely burned woman who had been washing when the bomb fell said that she went down to the river, where "there were many people just dripping from their burns. Many of them were so badly burned that you could see the meat. By this time it was raining pretty badly. I could not walk or lie down or do anything. Water poured into the shelter and I received water blisters as well as blisters from the burns. It rained a lot right after the bomb."

53   Although the fire burned for days, the major destruction did not take very long. A fisherman out on the bay said, "I saw suddenly a flash of light. I thought something burned my face. I hid in the boat face down. When I looked up, later, Hiroshima was completely burned."

IV

54   Hiroshima, of course, never had been prepared for a disaster of the magnitude which overtook it, but in addition the organized sources of aid that did exist were decimated along with everything else. As a result, rescue had to come from surrounding areas, and soon trucks and trains were picking up the wounded, while hospitals, schools, temples, assembly halls, and tents were preparing to receive them. However, the suburbs and surrounding areas were overwhelmed by the rush of immediate survivors out of the bombed region and so, for about a day, help did not penetrate far into the city. This, together with the fact that survivors who were physically uninjured were stunned and bewildered, resulted in great numbers of the wounded dying from lack of aid.

55   The vice-mayor of a neighboring town that began receiving the wounded about 11:30 in the morning said, "Everybody looked alike. The eyes appeared to be a mass of melted flesh. The lips were split up and also looked like a mass of molten flesh. Only the nose appeared the same as before. The death scene was awful. The patient would turn blue and when we touched the body the skin would stick to our hands."

56   Those who ventured into Hiroshima were greeted by sights they were reluctant to describe. A businessman reported: "The bodies of half-dead people lay on the roadside, on the bridges, in the water, in the gardens, and everywhere. It was a sight no one wants to see. Practically all of these people were nude. Their color was brownish blackish and some of their bodies were dripping. There was a fellow whose head was half burned so that I thought he was wearing a hat." Another man said, "The bodies of the dead were so burned that we could not distinguish men from women."

57   In the public parks great numbers of both wounded and dead were congregated. There were cries for aid and cries for water and there were places where unidentifiable shapes merely stirred.

58   In the late afternoon, aid began to come farther into the city from the outer edges. Rice balls and other food were brought. From their mission

up the valley a number of Jesuits came, and one of them, Father Siemes, gave a vivid and careful description of what he had seen, when he was later interviewed by members of the Bombing Survey in Tokyo. He said, "Beneath the wreckage of the houses along the way many had been trapped and they screamed to be rescued from the oncoming flames. They had to be left to their fate."

59   On a bridge, he encountered a procession of soldiers "dragging themselves along with the help of staves or carried by their less severely injured comrades. Abandoned on the bridge there stood with sunken heads a number of horses with large burns on their flanks.

60   "Fukai, the secretary of the mission, was completely out of his mind. He did not want to leave the house when the fires were burning closer, and explained that he did not want to survive the destruction of his fatherland." He had to be carried away by force.

61   After dark, the priests helped pull from the river two children who suffered chills and then died. There was a sand-spit in the river, covered with wounded, who cried for help and who were afraid that the rising tide would drown them. After midnight, "only occasionally did we hear calls for help."

62   Many patients were brought to an open field right behind Hiroshima station, and tents were set up for them. Doctors came in from the neighboring prefectures and from nearby towns such as Yamaguchi, Okayama, and Shimane. The Army also took part in relief measures, and all available military facilities and units were mobilized to that end.

63   A fisherman who came to Hiroshima to see what had happened said, "I cannot describe the situation in words, it was so pitiful. To see so many people dead was a terrible sight. Their clothes were shredded and their bodies puffed up, some with tongues hanging out. They were dead in all shapes."

64   As late as the second day the priests noted that among cadavers there were still many wounded alive. "Frightfully injured forms beckoned to us and then collapsed."

65   They carried some to the hospitals, but "we could not move everybody who lay exposed to the sun." It did not make much difference, anyway, for in the hospitals there was little that could be done. They just lay in the corridors, row on row, and died.

66   A businessman came into Hiroshima on the third day. "I went to my brother's house in the suburbs and found that all were wounded but none killed. They were stunned and could hardly speak. The next day, one of the four children died. She got black and blue in the face, just as if you had mashed your finger, and had died fifteen minutes after that. In another half hour, her sister did the same thing and she died also."

67   The wife of a soldier who had been with the Hiroshima troops said, "My husband was a soldier and so he was to die, but when it actually happened, I wondered why we did not all go with him. They called me

and I went to see. I was to find him in the heap, but I decided against looking at the bodies. I want to remember him as he was—big and healthy, not some horribly charred body. If I saw that, it would remain forever in my eyes."

68   A police chief told how the dead were collected and burned. "Many could not be identified. In cases where it was possible, the corpses or the ashes were given to the immediate family. Mostly, the cremation was done by the police or the soldiers, and the identified ashes were given to the family. The ashes of those not identified were turned over to the City Hall. There still are boxes in the City Hall. Occasionally even now one is identified, or is supposed to be identified, and is claimed."

69   The destroyed heart of Hiroshima consisted of 4.7 square miles, and the best estimates indicate that the mortality rate was 15,000 to the square mile. For many days funeral processions moved along the roads and through the towns and villages all around Hiroshima. The winds were pervaded by the smell of death and cremation. At night the skies were lit with the flames of funeral pyres.

V

70   Very few of the people we interviewed at Hiroshima attempted to make a play for sympathy or to make us feel guilty. The general manner was one which might be interpreted as due either to lingering apathy and absence of feeling consequent on shock, or to reserve which masked hate. It was probably a mixture of both, in varying degrees in different people. But on the surface everyone appeared willing to coöperate and oblige.

71   An official of a near-by small town thought that "if America had such a weapon, there was no use to go on. Many high school students in Hiroshima who were wounded in the raid spoke incoherently on their death-beds, saying, 'Please avenge that raid for us somehow.' However, most of the people felt that since it was war, it was just *shikata ga nai*, could not be helped. But we were unified in the idea that we had to win the war."

72   A newspaper reporter said that after the bomb fell, some felt that this was the end, while others wanted to go on regardless. "Those who had actually experienced the bomb were the ones who wanted to quit, while those who had not, wanted to go on."

73   The wife of a soldier killed in the blast said, "Though many are resentful against America, I feel no animosity. It was an understood war and the use of weapons was fair. I only wonder why they didn't let the people know about this bomb and give us a chance, before bombing us, to give up."

74   A police chief believed that the general reaction among the people was one of surprise and a feeling that "we have taken the worst beating, we have been the goats." He said, "They felt that America had done a terrible

thing and were very bitter, but after the surrender they turned on the Japanese military. They felt they had been fooled, and wondered if the military knew that the bomb was coming and why they did not take steps. The bomb made no difference in the fighting spirit of the people: it drew them together and made them more coöperative. My eldest son was killed, but I felt it was destiny that ruled. When I see people who got away without any injury, I feel a little pang of envy naturally, but I don't feel bitter toward them."

75   Poking in the ruins one day, I came on the stone figure of a dog, one of that grinning type derived from China which commonly guards the entrances to temples. It was tilted on its pedestal but undamaged, and the grin gleamed out as if it were hailing me. Its rakish air and its look of fiendish satisfaction with all that lay around drew me on to inspect it more closely. It was then apparent that the look was not directed at me, but out somewhere beyond. It was, of course, only a piece of stone, and it displayed no particular artistic merit; yet in looking at it I felt that I was a clod, while it had a higher, sentient wisdom locked up within.

76   The look and the feeling it inspired were familiar and I groped to remember where I had seen it before other than on temple dogs. The eyes were creased in a fashion that did not exactly connotate mirth, and the lips were drawn far back in a smile that seemed to blend bitterness, glee, and compassion. The word "sardonic" came to mind, and this led to recognition and a realization of terrible appropriateness.

77   All who have acquaintance with the dead know the curious smile that may crop over the human face as *rigor mortis* sets in, a smile of special quality called by doctors *risus sardonicus.* The dog had this look, and it seemed to me probable that some ancient Oriental sculptor, in seeking an expression for temple guardians that would drive off evil spirits, had taken this death grin as his model, and thus it had come down through hundreds of years to this beast looking out on Hiroshima.

78   Many a soldier has seen this face looking up at him from the field of battle, before he himself was wearing it, and many a priest and doctor has found himself alone with it in a darkened room. As with the dog, at first the look seems at you, and then beyond you, as if there lay at last behind it knowledge of the huge joke of life which the rest of us feel vaguely but cannot comprehend. And there is that tinge of compassion that is as dreadful as it is unknowable.

79   As I continued to study this stone face, it began to appear that the grin was not directed at the waste and the destruction around, at the red and yellow and the smells, any more than it was at me. It was not so much a face looking at Hiroshima as it was the face of Hiroshima. The carved eyes gazed beyond the rubble, beyond the gardens of radishes and fields of winter wheat, beyond the toiling adults and the rippling children with their tangerines and shouts of "Haro-goodabye!" surging up with new

life like flowers and weeds spreading over devastation, beyond the mountains with red pines in the blue sky, beyond all these, over the whole broad shoulder of the world to where, in cities and towns, watches on wrists and clocks on towers still ticked and moved. The face seemed to be smiling and waiting for the harvest of the wind that had been sown.

80   There was one woman in Hiroshima who said, "If there are such things as ghosts, why don't they haunt the Americans?"

81   Perhaps they do.

That Day at Hiroshima

Questions on Content, Style, and Structure

1. What are Leighton's purposes in telling about Hiroshima? Is he successful?

2. Point out several examples of similes in part I. What do they contribute to this section?

3. What attitude do the comments of the American driver reveal?

4. Why does Leighton describe Hiroshima before the bomb in such guidebook detail? How does he make the transition from this visit to the police headquarters to the description of the city as it used to be?

5. What point is Leighton making in paragraph 18?

6. From whose point of view is the bombing told? Is this an effective choice?

7. How does Leighton make the story of the bombing vivid without numbing the reader with horror?

8. How does Leighton shift from his trip to the story of August 6 and back again? Are the shifts too abrupt?

9. Evaluate Leighton's use of statistics. Are there too many or too few?

10. Explain the symbolism of the smiling stone dog. How does it represent Leighton's experience in Hiroshima? Why, in paragraph 79, does he mention watches and clocks?

11. Is Leighton's conclusion appropriate?

Vocabulary

cloven (1)	geishas (25)	cadavers (64)
bandy-legged (3)	incendiary (29)	funeral pyres (69)
animation (8)	seared (34)	incoherently (71)
tumult (11)	archeology (42)	animosity (73)
buttes (11)	engendered (51)	rakish (75)
cornice (15)	waterspouts (51)	sentient (75)
traversed (20)	decimated (54)	connotate (76)
fjord (20)	prefectures (62)	sardonic (76)

Suggestions for Writing

1. Some critics have protested President Truman's use of the bomb on Hiroshima and Nagasaki, saying that the Japanese should have been given an opportunity to learn about the bomb and give up in advance. Others say the bomb was necessary to end the war in the Pacific quickly without further loss of American life. Research both sides of this controversy and write an essay defending your view.

2. More than 1,200 southern Utah, Nevada, and Arizona residents who lived or worked over 30 years ago near the bomb test sites are now suing the federal government, blaming radioactive fallout for the increase in cancers they claim their families have suffered. Are Americans experiencing after-effects of radiation similar to those felt by Japanese people today? How much do scientists really know about the long-range effects of fallout? Research some aspect of this complex problem that interests you and then write an essay on your findings.

3. Research and write a report on the Japanese internment camps in the United States during World War II. Why do you suppose that for years many Americans were never told about these camps?

Silence on Campus
Joseph N. Bell

Joseph N. Bell is a professor of English at the University of California at Irvine whose articles have appeared in a variety of magazines. He has written eight books of nonfiction, including *Seven into Space* (1962), the first book on America's manned space program. This essay first appeared in *Harper's Magazine* in 1976.

1   A former student stopped by my office the other day. I remembered her instantly. Every teacher has a small collection of students, arranged carefully in a trophy case, to be brought down and examined in low periods. I've had maybe a dozen in eight years of teaching, and Susan was one.

2   She came to the Irvine campus of the University of California as a transfer student in 1970—a white, upper-middle-class product of southern California, blonde, pretty, athletic—and unhappy. She was tearing at her own roots, reluctantly, but she knew it was inevitable. It was a painful process that she tried to put on paper, not very successfully.

3   From those agonized writings of hers, I learned that her parents were politically and socially conservative, and that Susan—thoughtful but not

belligerent—had gone off to the Santa Barbara campus of the University of California in the late 1960s. There she found herself increasingly disturbed at American activities in Vietnam and at Washington's lack of response to the public mood of disenchantment with them. Because activism was not her style, Susan was pulled between the strong need to declare herself and dismay at what seemed to her the excesses of some of her fellow students.

4 Then the United States invaded Cambodia, and American campuses erupted in protest. Susan saw policemen swarm into her campus community and drag students from their rooms and beat them up outside. Outraged and sickened, she joined the demonstrators, was picked up in a police dragnet, and spent two nights in jail before being released without any charges preferred against her.

5 She transferred to my campus the following fall, and as a student in my writing class tried to articulate the changes that were taking place in her, to put them in perspective without breaking completely from her roots. To some of the people in her hometown, this concerned young woman had been radicalized by university left-wingers when she graduated a year later.

6 I didn't see Susan again until a few weeks ago. After working for several years, she had returned to her old campus for a graduate degree, earning her room and board as a counselor in a freshman dormitory. She was depressed over what she had seen and heard. She had been asked—and had agreed—to help organize a student movement against a law that would effectively disenfranchise students by preventing them from registering to vote at their university home. Susan felt deeply about this: she had once worked very hard to extend the vote to eighteen-year-olds. For university students, those efforts would be thwarted by the new law.

7 Petitions in hand, Susan worked her way through the dormitories. "It was awful," she said. "There wasn't the slightest interest among those students in what was being taken from them. They weren't aware, and they didn't want to listen to me. I came away defeated. I just couldn't believe the change that has taken place in college students in the last few years."

8 I have found it hard to believe, too—particularly because the change has been so abrupt and pervasive. I teach nonfiction writing, and I tend to give students a lot of latitude in subject matter. Three-fourths of the essays I read five years ago dealt with some form of social change. Now they bear such titles as "How Students Can Invest in the Stock Market" or "How I Became a Christian."

9 A lot of Americans—most of them, I suspect—are relieved at the quiet that has fallen over our college campuses after the chaos of the Vietnam war years. I am not. The passive students today alarm me far more than the activists of a few years ago ever did. They are, I'm sure, the inevitable

result of two things: public hostility toward the universities during the hyperactivist years and private disenchantment—not always rational—among young people over their inability to dent the system.

10   There is little question that many colleges today are being punished for the campus upheavals that took place during the war years. Public officials who always feared and suspected freewheeling intellectual give-and-take have used citizen revulsion at student excesses (a relatively small part of campus activism) as a club to beat down university budgets and anesthetize the troublemaking potential of students and faculty alike.

11   When Richard Nixon became President, the federal government spent $262 million annually to help support 51,400 graduate students in our universities; when he left office, federal support had shrunk to $33 million for 6,600 graduate students. At the same time, inflation was putting college out of reach for a growing segment of our society. During the same period at the University of California, I have watched faculty salaries go down relative to other top universities, research projects with considerable potential for public benefit aborted, and faculty-student ratios climb, as a result of a state administration that has denigrated its own fine university whenever possible. Moreover, this decrease in university funds and support has accompanied a wave of postactivist students who seem to reflect these public attitudes.

12   Last year, a high-school civics teacher wrote to a Los Angeles newspaper: "The majority of young people with whom I come in contact was never enthralled by politics. Now, they seem to be sinking even deeper into an apolitical torpor. Watergate taught them not to care. I see the silent majority growing in my classroom every school day. It is a frightening development."

13   Other evidence is all around. When the University of California at San Diego opened a new school recently that stressed "professional and pre-professional training," it was immediately oversubscribed—in a period of generally declining admissions elsewhere. This response, the provost explained, was due to "a new breed of student who is thinking more about jobs, money, and the future." A study by the Rockefeller Youth Task Force found that "the challenge of traditional cultural values has shifted to non-college youth," and the task force director, Daniel Yankelovich, added: "In a brief five-year period, the gap between the campus and the country has begun to close, but a new gap between working youth who have not gone to college and the country's social institutions is now opening up."

14   If this means that healthy challenges to pernicious national policies have moved from the campus to the young working class, it may also mean that the challenges will be more effective. But if it means that the young have simply detached themselves from social activism and criticism, we are in trouble.

15   I pondered these questions the other night on my way home from a talk I had given to a group of social-science classes at a local high school. My oldest daughter had been a student in this high school when John Kennedy was murdered. She had sat numbly in a classroom for a few minutes, then walked out of school and several miles to the ocean, where she sat on the beach alone until darkness drove her home. She had been expelled for this agonized act, and I vividly remember my own anger and outrage when I took her case before the school authorities.

16   Speaking in that same school a little more than a decade later, it came as a shock to me that many of the young people in my audience were no more inspired by John Kennedy than by Grover Cleveland or Millard Fillmore. A few minutes into my talk, I realized we weren't even on the same planet. I was assuming certain social awarenesses and interests they obviously didn't have, so I tried to penetrate the glaze over their eyes with more and more outrageous statements, hoping for some kind of response. *Anything* at all.

17   When nothing came back, I began asking them questions. And, slowly, I began to see that I was dealing with students who had happily accepted the social and political changes won by the activists of the 1960s, and totally discarded the commitment that produced the changes. At last I asked these students if they would be enough outraged to demonstrate if we started massive bombing of Vietnam again tomorrow. Nothing. In desperation, I said: "For God's sake, what *would* outrage you?" After a pause, a girl in the front row wearing a cheerleader uniform raised her hand and said tentatively, "Well, I'd be pretty mad if they bombed this *school.*"

18   I recognize that this is one upper-middle-class high school in a conservative area of California and that generalizing from such an experience is dangerous. But from this same background came young people who marched in Mississippi and unseated a President of the United States in New Hampshire, who demanded and got long overdue educational reforms, who broke down outmoded social castes and attitudes. True, they also disrupted classes, undermined useful social values and traditions, loved the sounds of their own voices, and frequently substituted rhetoric for reason and self-indulgent impulse for effective action. They were noisy and abrasive, and when it was all over, I was relieved. For a while.

19   But now I contemplate the reaction—and I wonder about our future. Now I'm told to honk if I love Jesus. I hear students dismiss Watergate as "the way it's always been, so why hassle it?" I see them single-mindedly pursuing grades and worrying about jobs with secure retirement plans. I even see a resurgence of those pillars of the American social caste system, fraternities and sororities.

20   When I express dismay about these changes, I catch it from all sides. My own children—formed ideologically by the Kennedy years—tell me

I'm a crashing idealist as far as young people are concerned, that I should never have imputed all those selfless motives to the activists of the Sixties. By way of corroboration, they point out that the demonstrations stopped almost immediately after the military draft was suspended. The point is well taken, and I've not heard any students of that period deny it when faced with this fact.

21   But it is also true that the threshold of social and political awareness—for whatever reason—was extraordinarily high, was acted on, and produced results that in my view were mostly progressive and badly needed. Student activism had a direct effect on our slow withdrawal from Vietnam, on the eighteen-year-old vote, on progress in the black and other minority communities, on women's rights, and on the critical examination of religious, ethical, and institutional values that were out of step with the world in which we lived. Admittedly, there were dangerous and distressing side effects, but too often the threat of these side effects was allowed to obscure the progress initiated by the students of the Sixties.

22   Some of my old activist student friends are still around and in touch. One is working as an organizer for a trade union, fighting that monolith from within, while he writes and tries to publish impassioned exposés of the perfidy and greed of the automobile industry. Another is writing poetry in a secluded southern California canyon and repairing automobiles for a living. A young woman who worked for Robert Kennedy and saw him killed is struggling through law school so she can join the young attorneys who are fighting our system on behalf of the powerless. A determined young man is trying to finish graduate school so he can teach, bedding down in various offices around the campus because inflation and rising university fees have made it impossible for him to afford a room. These people are oddly anachronistic on campus today, artifacts of a time and place that seem light years away.

23   Meanwhile, as noted by Professor Martin Marty,[1] the nation continues to discourage social activists like them. "The people," writes Professor Marty, "have tended to turn from those who disturbed the peace with manifestos, experiments, or searching questions. Where people now rise above apathy at all, they seem to want only to be soothed. Today's prophets are invited to dinner, where they offer the sweets."

24   The good citizens who are relieved at this state of affairs might ponder the possibility that a group like the Symbionese Liberation Army[2] arises, not from a society of young people working actively to correct injustice, but from a society where injustice is ignored. Without responsible activ-

[1] Professor Marty of the University of Chicago holds a Ph. D. in American Religious and Intellectual History and is the author of many books on religion, including *Righteous Empire*, which won a National Book Award in 1971.
[2] The Symbionese Liberation Army was a small revolutionary group responsible for a series of violent acts in California during the early 1970s, including the kidnapping of heiress Patricia Hearst.

ism to contain them, revolutionaries can turn into dangerous, demented, and frustrated people, toting machine guns and a death wish.

25   At the other extreme are those students writing about the stock market, joining frats and sororities, sweating grades, and honking for Christ. Most of them are pleasant and terribly earnest. Maybe, I tell myself, this is just the transition generation, which will soothe public attitudes toward our universities. Maybe a new and idealist group of young people will follow them, and shake up their elders all over again. Maybe that excitement, or at least some of it, will return.

Silence on Campus

Questions on Content, Style, and Structure

1. What strategy does Bell use to introduce his essay's subject?
2. What is Bell's attitude toward the passive students of today? toward the students of the 1960s?
3. What are the causes of student passivity, according to Bell?
4. What evidence does Bell offer in support of his claim that colleges are being "punished" for the upheavals of the 1960s?
5. What examples are offered to illustrate the apolitical attitudes of today's students? Are the examples persuasive?
6. According to Bell, what effects did the student activism of the 1960s produce?
7. Does Bell "apologize" too often for the excesses of the 1960s? Why did he include these remarks? Should he have omitted them?
8. Why does Bell mention the activist students he still knows?
9. How does Bell conclude his essay? Is it an appropriate conclusion?
10. Analyze the tone of this essay. Is it effective? Why/why not?

Vocabulary

belligerent (3)	enthralled (12)	monolith (22)
disenfranchise (6)	apolitical (12)	exposés (22)
thwarted (6)	torpor (12)	perfidy (22)
pervasive (8)	provost (13)	anachronistic (22)
denigrated (11)	pernicious (14)	demented (24)

Suggestions for Writing

1. Do you agree that today's students are politically or socially apathetic? If so, is such an attitude disturbing or dangerous? Write an essay supporting your view.

2. Bell notes a resurgence in fraternities and sororities, which he calls "pillars of the American social caste system." Write an essay in which you defend or attack his evaluation of social clubs.

3. If you have ever been active in a political or social movement, write an essay describing your experience and explaining what you learned from it.

Disgrace
David Hall

David Hall received his Ph.D. in English from the University of Texas, Austin, in 1978. He has published numerous poems and stories in literary magazines across the country; he won the Texas Institute of Letters award for best short fiction in 1980. This poem was first published in *Encore* in 1975, five years after Hall served as an artillery First Lieutenant in Vietnam.

If Juan Rodriguez is alive today
I'd like to tell him that
to step on a mine
your first step into war
5 is no disgrace.

What will my mother say?
he asked the medics
bending over him
knowing he shouldn't see
10 what all he'd lost.

What will she think of her clumsy son?

I'd like to say
I've seen good men
take longer,
long enough to think their country
16 putrefied.

I knew one boy
who ate gunpowder
19 and died.

I'd like to say
I've seen men cry
and try to swat the bullets
23   away like bees

and watched one black man
scared of dying
26   shoot off both his knees.

I huddled half my year in mud
28   and couldn't remember my mother's face.

Believe me Juan
your friends who stayed
31   went far beyond disgrace.

Disgrace

Questions on Content, Style, and Structure

1. From whose point of view is this poem written?
2. Who is Juan Rodriguez and why does he feel disgraced?
3. What is the poet's attitude toward Juan? Why?
4. What does the poet try to tell Juan about some of the other soldiers?
5. Why does the poet mention that he couldn't remember his mother's face? How does this comment relate to Juan's reference to his mother in line 6?
6. What kind of "disgrace" is the poet talking about in the last stanza?
7. Identify the only simile in the poem; what is its purpose?
8. Analyze the poem's use of rhyme. What pattern is present? Why does the poet maintain this pattern?
9. If you had not been told that the author of this poem served in Vietnam, would you have guessed it? Why/why not?

Vocabulary

medics (l. 7)
putrefied (l. 16)

Suggestions for Writing

1. During the Vietnam war, many young men declared themselves "conscientious objectors" and refused to fight in a war they felt unjust.

Should people of draft age have the right to object to fighting in a particular war? Or should only those with traditional religious opposition to fighting in general be exempt? Write an essay defending your position.
2. Some people believe that Vietnam should be the last war in which only men are drafted. Should women be liable for military service in the event of a draft? Write an essay arguing your side of the controversy.
3. Compare/contrast this war poem to Randall Jarrell's "The Death of the Ball Turret Gunner" on page 177. Write an essay explaining the similarities and differences you see in the subject matter, style, and structure of the two poems.

The Bride Comes to Yellow Sky
Stephen Crane

Stephen Crane was a nineteenth-century novelist, short story writer, and journalist. His two most famous novels are *Maggie, A Girl of the Streets* (1893), originally rejected by publishers because of its sympathetic treatment of a young girl turned prostitute, and *The Red Badge of Courage* (1895), still admired as one of the best war stories ever written. This story was published in *The Open Boat and Other Tales of Adventure* in 1898.

I

1   The great Pullman was whirling onward with such dignity of motion that a glance from the window seemed simply to prove that the plains of Texas were pouring eastward. Vast flats of green grass, dull-hued spaces of mesquit and cactus, little groups of frame houses, woods of light and tender trees, all were sweeping into the east, sweeping over the horizon, a precipice.

2   A newly married pair had boarded this coach at San Antonio. The man's face was reddened from many days in the wind and sun, and a direct result of his new black clothes was that his brick-colored hands were constantly performing in a most conscious fashion. From time to time he looked down respectfully at his attire. He sat with a hand on each knee, like a man waiting in a barber's shop. The glances he devoted to other passengers were furtive and shy.

3   The bride was not pretty, nor was she very young. She wore a dress of

blue cashmere, with small reservations of velvet here and there, and with steel buttons abounding. She continually twisted her head to regard her puff sleeves, very stiff, straight, and high. They embarrassed her. It was quite apparent that she had cooked, and that she expected to cook, dutifully. The blushes caused by the careless scrutiny of some passengers as she had entered the car were strange to see upon this plain, under-class countenance, which was drawn in placid, almost emotionless lines.

4   They were evidently very happy. "Ever been in a parlor-car before?" he asked, smiling with delight.

5   "No," she answered; "I never was. It's fine, ain't it?"

6   "Great! And then after a while we'll go forward to the diner, and get a big lay-out. Finest meal in the world. Charge a dollar."

7   "Oh, do they?" cried the bride. "Charge a dollar? Why, that's too much—for us—ain't it, Jack?"

8   "Not this trip, anyhow," he answered bravely. "We're going to go the whole thing."

9   Later he explained to her about the trains. "You see, it's a thousand miles from one end of Texas to the other; and this train runs right across it, and never stops but for four times." He had the pride of an owner. He pointed out to her the dazzling fittings of the coach; and in truth her eyes opened wider as she contemplated the sea-green figured velvet, the shining brass, silver, and glass, the wood that gleamed as darkly brilliant as the surface of a pool of oil. At one end a bronze figure sturdily held a support for a separated chamber, and at convenient places on the ceiling were frescos in olive and silver.

10   To the minds of the pair, their surroundings reflected the glory of their marriage that morning in San Antonio; this was the environment of their new estate; and the man's face in particular beamed with an elation that made him appear ridiculous to the negro porter. This individual at times surveyed them from afar with an amused and superior grin. On other occasions he bullied them with skill in ways that did not make it exactly plain to them that they were being bullied. He subtly used all the manners of the most unconquerable kind of snobbery. He oppressed them; but of this oppression they had small knowledge, and they speedily forgot that infrequently a number of travellers covered them with stares of derisive enjoyment. Historically there was supposed to be something infinitely humorous in their situation.

11   "We are due in Yellow Sky at 3:42," he said, looking tenderly into her eyes.

12   "Oh, are we?" she said, as if she had not been aware of it. To evince surprise at her husband's statement was part of her wifely amiability. She took from a pocket a little silver watch; and as she held it before her, and stared at it with a frown of attention, the new husband's face shone.

13   "I bought it in San Anton' from a friend of mine," he told her gleefully.

14   "It's seventeen minutes past twelve," she said, looking up at him with a kind of shy and clumsy coquetry. A passenger, noting this play, grew

excessively sardonic, and winked at himself in one of the numerous mirrors.

15   At last they went to the dining-car. Two rows of negro waiters, in glowing white suits, surveyed their entrance with the interest, and also the equanimity, of men who had been forewarned. The pair fell to the lot of a waiter who happened to feel pleasure in steering them through their meal. He viewed them with the manner of a fatherly pilot, his countenance radiant with benevolence. The patronage, entwined with the ordinary deference, was not plain to them. And yet, as they returned to their coach, they showed in their faces a sense of escape.

16   To the left, miles down a long purple slope, was a little ribbon of mist where moved the keening Rio Grande. The train was approaching it at an angle, and the apex was Yellow Sky. Presently it was apparent that, as the distance from Yellow Sky grew shorter, the husband became commensurately restless. His brick-red hands were more insistent in their prominence. Occasionally he was even rather absent-minded and far-away when the bride leaned forward and addressed him.

17   As a matter of truth, Jack Potter was beginning to find the shadow of a deed weigh upon him like a leaden slab. He, the town marshal of Yellow Sky, a man known, liked, and feared in his corner, a prominent person, had gone to San Antonio to meet a girl he believed he loved, and there, after the usual prayers, had actually induced her to marry him, without consulting Yellow Sky for any part of the transaction. He was now bringing his bride before an innocent and unsuspecting community.

18   Of course people in Yellow Sky married as it pleased them, in accordance with a general custom; but such was Potter's thought of his duty to his friends, or of their idea of his duty, or of an unspoken form which does not control men in these matters, that he felt he was heinous. He had committed an extraordinary crime. Face to face with this girl in San Antonio, and spurred by his sharp impulse, he had gone headlong over all the social hedges. At San Antonio he was like a man hidden in the dark. A knife to sever any friendly duty, any form, was easy to his hand in that remote city. But the hour of Yellow Sky—the hour of daylight— was approaching.

19   He knew full well that his marriage was an important thing to his town. It could only be exceeded by the burning of the new hotel. His friends could not forgive him. Frequently he had reflected on the advisability of telling them by telegraph, but a new cowardice had been upon him. He feared to do it. And now the train was hurrying him toward a scene of amazement, glee, and reproach. He glanced out of the window at the line of haze swinging slowly in toward the train.

20   Yellow Sky had a kind of brass band, which played painfully, to the delight of the populace. He laughed without heart as he thought of it. If the citizens could dream of his prospective arrival with his bride, they would parade the band at the station and escort them, amid cheers and laughing congratulations, to his adobe home.

21   He resolved that he would use all the devices of speed and plains-craft in making the journey from the station to his house. Once within that safe citadel, he could issue some sort of vocal bulletin, and then not go among the citizens until they had time to wear off a little of their enthusiasm.

22   The bride looked anxiously at him. "What's worrying you, Jack?"

23   He laughed again. "I'm not worrying, girl; I'm only thinking of Yellow Sky."

24   She flushed in comprehension.

25   A sense of mutual guilt invaded their minds and developed a finer tenderness. They looked at each other with eyes softly aglow. But Potter often laughed the same nervous laugh; the flush upon the bride's face seemed quite permanent.

26   The traitor to the feelings of Yellow Sky narrowly watched the speeding landscape. "We're nearly there," he said.

27   Presently the porter came and announced the proximity of Potter's home. He held a brush in his hand, and, with all his airy superiority gone, he brushed Potter's new clothes as the latter slowly turned this way and that way. Potter fumbled out a coin and gave it to the porter, as he had seen others do. It was a heavy and muscle-bound business, as that of a man shoeing his first horse.

28   The porter took their bag, and as the train began to slow they moved forward to the hooded platform of the car. Presently the two engines and their long string of coaches rushed into the station of Yellow Sky.

29   "They have to take water here," said Potter, from a constricted throat and in mournful cadence, as one announcing death. Before the train stopped his eye had swept the length of the platform, and he was glad and astonished to see there was none upon it but the station-agent, who, with a slightly hurried and anxious air, was walking toward the water-tanks. When the train had halted, the porter alighted first, and placed in position a little temporary step.

30   "Come on, girl," said Potter, hoarsely. As he helped her down they each laughed on a false note. He took the bag from the negro, and bade his wife cling to his arm. As they slunk rapidly away, his hang-dog glance perceived that they were unloading the two trunks, and also that the station agent, far ahead near the baggage car, had turned and was running towards him, making gestures. He laughed, and groaned as he laughed, when he noted the first effect of his marital bliss upon Yellow Sky. He gripped his wife's arm firmly to his side, and they fled. Behind them the porter stood, chuckling fatuously.

II

31   The California express on the Southern Railway was due at Yellow Sky in twenty-one minutes. There were six men at the bar of the Weary

Gentleman Saloon. One was a drummer* who talked a great deal and rapidly; three were Texans who did not care to talk at that time; and two were Mexican sheep-herders, who did not talk as a general practice in the Weary Gentleman Saloon. The barkeeper's dog lay on the board walk that crossed in front of the door. His head was on his paws, and he glanced drowsily here and there with the constant vigilance of a dog that is kicked on occasion. Across the sandy street were some vivid green grass-plots, so wonderful in appearance, amid the sands that burned near them in a blazing sun, that they caused a doubt in the mind. They exactly resembled the grass mats used to represent lawns on the stage. At the cooler end of the railway station, a man without a coat sat in a tilted chair and smoked his pipe. The fresh-cut bank of the Rio Grande circled near the town, and there could be seen beyond it a great plum-colored plain of mesquit.

32   Save for the busy drummer and his companions in the saloon, Yellow Sky was dozing. The newcomer leaned gracefully upon the bar, and recited many tales with the confidence of a bard who has come upon a new field.

33   "—and at the moment that the old man fell downstairs with the bureau in his arms, the old woman was coming up with two scuttles of coal, and of course—"

34   The drummer's tale was interrupted by a young man who suddenly appeared in the open door. He cried: "Scratchy Wilson's drunk, and has turned loose with both hands." The two Mexicans at once set down their glasses and faded out of the rear entrance of the saloon.

35   The drummer, innocent and jocular, answered: "All right, old man. S'pose he has? Come in and have a drink, anyhow."

36   But the information had made such an obvious cleft in every skull in the room that the drummer was obliged to see its importance. All had become instantly solemn. "Say," said he, mystified, "what is this?" His three companions made the introductory gesture of eloquent speech; but the young man at the door forestalled them.

37   "It means, my friend," he answered, as he came into the saloon, "that for the next two hours this town won't be a health resort."

38   The barkeeper went to the door, and locked and barred it; reaching out of the window, he pulled in heavy wooden shutters, and barred them. Immediately a solemn, chapel-like gloom was upon the place. The drummer was looking from one to another.

39   "But say," he cried, "what is this anyhow? You don't mean there is going to be a gun-fight?"

40   "Don't know whether there'll be a fight or not," answered one man, grimly; "but there'll be some shootin'—some good shootin'."

41   The young man who had warned them waved his hand. "Oh, there'll

* A drummer was a traveling salesman.

be a fight fast enough, if any one wants it. Anybody can get a fight out there in the street. There's a fight just waiting."

42   The drummer seemed to be swayed between the interest of a foreigner and a perception of personal danger.

43   "What did you say his name was?" he asked.

44   "Scratchy Wilson," they answered in chorus.

45   "And will he kill anybody? What are you going to do? Does this happen often? Does he rampage around like this once a week or so? Can he break in that door?"

46   "No; he can't break down that door," replied the barkeeper. "He's tried it three times. But when he comes you'd better lay down on the floor, stranger. He's dead sure to shoot at it, and a bullet may come through."

47   Thereafter the drummer kept a strict eye upon the door. The time had not yet been called for him to hug the floor, but, as a minor precaution, he sidled near to the wall. "Will he kill anybody?" he said again.

48   The men laughed low and scornfully at the question.

49   "He's out to shoot, and he's out for trouble. Don't see any good in experimentin' with him."

50   "But what do you do in a case like this? What do you do?"

51   A man responded: "Why, he and Jack Potter—"

52   "But," in chorus the other men interrupted, "Jack Potter's in San-Anton'."

53   "Well, who is he? What's he got to do with it?"

54   "Oh, he's the town marshal. He goes out and fights Scratchy when he gets on one of these tears."

55   "Wow!" said the drummer, mopping his brow. "Nice job he's got."

56   The voices had toned away to mere whisperings. The drummer wished to ask further questions, which were born of an increasing anxiety and bewilderment; but when he attempted them, the men merely looked at him in irritation and motioned him to remain silent. A tense waiting hush was upon them. In the deep shadows of the room their eyes shone as they listened for sounds from the street. One man made three gestures at the barkeeper; and the latter moving like a ghost, handed him a glass and a bottle. The man poured a full glass of whiskey, and set down the bottle noiselessly. He gulped the whiskey in a swallow, and turned again toward the door in immovable silence. The drummer saw that the barkeeper, without a sound, had taken a Winchester from beneath the bar. Later he saw this individual beckoning to him, so he tiptoed across the room.

57   "You better come with me back of the bar."

58   "No, thanks," said the drummer, perspiring; "I'd rather be where I can make a break for the back door."

59   Whereupon the man of bottles made a kindly but peremptory gesture. The drummer obeyed it, and, finding himself seated on a box with his

head below the level of the bar, balm was laid upon his soul at sight of various zinc and copper fittings that bore a resemblance to armor-plate. The barkeeper took a seat comfortably upon an adjacent box.

60 "You see," he whispered, "this here Scratchy Wilson is a wonder with a gun—a perfect wonder; and when he goes on the war-trail, we hunt our holes—naturally. He's about the last one of the old gang that used to hang out along the river here. He's a terror when he's drunk. When he's sober he's all right—kind of simple—wouldn't hurt a fly—nicest fellow in town. But when he's drunk—whoo!"

61 There were periods of stillness. "I wish Jack Potter was back from San Anton'," said the barkeeper. "He shot Wilson up once—in the leg—and he would sail in and pull out the kinks in this thing."

62 Presently they heard from a distance the sound of a shot, followed by three wild yowls. It instantly removed a bond from the men in the darkened saloon. There was a shuffling of feet. They looked at each other. "Here he comes," they said.

III

63 A man in a maroon-colored flannel shirt, which had been purchased for purposes of decoration, and made principally by some Jewish women on the East Side of New York, rounded a corner and walked into the middle of the main street of Yellow Sky. In either hand the man held a long, heavy, blue-black revolver. Often he yelled, and these cries rang through a semblance of a deserted village, shrilly flying over the roofs in a volume that seemed to have no relation to the ordinary vocal strength of a man. It was as if the surrounding stillness formed the arch of a tomb over him. These cries of ferocious challenge rang against walls of silence. And his boots had red tops with gilded imprints, of the kind beloved in winter by little sledding boys on the hillsides of New England.

64 The man's face flamed in a rage begot of whiskey. His eyes, rolling, and yet keen for ambush, hunted still doorways and windows. He walked with the creeping movement of the midnight cat. As it occurred to him, he roared menacing information. The long revolvers in his hands were as easy as straws; they were moved with an electric swiftness. The little fingers of each hand played sometimes in a musician's way. Plain from the low collar of the shirt, the cords of his neck straightened and sank, straightened and sank as passion moved him. The only sounds were his terrible invitations. The calm adobes preserved their demeanor at the passing of this small thing in the middle of the street.

65 There was no offer of fight—no offer of fight. The man called to the sky. There were no attractions. He bellowed and fumed and swayed his revolvers here and everywhere.

66 The dog of the barkeeper of the Weary Gentleman Saloon had not appreciated the advance of events. He yet lay dozing in front of his mas-

ter's door. At sight of the dog, the man paused and raised his revolver humorously. At sight of the man, the dog sprang up and walked diagonally away, with a sullen head, and growling. The man yelled, and the dog broke into a gallop. As it was about to enter an alley, there was a loud noise, a whistling, and something spat the ground directly before it. The dog screamed, and, wheeling in terror, galloped headlong in a new direction. Again there was a noise, a whistling, and sand was kicked viciously before it. Fear-stricken, the dog turned and flurried like an animal in a pen. The man stood laughing, his weapons at his hips.

67   Ultimately the man was attracted by the closed door of the Weary Gentleman Saloon. He went to it and, hammering with a revolver, demanded drink.

68   The door remaining imperturbable, he picked a bit of paper from the walk, and nailed it to the framework with a knife. He then turned his back contemptuously upon this popular resort, and, walking to the opposite side of the street and spinning there on his heel quickly and lithely, fired at the bit of paper. He missed it by a half-inch. He swore at himself, and went away. Later he comfortably fusilladed the windows of his most intimate friend. The man was playing with this town; it was a toy for him.

69   But still there was no offer of fight. The name of Jack Potter, his ancient antagonist, entered his mind, and he concluded that it would be a glad thing if he should go to Potter's house, and by bombardment induce him to come out and fight. He moved in the direction of his desire, chanting Apache scalp-music.

70   When he arrived at it, Potter's house presented the same still front as had the other adobes. Taking up a strategic position, the man howled a challenge. But this house regarded him as might a great stone god. It gave no sign. After a decent wait, the man howled further challenges, mingling with them wonderful epithets.

71   Presently there came the spectacle of a man churning himself into deepest rage over the immobility of a house. He fumed at it as the winter wind attacks a prairie cabin in the North. To the distance there should have gone the sound of tumult like the fighting of two hundred Mexicans. As necessity bade him, he paused for breath or to reload his revolvers.

IV

72   Potter and his bride walked sheepishly and with speed. Sometimes they laughed together shamefacedly and low.

73   "Next corner, dear," he said finally.

74   They put forth the efforts of a pair walking bowed against a strong wind. Potter was about to raise a finger to point the first appearance of the new home when, as they circled the corner, they came face to face with a man in a maroon-colored shirt, who was feverishly pushing car-

tridges into a large revolver. Upon the instant the man dropped his revolver to the ground, and, like lightning, whipped another from its holster. The second weapon was aimed at the bridegroom's chest.

75   There was a silence. Potter's mouth seemed to be merely a grave for his tongue. He exhibited an instinct to at once loosen his arm from the woman's grip, and he dropped the bag to the sand. As for the bride, her face had gone as yellow as old cloth. She was a slave to hideous rites, gazing at the apparitional snake.

76   The two men faced each other at a distance of three paces. He of the revolver smiled with a new and quiet ferocity.

77   "Tried to sneak up on me," he said. "Tried to sneak up on me!" His eyes grew more baleful. As Potter made a slight movement, the man thrust his revolver venomously forward. "No; don't you do it, Jack Potter. Don't you move a finger toward a gun just yet. Don't you move an eyelash. The time has come for me to settle with you, and I'm goin' to do it my own way, and loaf along with no interferin'. So if you don't want a gun bent on you, just mind what I tell you."

78   Potter looked at his enemy. "I ain't got a gun on me, Scratchy," he said. "Honest, I ain't." He was stiffening and steadying, but yet somewhere at the back of his mind a vision of the Pullman floated: the sea-green figured velvet, the shining brass, silver, and glass, the wood that gleamed as darkly brilliant as the surface of a pool of oil—all the glory of the marriage, the environment of the new estate. "You know I fight when it comes to fighting, Scratchy Wilson; but I ain't got a gun on me. You'll have to do all the shootin' yourself."

79   His enemy's face went livid. He stepped forward, and lashed his weapon to and fro before Potter's chest. "Don't you tell me you ain't got no gun on you, you whelp. Don't tell me no lie like that. There ain't a man in Texas ever seen you without no gun. Don't take me for no kid." His eyes blazed with light, and his throat worked like a pump.

80   "I ain't takin' you for no kid," answered Potter. His heels had not moved an inch backward. "I'm takin' you for a —— fool. I tell you I ain't got a gun, and I ain't. If you're goin' to shoot me up, you better begin now; you'll never get a chance like this again."

81   So much enforced reasoning had told on Wilson's rage; he was calmer. "If you ain't got a gun, why ain't you got a gun?" he sneered. "Been to Sunday school?"

82   "I ain't got a gun because I've just come from San Anton' with my wife. I'm married," said Potter. "And if I'd thought there was going to be any galoots like you prowling around when I brought my wife home, I'd had a gun, and don't you forget it."

83   "Married?" said Scratchy, not at all comprehending.

84   "Yes, married. I'm married," said Potter, distinctly.

85   "Married?" said Scratchy. Seemingly for the first time, he saw the drooping, drowning woman at the other man's side. "No!" he said. He

was like a creature allowed a glimpse of another world. He moved a pace backward, and his arm, with the revolver, dropped to his side. "Is this the lady?" he asked.

86   "Yes; this is the lady," answered Potter.

87   There was another period of silence.

88   "Well," said Wilson at last, slowly, "I s'pose it's all off now."

89   "It's all off if you say so, Scratchy. You know I didn't make the trouble." Potter lifted his valise.

90   "Well, I 'low it's off, Jack," said Wilson. He was looking at the ground. "Married!" He was not a student of chivalry; it was merely that in the presence of this foreign condition he was a simple child of the earlier plains. He picked up his starboard revolver, and, placing both weapons in their holsters, he went away. His feet made funnel-shaped tracks in the heavy sand.

The Bride Comes to Yellow Sky

Questions on Content, Style, and Structure

1. What does the marshal's marriage symbolize? What is happening to the Old West in this story?

2. Why is it significant that in the story's first sentence Crane says the train's motion seemed to prove that the Texas plains were "pouring eastward"?

3. How does the train car represent Potter's "new estate"?

4. What kinds of imagery are used to describe Potter's feelings as the train approaches Yellow Sky? Why are these images ironic?

5. Why does Crane include a drummer in the saloon? What does his presence reveal about Yellow Sky?

6. Characterize Scratchy Wilson. What is his past? What does he represent in this story?

7. Why are Wilson's clothes ironic?

8. Potter's house and the other adobes are personified in what way? Why?

9. When Wilson learns that Potter is married, he is "like a creature allowed a glimpse of another world." Explain this image.

10. Why does Wilson call off the gunfight?

11. Some critics have suggested that Wilson's "funnel-shaped" tracks in the sand are meant to allude to hourglasses. Why would hourglasses be appropriate images on which to end this story? What other references to time are there in this story?

12. What is the tone of this story? Support your answer with reference to Crane's language.

13. Summarize in a few sentences what you think this story is about.

Vocabulary

precipice (1)	deference (15)	semblance (63)
furtive (2)	keening (16)	demeanor (64)
countenance (3)	commensurately (16)	imperturbable (68)
placid (3)	heinous (18)	lithely (68)
derisive (10)	citadel (21)	antagonist (69)
sardonic (14)	fatuously (30)	epithets (69)
equanimity (15)	jocular (35)	apparitional (75)
		baleful (77)

Suggestions for Writing

1. Throughout his story Crane uses a variety of images to communicate the passing of the Old West. Select a few major examples and write an essay showing how they clarify Crane's story.

2. Write an essay on Crane's use of irony and/or humor in this story.

3. Write a character analysis of one or two of the following: Potter, Wilson, the bride, the drummer, the people on the train. Include in your analysis an explanation of the characters' purposes in the story.

How to Write an "F" Paper: Fresh Advice for Students of Freshman English

Joseph C. Pattison

Joseph C. Pattison taught composition and literature at California State University at Sacramento until he retired in 1977; he now lives on Cape Cod. This essay first appeared in *College English*, a journal published by the National Council of Teachers of English, in 1963.

1 Writing an "F" paper is admittedly not an easy task, but one can learn to do it by grasp of the principles to use. The thirteen below, if practiced at all diligently, should lead any student to that fortune in his writing.

Obscure the Ideas:

2 1. Select a topic that is big enough to let you wander around the main idea without ever being forced to state it precisely. If an assigned topic has been limited for you, take a detour that will allow you to amble away from it for a while.

3 2. Pad! Pad! Pad! Do not develop your ideas. Simply restate them in safe, spongy generalizations to avoid the need to find evidence to support what you say. Always point out repetition with the phrase, "As previously noted. . . ." Better yet, repeat word-for-word at least one or two of your statements.

4 3. Disorganize your discussion. For example, if you are using the time order to present your material, keep the reader alert by making a jump from the past to the present only to spring back into the past preparatory to a leap into the future preceding a return hop into the present just before the finish of the point about the past. Devise comparable stratagems to use with such other principles for organizing a discussion as space, contrast, cause-effect, and climax.

5 4. Begin a new paragraph every sentence or two.

6 By generous use of white space, make the reader aware that he is looking at a page blank of sustained thought.

7 Like this.

Mangle the Sentences:

8 5. Fill all the areas of your sentences with deadwood. Incidentally, "the area of" will deaden almost any sentence, and it is particularly flat when displayed prominently at the beginning of a sentence.

9 6. Using fragments and run-on or comma-spliced sentences. Do not use a main subject and a main verb, for the reader will get the complete thought too easily. Just toss him part of the idea at a time, as in "Using fragments. . . ." To gain sentence variety, throw in an occasional run-on sentence thus the reader will have to read slowly and carefully to get the idea.

10 7. Your sentence order invert for statement of the least important matters. That will force the reader to be attentive to understand even the simplest points you make.

11 8. You, in the introduction, body, and conclusion of your paper, to show that you can contrive ornate, graceful sentences, should use involution. Frequent separation of subjects from verbs by insertion of involved phrases and clauses will prove that you know what can be done to a sentence.

Slovenize the Diction:

12 9. Add the popular "-wise" and "-ize" endings to words. Say, "Timewise, it is fastest to go by U.S. 40," rather than simply, "It is fastest to go by U.S. 40." Choose "circularize" in preference to "circulate." Practice will smartenize your style.

13 10. Use vague words in place of precise ones. From the start, establish vagueness of tone by saying, "The thing is . . ." instead of, "The issue is. . . ." Make the reader be imaginative throughout his reading of your paper.

14 11. Employ lengthy Latinate locutions wherever possible. Shun the simplicity of style that comes from apt use of short, old, familiar words, especially those of Anglo-Saxon origin. Show that you can get the *maximum* (L.), not merely the *most* (A.S.), from every word choice you make.

15 12. Inject humor into your writing by using the wrong word occasionally. Write "then" when you mean "than" or "to" when you mean "too." Every reader likes to laugh.

16 13. Find a "tried and true" phrase to use to clinch a point. It will have a comfortingly folksy sound for the reader. Best of all, since you want to end in a conversational and friendly way, sprinkle your conclusions with clichés. "Put a little frosting on the cake," as the saying goes.

17 Well, to ensconce this whole business in a nutshell, you, above all, an erudite discourse on nothing in the field of your topic should pen. Thereby gaining the reader's credence in what you say.

18 Suggestion-wise, one last thing: file-ize this list for handy reference the next time you a paper write.

How to Write an "F" Paper: Fresh Advice for Students of Freshman English

Questions on Content, Style, and Structure

1. A process essay may be identified as either directional (tells the readers how they may do or make something) or informative (tells the readers how someone else does or makes something). This essay is which type?
2. How is this essay organized? Does Pattison follow his own advice in rule three?
3. Point out examples in which Pattison follows his own recommendations. Why does he do this?
4. Does Pattison use enough examples to illustrate his rules?
5. List the errors you find in the last two paragraphs.
6. Were the last paragraphs an effective means of ending this selection? Why/why not?
7. What role does irony play in this selection?
8. What other rules could Pattison have added to insure an "F" paper? Give at least two examples.

Vocabulary

diligently (1)   ensconce (17)
amble (2)   erudite (17)
slovenize (12)   credence (17)
locutions (14)

Suggestions for Writing

1. Using Pattison's approach, write an essay on "How to Flunk a Test," "How to Ruin a Blind Date," "How to Remain a Bench Warmer" or some such topic.
2. Write a directional process essay telling your reader how to make some kind of artistic or useful creation.
3. Write an informative essay telling your reader how a particular historical event occurred.

Beating Writer's Block: How to Confront the Typewriter Fearlessly
John Leo

John Leo is an associate editor of *Time* magazine. This article appeared in that magazine in 1977.

9:03 A.M.

1   As every schoolboy knows, writer's block is an affliction every bit as debilitating as . . . *(Well, as what? Maybe a cup of coffee will help.)*

2   Writer's block is a condition that . . .

3   *(Retrieve paper airplanes, empty wastebasket, reread* Playboy *centerfold. Remember the writer who set fire to his apartment to avoid meeting a deadline?)*

9:25 A.M.

4   *(Try to beat the block by leading off with other people's quotes.)* "Blocks are simply forms of egotism," said Lawrence Durrell. . . .

10:32 A.M.

5   *(Maybe this will do it.)* What can be done to break writer's block? There are many traditional answers: change of scenery, change of work habits, drop everything and see a James Bond movie. Durrell recommends insulting oneself while shaving and concentrating on unpaid bills. T. S. Eliot broke his block by writing poems in French. *(Dabbling in lesser languages removes pressure to perform in mother tongue.)* Tom Wolfe, totally blocked on his first famous article, a story about customized cars for *Esquire*, wrote a really socko memorandum to his editor on the subject. The editor ran the memo as the article. Wolfe now writes all his articles as memos. *(On the other hand he is at least three years late with his current book . . .)*

11:09 A.M.

6   Los Angeles Psychoanalyst Martin Grotjahn thinks he knows the cause of the malady. Says he: "People who have strong needs to love or fight are more prone to writer's block." Most psychiatrists believe that, just as there is no single explanation for murder or theft, there is no one cause

for writer's block. But Grotjahn, who discusses the problem in his book *Beyond Laughter*, believes hostility is the fundamental reason. Writing is an aggressive demand for attention. It can be blocked when a writer projects his anger onto reviewers and readers. "It's the fear of being attacked," says Manhattan Psychoanalyst Walter Stewart, "the fear that you will be treated as contemptuously as you would like to treat everyone else."

7   In fact, Herman Melville was so wounded by critics that he wrote no fiction at all for 30 years. Says Psychoanalyst Yale Kramer, who is studying Melville's life: "He behaved like a child stubbornly remaining silent in a passive attempt at revenge." But even good reviews can bring on writer's block; they tend to paralyze by awakening great expectations. As Author Cyril Connolly, a part-time blockee, expressed it: "Whom the gods wish to destroy they first call promising."

12:15 P.M.

8   *(Word count so far: 385.)* Short break for inner movie about receiving Nobel Prize for literature. Psychiatrists call this the "grandiose fantasy." This imaginary acclaim is a neurotic compromise between the real self—scared, limited—and the ideal self—a literary conqueror. Says Manhattan Analyst Donald Kaplan: "The fantasy of playing Carnegie Hall may be so gratifying that you can't manage to practice your scales."

9   This is not to be confused with what Kaplan calls "the Nobel Prize complex"—a compulsive perfectionism that drives the writer to type the opening line of a book 403 times. Every word has to be as good as Shakespeare or Shaw, or there is no use playing the game at all. A subvariation, of course, is that it also has to be perfectly typed. Psychoanalyst Edmund Bergler, a brilliant but erratic writer on the 1950s, has a scatological interpretation of the first-line problem: the writer smearing the empty page with words is the baby smearing mommy's living room wall with diaper residue. Bergler, much admired for his own literary wall smearing, churned out a dozen popular books on psychiatry, all of them arguing that masochism explained *most* of human affairs. He could have used a block or two himself.

1:30 P.M.

10   *(Time to lapse into coherence.)* The opposite of the "first-line" problem is the "last-lap paralysis." One screenwriter wrote two-thirds of a script and made the mistake of showing it to friends, who said it was the greatest property ever to hit Hollywood, thus immobilizing the writer.

11   Fear of success comes in here. One symptom is short sentences. Fear makes you lose your rhythm and forget how English sentences run.

(Bathroom break, check mail.) But psychiatrists know that the plucky writer can pull up his socks and finish everything he begi

Beating Writer's Block: How to Confront the Typewriter Fearlessly

Questions on Content, Style, and Structure

1. What, according to this article, are some of the causes of writer's block? some of the cures?
2. What are the purposes of the comments in italics in the parentheses?
3. How is this selection organized? Is it an effective choice?
4. Analyze the source of the humor in this essay. When does the reader first realize that the article is meant to be funny?
5. Why does the writer refer to other writers and to psychoanalysts?
6. What is the "grandiose fantasy"? "last-lap paralysis"? Are these complexes real?
7. How effective is the conclusion?
8. Why do you think the writer wrote this article?

Vocabulary

debilitating (1)   erratic (9)
malady (6)   scatological (9)
contemptuously (6)   immobilizing (10)
grandiose (8)

Suggestions for Writing

1. Write a humorous process essay in which you explain how to confront some other kind of "block" or irrational fear.
2. Write a serious essay that explains how you faced an important decision or problem in your life.
3. Describe in a short essay the steps in your own composing process. How do you avoid the "first-line problem" or "last-lap paralysis" in your own writing?

Semantic Spinach:
Or, Mellowing Out in Sunny California
Cyra McFadden

Cyra McFadden is a former English teacher whose articles have
appeared in a variety of magazines. Her novel *The Serial* (1976) was
made into a movie in 1980. This essay was published in 1977 in *The
New York Times Magazine*.

1   A woman who lives here in the San Francisco Bay Area, where every
prospect pleases and only man is vile, is teaching "inner cooking." "I'm
out of the closet," a newspaper interview quotes her as saying. "All this
time I've been interested in people and feelings, but I've been in the
disguise of a cooking teacher."

2   Joyce Goldstein conducts her classes in "Kitchen Consciousness" in
her Berkeley home. Cooking, she believes, is a metaphor for life. It involves "taking risks," "expressing feelings," "releasing body energy" and
"sharing space." That her techniques of guided fantasy and gestalt in the
kitchen fill yet another need in the collective Bay Area consciousness is
apparent in a student testimonial quoted in the same interview: "Joyce's
classes have changed my whole outlook in the kitchen. I don't feel all
those ought-tos and should-haves anymore. I am a free woman."

3   I know, I know. It's also a free country. If, as Goldstein suggests, you
find cleaning shrimp "a meditative experience," and if you, too, believe
that foods have personalities ("the tomato . . . is thin-skinned and bruises
easily, but likes to bring things together") that, as we say in the consciousness-raising capital of the Western World, is your own trip. Dig it,
relate to it, groove on it, get behind it, even, if you choose. Only spare
me your account of the whole transcendent experience. Living here in
beautiful Marin County, between the fern bars and the deep blue sea, I
hear all the mindless prattle about feelings, human and vegetable, that
I can tolerate without "acting out" and drowning the users of the New-
speak of the 70's, like unwanted kittens, in their own hot tubs.

4   "You've really got a Thing about language, haven't you?" said a man
who sat next to me at a luncheon recently. "What's your hang-up? I think
the whole new language trip is because people are really into being upfront about their feelings these days instead of intellectualizing, so we
need a whole new way of decribing all that stuff . . . the feelings. I mean,
10 years ago we didn't even know they were there. And anyway, you
can't say it doesn't communicate.

5   "Like, right now we're having this discussion, for example, and I say,

'I know where you're coming from.' Are you going to tell me you don't know what I mean by that?"

6   Arguing with such people, I have learned, is as futile as trying to scrape fresh bubble gum off one's shoe. Still, I insisted that I didn't know what my luncheon partner meant in any concrete sense and that 'I know where you're coming from' was meaningless in the context. Did he mean he knew where I'd grown up, or where I'd been immediately before malevolent fate planted me at the table beside him, or what education and experience had shaped my thinking about the issue between us?

7   Intellectualizing, said my companion. Nit-picking. I knew very well that he meant that he could relate, that he knew what space I was in. Where my head was coming from.

8   By this time I wished my head and everything appended to it were elsewhere. "Are you trying to say you understand why I feel the way I do about empty rubber-stamp language?" I asked, coming down hard on the consonants.

9   My luncheon partner smiled infuriatingly. "You see?" he said. "I *knew* you knew where I was coming from."

10   Writer Richard Rosen calls such language psychobabble (his funny and incisive book by the same title has just been published by Atheneum). He defines it as "monotonous patois . . . psychological patter, whose concern is to faithfully catalogue the ego's condition."

11   I define it as semantic spinach, and I say the hell with it. Conversations like the above, if one can call such an exchange a conversation, have all but supplanted anything resembling intelligent human discourse here, where the human-potential movement takes the place of other light industry and where the redwood-shingled offices of the healer/masseurs, the gurus and the "life-goals consultants" line the main approach to Mill Valley along with the hamburger stands. They make any real exchange of ideas impossible; block any attempt at true communication; substitute what Orwell called "prefabricated words and phrases" for thought.[1]

12   Just as surely as the Styrofoam boxes one sees everywhere are evidence of the popularity of McDonald's, such conversations, too, are the fallout from the fast-food-outlet approach to therapy of the 70's. With the self the only subject worth examining, one's purely intuitive "off the wall" response the only reference point, all verbal exchange is soon reduced to a kind of mechanical chatter in the infield.

13   Speakers of psychobabble, I believe, are not so much concerned with describing feelings "we didn't even know were there" 10 years ago as with avoiding any mental exertion whatsoever; any effort at precision of expression, or even thought itself, falls under the pejorative label

[1] See "Politics and the English Language" by George Orwell, famous British novelist and essayist, on pages 339–349.

"intellectualizing." Thus the number of words and phrases in the Bay Area vocabulary that describe mental inertia: "mellowing out," "kicking back," "going with the flow," being "laid back." All suggest that the laid-back, mellowed-out speaker achieves a perfect relation with the universe while in a state of passivity just short of that produced by full anesthetic.

14   How much easier it is, after all, to "verbalize" in platitudes rather than to think. Trite, cliché-ridden language is always a sign of inattention at best, intellectual laziness at worst. One either speaks or writes the occasional cliché because his mind, for some reason or other, has momentarily switched over to automatic pilot, or he uses prefabricated words and phrases routinely because as far as he's concerned, it's six of one, half a dozen of the other.

15   Psychobabble is no more difficult to use than drawing the girl on the matchbook cover, and it has another attraction as well: Speakers associate its platitudes with profundity and mouth its Words to Live By in the apparent conviction that having said nothing, they have said it all.

16   "I can't get behind school right now," said a student in a college composition class of mine, when I warned him that if he continued to show no vital signs, he would fail the course. "But I'm not into F's," he added, "and, anyway, I don't think you ought to lay that authority trip on me. I mean, failing someone . . wow, that's a value judgment."

17   "I can't relate to the dude," said another, in a contemporary literature class, pressed for his opinion of a Ray Bradbury short story.

18   "How about being more specific?" I said. "Do you mean you weren't interested in his ideas, or that you didn't find them sympathetic? Were you bored? Did you have trouble following the action of the story?"

19   "Actually I didn't exactly read it," said the student.

20   "For God's sake, how do you know you 'can't relate' then?" I asked, knowing better.

21   My student turned his serene blue gaze upon me. "I just flashed on it," he explained.

22   A *value judgment*. Give me the trench-coat type flasher any time over the one who whips open an empty mind to display his poor excuse for an insight.

23   What is most alarming about psychobabble, however, is not its appalling smugness but that it spreads like Dutch elm disease. Unlike most cult language—private vocabularies small groups use to distinguish themselves from the larger language community—the fatuous fallout from the human potential movement seems to have jumped all the usual fences. And while elsewhere in the country one hears psychobabble spoken by the members of the "counterculture," here the counterculture has come out from under the counter and become the dominant culture itself, its dialect the language of polite society that one must speak in

order to belong. Rock-band roadies, stockbrokers, academics, teeny-boppers, butchers—sometimes it appears that everyone one meets has taken the same course in Deep Feelereze at Berlitz.

24 "Your arms are crossed. Do you realize that's a very defensive posture?" says the friend I meet in the supermarket. "You're afraid of me. I can tell from your body language."

25 I'm not afraid, I assure her. My arms are crossed because I couldn't find a cart, and if I adopt a less defensive posture, I will drop a dozen cat-food cans on her foot.

26 My friend smiles wisely, bemused by my transparent self-deception. Some of the people can fool themselves all of the time, she is thinking. "Look," she says, "it's O.K. *You're* O.K. I just think maybe some time when the vibes are right, we ought to get clear. . . ."

27 At a dinner party, a new acquaintance tells me about her intimate life. Although she is still "processing" her ex-husband (not, I hope, in the Waring blender her language brings to mind), she just spent a weekend with another man from whom she gets "a lot of ego reinforcement. My therapist keeps telling me to go where the energies are," she says, "so that's what I'm doing, because that's what went wrong last time. I didn't just kick back and go with the energies."

28 Suddenly I realize why Marin's own George Lucas is getting rich from *Star Wars*, a film in which people go where the energies are, at speeds faster than "hyperspace," and deliver themselves of simple-minded philosophy in one-syllable words.

29 Why has psychobabble saturated Bay Area conversation so? One hears it nearly everywhere else to some extent, it is true, but only in San Francisco, Los Angeles and environs has it all but replaced English. (Los Angeles has its own bizarre variation, incidentally, incorporating film and television industry money talk. Example: "I'm gonna be totally upfront with you, sweetheart. The bottom line is 50 thou and points.")

30 In part, the appeal is the gravitational pull urban California has always felt toward the new, the Now, the "trendy," no matter how ludicrous its current manifestation. In an area where opening night at the opera featured at least one socialite in an elegant designer gown and a punk-rock safety pin in her hair, one shouldn't be too surprised when a butcher asks, "Could you relate to a pork loin roast?"

31 Partly responsible, too, is the legacy of the Haight-Ashbury and the Summer of Love. Former flower children whose own vocabulary of peace and love focused on the primacy of feelings, who found concrete reality largely irrelevant, now abound in the hills and canyons of Marin, driving car pool to Montessori school on alternate Thursdays or working as claims adjusters at Fireman's Fund.

32 Fallen victim to cellulite and revolving credit, wistful for the days of LSD and roses, they naturally embrace a language pattern that declares they have not repudiated their 60's selves.

33 "Listen," one of them told a friend of mine recently, as they exchanged

driver's licenses and phone numbers after a minor traffic accident, "I just want you to know that you've been so beautiful about all this, it's really been a beautiful experience."

34 My friend said he didn't agree and that most of the traffic accidents he had known couldn't really be described as beautiful, though some were pretty and others compensated for their plainness with lots of charm.

35 Finally, in these pleasant, prosperous suburbs, enough people have enough money to spend on weekend after weekend at psychological boot camps for civilians like *est* and Silva mind control; consulting holistic healers and doing dream or body work; being Rolfed, getting centered, or—in Marin County—taking their horses to be treated for anxiety by a veterinarian who specializes in equine acupuncture.

36 What Tom Wolfe[2] calls "the Me decade" can burgeon here under ideal conditions: affluence, leisure and what has been traditionally a high level of tolerance for fads and human foibles. Joyce Goldstein, the Berkeley teacher of inner cooking, might have a little trouble collecting disciples in, say, Missoula, Mont., but she is doing nicely, thank you, in balmy Berkeley. "Joyce is nifty and a half," says another of her students, a woman assistant vice president at Wells Fargo Bank. "I was a cooking cripple until I met her. Now I can't cook, but Joyce has showed me that it's O.K."

37 Los Angeles, too, has the money, the leisure and the fondness for fakery that nurture the rapid growth of the new subculture, and in greater abundance. There, Maseratis and chauffeured limousines double-park in front of the mystical bookstores, the offices of the Astrological Guidance counselors and the Kirlian "aura photo" workshops. Understandably.

38 After all, when you've built the palatial house in Beverly Hills, bought cocaine as if it were baby powder, had cosmetic surgery on everything and still have money left, you've got to spend it somewhere.

39 One could argue that such preoccupations and diversions are essentially harmless in that they keep people off the streets, or what are called in Los Angeles (to distinguish them from the freeways) the surface roads. In this era of do your own thing, however, my thing, as my luncheon partner some weeks past either understood or didn't, is despair at the effects of 70's egocentrism on the language.

40 I have read too many essays by and held too many conferences with college students whose written and spoken English had the clarity of Cream of Wheat.

41 I have listened to too many *est* graduates, living walkie-talkies, tell me, unsolicited, what they were "getting." (Clear, creative divorces, double messages, in touch with themselves, not necessarily in that order.)

42 I have argued too many times about things that matter to me passion-

[2] Wolfe is a popular American journalist-author whose books include *The Kandy-Kolored Tangerine-Flake Streamlined Baby* (1965), *The Electric Kool-Aid Acid Test* (1968), *The Right Stuff* (1979), and *From BauHouse to Our House* (1981).

ately with people who dismissed both arguments and me with "How come you're so uptight?" or "Your head's really in a funny place, you know?"

43   Crack-brained California, you say complacently; it's always been Cloud Cuckooland out there. True, but California foolishness has an historic tendency to seep through the water tables and across state lines. What if one day soon it is impossible to carry on a reasonably coherent conversation north of Yucatán and south of the Bering Sea?

44   Meanwhile I stand on the roof of my Mill Valley house, watching the flood of psychobabble rising, ever rising, and wishing I knew how to turn the situation around. It won't be easy. The psychobabblers not only outnumber the rest of us, but, what is worse, they have The Force on their side.

Semantic Spinach:
Or, Mellowing Out in Sunny California

Questions on Content, Style, and Structure

1. What is McFadden's attitude toward the use of the language she describes?
2. How does she introduce her essay? How does her introduction set the tone of the essay?
3. Why does McFadden write from a first person point of view?
4. Why does McFadden criticize "psychobabble"? Why is it so easy to use?
5. How is analogy used in paragraph 12?
6. Why are the stories of the college student, grocery shopper, and dinner guest included?
7. Why does McFadden use so much dialogue in the stories mentioned above and throughout the essay?
8. Why is California the center for psychobabble?
9. Why is McFadden so concerned about the state of the language in California?
10. In paragraph 28 and in the concluding paragraph, McFadden refers to the movie *Star Wars*. Why? Is her reference an effective way to end her essay? Why/why not?
11. Discuss the source of McFadden's humor. How does her humorous tone help her make her points?
12. Point out some examples of McFadden's own use of figurative language (college students' language with the "clarity of Cream of Wheat," for instance). Is her language clichéd or fuzzy?

Vocabulary

gestalt (2)	pejorative (13)	holistic (35)
malevolent (6)	platitudes (14)	equine (35)
patois (10)	profundity (15)	burgeon (36)
semantic (11)	fatuous (23)	foibles (36)
supplanted (11)	bemused (26)	complacently (43)
discourse (11)	ludicrous (30)	

Suggestions for Writing

1. McFadden worries that "semantic spinach" will creep into other parts of the country. Write an essay in which you analyze and illustrate the slang currently popular in your area. Does the slang obscure communication, as McFadden claims?

2. Write a paragraph defining a popular slang word or phrase. Assume your reader is a foreign visitor who has heard but not understood the term.

3. In paragraph 11 McFadden refers to George Orwell's criticism of "prefabricated words." Read "Politics and the English Language," pages 339–349, and write an essay comparing his thesis, methods of organization and development, and tone to those of McFadden.

The Seven Sins of Technical Writing
Morris Freedman

Morris Freedman is a professor of English and Comparative Literature at the University of Maryland. His books include *The Compact English Handbook* (1967) and *The Moral Impulse* (1967); his articles have appeared in *The American Scholar, Harper's Magazine,* and a variety of professional journals. This selection, originally a speech delivered to an association of technical writers in New Mexico, was published in *College Composition and Communication,* a journal of the National Council of Teachers of English, in 1958.

1   Let me start by saying at once that I do not come to you tonight just as a professor of English, for, frankly, I do not think that I would have very much to say to you only as someone expert in the history of the use—and misuse—of the language. And any remarks on literature might be confusing, at least without extensive elaboration, for the values and objectives of literature seem so very different at first from those of technical

writing—although fundamentally many of these values and objectives coincide. And I am sure that you are more than familiar with such things as clichés, comma splices, fragmentary sentences, and the other abominations we deal with in freshman composition. These obviously have nothing to do specifically with technical writing.

2   But I want to say, before anyone thinks that I class technical writing entirely by itself, immune from rules and requirements of communication that govern other kinds of writing, that technical writing calls for the same kind of attention and must be judged by the same standards as any other kind of writing; *indeed, it calls for a great attention and for higher standards.* And I say this as a former science and medical writer for the popular press; as a former writer of procedure manuals and directives for the government; as a former editor of technical studies in sociology, statistics, law, and psychology; as a former general magazine editor; as a writer of fiction, essays, and scholarly articles; and, not least, as a professor of English. We can see at once why technical writing must be measured by higher standards, or, at least, by different ones, if anyone will not grant me that they are higher. Technical writing is so immediately functional. Confusing directions accompanying an essential device in a jet plane may result in disaster; bad writing elsewhere can have as its most extreme effect merely boredom.

3   Yet, while technical writing implicitly calls for great care, it differs from other kinds of writing in that its practitioners are, by and large, first technicians and only incidentally writers. And principally because of this arrangement, I think, technical writing has become characterized by a collection of sins peculiar to this dicipline alone. I say the *collection* is peculiar to technical writing, not any one of the sins alone. Any newspaper, weekly magazine, encyclopedia, textbook, any piece of writing you might name, will contain one or another of these sins, in greater or lesser profusion. But I know of no kind of writing that contains as many different sins in such great number as technical writing, and with such great potential for danger. To repeat, the sins in the world at large—at least, of the sort I'm talking about—often don't matter much. And sometimes, too, they don't matter in technical writing. As my students argue when I correct them in informative writing: "You got the meaning, didn't you?" Yes, I did, and so do we all get the meaning when a newspaper, a magazine, a set of directions stammers out its message. And I suppose, too, we could travel by ox-cart, or dress in burlap, or drive around with rattling fenders, and still get through a day.

4   But technical writing in this age can no more afford widespread sloppiness of expression, confusion of meaning, rattle-trap construction than a supersonic missile can afford to be made of the wrong materials, or be put together haphazardly with screws jutting out here and there, or have wiring circuits that may go off any way at all, or—have a self-destructive system that fails because of some fault along the way in construction. Technical writing today—as I need hardly reiterate to this audience—if

it is much less than perfect in its streamlining and design may well result in machines that are less than trim, and in operation that is not exactly neat. This is at worst; at best, poor technical writing, when its effect is minimized by careful reading, hinders efficiency, wastes time. Let me remark too that the commission of any one of these sins, and of any one of many, many lesser ones, is really not likely alone to be fatal, just as one loose screw by itself is not likely to destroy a machine; but always, we know, sins come in bunches, the sin of avarice often links hands with the sin of gluttony, one loose screw may mean others, and, anyway, the ideal of no sins at all—especially in something like technical writing, where the pain of self-denial should be minimal—is always to be strived for.

5   A final word before I launch into the sins (whose parade, so long delayed, will prove, I hope, so much more edifying—like a medieval tableau). The seven I list might be described as cardinal ones, and as such they are broad and overlapping, perhaps, rather than specific and very clearly distinguished from one another. They all contribute to making technical writing less clear, concise, coherent, and correct than it should be.

6   Sin 1, then, might be described as that of *Indifference,* neglecting the reader. I do not mean anything so simple as writing down to an engineer or physicist, although this is all too common and may be considered part of this sin. This writing down—elaborating the obvious—is one reason the abstract or summary has become so indispensable a part of technical reports; very often, it is all the expert needs to read of the whole report, the rest being a matter of all too obvious detailing. Nor do I mean writing above the heads of your audience either, which is a defect likely to be taken care of by a thoughtful editor. Both writing over or under the heads of your reader, or to the side, are really matters of careless aiming and, as such, of indifference, too. But what I mean here by indifference are shortcuts of expression, elliptical diction, sloppy organization, bringing up points and letting them hang unresolved, improper or inadequate labelling of graphic material, and the like. This is communication by gutturals, grunts, shrugs, as though it were not worth the trouble to articulate carefully, as though the reader didn't matter—or didn't exist. This is basically an attitude of disrespect: *Caveat lector*—let the reader beware. Let the reader do his own work; the writer isn't going to help him.

7   Here is the concluding sentence from a quite respectable report, one most carefully edited and indeed presented as a model in a handbook for technical writers used by a great chemical firm. The sentence is relatively good, for it takes only a second reading to work out its meaning (perhaps only a slow first one for someone trained in reading this kind of writing):

> When it is assumed that all of the cellulose is converted to ethyl cellulose, reaction conversion of cellulose to ethyl cellulose, per cent of cellulose reacted, and reaction yield of ethyl cellulose based on cellulose are each equal to 100%.

8   This is admittedly a tough sentence to get across simply, considering that "cellulose" is repeated in several different contexts. Yet two guiding principles would have made it much clearer: (1) always put for your reader first things first (here, the meaning hangs on the final phrase, "each equal to 100%," which comes at the end of a complicated series); and (2) clearly separate items in a series. (The second rule seems to me one of the most important in technical writing where so many things have to be listed so often.) Here is the recast sentence:

> If all the cellulose is converted to ethyl cellulose, each of the following factors is then equal to 100%:
>
>   1. reaction conversion of cellulose to ethyl cellulose.
>   2. proportion of cellulose reacted.
>   3. reaction yield of ethyl cellulose based on cellulose.

The changes are not great, certainly, but in the process we have eliminated the indisputable notion of a percent being equal to a percent, and have arranged the series so that both the eye and the mind together can grasp the information immediately. Sin 1 then can be handled, one way, by cutting out indirect Rube Goldbergish contraptions and hitting your points directly on their heads, one, two, three.

9   The remaining sins I shall discuss are extensions of this primal one, disregard for the reader. Sin 2 may be designated as *Fuzziness*, that is, a general fuzziness of communication—vague words, meaningless words, wrong ones. The reader uses his own experience to supply the meaning in such writing; the writing itself acts only as a collection of clues. The military specializes in this sort of thing. I recall an eerie warning in an air force mess hall: "Anyone smoking in or around this mess hall will be dealt with accordingly." It still haunts me. Here is a caution in a handbook of technical writing with which you may be familiar: "Flowery, euphemistic protestations of gratitude are inappropiate." We know what this means, of course, but we ourselves supply the exact meaning. It happens that a "euphemism" is "the substitution of an inoffensive or mild expression for one that may offend or suggest something unpleasant." At least, that's what *Webster's Collegiate* says it is.

10   Here are some other examples: "The intrinsic labyrinth of wires must be first disentangled." The writer meant "network," not "labyrinth"; and I think he meant "internal" for "intrinsic" and "untangled" for "disentangled." Item: "The liquid contents of the container should then be disgorged via the spout by the operator." Translation: "The operator should then empty the container." Here is a final long one:

> When the element numbered one is brought into tactual contact with the element numbered two, when the appropriate conditions of temperature have been met above the previously determined safety point, then there will be exhibited a tendency for the appropriate circuit to be closed and consequently to serve the purpose of activating an audible warning device.

Translation:

> When the heat rises above the set safety point, element one touches element two, closing a circuit and setting off a bell.

Prescription to avoid Sin 2: use concrete, specific words and phrases whenever you can, and use only those words whose meaning you are sure of. (A dictionary, by the way, is only a partial help in determining the correct and *idiomatic* use of a word.) English is perhaps the richest of languages in offering a variety of alternatives for saying the same thing.

11   Sin 3 might be called the sin of *Emptiness*. It is the use of jargon and big words, pretentious ones, where perfectly appropriate and acceptable small and normal words are available. (There is nothing wrong with big words in themselves, provided they are the best ones for the job. A steam shovel is right for moving a boulder, ridiculous for picking up a handkerchief.) We may want to connect this sin with the larger, more universal one of pride, the general desire to seem important and impressive. During World War II a high government official devoted much time to composing an effective warning for a sticker to be put above light switches. He emerged with "Illumination is required to be extinguished on these premises on the termination of daily activities," or something of the sort. He meant "Put the lights out when you go home."

12   The jargon I'm talking about is not the technical language you use normally and necessarily for efficient communication. I have in mind only the use of a big word or a jumble of words for something that can be said more efficiently with familiar words and straightforward expressions. I have in mind also a kind of code language used to show that you're an insider, somewhere or other: "Production-wise, that's a high-type machine that can be used to finalize procedure. The organization is enthused." There is rarely any functional justification for saying "utilize" or "utilization" for "use," "prior to" for "before," "the answer is in the affirmative or negative" for "yes or no," or for using any of the "operators, or false verbal limbs," as George Orwell* called them, like "render inoperative," "prove unacceptable," "exhibit a tendency to," "serve the purpose of," and so on and on.

13   Again, one can handle this sin simply by overcoming a reluctance to saying things directly; the most complex things in the world can be said in simple words, often of one syllable. Consider propositions in higher math or logic, the Supreme Court decisions of men like Brandeis and Holmes, the poetry of Shakespeare. I cannot resist quoting here Sir Arthur Quiller-Couch's rendition in jargon of Hamlet's "To be or not to be, that is the question." I am sure you all know the full jargon rendition of the soliloquy. "To be, or the contrary? Whether the former or the latter be preferable would seem to admit of some difference of opinion."

*See Orwell's "Politics and the English Language" on page 339–349.

14   Sin 4 is an extension of 3: just plain *Wordiness*. The principle here is that if you can say anything with more words than necessary for the job, then by all means do so. I've already cited examples of this sin above, but compounded with other sins. Here is a purer example, the opening of a sentence in a technical writing handbook: "Material to be contained on the cover of the technical report includes . . ." This can be reduced to "The cover of the technical report should include . . ." Another example, less pure: "The front-mounted blade of the bulldozer is employed for earth moving operations on road construction jobs." Translation: "The bulldozer's front blade moves earth in road building." Item: "There is another way of accomplishing this purpose, and that is by evaporation." Translation: "Evaporation is another way of doing this." Instead of saying simply that "the bulldozer's front blade moves earth," you say it "is employed for earth moving operations," throwing in "employed" and "operations," as though "moves" alone is too weak to do this tremendous job. The cure for this sin? Simply reverse the mechanism: say what you have to in the fewest words.

15   Sin 5, once again an extension of the immediately preceding sin, is a matter of *Bad Habits*, the use of pat phrases, awkward expressions, confusing sentence structure, that have, unfortunately, become second nature. Again, I'm not alluding to the perfectly natural use of familiar technical expressions, which may literally be called clichés, but which are not efficiently replaceable. Sin 5 is a matter of just not paying attention to what you say, with the result that when you do suddenly pay attention, you see the pointlessness or even humor of what you have set down. Perhaps the most common example of this sin is what has been called "deadwood," or what may be called "writing for the simple minded." Examples: "red in color," "three in number," "square in shape," "the month of January," "the year 1956," "ten miles in distance," and the like. What else is red but a color, three but a number, square but a shape, January but a month, 1956 but a year, ten miles but a distance? To say that something is "two inches wide and three inches long" is to assume that your reader can't figure out length and width from the simple dimensions "two inches by three inches." I once read that a certain machine was 18 feet high, "vertically," the writer made sure to add; and another time that a certain knob should be turned "right, in direction."

16   A caution is needed here. There are many obvious instances when qualification is necessary. To say that something is "light," for example, is plainly mysterious unless you add "in color" or "in weight" or, perhaps, "in density" (unless the context makes such addition "deadwood").

17   I would include under Sin 5 the locutions "as far as that is concerned" (lately shortened to "as far as that"), "as regards," "with regard to," "in the case of" ("In the case of the case enclosing the instrument, the case is being studied"). These are all too often just lazy ways of making transitions (and, thus, incidentally, quite justifiable when speed of writing is a factor).

18   Sin 6 is the *Deadly Passive,* or, better, deadening passive; it takes the life out of writing, making everything impersonal, eternal, remote and dead. The deadly passive is guaranteed to make any reading matter more difficult to understand, to get through, and to retain. Textbook writers in certain fields have long ago learned to use the deadly passive to create difficulties where none exist; this makes their subject seem weightier, and their accomplishment more impressive. (And, of course, if this is ever what you have in mind on an assignment, then by all means use the deadly passive.) Sin 6 is rarely found alone; it is almost indispensable for fully carrying out the sins of wordiness and jargon. Frequently, of course, the passive is not a sin and not deadly, for there simply is no active agent and the material must be put impersonally.

19   Examples of this sin are so easy to come by, it is difficult to find one better than another. Here is a relatively mild example of Sin 6.

> The standardization of procedure in print finishing can be a very important factor in the efficient production of service pictures. In so far as possible, the smallest number of types and sizes of paper should be employed, and the recommended processing followed. The fewer paper grades and processing procedures used, the fewer errors and make-overs that are likely. Make-overs are time-consuming and costly.

20   Here it is with the deadly passive out and some other changes made:

> To produce service pictures efficiently, a standard way of finishing prints can be very important. You should use as few types and sizes of paper as possible, and you should follow the recommended procedure for processing. In this way, you will make fewer errors, and have to re-do less work. You save time and money.

Associated with the deadly passive, as you might see from the two passages above, is the use of abstract nouns and adjectives for verbs. Verbs always live; nouns and adjectives just sit there, and abstract nouns aren't even there. Of course, there are a number of other ways of undoing the passivity of the passage I quoted, and of making other improvements, just as there were other ways of handling any of the specimens I have cited in the train of horrors accompanying my pageant of sins.

21   Finally we come to Sin 7, the one considered the deadliest by many, and not only by teachers of English but by technical writers and technologists of various sorts: *Mechanical Errors.* I don't think this sin the deadliest of all. It does happen to be the easiest one to recognize, the one easiest to deal with "quantitatively," so to speak, and the easiest one to resist. I suppose it is considered deadliest because then those who avoid it can so quickly feel virtuous. It can promptly be handled by good works alone. Actually most technical writing happens to be mechanically impeccable; not one of the examples I have used tonight had very much mechanically wrong with it. If anything, technical people tend to make too much of formal mechanisms. I remember working with a physicist who had much trouble saying anything in writing. While his general

incapacity to write was almost total, one thing he did know, and know firmly, and that was that a split infinitive was to be abhorred. That, and using a preposition to end a sentence with. He could never communicate the simplest notion coherently, but he never split an infinitive or left a preposition at the end of a sentence. If Nobel Prizes were to be awarded for never splitting infinitives or for encapsulating prepositions within sentences, he would be a leading candidate.

22   There are a handful of mechanical errors which are relevant to technical writing, and these are important because they are so common, especially in combination with other sins. (Split infinitives or sentence-ending prepositions, need I say, are not among them.) These are dangling participles and other types of poorly placed modifiers, and ambiguous references. There are others, a good number of others, but the ones I mention creep in most insidiously and most often.

23   Here are some examples stripped down to emphasize the errors:

> *Raising the temperature, the thermostat failed to function.*
> Who or what raised the temperature? Not the thermostat; I presume; and if it did somehow, as the result of current flowing in its wiring, then this ought to be said quite plainly.

> *The apparatus is inappropriately situated in the corner since it is too small.*
> What is too small? Apparatus or corner?

> *Every element in the device must not be considered to be subject to abnormal stress.*
> What is meant here is that "Not every element in the apparatus must be considered subject to abnormal stress," almost the opposite of the original taken literally.

24   I should like to conclude by emphasizing something I glanced at in my introduction, that the seven sins of technical writing are to be avoided not so much by a specific awareness of each, accompanied by specific penance for each, as by a much more general awareness, by an attitude toward subject matter, writing process, and reader that can best be described only as "respectful." You will not help yourself very much if you rely on such purely mechanical aids as Rudolf Flesch's formulas for "readable writing," or on slide rules measuring readability, much as you may be tempted to do so. These can be devil's snares, ways to make you think you are avoiding sin. There are no general texts, either, at present that will help you in more than very minor ways. The only aids you can safely depend on are the good book itself, that is, a good dictionary (there are many poor ones), any of the several volumes by H. W Fowler, and occasional essays, here and there, by George Orwell, Jacques Barzun, Herbert Read, Somerset Maugham, and others. And these, I stress, can only be *aids*. What is most important in eliminating sin in technical writing is general attitude—as it may well be in eliminating sin anywhere.

25   I repeat that technical writing must be as rationally shaped as a technical object. A piece of technical writing, after all, is something that is shaped into being for a special purpose, much as a technical object. The design engineer should be guided in his work by the requirements of function almost alone. (Of course, if he happens to have a boss who likes to embellish the object with useless doo-dads, why then he may have to modify his work accordingly to keep his job—as automobile designers do every day; but we try never to have in mind unreasonable situations of this sort.) It is as pointless for the design engineer to use three bolts where one would do (both for safety and function), to make an object square when its use dictates it should be round, to take the long way through a process when there is a short way, as it is for the technical writer to commit any of the sins I have mentioned. Technical writing— informative writing of any sort—should be as clean, as functional, as inevitable as any modern machine designed to do a job well. If I will not be misunderstood in throwing out this thought, I should like to suggest to you that good technical writing should be like good poetry—every word in its exact place for maximum effect, no word readily replaceable by another, not a word too many or too few, and the whole combination, so to speak, invisible, not calling attention to its structure, seemingly effortless, perfectly adapted to its subject.

26   If one takes this general approach to the shaping of a piece of technical writing, and there really can't be much excuse for any other, then there is no need to worry about any of the sins I mention. Virtue may not come at once or automatically, for good writing never comes without effort, however fine one's intentions, but it will certainly come, and perhaps even bring with it that same satisfaction the creative engineer experiences. Technical writing cleansed of its sins is no less worthy, no less impressive, an enterprise than good engineering itself. Like mathematics to physics, technical writing is a handmaid to technology, but like mathematics, too, it can be a helpmate, that is, an equal partner. But it can achieve this reward of virtue only by emphasizing the virtues of writing equally with those of technology.

The Seven Sins of Technical Writing

Questions on Content, Style, and Structure

1. How do the standards for technical writing compare to those for other kinds of writing, according to Freedman? Why?
2. Why does Freedman mention his job experiences in paragraph 2?
3. Why does Freedman refer to travelling by ox-cart and wearing burlap dress in paragraph 3?

4. What are the results of poor technical writing?
5. List the seven sins. Does Freedman commit any of them in his essay?
6. The seven sins may be avoided by adopting what attitude toward the writing process?
7. Evaluate Freedman's use of illustration. Does he use enough examples to make his points clear? What other means does he use to clarify his advice?
8. According to Freedman, which mechanical errors are the most "sinful" to technical writers?
9. Point out the analogies used in paragraph 25. Are they effective?
10. What are some of the transition devices Freedman uses to help him move from paragraph to paragraph in this essay?
11. Do you think that Freedman's list of "sins" is applicable only to technical writing? Why/why not?

Vocabulary

implicitly (3)   elliptical (6)   pretentious (11)
profusion (3)   diction (6)   locutions (17)
reiterate (4)   indisputable (8)   impeccable (21)
avarice (4)   intrinsic (10)   abhorred (21)
edifying (5)   idiomatic (10)   encapsulating (21)
                                                insidiously (22)

Suggestions for Writing

1. Select a piece of technical writing and evaluate it according to Freedman's standards.
2. Write a short essay on some scientific or technical subject in which you avoid all seven sins.
3. Write a paragraph on some scientific or technical subject in which you commit the seven sins; exchange your paragraph with a classmate and then rewrite each other's sentences in clear, precise prose.

Politics and the English Language
George Orwell

George Orwell was the pseudonym of Eric Blair, well-known British novelist and essayist. Two of his most popular books include *Animal Farm* (1945), a political satire, and *1984* (1949), a novel depicting life in a totalitarian society under the watchful eye of "Big Brother." This essay originally appeared in *Horizon* in 1946 and is included in *Shooting an Elephant and Other Essays* (1950).

1   Most people who bother with the matter at all would admit that the English language is in a bad way, but it is generally assumed that we cannot by conscious action do anything about it. Our civilization is decadent and our language—so the argument runs—must inevitably share in the general collapse. It follows that any struggle against the abuse of language is a sentimantal archaism, like preferring candles to electric light or hansom cabs to aeroplanes. Underneath this lies the half-conscious belief that language is a natural growth and not an instrument which we shape for our own purposes.

2   Now, it is clear that the decline of a language must ultimately have political and economic causes: it is not due simply to the bad influence of this or that individual writer. But an effect can become a cause, reinforcing the original cause and producing the same effect in an intensified form, and so on indefinitely. A man may take to drink because he feels himself to be a failure, and then fail all the more completely because he drinks. It is rather the same thing that is happening to the English language. It becomes ugly and inaccurate because our thoughts are foolish, but the slovenliness of our language makes it easier for us to have foolish thoughts. The point is that the process is reversible. Modern English, especially written English, is full of bad habits which spread by imitation and which can be avoided if one is willing to take the necessary trouble. If one gets rid of these habits one can think more clearly, and to think clearly is a necessary first step towards political regeneration: so that the fight against bad English is not frivolous and is not the exclusive concern of professional writers. I will come back to this presently, and I hope that by that time the meaning of what I have said here will have become clearer. Meanwhile, here are five specimens of the English language as it is now habitually written.

3   These five passages have not been picked out because they are especially bad—I could have quoted far worse if I had chosen—but because they illustrate various of the mental vices from which we now suffer. They are a little below the average, but are fairly representative samples.

I number them so that I can refer back to them when necessary:

1. I am not, indeed, sure whether it is not true to say that the Milton who once seemed not unlike a seventeenth-century Shelley had not become, out of an experience ever more bitter in each year, more alien [sic] to the founder of that Jesuit sect which nothing could induce him to tolerate.

Professor Harold Laski (Essay in Freedom of Expression).

2. Above all, we cannot play ducks and drakes with a native battery of idioms which prescribes such egregious collocations of vocables as the Basic *put up with* for *tolerate* or *put at a loss* for *bewilder*.

Professor Lancelot Hogben (Interglossa).

3. On the one side we have the free personality: by definition it is not neurotic, for it has neither conflict nor dream. Its desires, such as they are, are transparent, for they are just what institutional approval keeps in the forefront of consciousness; another institutional pattern would alter their number and intensity; there is little in them that is natural, irreducible, or culturally dangerous. But *on the other side*, the social bond itself is nothing but the mutual reflection of these self-secure integrities. Recall the definition of love. Is not this the very picture of a small academic? Where is there a place in this hall of mirrors for either personality or fraternity?

Essay on psychology in Politics (New York).

4. All the 'best people' from the gentlemen's clubs, and all the frantic fascist captains, united in common hatred of Socialism and bestial horror of the rising tide of the mass revolutionary movement, have turned to acts of provocation, to foul incendiarism, to medieval legends of poisoned wells, to legalize their own destruction of proletarian organizations, and rouse the agitated petty-bourgeoisie to chauvinistic fervour on behalf of the fight against the revolutionary way out of the crisis.

Communist pamphlet.

5. If a new spirit *is* to be infused into this old country, there is one thorny and contentious reform which must be tackled, and that is the humanization and galvanization of the B.B.C. Timidity here will bespeak cancer and atrophy of the soul. The heart of Britain may be sound and of strong beat, for instance, but the British lion's roar at present is like that of Bottom in Shakespeare's *Midsummer Night's Dream*—as gentle as any sucking dove. A virile new Britain cannot continue indefinitely to be traduced in the eyes, or rather ears, of the world by the effete languors of Langham Place, brazenly masquerading as "standard English". When the Voice of Britain is heard at nine o'clock, better far and infinitely less ludicrous to hear aitches honestly dropped than the present priggish, inflated, inhibited, school-ma'amish arch braying of blameless bashful mewing maidens!

Letter in Tribune.

4   Each of these passages has faults of its own, but, quite apart from avoidable ugliness, two qualities are common to all of them. The first is staleness of imagery: the other is lack of precision. The writer either has a meaning and cannot express it, or he inadvertently says something else, or he is almost indifferent as to whether his words mean anything or not. This mixture of vagueness and sheer incompetence is the most marked characteristic of modern English prose, and especially of any kind of political writing. As soon as certain topics are raised, the concrete melts into the abstract and no one seems to think of turns of speech that are not hackneyed: prose consists less and less of *words* chosen for the sake of their meaning, and more and more of *phrases* tacked together like the sections of a prefabricated hen-house. I list below, with notes and examples, various of the tricks by means of which the work of prose-construction is habitually dodged:

Dying Metaphors

5   A newly invented metaphor assists thought by evoking a visual image, while on the other hand a metaphor which is technically "dead" (e.g. *iron resolution*) has in effect reverted to being an ordinary word and can generally be used without loss of vividness. But in between these two classes there is a huge dump of worn-out metaphors which have lost all evocative power and are merely used because they save people the trouble of inventing phrases for themselves. Examples are: *Ring the changes on, take up the cudgels for, toe the line, ride roughshod over, stand shoulder to shoulder with, play into the hands of, no axe to grind, grist to the mill, fishing in troubled waters, on the order of the day, Achilles' heel, swan song, hotbed.* Many of these are used without knowledge of their meaning (what is a "rift", for instance?), and incompatible metaphors are frequently mixed, a sure sign that the writer is not interested in what he is saying. Some metaphors now current have been twisted out of their original meaning without those who use them even being aware of the fact. For example, *toe the line* is sometimes written *tow the line.* Another example is *the hammer and the anvil*, now always used with the implication that the anvil gets the worst of it. In real life it is always the anvil that breaks the hammer, never the other way about: a writer who stopped to think what he was saying would be aware of this, and would avoid perverting the original phrase.

Operators, *or* Verbal False Limbs

6   These save the trouble of picking out appropriate verbs and nouns, and at the same time pad each sentence with extra syllables which give it an appearance of symmetry. Characteristic phrases are: *render inoperative, militate against, make contact with, be subjected to, give rise to, give grounds for, have the effect of, play a leading part (role) in, make itself*

felt, take effect, exhibit a tendency to, serve the purpose of, etc., etc. The keynote is the elimination of simple verbs. Instead of being a single word, such as *break, stop, spoil, mend, kill,* a verb becomes a *phrase,* made up of a noun or adjective tacked on to some general-purpose verb such as *prove, serve, form, play, render.* In addition, the passive voice is wherever possible used in preference to the active, and noun constructions are used instead of gerunds (*by examination of* instead of *by examining*). The range of verbs is further cut down by means of the *-ise* and *de-* formation, and the banal statements are given an appearance of profundity by means of the *not un-* formation. Simple conjunctions and prepositions are replaced by such phrases as *with respect to, having regard to, the fact that, by dint of, in view of, in the interests of, on the hypothesis that;* and the ends of sentences are saved from anticlimax by such resounding commonplaces as *greatly to be desired, cannot be left out of account, a development to be expected in the near future, deserving of serious consideration, brought to a satisfactory conclusion,* and so on and so forth.

Pretentious Diction

7   Words like *phenomenon, element, individual* (as noun), *objective, categorical, effective, virtual, basic, primary, promote, constitute, exhibit, exploit, utilize, eliminate, liquidate,* are used to dress up simple statements and give an air of scientific impartiality to biased judgments. Adjectives like *epoch-making, epic, historic, unforgettable, triumphant, age-old, inevitable, inexorable, veritable,* are used to dignify the sordid processes of international politics, while writing that aims at glorifying war usually takes on an archaic colour, its characteristic words being: *realm, throne, chariot, mailed fist, trident, sword, shield, buckler, banner, jackboot, clarion.* Foreign words and expressions such as *cul de sac, ancien régime, deus ex machina, mutatis mutandis, status quo, Gleichschaltung, Weltanschauung,* are used to give an air of culture and elegance. Except for the useful abbreviations *i.e., e.g.,* and *etc.,* there is no real need for any of the hundreds of foreign phrases now current in English. Bad writers, and especially scientific, political and sociological writers, are nearly always haunted by the notion that Latin or Greek words are grander than Saxon ones, and unnecessary words like *expedite, ameliorate, predict, extraneous, deracinated, clandestine, subaqueous* and hundreds of others constantly gain ground from their Anglo-Saxon opposite numbers.[1] The jargon peculiar to Marxist writing (*hyena, hangman, cannibal, petty bourgeois, these gentry, lacquey, flunkey, mad dog,*

---

[1] An interesting illustration of this is the way in which the English flower names which were in use till very recently are being ousted by Greek ones, *snapdragon* becoming *antirrhinum, forget-me-not* becoming *myosotis,* etc. It is hard to see any practical reason for this change of fashion: it is probably due to an instinctive turning-away from the more homely word and a vague feeling that the Greek word is scientific. [Orwell's note]

White Guard, etc.) consists largely of words and phrases translated from Russian, German or French; but the normal way of coining a new word is to use a Latin or Greek root with the appropriate affix and, where necessary, the *-ise* formation. It is often easier to make up words of this kind (*deregionalise, impermissible, extramarital, nonfragmentatory* and so forth) than to think up the English words that will cover one's meaning. The result, in general, is an increase in slovenliness and vagueness.

Meaningless Words

8   In certain kinds of writing, particularly in art criticism and literary criticism, it is normal to come across long passages which are almost completely lacking in meaning.[2] Words like *romantic, plastic, values, human, dead, sentimental, natural, vitality,* as used in art criticism, are strictly meaningless in the sense that they not only do not point to any discoverable object, but are hardly ever expected to do so by the reader. When one critic writes, "The outstanding feature of Mr. X's work is its living quality", while another writes, "The immediately striking thing about Mr. X's work is its peculiar deadness", the reader accepts this as a simple difference of opinion. If words like *black* and *white* were involved, instead of the jargon words *dead* and *living,* he would see at once that language was being used in an improper way. Many political words are similarly abused. The word *Fascism* has now no meaning except in so far as it signifies "something not desirable". The words *democracy, socialism, freedom, patriotic, realistic, justice,* have each of them several different meanings which cannot be reconciled with one another. In the case of a word like *democracy,* not only is there no agreed definition, but the attempt to make one is resisted from all sides. It is almost universally felt that when we call a country democratic we are praising it: consequently the defenders of every kind of régime claim that it is a democracy, and fear that they might have to stop using the word if it were tied down to any one meaning. Words of this kind are often used in a consciously dishonest way. That is, the person who uses them has his own private definition, but allows his hearer to think he means something quite different. Statements like *Marshal Pétain was a true patriot, The Soviet Press is the freest in the world, The Catholic Church is opposed to persecution,* are almost always made with intent to deceive. Other words used on variable meanings, in most cases more or less dishonestly,

[2] Example: "Comfort's catholicity of perception and image, strangely Whitmanesque in range, almost the exact opposite in aesthetic compulsion, continues to evoke that trembling atmospheric accumulative hinting at a cruel, an inexorably serene timelessness ... Wrey Gardiner scores by aiming at simple bull's-eyes with precision. Only they are not so simple, and through this contented sadness runs more than the surface bitter-sweet of resignation." (*Poetry Quarterly.*) [Orwell's note]

are: *class, totalitarian, science, progressive, reactionary, bourgeois, equality.*

9   Now that I have made this catalogue of swindles and perversions, let me give another example of the kind of writing that they lead to. This time it must of its nature be an imaginary one. I am going to translate a passage of good English into modern English of the worst sort. Here is a well-known verse from *Ecclesiastes:*

> I returned and saw under the sun, that the race is not to the swift, nor the battle to the strong, neither yet bread to the wise, nor yet riches to men of understanding, nor yet favour to men of skill; but time and chance happeneth to them all.

Here it is in modern English:

> Objective consideration of contemporary phenomena compels the conclusion that success or failure in competitive activities exhibits no tendency to be commensurate with innate capacity, but that a considerable element of the unpredictable must invariably be taken into account.

10   This is a parody, but not a very gross one. Exhibit 3, above, for instance, contains several patches of the same kind of English. It will be seen that I have not made a full translation. The beginning and ending of the sentence follow the original meaning fairly closely, but in the middle the concrete illustrations—race, battle, bread—dissolve into the vague phrase "success or failure in competitive activities". This had to be so, because no modern writer of the kind I am discussing—no one capable of using phrases like "objective consideration of contemporary phenomena"—would ever tabulate his thoughts in that precise and detailed way. The whole tendency of modern prose is away from concreteness. Now analyse these two sentences a little more closely. The first contains 49 words but only 60 syllables, and all its words are those of everyday life. The second contains 38 words of 90 syllables: eighteen of its words are from Latin roots, and one from Greek. The first sentence contains six vivid images, and only one phrase ("time and chance") that could be called vague. The second contains not a single fresh, arresting phrase, and in spite of its ninety syllables it gives only a shortened version of the meaning contained in the first. Yet without a doubt it is the second kind of sentence that is gaining ground in modern English. I do not want to exaggerate. This kind of writing is not yet universal, and outcrops of simplicity will occur here and there in the worst-written page. Still, if you or I were told to write a few lines on the uncertainty of human fortunes, we should probably come much nearer to my imaginary sentence than to the one from *Ecclesiastes.*

11   As I have tried to show, modern writing at its worst does not consist in picking out words for the sake of their meaning and inventing images in order to make the meaning clearer. It consists in gumming together

long strips of words which have already been set in order by someone
else, and making the results presentable by sheer humbug. The attraction
of this way of writing is that it is easy. It is easier—even quicker, once
you have the habit—to say *In my opinion it is a not unjustifiable assumption that* than to say *I think.* If you use ready-made phrases,
you not only don't have to hunt about for words; you also don't have to
bother with the rhythms of your sentences, since these phrases are generally so arranged as to be more or less euphonious. When you are composing in a hurry—when you are dictating to a stenographer, for instance,
or making a public speech—it is natural to fall into a pretentious, Latin-
ized style. Tags like *a consideration which we should do well to bear
in mind* or *a conclusion to which all of us would readily assent* will
save many a sentence from coming down with a bump. By using stale
metaphors, similes and idioms, you save much mental effort, at the cost
of leaving your meaning vague, not only for your reader but for yourself.
This is the significance of mixed metaphors. The sole aim of a metaphor
is to call up a visual image. When these images clash—as in *The Fascist
octopus has sung its swan song, the jackboot is thrown into the melting
pot*—it can be taken as certain that the writer is not seeing a mental
image of the objects he is naming; in other words he is not really thinking. Look again at the examples I gave at the beginning of this essay.
Professor Laski (1) uses five negatives in fifty-three words. One of these
is superfluous, making nonsense of the whole passage, and in addition
there is the slip *alien* for *akin,* making further nonsense, and several
avoidable pieces of clumsiness which increase the general vagueness.
Professor Hogben (2) plays ducks and drakes with a battery which is able
to write prescriptions, and, while disapproving of the everyday phrase
put up with, is unwilling to look *egregious* up in the dictionary and see
what it means. (3), if one takes an uncharitable attitude towards it, is
simply meaningless: probably one could work out its intended meaning
by reading the whole of the article in which it occurs. In (4), the writer
knows more or less what he wants to say, but an accumulation of stale
phrases chokes him like tea leaves blocking a sink. In (5), words and
meaning have almost parted company. People who write in this manner
usually have a general emotional meaning—they dislike one thing and
want to espress solidarity with another—but they are not interested in
the detail of what they are saying. A scrupulous writer, in every sentence
that he writes, will ask himself at least four questions, thus: What am
I trying to say? What words will express it? What image or idiom will
make it clearer? Is this image fresh enough to have an effect? And he will
probably ask himself two more: Could I put it more shortly? Have I said
anything that is avoidably ugly? But you are not obliged to go to all this
trouble. You can shirk it by simply throwing your mind open and letting
the ready-made phrases come crowding in. They will construct your sen-

tences for you—even think your thoughts for you, to a certain extent—and at need they will perform the important service of partially concealing your meaning even from yourself. It is at this point that the special connection between politics and the debasement of language becomes clear.

12   In our time it is broadly true that political writing is bad writing. Where it is not true, it will generally be found that the writer is some kind of rebel, expressing his private opinions and not a "party line". Orthodoxy, of whatever colour, seems to demand a lifeless, imitative style. The political dialects to be found in pamphlets, leading articles, manifestos, White Papers and the speeches of under-secretaries do, of course, vary from party to party, but they are all alike in that one almost never finds in them a fresh, vivid, home-made turn of speech. When one watches some tired hack on the platform mechanically repeating the familiar phrases—*bestial atrocities, iron heel, bloodstained tyranny, free peoples of the world, stand shoulder to shoulder*—one often has a curious feeling that one is not watching a live human being but some kind of dummy: a feeling which suddenly becomes stronger at moments when the light catches the speaker's spectacles and turns them into blank discs which seem to have no eyes behind them. And this is not altogether fanciful. A speaker who uses that kind of phraseology has gone some distance towards turning himself into a machine. The appropriate noises are coming out of his larynx, but his brain is not involved as it would be if he were choosing his words for himself. If the speech he is making is one that he is accustomed to make over and over again, he may be almost unconscious of what he is saying, as one is when one utters the responses in church. And this reduced state of consciousness, if not indispensable, is at any rate favourable to political conformity.

13   In our time, political speech and writing are largely the defense of the indefensible. Things like the continuance of British rule in India, the Russian purges and deportations, the dropping of the atom bombs on Japan, can indeed be defended, but only by arguments which are too brutal for most people to face, and which do not square with the professed aims of political parties. Thus political language has to consist largely of euphemism, question-begging and sheer cloudy vagueness. Defenseless villages are bombarded from the air, the inhabitants driven out into the countryside, the cattle machine-gunned, the huts set on fire with incendiary bullets: this is called *pacification*. Millions of peasants are robbed of their farms and sent trudging along the roads with no more than they can carry: this is called *transfer of population* or *rectification of frontiers*. People are imprisoned for years without trial, or shot in the back of the neck or sent to die of scurvy in Arctic lumber camps: this called *elimination of unreliable elements*. Such phraseology is needed if one wants to name things without calling up mental pictures of them. Consider for instance some comfortable English professor defending Russian totali-

tarianism. He cannot say outright, "I believe in killing off your opponents when you can get good results by doing so". Probably, therefore, he will say something like this:

> While freely conceding that the Soviet régime exhibits certain features which the humanitarian may be inclined to deplore, we must, I think, agree that a certain curtailment of the right to political opposition is an unavoidable concomitant of transitional periods, and that the rigours which the Russian people have been called upon to undergo have been amply justified in the sphere of concrete achievement.

14   The inflated style is itself a kind of euphemism. A mass of Latin words falls upon the facts like soft snow, blurring the outlines and covering up all the details. The great enemy of clear language is insincerity. When there is a gap between one's real and one's declared aims, one turns as it were instinctively to long words and exhausted idioms, like a cuttlefish squirting out ink. In our age there is no such thing as "keeping out of politics". All issues are political issues, and politics itself is a mass of lies, evasions, folly, hatred and schizophrenia. When the general atmosphere is bad, language must suffer. I should expect to find—this is a guess which I have not sufficient knowledge to verify—that the German, Russian and Italian languages have all deteriorated in the last ten or fifteen years, as a result of dictatorship.

15   But if thought corrupts language, language can also corrupt thought. A bad usage can spread by tradition and imitation, even among people who should and do know better. The debased language that I have been discussing is in some ways very convenient. Phrases like *a not unjustifiable assumption, leaves much to be desired, would serve no good purpose, a consideration which we should do well to bear in mind,* are a continuous temptation, a packet of aspirins always at one's elbow. Look back through this essay, and for certain you will find that I have again and again committed the very faults I am protesting against. By this morning's post I have received a pamphlet dealing with conditions in Germany. The author tells me that he "felt impelled" to write it. I open it at random, and here is almost the first sentence that I see: "(The Allies) have an opportunity not only of achieving a radical transformation of Germany's social and political structure in such a way as to avoid a nationalistic reaction in Germany itself, but at the same time of laying the foundations of a co-operative and unified Europe." You see, he "feels impelled" to write—feels, presumably, that he has something new to say—and yet his words, like cavalry horses answering the bugle, group themselves automatically into the familiar dreary pattern. This invasion of one's mind by ready-made phrases *(lay the foundations, achieve a radical transformation)* can only be prevented if one is constantly on guard against them, and every such phrase anaesthetizes a portion of one's brain.

16   I said earlier that the decadence of our language is probably curable. Those who deny this would argue, if they produced an argument at all, that language merely reflects existing social conditions, and that we cannot influence its development by any direct tinkering with words and constructions. So far as the general tone or spirit of a language goes, this may be true, but it is not true in detail. Silly words and expressions have often disappeared, not through any evolutionary process but owing to the conscious action of a minority. Two recent examples were *explore every avenue* and *leave no stone unturned*, which were killed by the jeers of a few journalists. There is a long list of flyblown metaphors which could similarly be got rid of if enough people would interest themselves in the job; and it should also be possible to laugh the *not un-* formation out of existence,[3] to reduce the amount of Latin and Greek in the average sentence, to drive out foreign phrases and strayed scientific words, and, in general, to make pretentiousness unfashionable. But all these are minor points. The defense of the English language implies more than this, and perhaps it is best to start by saying what it does *not* imply.

17   To begin with it has nothing to do with archaism, with the salvaging of obsolete words and turns of speech, or with the setting up of a "standard English" which must never be departed from. On the contrary, it is especially concerned with the scrapping of every word or idiom which has outworn its usefulness. It has nothing to do with correct grammar and syntax, which are of no importance so long as one makes one's meaning clear, or with the avoidance of Americanisms, or with having what is called a "good prose style". On the other hand it is not concerned with fake simplicity and the attempt to make written English colloquial. Nor does it even imply in every case preferring the Saxon word to the Latin one, though it does imply using the fewest and shortest words that will cover one's meaning. What is above all needed is to let the meaning choose the word, and not the other way about. In prose, the worst thing one can do with words is to surrender to them. When you think of a concrete object, you think wordlessly, and then, if you want to describe the thing you have been visualizing, you probably hunt about till you find the exact words that seem to fit. When you think of something abstract you are more inclined to use words from the start, and unless you make a conscious effort to prevent it, the existing dialect will come rushing in and do the job for you, at the expense of blurring or even changing your meaning. Probably it is better to put off using words as long as possible and get one's meaning as clear as one can through pictures or sensations. Afterwards one can choose—not simply *accept*—the phrases that will best cover the meaning, and then switch round and

---

[3] One can cure oneself of the *not un-* formation by memorizing this sentence: *A not unblack dog was chasing a not unsmall rabbit across a not ungreen field.* [Orwell's note]

decide what impression one's words are likely to make on another person. The last effort of the mind cuts out all stale or mixed images, all prefabricated phrases, needless repetitions, and humbug and vagueness generally. But one can often be in doubt about the effect of a word or a phrase, and one needs rules that one can rely on when instinct fails. I think the following rules will cover most cases:

i. Never use a metaphor, simile or other figure of speech which you are used to seeing in print.

ii. Never use a long word where a short one will do.

iii. If it is possible to cut a word out, always cut it out.

iv. Never use the passive where you can use the active.

v. Never use a foreign phrase, a scientific word or a jargon word if you can think of an everyday English equivalent.

vi. Break any of these rules sooner than say anything outright barbarous.

18   These rules sound elementary, and so they are, but they demand a deep change of attitude in anyone who has grown used to writing in the style now fashionable. One could keep all of them and still write bad English, but one could not write the kind of stuff that I quoted in those five specimens at the beginning of this article.

19   I have not here been considering the literary use of language, but merely language as an instrument for expressing and not for concealing or preventing thought. Stuart Chase and others have come near to claiming that all abstract words are meaningless, and have used this as a pretext for advocating a kind of political quietism. Since you don't know what Fascism is, how can you struggle against Fascism? One need not swallow such absurdities as this, but one ought to recognize that the present political chaos is connected with the decay of language, and that one can probably bring about some improvement by starting at the verbal end. If you simplify your English, you are freed from the worst follies of orthodoxy. You cannot speak any of the necessary dialects, and when you make a stupid remark its stupidity will be obvious, even to yourself. Political language—and with variations this is true of all political parties, from Conservatives to Anarchists—is designed to make lies sound truthful and murder respectable, and to give an appearance of solidity to pure wind. One cannot change this all in a moment, but one can at least change one's own habits, and from time to time one can even, if one jeers loudly enough, send some worn-out and useless phrase—some *jackboot, Achilles' heel, hotbed, melting pot, acid test, veritable inferno* or other lump of verbal refuse—into the dustbin where it belongs.

Politics and the English Language

Questions on Content, Style, and Structure

1. What is Orwell's thesis?
2. What is the difference between a fresh metaphor and a dying one?
3. What's wrong with using what Orwell calls "operators, or verbal false limbs"?
4. How does Orwell use parody to communicate one of his points?
5. According to Orwell, modern writing at its worst is composed in what way?
6. Why does Orwell criticize political speech? What is a euphemism and why is it used frequently in politics?
7. How does Orwell counter the argument that we cannot influence the development of language? What plan does he advocate?
8. What rules does Orwell give writers?
9. What is Orwell's chief means of supporting his points throughout this essay? Is it effective?
10. Cite some examples of Orwell's use of figurative language. Is his imagery fresh? Effective?
11. This essay was written in 1945; are any of Orwell's examples irrelevant now? If so, does that seriously affect the effectiveness of his essay?

Vocabulary

decadent (1)
archaism (1)
slovenliness (2)
hackneyed (4)
evocative (5)
profundity (6)

sordid (7)
commensurate (9)
innate (10)
euphonious (11)
superfluous (11)
scrupulous (11)

idiom (11)
debasement (11)
incendiary (13)
curtailment (13)
concomitant (13)
barbarous (17)

Suggestions for Writing

1. Select a piece of political writing or an advertisement and analyze it according to Orwell's criteria.
2. Using Orwell's parody of the verse from *Ecclesiastes* as a model, rewrite in modern jargon a well-known passage from the Bible or some other famous text.
3. Find five samples of bad writing. Rewrite each one, and explain your reasons for making the changes you felt necessary.

Love Is a Fallacy
Max Shulman

Max Shulman is an American humorist whose books include *Barefoot Boy with Cheek* (1943), *The Feather Merchants* (1944), and *Rally Round the Flag, Boys* (1957). This selection is from *The Many Lives of Dobie Gillis* (1951), which Shulman also made into a television series.

1   Cool was I and logical. Keen, calculating, perspicacious, acute and astute—I was all of these. My brain was as powerful as a dynamo, as precise as a chemist's scales, as penetrating as a scalpel. And—think of it—I was only eighteen.

2   It is not often that one so young has such a giant intellect. Take, for example, Petey Burch, my roommate at the University of Minnesota. Same age, same background, but dumb as an ox. A nice enough fellow, you understand, but nothing upstairs. Emotional type. Unstable. Impressionable. Worst of all, a faddist. Fads, I submit, are the very negation of reason. To be swept up in every new craze that comes along, to surrender yourself to idiocy just because everybody else is doing it—this, to me, is the acme of mindlessness. Not, however, to Petey.

3   One afternoon I found Petey lying on his bed with an expression of such distress on his face that I immediately diagnosed appendicitis. "Don't move," I said. "Don't take a laxative. I'll get a doctor."

4   "Raccoon," he mumbled thickly.

5   "Raccoon?" I said, pausing in my flight.

6   "I want a raccoon coat," he wailed.

7   I perceived that his trouble was not physical, but mental. "Why do you want a raccoon coat?"

8   "I should have known it," he cried, pounding his temples. "I should have known they'd come back when the Charleston came back. Like a fool I spent all my money for textbooks, and now I can't get a raccoon coat."

9   "Can you mean," I said incredulously, "that people are actually wearing raccoon coats again?"

10 "All the Big Men on Campus are wearing them. Where've you been?"

11 "In the library," I said, naming a place not frequented by Big Men on Campus.

12 He leaped from the bed and paced the room. "I've got to have a raccoon coat," he said passionately. "I've got to!"

13 "Petey, why? Look at it rationally. Raccoon coats are unsanitary. They shed. They smell bad. They weigh too much. They're unsightly. They—"

14   "You don't understand," he interrupted impatiently. "It's the thing to do. Don't you want to be in the swim?"

15   "No," I said truthfully.

16   "Well, I do," he declared. "I'd give anything for a raccoon coat. Anything!"

17   My brain, that precision instrument, slipped into high gear. "Anything?" I asked, looking at him narrowly.

18   "Anything," he affirmed in ringing tones.

19   I stroked my chin thoughtfully. It so happened that I knew where to get my hands on a raccoon coat. My father had had one in his undergraduate days; it lay now in a trunk in the attic back home. It also happened that Petey had something I wanted. He didn't *have* it exactly, but at least he had first rights on it. I refer to his girl, Polly Espy.

20   I had long coveted Polly Espy. Let me emphasize that my desire for this young woman was not emotional in nature. She was, to be sure, a girl who excited the emotions, but I was not one to let my heart rule my head. I wanted Polly for a shrewdly calculated, entirely cerebral reason.

21   I was a freshman in law school. In a few years I would be out in practice. I was well aware of the importance of the right kind of wife in furthering a lawyer's career. The successful lawyers I had observed were, almost without exception, married to beautiful, gracious, intelligent women. With one omission, Polly fitted these specifications perfectly.

22   Beautiful she was. She was not yet of pin-up proportions, but I felt sure that time would supply the lack. She already had the makings.

23   Gracious she was. By gracious I mean full of graces. She had an erectness of carriage, an ease of bearing, a poise that clearly indicated the best of breeding. At table her manners were exquisite. I had seen her at the Kozy Korner eating the specialty of the house—a sandwich that contained scraps of pot roast, gravy, chopped nuts, and a dipper of sauerkraut—without even getting her fingers moist.

24   Intelligent she was not. In fact, she veered in the opposite direction. But I believed that under my guidance she would smarten up. At any rate, it was worth a try. It is, after all, easier to make a beautiful dumb girl smart than to make an ugly smart girl beautiful.

25   "Petey," I said, "are you in love with Polly Espy?"

26   "I think she's a keen kid," he replied, "but I don't know if you'd call it love. Why?"

27   "Do you," I asked, "have any kind of formal arrangement with her? I mean are you going steady or anything like that?"

28   "No. We see each other quite a bit, but we both have other dates. Why?"

29   "Is there," I asked, "any other man for whom she has a particular fondness?"

30   "Not that I know of. Why?"

31   I nodded with satisfaction. "In other words, if you were out of the picture, the field would be open. Is that right?"

32   "I guess so. What are you getting at?"

33   "Nothing, nothing," I said innocently, and took my suitcase out of the closet.

34   "Where are you going?" asked Petey.

35   "Home for the weekend." I threw a few things into the bag.

36   "Listen," he said, clutching my arm eagerly, "while you're home, you couldn't get some money from your old man, could you, and lend it to me so I can buy a raccoon coat?"

37   "I may do better than that," I said with a mysterious wink and closed my bag and left.

38   "Look," I said to Petey when I got back Monday morning. I threw open the suitcase and revealed the huge, hairy, gamy object that my father had worn in his Stutz Bearcat in 1925.

39   "Holy Toledo!" said Petey reverently. He plunged his hands into the raccoon coat and then his face. "Holy Toledo!" he repeated fifteen or twenty times.

40   "Would you like it?" I asked.

41   "Oh yes!" he cried, clutching the greasy pelt to him. Then a canny look came into his eyes. "What do you want for it?"

42   "Your girl," I said, mincing no words.

43   "Polly?" he said in a horrified whisper. "You want Polly?"

44   "That's right."

45   He flung the coat from him. "Never," he said stoutly.

46   I shrugged. "Okay. If you don't want to be in the swim, I guess it's your business."

47   I sat down in a chair and pretended to read a book, but out of the corner of my eye I kept watching Petey. He was a torn man. First he looked at the coat with the expression of a waif at a bakery window. Then he turned away and set his jaw resolutely. Then he looked back at the coat, with even more longing in his face. Then he turned away, but with not so much resolution this time. Back and forth his head swiveled, desire waxing, resolution waning. Finally he didn't turn away at all; he just stood and stared with mad lust at the coat.

48   "It isn't as though I was in love with Polly," he said thickly. "Or going steady or anything like that."

49   "That's right," I murmured.

50   "What's Polly to me, or me to Polly?"

51   "Not a thing," said I.

52   "It's just been a casual kick—just a few laughs, that's all."

53   "Try on the coat," said I.

54   He complied. The coat bunched high over his ears and dropped all the way down to his shoe tops. He looked like a mound of dead raccoons. "Fits fine," he said happily.

55   I rose from my chair. "Is it a deal?" I asked, extending my hand.

56   He swallowed. "It's a deal," he said and shook my hand.

57   I had my first date with Polly the following evening. This was in the nature of a survey; I wanted to find out just how much work I had to do to get her mind up to the standard I required. I took her first to dinner. "Gee, that was a delish dinner," she said as we left the restaurant. Then I took her to a movie. "Gee, that was a marvy movie," she said as we left the theater. And then I took her home. "Gee, I had a sensaysh time," she said as she bade me good night.

58   I went back to my room with a heavy heart. I had gravely underestimated the size of my task. This girl's lack of information was terrifying. Nor would it be enough merely to supply her with information. First she had to be taught to *think*. This loomed as a project of no small dimensions, and at first I was tempted to give her back to Petey. But then I got to thinking about her abundant physical charms and about the way she entered a room and the way she handled a knife and fork, and I decided to make an effort.

59   I went about it, as in all things, systematically. I gave her a course in logic. It happened that I, as a law student, was taking a course in logic myself, so I had all the facts at my finger tips. "Polly," I said to her when I picked her up on our next date, "tonight we are going over to the Knoll and talk."

60   "Oo, terrif," she replied. One thing I will say for this girl: you would go far to find another so agreeable.

61   We went to the Knoll, the campus trysting place, and we sat down under an old oak, and she looked at me expectantly. "What are we going to talk about?" she asked.

62   "Logic."

63   She thought this over for a minute and decided she liked it. "Magnif," she said.

64   "Logic," I said, clearing my throat, "is the science of thinking. Before we can think correctly, we must first learn to recognize the common fallacies of logic. These we will take up tonight."

65   "Wow-dow!" she cried, clapping her hands delightedly.

66   I winced, but went bravely on. "First let us examine the fallacy called Dicto Simpliciter."

67   "By all means," she urged, batting her lashes eagerly.

68   "Dicto Simpliciter means an argument based on an unqualified generalization. For example: Exercise is good. Therefore everybody should exercise."

69   "I agree," said Polly earnestly. "I mean exercise is wonderful. I mean it builds the body and everything."

70   "Polly," I said gently, "the argument is a fallacy. *Exercise is good* is an unqualified generalization. For instance, if you have heart disease, exercise is bad, not good. Many people are ordered by their doctors *not*

to exercise. You must *qualify* the generalization. You must say exercise is *usually* good, or exercise is good *for most people.* Otherwise you have committed a Dicto Simpliciter. Do you see?"

71   "No," she confessed. "But this is marvy. Do more! Do more!"

72   "It will be better if you stop tugging at my sleeve," I told her, and when she desisted, I continued. "Next we take up a fallacy called Hasty Generalization. Listen carefully: You can't speak French. I can't speak French. Petey Burch can't speak French. I must therefore conclude that nobody at the University of Minnesota can speak French."

73   "Really?" said Polly, amazed. *"Nobody?"*

74   I hid my exasperation. "Polly, it's a fallacy. The generalization is reached too hastily. There are too few instances to support such a conclusion."

75   "Know any more fallacies?" she asked breathlessly. "This is more fun than dancing even."

76   I fought off a wave of despair. I was getting nowhere with this girl, absolutely nowhere. Still, I am nothing if not persistent. I continued. "Next comes Post Hoc. Listen to this: Let's not take Bill on our picnic. Every time we take him out with us, it rains."

77   "I know somebody just like that," she exclaimed. "A girl back home— Eula Becker, her name is. It never fails. Every single time we take her on a picnic—"

78   "Polly," I said sharply, "it's a fallacy. Eula Becker doesn't *cause* the rain. She has no connection with the rain. You are guilty of Post Hoc if you blame Eula Becker."

79   "I'll never do it again," she promised contritely. "Are you mad at me?"

80   I sighed deeply. "No, Polly, I'm not mad."

81   "Then tell me some more fallacies."

82   "All right. Let's try Contradictory Premises."

83   "Yes, let's," she chirped, blinking her eyes happily.

84   I frowned, but plunged ahead. "Here's an example of Contradictory Premises: If God can do anything, can He make a stone so heavy that He won't be able to lift it?"

85   "Of course," she replied promptly.

86   "But if He can do anything, He can lift the stone," I pointed out.

87   "Yeah," she said thoughtfully. "Well, then I guess He can't make the stone."

88   "But He can do anything," I reminded her.

89   She scratched her pretty, empty head. "I'm all confused," she admitted.

90   "Of course you are. Because when the premises of an argument contradict each other, there can be no argument. If there is an irresistible force, there can be no immovable object. If there is an immovable object, there can be no irresistible force. Get it?"

91   "Tell me some more of this keen stuff," she said eagerly.

92   I consulted my watch. "I think we'd better call it a night. I'll take you home now, and you go over all the things you've learned. We'll have another session tomorrow night."

93   I deposited her at the girls' dormitory, where she assured me that she had had a perfectly terrif evening, and I went glumly home to my room. Petey lay snoring in his bed, the raccoon coat huddled like a great hairy beast at his feet. For a moment I considered waking him and telling him that he could have his girl back. It seemed clear that my project was doomed to failure. The girl simply had a logic-proof head.

94   But then I reconsidered. I had wasted one evening; I might as well waste another. Who knew? Maybe somewhere in the extinct crater of her mind, a few embers still smoldered. Maybe somehow I could fan them into flame. Admittedly it was not a prospect fraught with hope, but I decided to give it one more try.

95   Seated under the oak the next evening I said, "Our first fallacy tonight is called Ad Misericordiam."

96   She quivered with delight.

97   "Listen closely," I said. "A man applies for a job. When the boss asks him what his qualifications are, he replies that he has a wife and six children at home, the wife is a helpless cripple, the children have nothing to eat, no clothes to wear, no shoes on their feet, there are no beds in the house, no coal in the cellar, and winter is coming."

98   A tear rolled down each of Polly's pink cheeks. "Oh, this is awful, awful," she sobbed.

99   "Yes, it's awful," I agreed, "but it's no argument. The man never answered the boss's question about his qualifications. Instead he appealed to the boss's sympathy. He committed the fallacy of Ad Misericordiam. Do you understand?"

100   "Have you got a handkerchief?" she blubbered.

101   I handed her a handkerchief and tried to keep from screaming while she wiped her eyes. "Next," I said in a carefully controlled tone, "we will discuss False Analogy. Here is an example: Students should be allowed to look at their textbooks during examinations. After all, surgeons have X-rays to guide them during an operation, lawyers have briefs to guide them during a trial, carpenters have blueprints to guide them when they are building a house. Why, then, shouldn't students be allowed to look at their textbooks during an examination?"

102   "There now," she said enthusiastically, "is the most marvy idea I've heard in years."

103   "Polly," I said testily, "the argument is all wrong. Doctors, lawyers, and carpenters aren't taking a test to see how much they have learned, but students are. The situations are altogether different, and you can't make an analogy between them."

104   "I still think it's a good idea," said Polly.

105   "Nuts," I muttered Doggedly I pressed on. "Next we'll try Hypothesis Contrary to Fact."

106   "Sounds yummy," was Polly's reaction.

107   "Listen: If Madame Curie had not happened to leave a photographic plate in a drawer with a chunk of pitchblende, the world today would not know about radium."

108   "True, true," said Polly, nodding her head. "Did you see the movie? Oh, it just knocked me out. That Walter Pidgeon is so dreamy. I mean he fractures me."

109   "If you can forget Mr. Pidgeon for a moment," I said coldly, "I would like to point out that the statement is a fallacy. Maybe Madame Curie would have discovered radium at some later date. Maybe somebody else would have discovered it. Maybe any number of things would have happened. You can't start with a hypothesis that is not true and then draw any supportable conclusions from it."

110   "They ought to put Walter Pidgeon in more pictures," said Polly. "I hardly ever see him any more."

111   One more chance, I decided. But just one more. There is a limit to what flesh and blood can bear. "The next fallacy is called Poisoning the Well."

112   "How cute!" she gurgled.

113   "Two men are having a debate. The first one gets up and says, 'My opponent is a notorious liar. You can't believe a word that he is going to say.' . . . Now, Polly, think. Think hard. What's wrong?"

114   I watched her closely as she knit her creamy brow in concentration. Suddenly a glimmer of intelligence—the first I had seen—came into her eyes. "It's not fair," she said with indignation. "It's not a bit fair. What chance has the second man got if the first man calls him a liar before he even begins talking?"

115   "Right!" I cried exultantly. "One hundred percent right. It's not fair. The first man has *poisoned the well* before anybody could drink from it. He has hamstrung his opponent before he could even start. . . . Polly, I'm proud of you."

116   "Pshaw," she murmured, blushing with pleasure.

117   "You see, my dear, these things aren't so hard. All you have to do is concentrate. Think—examine—evaluate. Come now, let's review everything we have learned."

118   "Fire away," she said with an airy wave of her hand.

119   Heartened by the knowledge that Polly was not altogether a cretin, I began a long, patient review of all I had told her. Over and over and over again. I cited instances, pointed out flaws, kept hammering away without let-up. It was like digging a tunnel. At first everything was work, sweat, and darkness. I had no idea when I would reach the light, or even *if* I would. But I persisted. I pounded and clawed and scraped, and finally I was rewarded. I saw a chink of light. And then the chink got bigger and the sun came pouring in and all was bright.

120   Five grueling nights this took, but it was worth it. I had made a logician out of Polly; I had taught her to think. My job was done. She was worthy

of me at last. She was a fit wife for me, a proper hostess for many mansions, a suitable mother for my well-heeled children.

121   It must not be thought that I was without love for this girl. Quite the contrary. Just as Pygmalion loved the perfect woman he had fashioned, so I loved mine. I determined to acquaint her with my feelings at our very next meeting. The time had come to change our relationship from academic to romantic.

122   "Polly," I said when next we sat beneath our oak, "tonight we will not discuss fallacies."

123   "Aw, gee," she said, disappointed.

124   "My dear," I said, favoring her with a smile, "we have now spent five evenings together. We have gotten along splendidly. It is clear that we are well matched."

125   "Hasty Generalization," said Polly brightly.

126   "I beg your pardon," said I.

127   "Hasty Generalization," she repeated. "How can you say that we are well matched on the basis of only five dates?"

128   I chuckled with amusement. The dear child had learned her lessons well. "My dear," I said, patting her hand in a tolerant manner, "five dates is plenty. After all, you don't have to eat a whole cake to know that it's good."

129   "False Analogy," said Polly promptly. "I'm not a cake. I'm a girl."

130   I chuckled with somewhat less amusement. The dear child had learned her lessons perhaps too well. I decided to change tactics. Obviously the best approach was a simple, strong, direct declaration of love. I paused for a moment while my massive brain chose the proper words. Then I began:

131   "Polly, I love you. You are the whole world to me, and the moon and the stars and the constellations of outer space. Please, my darling, say that you will go steady with me, for if you will not, life will be meaningless. I will languish. I will refuse my meals. I will wander the face of the earth, a shambling, hollow-eyed hulk."

132   There, I thought, folding my arms, that ought to do it.

133   "Ad Misericordiam," said Polly.

134   I ground my teeth. I was no Pygmalion; I was Frankenstein, and my monster had me by the throat. Frantically I fought back the tide of panic surging through me. At all costs I had to keep cool.

135   "Well, Polly," I said, forcing a smile, "you certainly have learned your fallacies."

136   "You're darn right," she said with a vigorous nod.

137   "And who taught them to you, Polly?"

138   "You did."

139   "That's right. So you do owe me something, don't you, my dear? If I hadn't come along you never would have learned about fallacies."

140   "Hypothesis Contrary to Fact," she said instantly.

141   I dashed perspiration from my brow. "Polly," I croaked, "you mustn't take all these things so literally. I mean this is just classroom stuff. You know that the things you learn in school don't have anything to do with life."

142   "Dicto Simpliciter," she said, wagging her finger at me playfully.

143   That did it. I leaped to my feet, bellowing like a bull. "Will you or will you not go steady with me?"

144   "I will not," she replied.

145   "Why not?" I demanded.

146   "Because this afternoon I promised Petey Burch that I would go steady with him."

147   I reeled back, overcome with the infamy of it. After he promised, after he made a deal, after he shook my hand! "The rat!" I shrieked, kicking up great chunks of turf. "You can't go with him, Polly. He's a liar. He's a cheat. He's a rat."

148   "Poisoning the Well," said Polly, "and stop shouting. I think shouting must be a fallacy too."

149   With an immense effort of will, I modulated my voice. "All right," I said. "You're a logician. Let's look at this thing logically. How could you choose Petey Burch over me? Look at me—a brilliant student, a tremendous intellectual, a man with an assured future. Look at Petey—a knothead, a jitterbug, a guy who'll never know where his next meal is coming from. Can you give me one logical reason why you should go steady with Petey Burch?"

150   "I certainly can," declared Polly. "He's got a raccoon coat."

Love Is a Fallacy

Questions on Content, Style, and Structure

1. What does paragraph 1 tell you about the narrator's opinion of himself?

2. Why does the narrator want Polly for his girl?

3. Characterize Polly's diction.

4. Summarize the narrator's character. Why does Shulman present him this way?

5. How does Shulman's choice of point of view add to the humor of this story?

6. Why does the narrator refer to Pygmalion and Frankenstein in paragraph 134?

7. Why is this story told through the use of so much dialogue rather than description?

8. How does Shulman present his dialogue so that the reader is not forced through a series of *he said*s and *she said*s?

9. Why do you think Shulman named this story as he did? Is love a fallacy?

Vocabulary

perspicacious (1)	gamy (38)	doggedly (105)
acute (1)	canny (41)	cretin (119)
astute (1)	trysting (61)	languish (131)
incredulously (9)	fallacy (70)	infamy (147)
cerebral (20)	contritely (79)	modulated (149)

Suggestions for Writing

1. Write a scene of dialogue in which two people in love trade fallacious arguments.

2. Write a note to your composition teacher in which you use a number of fallacies in your efforts to convince him/her to excuse you from your composition assignment or to change your latest grade.

3. Select an argumentative essay from this text or from another source (newspaper editorials, political propaganda, magazine columns, etc.) and analyze its logic. Does it contain any of the fallacies Shulman mentions? Any other fallacies? Present your analysis in a short essay.

Index

361